EUROPE TRANSFORMED

Also published by Tri-Service Press

NBC 90. The Directory of Nuclear, Biological and Chemical Arms and Disarmament 1990

Defence Procurement

Double Zero and Soviet Military Strategy (revised edition)

Central Region vs Out-of-Area: Future Commitments

Soviet Air Power: Prospects for the Future
Perestroyka and the Soviet Air Forces

Indian Defence Review

EUROPE TRANSFORMED

Documents on the End of the Cold War

edited by

LAWRENCE FREEDMAN

TRI-SERVICE

PRESS

First published 1990 by Tri-Service Press Limited, 42–43 Lower Marsh,
Waterloo, London SE1 7RG, United Kingdom

British Library Catloguing in Publication Data

Europe Transformed: Documents on the End of the Cold War
  1. Nuclear weapons. Arms control. History
  I. Freedman, Lawrence
  327.1'74

  ISBN 1-85488-028-4
  ISBN 1-85488-061-6 paperback

Typeset by Florencetype Limited, Kewstoke, Avon
Printed by Biddles Limited

TABLE OF CONTENTS

ACKNOWLEDGEMENTS

I am grateful to Anne-Lucie Norton of Tri-Service Press for being prepared to move so quickly to get this book published and the support from Josephine O'Connor Howe which made this possible. Special thanks must go to my researcher David Boren who did a magnificent job tracking down much of the material collected here and worked closely with me on all stages of the book.

In putting together this collection it was assumed that all the material was already in the public domain. The sources used are indicated throughout. The Editor apologises if any material contained herein is subject to copyright and will be pleased to include appropriate acknowledgements in any further edition.

EUROPE TRANSFORMED
Documents on the End of the Cold War

Introduction

During 1989 the political situation was completely transformed as one Communist government after another was obliged to give way to popular pressures for multi-party democracy and market economies. By the end of the year the talking points were the possible unification of Germany, the demise of the Warsaw Pact and even the eventual break-up of the Soviet Union itself. The underlying cause of these dramatic developments was the chronic economic failure of Soviet-style social-ism, a yearning for democracy and a deep nationalist resentment within those countries which had been tied to the Soviet Union by force. Undoubtedly Mikhail Gorbachev's name will be associated with this change because without his recognition that change was inevitable and should be allowed to take place peacefully this process could have been extremely violent, with awesome consequences for world peace. As it happened, only in Rumania, which had long travelled an independent course, was popular protest resisted with real severity.

This process has yet to come to a conclusion. At the time of writing Albania remains wedded to its old regime, Yugoslavia is on the verge of a civil war, secession is being actively considered within a number of Soviet Republics and being forcibly prevented in Azerbaijan, and the urge to unity in Germany is growing stronger daily.

A meeting of the 35-nation Conference on Security and Co-operation in Europe (CSCE) is now scheduled for late 1990 when it is hoped to seal an agreement on conventional force reductions and, most signifi-cantly, a plan for German unification. This plan will be shaped in discussions between the governments of East and West Germany (following the East German elections) and the four war-time allies (Britain, France, the Soviet Union and the United States). There has been some debate as to whether these talks should be known as the 'two plus four' or 'four plus two', according to whether the talks are judged to be led by inner-German or international considerations. For diplomatic convenience they will come to be known as the 'six'.

Governments are at the same time both trying to anticipate events in areas where they seem to have little control and trying to influence events in those areas where they have the means. They cannot just 'wait and see' but must consider now as practical matters:

1

- the processes of German unification, which are increasingly being driven by the collapse of the East German economy as much of its population streams towards the West in search of a higher standard of living;
- the role of stationed troops in Germany, especially the Soviet troops based in the East;
- how the stagnant, mismanaged economies of the East can be revived (or in some cases given life for the first time);
- how the hopes within these societies for close, productive relations with the European Community can be reconciled with the integration of existing members within the single integrated market by 31 December 1992;
- the future of the NATO/Warsaw Pact alliance system as the grand confrontation upon which it had been based comes to an end;
- the possible shape of a new security system in Europe and the role of various countries and institutions within it;
- the implications for arms control, which had hitherto provided the basis for an orderly reduction of armed force and now appears threatened by pressure for unilateral cuts;
- the future status of a united Germany.

The purpose of this volume is to bring together materials relevant to an understanding of these issues. As a result of discussions with a number of people who address these matters in an official capacity as well as students, there seemed to be a need for a source book containing the most relevant treaties, agreements and statements. In times such as these it often becomes necessary to return to the documents which established key institutions or addressed particularly sensitive matters, such as the future shape of Germany.

Obviously, when a situation is so fast-moving, many documents of apparently critical importance soon become dated. This is already the case with a number of those in this book. They have been included because they are of historical interest in themselves, and also because the evolution of the thinking of key figures in this drama, such as Gorbachev, is important when forming judgements as to how the future might evolve.

It should be emphasised that although much in this book should be of great interest and value to a historian of this period, it has not been organized with this purpose primarily in mind. It concentrates on the diplomatic framework within which current discussions on the future of Europe are taking place and statements of official policy with regard to the future. It does not provide popular manifestoes nor the surrender documents of the various Communist parties, nor policy statements relating to solely internal developments within individual countries. Despite all these limitations it certainly conveys some of the drama of this fascinating period.

In order to keep the book to a reasonable length it has obviously not proved possible to include all relevant material. Those who use this book may well have strong views with regard to particular omissions. We would like to hear any suggestions for improvement which might be incorporated in any further editions.

The book is organized simply into three sections. The first contains the critical treaties and agreements that provide the diplomatic framework. The second includes the mandates, official proposals and draft materials for arms control negotiations. The third contains a series of important proposals and statements by political leaders. This includes the US-Soviet summit communiqués beginning with Geneva in October 1985. It also includes two of Gorbachev's land-mark speeches – his proposals on nuclear disarmament of January 1986 and his announcement of conventional force reductions at the UN in December 1988. A great number of the statements reproduced here are those which followed the breaching of the Berlin Wall on 9 November 1989 and reflected the urgency of the situation which this created.

Lawrence Freedman

SECTION I
The Diplomatic Framework

Since 1945 there have been three major waves of diplomatic activity concerning the shape of European security. The third of these waves began during the second half of the 1980s. Its major achievements thus far have been largely in the field of arms control, covered in Section II of this book. Following the breaching of the Berlin Wall on 9 November 1989 it became possible to envisage the resolution of the basic division on the continent, including the German question, and restructure all security arrangements. The intense activity generated by this possibility is covered in Section III. In this section can be found the framework of treaties and agreements developed during the first two stages which provides the critical reference points for the most recent activity.

The first stage lasted from the end of the Second World War to the mid-1950s and was largely bound up with the failure to resolve the future of Germany and the consequent division of the continent into two competing, antagonistic blocs, each led by a superpower.

The North Atlantic Treaty which links the United States with the West European democracies was signed in 1949 and its provisions have remained unaltered ever since, except for the accession of new members. Although it developed an associated military organization it should be noted that the Treaty itself has a high political content.

It was preceded by the 1948 Brussels Treaty, which is the basis of the Western European Union, and which brought together the West European democracies in order to demonstrate their commitment to collective defence. The obligations in this Treaty are somewhat tighter than the North Atlantic Treaty and are less constrained geographically in their application. It was the Brussels Treaty which was used in 1954 as the essential instrument for incorporating the Federal Republic of Germany into the western Alliance. The 1954 Paris Agreements amended the Treaty and provided a framework of controls and guarantees in order to facilitate German rearmament. In 1984, the Western European Union attempted to modernize itself. It eased a number of controls on Germany. The Paris Agreements are still cited as defining the composition and role of the British Army of the Rhine.

The Soviet bloc was put together in a different form from NATO. The Warsaw Pact was officially formed in 1955, ostensibly in response to German rearmament. It came on top of a series of bilateral treaties between the Soviet Union and its satellites and was followed by another series which allowed for the stationing of its troops on the soil of its respective allies.

The second stage of diplomatic activity began in the late 1960s as the Federal Republic of Germany changed its stance on its policy towards the East and began to establish normal diplomatic relations with the countries of the Soviet bloc. Although West Germany maintained its position on eventual unification, it acknowledged the durability of the post-war boundaries. This development required a new four-power agreement on Berlin to regularise the situation in the old capital which had served as a flashpoint in East-West relations since 1948.

The basic principles for a European detente were enshrined in the 1975 Final Act of the Conference on Security and Co-operation in Europe (CSCE). It should be noted that while the CSCE Final Act has played an important role in shaping European attitudes and behaviour it has no legal status.

THE ESTABLISHMENT OF THE POST-WAR SYSTEM

TREATY OF FRIENDSHIP, MUTUAL ASSISTANCE AND POST-WAR COOPERATION BETWEEN THE UNION OF SOVIET SOCIALIST REPUBLICS AND THE REPUBLIC OF POLAND, SIGNED AT MOSCOW, ON 21 APRIL 1945

(Instruments of ratification exchanged at Warsaw, 20 September 1945)

The President of the National Council of the People's Republic of Poland and the Presidium of the Supreme Soviet of the Union of Soviet Socialist Republics,

Being inflexibly resolved jointly to carry on the the war against the German aggressor until complete and final victory is achieved;

Desiring, at this critical turning-point in the history of Soviet–Polish relations, to consolidate the friendly, allied co-operation established between Poland and the USSR during the common struggle against German imperialism;

Being persuaded that the further strengthening of good-neighbourly and friendly relations between Poland and the adjacent Soviet Union is in accordance with the vital interests of the Polish and Soviet peoples;

Being convinced that the maintenance of friendship and close co-operation between the Polish and Soviet peoples will further the successful economic development of both countries, both during and after the war;

Being anxious to give all possible support after the war to the cause of international peace and security;

Have resolved for this purpose to conclude the present Treaty and . . . have agreed on the following provisions:

Article 1

The High Contracting Parties will continue, jointly with all the United Nations, the fight against Germany until final victory. In this fight the

7

High Contracting Parties agree to render each other military and other assistance by all the means in their power.

Article 2

Believing that it is necessary, in the interests of the security and prosperity of the Polish and Soviet peoples, to maintain and strengthen a firm and lasting friendship both during and after the war, the High Contracting Parties will strengthen friendly co-operation between both countries in accordance with the principles of mutual respect for their independence and sovereignty and also of non-intervention in the internal affairs of the other State.

Article 3

The High Contracting Parties agree to take, on the conclusion also of the present war with Germany, all joint action within their power to obviate any threat of further aggression by Germany or any other Power which might be associated with Germany either directly or in any other way.

To this end the High Contracting Parties will, in a spirit of sincerest co-operation, participate in all international action for ensuring international peace and security and will fully contribute to the realization of these lofty aims.

In carrying out the present Treaty, the High Contracting Parties will act conformably to the international principles, in the adoption of which both Contracting Parties participated.

Article 4

Should either of the High Contracting Parties during the post-war period be involved in hostilities with a Germany, which had renewed her policy of aggression, or with any other State which had joined Germany in such a war either directly or in any other way, the other High Contracting Party shall without delay extend to the Contracting Party involved in hostilities military and other assistance and support with all the means at its disposal.

Article 5

The High Contracting Parties agree not to conclude without each other's consent any armistice or peace treaty either with the Hitlerite Government or with any other authority in Germany violating or likely to violate the independence, territorial integrity or security of either High Contracting Party.

Article 6

The High Contracting Parties respectively agree not to enter into any alliance or take part in any coalition directed against the other High Contracting Party.

Article 7

The High Contracting Parties will continue, on the termination of the present war, also to co-operate in a spirit of friendship with a view to the further development and strengthening of the economic and cultural ties between the two countries, and to assist one another in restoring the national economies of both countries.

Article 8

The present Treaty shall come into force immediately upon signature and shall be subject to ratification in the shortest possible time. The instruments of ratification will be exchanged in Moscow as soon as possible.

The present Treaty shall remain in force for twenty years from the date of signature. If neither of the High Contracting Parties gives notice twelve months before the expiration of the twenty-year period that it wishes to denounce the Treaty, it shall remain in force for a further five years until such time as either High Contracting Party gives notice in writing twelve months before the expiration of the current five-year period of its intention to denounce the Treaty.

IN FAITH WHEREOF the Plenipotentiaries have signed the present Treaty and attached their seals thereto.

DONE in Moscow on 21 April 1945 in two copies, each in the Polish and Russian languages, both texts being equally authentic.

By authorization of the President of the National
Council of the People's Republic of Poland:
[L.S.] E. OSÓBKA-MORAWSKI

By authorization of the Presidium of the Supreme
Soviet of the USSR:
[L.S.] J. STALIN

Source: UN Treaty Series

★ ★ ★

Later treaties with Rumania (4 February 1948), Hungary (18 February 1948), and Bulgaria (18 March 1948) follow this form. An agreement with the Czechoslavak Government signed during the war (12 December 1943) anticipates many of the provisions of the Polish Treaty as well as referring to earlier Soviet-Czechoslovak agreements.

POTSDAM CONFERENCE

2 August 1945 (Extract)

The three Heads of Government (United States, Britain, Soviet Union) agree that, pending the final determination of Poland's western frontier, the former German territories east of a line running from the Baltic Sea immediately west of Swinemünde, and thence along the Oder River to the confluence of the western Neisse River and along the western Neisse to the Czechoslovak frontier, including that portion of East Prussia not placed under the administration of the Union of Soviet Socialist Republics in accordance with the understanding reached at this conference and including the area of the former Free City of Danzig, shall be under the administration of the Polish State and for such purposes should not be considered as part of the Soviet zone of occupation in Germany.

Source: US Dept. of State, Documents on Germany, 1944–1985

EXTRACTS FROM THE BRUSSELS TREATY

17 March 1948

The titular heads of the participating States:
Resolved to reaffirm their faith in fundamental human rights, in the dignity and worth of the human person and in the other ideals proclaimed in the Charter of the United Nations; *To fortify and preserve* the principles of democracy, personal freedom and political liberty, the constitutional traditions and the rule of law, which are their common heritage; *To strengthen*, with these aims in view, the economic, social and cultural ties by which they are already united; *To cooperate* loyally and to coordinate their efforts to create in Western Europe a firm basis for European economic recovery; *To afford assistance* to each other, in accordance with the Charter of the United Nations, in maintaining international peace and security and in resisting any policy of aggression; *To take such steps* as may be held to be necessary in the event of a renewal by Germany of a policy of aggression; *To associate* progressively in the pursuance of these aims other States inspired by the same ideals and animated by the like determination;
Desiring for these purposes to conclude a treaty for collaboration in economic, social and cultural matters and for collective self-defence;
Have appointed . . . their plenipotentiaries . . . who . . . have agreed as follows:

Article I
Convinced of the close community of their interests and of the necessity of uniting in order to promote the economic recovery of Europe, the High Contracting Parties will so organize and co-ordinate their economic activities as to produce the best possible results, by the elimination of conflict in their economic policies, the co-ordination of production and the development of commercial exchanges.

The co-operation provided for in the preceding paragraph, which will be effected through the Consultative Council referred to in Article VII as well as through other bodies, shall not involve any duplication of, or prejudice to, the work of other economic organizations in which the High Contracting Parties are or may be represented but shall on the contrary assist the work of those organizations.

Article II
The High Contracting Parties will make every effort in common, both by direct consultation and in specialized agencies, to promote the

attainment of a higher standard of living by their peoples and to develop on corresponding lines the social and other related services of their countries.

The High Contracting Parties will consult with the object of achieving the earliest possible application of recommendations of immediate practical interest, relating to social matters, adopted with their approval in the specialized agencies.

They will endeavour to conclude as soon as possible conventions with each other in the sphere of social security.

Article III

The High Contracting Parties will make every effort in common to lead their peoples towards a better understanding of the principles which form the basis of their common civilization and to promote cultural exchanges by conventions between themselves or by other means.

Article IV

If any of the High Contracting Parties should be the object of an armed attack in Europe, the other High Contracting Parties will, in accordance with the provisions of Article 51 of the Charter of the United Nations, afford the party so attacked all the military and other aid and assistance in their power.

Article V

All measures taken as a result of the preceding Article shall be immediately reported to the Security Council. They shall be terminated as soon as the Security Council has taken the measures necessary to maintain or restore international peace and security. The present Treaty does not prejudice in any way the obligations of the High Contracting Parties under the provisions of the Charter of the United Nations. It shall not be interpreted as affecting in any way the authority and responsibility of the Security Council under the Charter to take at any time such action as it deems necessary in order to maintain or restore international peace and security.

Article VI

The High Contracting Parties declare, each so far as he is concerned, that none of the international engagements now in force between him and any of the other High Contracting Parties or any third State is in conflict with the provisions of the present Treaty.

None of the High Contracting Parties will conclude any alliance or participate in any coalition directed against any other of the High Contracting Parties.

Article VII

For the purpose of consulting together on all the questions dealt with in the present Treaty, the High Contracting Parties will create a Consultative

Council, which shall be so organized as to be able to exercise its functions continuously. The Council shall meet at such times as it shall deem fit.

At the request of any of the High Contracting Parties, the Council shall be immediately convened in order to permit the High Contracting Parties to consult with regard to any situation which may constitute a threat to peace, in whatever area this threat should arise; with regard to the attitude to be adopted and the steps to be taken in case of a renewal by Germany of an aggressive policy; or with regard to any situation constituting a danger to economic stability.

Article VIII

In pursuance of their determination to settle disputes only by peaceful means, the High Contracting Parties will apply to disputes between themselves the following provision:

The High Contracting Parties will, while the present Treaty remains in force, settle all disputes falling within the scope of Article 36, paragraph 2, of the Statute of the International Court of Justice by referring them to the Court . . .

Article IX

The High Contracting Parties may, by agreement, invite any other State to accede to the present Treaty on conditions to be agreed between them and the State so invited . . .

Article X

The present Treaty . . . shall enter into force on the date of the deposit of the last instrument of ratification and shall thereafter remain in force for fifty years . . .

Done at Brussels, this seventeenth day of March, 1948 . . .

Source: NATO

THE NORTH ATLANTIC TREATY

Signed Washington D.C., 4 April 1949

The Parties to this Treaty *reaffirm* their faith in the purposes and principles of the Charter of the United Nations and their desire to live in peace with all peoples and all governments.

They *are determined* to safeguard the freedom, common heritage and civilization of their peoples, founded on the principles of democracy, individual liberty and the rule of law.

They *seek to promote* stability and well-being in the North Atlantic area.

They are *resolved* to unite their efforts for collective defence and for the preservation of peace and security.

They therefore agree to this North Atlantic Treaty:

Article 1

The Parties undertake, as set forth in the Charter of the United Nations, to settle any international dispute in which they may be involved by peaceful means in such a manner that international peace and security and justice are not endangered, and to refrain in their international relations from the threat or use of force in any manner inconsistent with the purposes of the United Nations.

Article 2

The Parties will contribute toward the further development of peaceful and friendly international relations by strengthening their free institutions, by bringing about a better understanding of the principles upon which these institutions are founded, and by promoting coalitions of stability and well-being. They will seek to eliminate conflict in their international economic policies and will encourage economic collaboration between any or all of them.

Article 3

In order more effectively to achieve the objectives of this Treaty, the Parties, separately and jointly, by means of continuous and effective self-help and mutual aid, will maintain and develop their individual and collective capacity to resist armed attack.

Article 4

The Parties will consult together whenever, in the opinion of any of them, the territorial integrity, political indepedence or security of any of the Parties is threatened.

Article 5

The Parties agree that an armed attack against one or more of them in Europe or North America shall be considered an attack against them all and consequently they agree that, if such an armed attack occurs, each of them, in exercise of the right of individual or collective self-defence recognized by Article 51 of the Charter of the United Nations, will assist the Party or Parties so attacked by taking forthwith, individually and in concert with the other Parties, such action as it deems necessary, including the use of armed force, to restore and maintain the security of the North Atlantic area.

Any such armed attack and all measures taken as a result thereof shall immediately be reported to the Security Council. Such measures shall be terminated when the Security Council has taken the measures necessary to restore and maintain international peace and security.

Article 6[1]

For the purpose of Article V an armed attack on one or more of the Parties is deemed to include an armed attack on the territory of any of the Parties in Europe or North America, on the Algerian Departments of France[2], on the occupation forces of any Party in Europe, on the islands under the jurisdiction of any Party in the North Atlantic area north of the Tropic of Cancer or on the vessels or aircraft in this area of any of the Parties.

Article 7

This Treaty does not affect, and shall not be interpreted as affecting, in any way the rights and obligations under the Charter of the Parties which are members of the United Nations, or the primary responsibility of the Security Council for the maintenance of international peace and security.

Article 8

Each Party declares that none of the international engagements now in force between it and any other of the Parties or any third State is in conflict with the provisions of this Treaty, and undertakes not to enter into any international engagement in conflict with this Treaty.

Article 9

The Parties hereby establish a Council, on which each of them shall be represented, to consider matters concerning the implementation of this Treaty. The Council shall be so organized as to be able to meet promptly at any time. The Council shall set up such subsidiary bodies as may be necessary; in particular it shall establish immediately a defence committee which shall recommend measures for the implementation of Articles III and V.

Article 10

The Parties may, by unanimous agreement, invite any other European State in a position to further the principles of this Treaty and to contribute to the security of the North Atlantic area to accede to this Treaty. Any State so invited may become a Party to the Treaty by deposing its instrument of accession with the Government of the United States of America. The Government of the United States of America will inform each of the Parties of the deposit of each such instrument of accession.

Article 11

This Treaty shall be ratified and its provisions carried out by the Parties in accordance with their respective constitutional processes. The instruments of ratification shall be deposited as soon as possible with the Government of the United States of America, which will notify all the other signatories of each deposit. The Treaty shall enter into force between the States which have ratified it as soon as the ratification of the majority of the signatories, including the ratifications of Belgium, Canada, France, Luxembourg, the Netherlands, the United Kingdom and the United States, have been deposited and shall come into effect with respect to other States on the date of the deposit of their ratifications.

Article 12

After the Treaty has been in force for ten years, or at any time thereafter, the Parties shall, if any of them so requests, consult together for the purpose of reviewing the Treaty, having regard for the factors then affecting peace and security in the North Atlantic area, including the development of universal as well as regional arrangements under the Charter of the United Nations for the maintenance of international peace and security.

Article 13

After the Treaty has been in force for twenty years, any Party may cease to be a Party one year after its notice of denunciation has been given to the Government of the United States of America, which will inform the Governments of the other Parties of the deposit of each notice of denunciation.

Article 14

This Treaty, of which the English and French texts are equally authentic, shall be deposited in the archives of the Government of the United States of America. Duly certified copies will be transmitted by that Government to the governments of the other signatories.

Source: NATO

Notes

(1) *The definition of the territories to which Article V applies has been revised by Article II of the Protocol to the North Atlantic Treaty on the accession of Greece and Turkey.*

(2) *On 16 January, 1963, the North Atlantic Council heard a declaration by the French Representative who recalled that by the vote on self-determination on 1 July, 1962, the Algerian people had pronounced itself in favour of the independence of Algeria in co-operation with France. In consequence, the President of the French Republic had on 3 July, 1962, formally recognized the independence of Algeria. The result was that the 'Algerian departments of France' no longer existed as such, and that at the same time the fact that they were mentioned in the North Atlantic Treaty had no longer any bearing.*

Following this statement the Council noted that insofar as the former Algerian Departments of France were concerned, the relevant clauses of this Treaty had become inapplicable as from 3 July, 1962.

CONVENTION FOR THE PROTECTION OF HUMAN RIGHTS AND FUNDAMENTAL FREEDOMS

4 November 1950

The Governments signatory hereto, being Members of the Council of Europe,

Considering the Universal Declaration of Human Rights proclaimed by the General Assembly of the United Nations on 10th December 1948;

Considering that this Declaration aims at securing the universal and effective recognition and observance of the Rights therein declared;

Considering that the aim of the Council of Europe is the achievement of greater unity between its Members and that one of the methods by which that aim is to be pursued is the maintenance and further realisation of Human Rights and Fundamental Freedoms;

Reaffirming their profound belief in those Fundamental Freedoms which are the foundation of justice and peace in the world and are best maintained on the one hand by an effective political democracy and on the other by a common understanding and observance of the Human Rights upon which they depend;

Being resolved, as the Governments of European countries which are likeminded and have a common heritage of political traditions, ideals, freedom and the rule of law to take the first steps for the collective enforcement of certain of the Rights stated in the Universal Declaration,

Have agreed as follows:

Article 1

The High Contracting Parties shall secure to everyone within their jurisdiction the rights and freedoms defined in Section 1 of this Convention.

Section 1

Article 2

1. Everyone's right to life shall be protected by law. No one shall be deprived of his life intentionally save in the execution of a sentence of a court following his conviction of a crime for which this penalty is provided by law.

2. Deprivation of life shall not be regarded as inflicted in contravention of this Article when it results from the use of force which is no more than absolutely necessary:

(a) in defence of any person from unlawful violence;
(b) in order to effect a lawful arrest or to prevent the escape of a person lawfully detained;
(c) in action lawfully taken for the purpose of quelling a riot or insurrection.

Article 3
No one shall be subjected to torture or to inhuman or degrading treatment or punishment.

Article 4
1. No one shall be held in slavery or servitude.
2. No one shall be required to perform forced or compulsory labour.
3. For the purpose of this Article the term 'forced or compulsory labour' shall not include:

(a) any work required to be done in the ordinary course of detention imposed according to the provisions of Article 5 of this Convention or during conditional release from such detention;
(b) any service of a military character or, in case of conscientious objectors in countries where they are recognised, service exacted instead of compulsory military service;
(c) any service exacted in case of an emergency or calamity threatening the life or well-being of the community;
(d) any work or service which forms part of normal civic obligations.

Article 5
1. Everyone has the right to liberty and security of person.
No one shall be deprived of his liberty save in the following cases and in accordance with a procedure prescribed by law;

(a) the lawful detention of a person after conviction by a competent court;
(b) the lawful arrest or detention of a person for non-compliance with the lawful order of a court or in order to secure the fulfilment of any obligation prescribed by law;
(c) the lawful arrest or detention of a person effected for the purpose of bringing him before the competent legal authority on reasonable suspicion of having committed an offence or when it is reasonably considered necessary to prevent his committing an offence or fleeing after having done so;
(d) the detention of a minor by lawful order for the purpose of educational supervision or his lawful detention for the purpose of bringing him before the competent legal authority;

(e) the lawful detention of persons for the prevention of the spreading of infectious diseases, of persons of unsound mind, alcoholics or drug addicts or vagrants;

(f) the lawful arrest or detention of a person to prevent his effecting an unauthorised entry into the country or of a person against whom action is being taken with a view to deportation or extradition.

2. Everyone who is arrested shall be informed promptly, in a language which he understands, of the reasons for his arrest and of any charge against him.

3. Everyone arrested or detained in accordance with the provisions of paragraph 1 (c) of this Article shall be brought promptly before a judge or other officer authorised by law to exercise judicial power and shall be entitled to trial within a reasonable time or to release pending trial. Release may be conditioned by guarantees to appear for trial.

4. Everyone who is deprived of his liberty by arrest or detention shall be entitled to take proceedings by which the lawfulness of his detention shall be decided speedily by a court and his release ordered if the detention is not lawful.

5. Everyone who has been the victim of arrest or detention in contravention of the provisions of this Article shall have an enforceable right to compensation.

Article 6

1. In the determination of his civil rights and obligations or of any criminal charge against him, everyone is entitled to a fair and public hearing within a reasonable time by an independent and impartial tribunal established by law. Judgment shall be pronounced publicly but the press and public may be excluded from all or part of the trial in the interest of morals, public order or national security in a democratic society, where the interests of juveniles or the protection of the private life of the parties so require, or to the extent strictly necessary in the opinion of the court in special circumstances where publicity would prejudice the interests of justice.

2. Everyone charged with a criminal offence shall be presumed innocent until proved guilty according to law.

3. Everyone charged with a criminal offence has the following minimum rights:

(a) to be informed promptly, in a language which he understands and in detail, of the nature and cause of the accusation against him;

(b) to have adequate time and facilities for the preparation of his defence;

(c) to defend himself in person or through legal assistance of his own choosing or, if he has not sufficient means to pay for legal assistance, to be given it free when the interests or justice so require;

(d) to examine or have examined witnesses against him and to obtain the attendance and examination of witnesses on his behalf under the same conditions as witnesses against him;

(e) to have the free assistance of an interpreter if he cannot understand or speak the language used in court.

Article 7

1. No one shall be held guilty of any criminal offence on account of any act or omission which did not constitute a criminal offence under national or international law at the time when it was committed. Nor shall a heavier penalty be imposed than the one that was applicable at the time the criminal offence was committed.

2. This Article shall not prejudice the trial and punishment of any person for any act or omission which at the time when it was committed, was criminal according to the general principles of law recognised by civilised nations.

Article 8

1. Everyone has the right to respect for his private and family life, his home and his correspondence.

2. There shall be no interference by a public authority with the exercise of this right except such as is in accordance with the law and is necessary in a democratic society in the interests of national security, public safety or the economic well-being of the country, for the prevention of disorder, or crime, for the protection of health or morals, or for the protection of the rights and freedoms of others.

Article 9

1. Everyone has the right to freedom of thought, conscience and religion; this right includes freedom to change his religion or belief and freedom, either alone or in community with others and in public or private, to manifest his religion or belief, in worship, teaching, practice and observance.

2. Freedom to manifest one's religion or beliefs shall be subject only to such limitations as are prescribed by law and are necessary in a democratic society in the interests of public safety, for the protection of public order, health or morals, or for the protection of the rights and freedoms of others.

Article 10

1. Everyone has the right to freedom of expression. This right shall include freedom to hold opinions and to receive and impart information and ideas without interference by public authority and regardless of frontiers. This Article shall not prevent States from requiring the licensing of broadcasting, television or cinema enterprises.

2. The exercise of these freedoms, since it carries with it duties and responsibilities, may be subject to such formalities, conditions, restrictions or penalties as are prescribed by law and are necessary in a

democratic society, in the interests of national security, territorial integrity or public safety, for the prevention of disorder or crime, for the protection of health or morals, for the protection of the reputation or rights of others, for preventing the disclosure of information received in confidence, or for maintaining the authority and impartiality of the judiciary.

Article 11

1. Everyone has the right to freedom of peaceful assembly and to freedom of association with others, including the right to form and to join trade unions for the protection of his interests.

2. No restrictions shall be placed on the exercise of these rights other than such as are prescribed by law and are necessary in a democratic society in the interests of national security or public safety, for the prevention of disorder or crime, for the protection of health or morals or for the protection of the rights and freedoms of others. This Article shall not prevent the imposition of lawful restrictions on the exercise of these rights by members of the armed forces, of the police or of the administration of the State.

Article 12

Men and women of marriageable age have the right to marry and to found a family, according to the national laws governing the exercise of this right.

Article 13

Everyone whose rights and freedoms as set forth in this Convention are violated shall have an effective remedy before a national authority notwithstanding that the violation has been committed by persons acting in an official capacity.

Article 14

The enjoyment of the rights and freedoms set forth in this Convention shall be secured without discrimination on any ground such as sex, race, colour, language, religion, political or other opinion, national or social origin, association with a national minority, property, birth or other status.

Article 15

1. In time of war or other public emergency threatening the life of the nation any High Contracting Party may take measures derogating from its obligations under this Convention to the extent strictly required by the exigencies of the situation, provided that such measures are not inconsistent with its other obligations under international law.

2. No derogation from Article 2, except in respect of deaths resulting from lawful acts of war, or from Articles 3, 4 (paragraph 1) and 7 shall be made under this provision.

3. Any High Contracting Party availing itself of this right of derogation shall keep the Secretary General of the Council of Europe fully informed of the measures which it has taken and the reasons therefor. It shall also inform the Secretary General of the Council of Europe, when such measures have ceased to operate and the provisions of the Convention are again being fully executed.

Article 16
Nothing in Articles 10, 11 and 14 shall be regarded as preventing the High Contracting Parties from imposing restrictions on the political activity of aliens.

Article 17
Nothing in this Convention may be interpreted as implying for any State, group or person any right to engage in any activity or perform any act aimed at the destruction of any of the rights and freedoms set forth herein or at their limitation to a greater extent than is provided for in the Convention.

Article 18
The restrictions permitted under this Convention to the said rights and freedoms shall not be applied for any purpose other than those for which they have been prescribed.

Section II

Article 19
To ensure the observance of the engagements undertaken by the High Contracting Parties in the present Convention, there shall be set up:
1. A European Commission of Human Rights hereinafter referred to as 'The Commission';
2. A European Court of Human Rights, hereinafter referred to as 'the Court'.

Section III

Article 20
The Commission shall consist of a number of members equal to that of the High Contracting Parties. No two members of the Commission may be nationals of the same State.

Article 21
1. The members of the Commission shall be elected by the Committee of Ministers by an absolute majority of votes, from a list of names drawn up by the Bureau of the Consultative Assembly; each group of the Representatives of the High Contracting Parties in the Consultative

Assembly shall put forward three candidates, of whom two at least shall be its nationals.

2. As far as applicable, the same procedure shall be followed to complete the Commission in the event of other States subsequently becoming Parties to this Convention, and in filling casual vacancies.

Article 22

1. The members of the Commission shall be elected for a period of six years. They may be re-elected. However, of the members elected at the first election, the terms of seven members shall expire at the end of three years.

2. The members whose terms are to expire at the end of the initial period of three years shall be chosen by lot by the Secretary General of the Council of Europe immediately after the first election has been completed.

3. A member of the Commission elected to replace a member whose term of office has not expired shall hold office for the remainder of his predecessor's term.

4. The members of the Commission shall hold office until replaced. After having been replaced, they shall continue to deal with such cases as they already have under consideration.

Article 23

The members of the Commission shall sit on the Commission in their individual capacity.

Article 24

Any High Contracting Party may refer to the Commission, through the Secretary General of the Council of Europe, any alleged breach of the provisions of the Convention by another High Contracting Party.

Article 25

1. The Commission may receive petitions addressed to the Secretary General of the Council of Europe from any person, non-governmental organisation or group of individuals claiming to be the victim of a violation by one of the High Contracting Parties of the rights set forth in this Convention, provided that the High Contracting Party against which the complaint has been lodged has declared that it recognises the competence of the Commission to receive such petitions. Those of the High Contracting Parties who have made such a declaration undertake not to hinder in any way the effective exercise of this right.

2. Such declarations may be made for a specific period.

3. The declarations shall be deposited with the Secretary General of the Council of Europe who shall transmit copies thereof to the High Contracting Parties and publish them.

4. The Commission shall only exercise the powers provided for in this Article when at least six High Contracting Parties are bound by declarations made in accordance with the preceding paragraphs.

Article 26

The Commission may only deal with the matter after all domestic remedies have been exhausted, according to the generally recognised rules of international law, and within a period of six months from the date on which the final decision was taken.

Article 27

1. The Commission shall not deal with any petition submitted under Article 25 which

(a) is anonymous, or

(b) is substantially the same as a matter which has already been examined by the Commission or has already been submitted to another procedure of international investigation or settlement and if it contains no relevant new information.

2. The Commission shall consider inadmissible any petition submitted under Article 25 which it considers incompatible with the provisions of the present Convention, manifestly ill-founded, or an abuse of the right of petition.

3. The Commission shall reject any petition referred to it which it considers inadmissible under Article 26.

Article 28

In the event of the Commission accepting a petition referred to it:

(a) it shall, with a view to ascertaining the facts, undertake together with the representatives of the parties an examination of the petition and, if need be, an investigation, for the effective conduct of which the States concerned shall furnish all necessary facilities, after an exchange of views with the Commission;

(b) it shall place itself at the disposal of the parties concerned with a view to securing a friendly settlement of the matter on the basis of respect for Human Rights as defined in this Convention.

Article 29

1. The Commission shall perform the functions set out in Article 28 by means of a Sub-Commission consisting of seven members of the Commission.

2. Each of the parties concerned may appoint as members of this Sub-Commission a person of its choice.

3. The remaining members shall be chosen by lot in accordance with arrangements prescribed in the Rules of Procedure of the Commission.

Article 30

If the Sub-Commission succeeds in effecting a friendly settlement in accordance with Article 28, it shall draw up a Report which shall be sent to the States concerned, to the Committee of Ministers and to the Secretary General of the Council of Europe for publication. This Report shall be confined to a brief statement of the facts and of the solution reached.

Article 31

1. If a solution is not reached, the Commission shall draw up a Report on the facts and state its opinion as to whether the facts found disclose a breach by the State concerned of its obligations under the Convention. The opinions of all the members of the Commission on this point may be stated in the Report.

2. The Report shall be transmitted to the Committee of Ministers. It shall also be transmitted to the States concerned, who shall not be at liberty to publish it.

3. In transmitting the Report to the Committee of Ministers the Commission may make such proposals as it thinks fit.

Article 32

1. If the question is not referred to the Court in accordance with Article 48 of this Convention within a period of three months from the date of the transmission of the Report to the Committee of Ministers, the Committee of Ministers shall decide by a majority of two-thirds of the members entitled to sit on the Committee whether there has been a violation of the Convention.

2. In the affirmative case the Committee of Ministers shall prescribe a period during which the Contracting Party concerned must take the measures required by the decision of the Committee of Ministers.

3. If the High Contracting Party concerned has not taken satisfactory measures within the prescribed period, the Committee of Ministers shall decide by the majority provided for in paragraph 1 above what effect shall be given to its original decision and shall publish the Report.

4. The High Contracting Parties undertake to regard as binding on them any decision which the Committee of Ministers may take in application of the preceding paragraphs.

Article 33

The Commission shall meet *in camera.*

Article 34

The Commission shall take its decisions by a majority of the members present and voting; the Sub-Commission shall take its decisions by a majority of its members.

Article 35

The Commission shall meet as the circumstances require. The meetings shall be convened by the Secretary General of the Council of Europe.

Article 36

The Commission shall draw up its own rules of procedure.

Article 37

The secretariat of the Commission shall be provided by the Secretary General of the Council of Europe.

Section IV

Article 38

The European Court of Human Rights shall consist of a number of judges equal to that of the Members of the Council of Europe. No two judges may be nationals of the same State.

Article 39

1. The members of the Court shall be elected by the Consultative Assembly by a majority of the votes cast from a list of persons nominated by the Members of the Council of Europe; each Member shall nominate three candidates, of whom two at least shall be its nationals.

2. As far as applicable, the same procedure shall be followed to complete the Court in the event of the admission of new Members of the Council of Europe, and in filling casual vacancies.

3. The candidates shall be of high moral character and must either possess the qualifications required for appointment to high judicial office or be jurisconsults of recognised competence.

Article 40

1. The members of the Court shall be elected for a period of nine years. They may be re-elected. However, of the members elected at the first election the terms of four members shall expire at the end of three years, and the terms of four more members shall expire at the end of six years.

2. The members whose terms are to expire at the end of the initial periods of three and six years shall be chosen by lot by the Secretary General immediately after the first election has been completed.

3. A member of the Court elected to replace a member whose term of office has not expired shall hold office for the remainder of his predecessor's term.

4. The members of the Court shall hold office until replaced. After having been replaced, they shall continue to deal with such cases as they already have under consideration.

Article 41

The Court shall elect its President and Vice-President for a period of three years. They may be re-elected.

Article 42

The members of the Court shall receive for each day of duty a compensation to be determined by the Committee of Ministers.

Article 43

For the consideration of each case brought before it the Court shall consist of a Chamber composed of seven judges. There shall sit as an ex officio member of the Chamber the judge who is a national of any State party concerned, or, if there is none, a person of its choice who shall sit in the capacity of judge; the names of the other judges shall be chosen by lot by the President before the opening of the case.

Article 44

Only the High Contracting Parties and the Commission shall have the right to bring a case before the Court.

Article 45

The jurisdiction of the Court shall extend to all cases concerning the interpretation and application of the present Convention which the High Contracting Parties or the Commission shall refer to it in accordance with Article 48.

Article 46

1. Any of the High Contracting Parties may at any time declare that it recognises as compulsory *ipso facto* and without special agreement the jurisdiction of the Court in all matters concerning the interpretation and application of the present Convention.

2. The declarations referred to above may be made unconditionally or on condition of reciprocity on the part of several or certain other High Contracting Parties or for a specified period.

3. These declarations shall be deposited with the Secretary General of the Council of Europe who shall transmit copies thereof to the High Contracting Parties.

Article 47

The Court may only deal with a case after the Commission has acknowledged the failure of efforts for a friendly settlement and within the period of three months provided for in Article 32.

Article 48

The following may bring a case before the Court, provided that the High Contracting Party concerned, if there is only one, or the High Contracting Parties concerned, if there is more than one, are subject to the compulsory jurisdiction of the Court or, failing that, with the consent of the High Contracting Party concerned, if there is only one, or of the High Contracting Parties concerned if there is more than one:

(a) the Commission;
(b) a High Contracting Party whose national is alleged to be a victim;
(c) a High Contracting Party which referred the case to the Commission;
(d) a High Contracting Party against which the complaint has been lodged.

Article 49
In the event of dispute as to whether the Court has jurisdiction, the matter shall be settled by the decision of the Court.

Article 50
If the Court finds that a decision or a measure taken by a legal authority or any other authority of a High Contracting Party, is completely or partially in conflict with the obligations arising from the present Convention, and if the internal law of the said Party allows only partial reparation to be made for the consequences of this decision or measure, the decision of the Court shall, if necessary, afford just satisfaction to the injured party.

Article 51
1. Reasons shall be given for the judgment of the Court.
2. If the judgment does not represent in whole or in part the unanimous opinion of the judges, any judge shall be entitled to deliver a separate opinion.

Article 52
The judgment of the Court shall be final.

Article 53
The High Contracting Parties undertake to abide by the decision of the Court in any case to which they are parties.

Article 54
The judgment of the Court shall be transmitted to the Committee of Ministers which shall supervise its execution.

Article 55
The Court shall draw up its own rules and shall determine its own procedure.

Article 56
1. The first election of the members of the Court shall take place after the declarations by the High Contracting Parties mentioned in Article 46 have reached a total of eight.
2. No case can be brought before the Court before this election.

Section V

Article 57
On receipt of a request from the Secretary General of the Council of Europe any High Contracting Party shall furnish an explanation of the manner in which its internal law ensures the effective implementation of any of the provisions of this Convention.

Article 58
The expenses of the Commission and the Court shall be borne by the Council of Europe.

Article 59
The members of the Commission and of the Court shall be entitled, during the discharge of their functions, to the privileges and immunities provided for in Article 40 of the Statute of the Council of Europe and in the agreements made thereunder.

Article 60
Nothing in this Convention shall be construed as limiting or derogating from any of the human rights and fundamental freedoms which may be ensured under the laws of any High Contracting Party or under any other agreement to which it is a Party.

Article 61
Nothing in this Convention shall prejudice the powers conferred on the Committee of Ministers by the Statute of the Council of Europe.

Article 62
The High Contracting Parties agree that, except by special agreement, they will not avail themselves of treaties, conventions or declarations in force between them for the purpose of submitting, by way of petition, a dispute arising out of the interpretation or application of this Convention to a means of settlement other than those provided for in this Convention.

Article 63
1. Any State may at the time of its ratification or at any time thereafter declare by notification addressed to the Secretary General of the Council of Europe that the present Convention shall extend to all or any of the territories for whose international relations it is responsible.
2. The Convention shall extend to the territory or territories named in the notification as from the thirtieth day after the receipt of this notification by the Secretary-General of the Council of Europe.
3. The provisions of this Convention shall be applied in such territories with due regard, however, to local requirements.
4. Any State which has made a declaration in accordance with

paragraph 1 of this Article may at any time thereafter declare on behalf of one or more of the territories to which the declaration relates that it accepts the competence of the Commission to receive petitions from individuals, non-governmental organisations or groups of individuals in accordance with Article 25 of the present Convention.

Article 64

1. Any State may, when signing this Convention or when depositing its instrument of ratification, make a reservation in respect of any particular provision of the Convention to the extent that any law then in force in its territory is not in conformity with the provision. Reservations of a general character shall not be permitted under this Article.

2. Any reservation made under this Article shall contain a brief statement of the law concerned.

Article 65

1. A High Contracting Party may denounce the present Convention only after the expiry of five years from the date on which it became a Party to it and after six months' notice contained in a notification addressed to the Secretary General of the Council of Europe, who shall inform the other High Contracting Parties.

2. Such a denunciation shall not have the effect of releasing the High Contracting Party concerned from its obligations under this Convention in respect of any act which, being capable of constituting a violation of such obligations, may have been performed by it before the date at which the denunciation became effective.

3. Any High Contracting Party which shall cease to be a Member of the Council of Europe shall cease to be a Party to this Convention under the same conditions.

4. The Convention may be denounced in accordance with the provisions of the preceding paragraphs in respect of any territory to which it has been declared to extend under the terms of Article 63.

Article 66

1. This Convention shall be open to the signature of the Members of the Council of Europe. It shall be ratified. Ratifications shall be deposited with the Secretary General of the Council of Europe.

2. The present Convention shall come into force after the deposit of ten instruments of ratification.

3. As regards any signatory ratifying subsequently, the Convention shall come into force at the date of the deposit of its instrument of ratification.

4. The Secretary General of the Council of Europe shall notify all the Members of the Council of Europe of the entry into force of the Convention, the names of the High Contracting Parties who have ratified it, and the deposit of all instruments of ratification which may be effected subsequently.

DONE at Rome this 4th day of November, 1950 in English and French, both texts being equally authentic, in a single copy which shall remain deposited in the archives of the Council of Europe. The Secretary General shall transmit certified copies to each of the signatories.

Source: Council of Europe

[The Convention has been amended a number of times since 1948]

THE PARIS AGREEMENTS

23 October 1954

The PARIS AGREEMENTS were signed in Paris on 23 October, 1954 after the London Conference (28 September – 3 October, 1954), the Paris Conference (20 – 22 October, 1954) and a Ministerial Meeting of the NATO Council (23 October, 1954). In London, the so-called Nine-Power Conference, in addition to the seven countries signatories of agreements, was attended by the United States and Canada. In Paris, the so-called Four-Power Conference was attended by the United States, France, the United Kingdom and the Federal Republic of Germany. There were a number of agreements signed. The following are the most relevant to the current situation.

1. Convention on the Presence of Foreign Forces in the Federal Republic of Germany, Paris, 23 October, 1954

In view of the present international situation and the need to ensure the defence of the free world which require the continuing presence of foreign forces in the Federal Republic of Germany, the United States of America, the United Kingdom of Great Britain and Northern Ireland, the French Republic and the Federal Republic of Germany agree as follows:

Article I

1. From the entry into force of the arrangements for the German Defence Contribution, forces of the same nationality and effective strength as at that time may be stationed in the Federal Republic.

2. The effective strength of the forces stationed in the Federal Republic of Germany pursuant to paragraph 1 of this Article may at any time be increased with the consent of the Government of the Federal Republic.

3. Additional forces of the States Parties to the present Convention may enter and remain in the Federal territory with the consent of the Government of the Federal Republic for training purposes in accordance with the procedures applicable to forces assigned to the Supreme Allied Commander Europe, provided that such forces do not remain there for more than thirty days at any one time.

4. The Federal Republic grants to the French, the United Kingdom and the United States forces the right to enter, pass through, and depart

33

from the territory of the Federal Republic in transit to or from Austria (so long as their forces continue to be stationed there) or any country Member of the North Atlantic Treaty Organization, on the same basis as is usual between Parties to the North Atlantic Treaty or as may be agreed with effect for all Member States by the North Atlantic Council.

Article II

The present Convention shall be open to accession by any State not a Signatory, which had forces stationed in the Federal territory on the date of the signature of the Protocol on the Termination of the Occupation Régime in the Federal Republic of Germany signed at Paris on 23 October, 1954. Any such State, desiring to accede to the present Convention, may deposit with the Government of the Federal Republic an Instrument of Accession.

Article III

1. The present Convention shall expire with the conclusion of a German peace settlement or if at an earlier time the Signatory States agree that the development of the international situation justifies new arrangements . . .

2. Protocol Modifying and Completing the Brussels Treaty, Paris, 23 October, 1954

His Majesty the King of the Belgians, the President of the French Republic, President of the French Union, Her Royal Highness the Grand Duchess of Luxembourg, Her Majesty the Queen of the Netherlands and Her Majesty the Queen of the United Kingdom of Great Britain and Northern Ireland and of Her other Realms and Territories, Head of the Commonwealth, Parties to the Treaty of Economic, Social and Cultural Collaboration and Collective Self-Defence, signed at Brussels on March the 17th, 1948, hereinafter referred to as the Treaty, on the one hand. and the President of the Federal Republic of Germany and the President of the Italian Republic on the other hand,

Inspired by a common will to strengthen peace and security;

Desirous to this end of promoting the unity and of encouraging the progressive integration of Europe;

Convinced that the accession of the Federal Republic of Germany and the Italian Republic to the Treaty will represent a new and substantial advance towards these aims;

Having taken into consideration the decisions of the London Conference as set out in the Final Act of October the 3rd, 1954 and its Annexes;

Have appointed as their Plenipotentiaries: . . .

Who, having exhibited their full powers found in good and due form, Have agreed as follows:

Article I

The Federal Republic of Germany and the Italian Republic hereby accede to the Treaty as modified and completed by the present Protocol.

The High Contracting Parties to the present Protocol consider the Protocol on Forces of Western European Union (hereinafter referred to as Protocol No. II), the Protocol on the Control of Armaments and its Annexes (hereinafter referred to as Protocol No. III), and the Protocol on the Agency of Western European Union for the Control of Armaments (hereinafter referred to as Protocol No. IV) to be an integral part of the present Protocol.

Article II

The sub-paragraph of the Preamble to the Treaty: 'to take such steps as may be held necessary in the event of renewal by Germany of a policy of aggression' shall be modified to read: 'to promote the unity and to encourage the progressive integration of Europe'. The opening words of the 2nd paragraph of Article I shall read: 'The co-operation provided for in the preceding paragraph, which will be effected through the Council referred to in Article VII . . .'

Article III

The following new Article shall be inserted in the Treaty as Article IV: 'In the execution of the Treaty the High Contracting Parties and any organs established by Them under the Treaty shall work in close co-operation with the North Atlantic Treaty Organization'.

Recognising the undesirability of duplicating the Military Staffs of NATO, the Council and its agency will rely on the appropriate Military Authorities of NATO for information and advice on military matters.

Articles IV, V, VI and VII of the Treaty will become respectively Articles V, VI, VII and VIII.

Article IV

Article VIII of the Treaty (formerly Article VII) shall be modified to read as follows:

1. 'For the purposes of strengthening peace and security and of promoting unity and of encouraging the progressive integration of Europe and closer co-operation between Them and with other European organizations, the High Contracting Parties to the Brussels Treaty shall create a Council to consider matters concerning the execution of this Treaty and of its Protocols and their Annexes.

2. This Council shall be known as the "Council of Western European Union"; it shall be so organized as to be able to exercise its functions continuously; it shall set up such subsidiary bodies as may be necessary: in particular it shall establish immediately an Agency for the Control of Armaments whose functions are defined in Protocol No. IV.

3. At the request of any of the High Contracting Parties the Council

shall be immediately convened in order to permit Them to consult with regard to any situation which may constitute a threat to peace, in whatever area this threat should arise, or a danger to economic stability.

4. The Council shall decide by unanimous vote questions for which no other voting procedure has been or may be agreed. In the cases provided for in Protocols II, III and IV it will follow the various voting procedures, unanimity, two-thirds majority, simple majority, laid down therein. It will decide by simple majority questions submitted to it by the Agency for the Control of Armaments'.

Article V

A new Article shall be inserted in the Treaty as Article IX: 'The Council of Western European Union shall make an Annual Report on its activities and in particular concerning the control of armaments to an Assembly composed of representatives of the Brussels Treaty Powers to the Consultative Assembly of the Council of Europe'. The Articles VIII, IX and X of the Treaty shall become respectively Articles X, XI and XII
. . .

3. Protocol on Forces of Western European Union Paris, 23 October, 1954

His Majesty the King of the Belgians, the President of the French Republic, President of the French Union, the President of the Federal Republic of Germany, the President of the Italian Republic. Her Royal Highness the Grand Duchess of Luxembourg, Her Majesty the Queen of the Netherlands, and Her Majesty the Queen of the United Kingdom of Great Britain and Northern Ireland and of Her other Realms and Territories, Head of the Commonwealth, Signatories of the Protocol Modifying and Completing the Brussels Treaty,
Having consulted the North Atlantic Council,
Have appointed . . .,
Have agreed as follows:

Article I

1. The land and air forces which each of the High Contracting Parties to the present Protocol shall place under the Supreme Allied Commander Europe in peacetime on the mainland of Europe shall not exceed in total strength and number of formations:

a.   for Belgium, France, the Federal Republic of Germany, Italy and the Netherlands, the maxima laid down for peacetime in the Special Agreement annexed to the Treaty on the Establishment of a European Defence Community signed at Paris, on 27 May, 1952; and

b. for the United Kingdom, four divisions and the Second Tactical Air
    Force;
c. for Luxembourg, one regimental combat team.

2. The number of formations mentioned in paragraph 1 may be
brought up to date and adapted as necessary to make them suitable for
the North Atlantic Treaty Organization, provided that the equivalent
fighting capacity and total strengths are not exceeded.
3. The statement of these maxima does not commit any of the High
Contracting Parties to build up or maintain forces at these levels, but
maintains their right to do so if required.

Article II

As regards naval forces, the contribution to NATO Commands of each of
the High Contracting Parties to the present Protocol shall be determined each year in the course of the Annual Review (which takes into
account the recommendations of the NATO military authorities). The
naval forces of the Federal Republic of Germany shall consist of the
vessels and formations necessary for the defensive missions assigned
to it by the North Atlantic Treaty Organization within the limits laid
down in the Special Agreement mentioned in Article I, or equivalent
fighting capacity.

Article III

If at any time during the Annual Review recommendations are put
forward, the effect of which would be to increase the level of forces
above the limits specified in Articles I and II, the acceptance by the
country concerned of such recommended increases shall be subject to
the unanimous approval of the High Contracting Parties to the present
Protocol expressed either in the Council of Western European Union or
in the North Atlantic Treaty Organization.

Article IV

In order that it may establish that the limits specified in Articles I and II
are being observed, the Council of Western European Union will
regularly receive information acquired as a result of inspections carried
out by the Supreme Allied Commander Europe. Such information will
be transmitted by a high-ranking officer designated for the purpose by
the Supreme Allied Commander Europe

Article V

The strength and armaments of the internal defence and police forces
on the mainland of Europe of the High Contracting Parties to the
present Protocol shall be fixed by agreements within the Organization
of Western European Union, having regard to their proper functions
and needs and to their existing levels.

Article VI

Her Majesty the Queen of the United Kingdom of Great Britain and Northern Ireland will continue to maintain on the mainland of Europe, including Germany, the effective strength of the United Kingdom forces which are now assigned to the Supreme Allied Commander Europe, that is to say four divisions and the Second Tactical Air Force, or such other forces as the Supreme Allied Commander Europe regards as having equivalent fighting capacity. She undertakes not to withdraw these forces against the wishes of the majority of the High Contracting Parties who should take their decision in the knowledge of the views of the Supreme Allied Commander Europe. This undertaking shall not, however, bind her in the event of an acute overseas emergency. If the maintenance of the United Kingdom forces on the mainland of Europe throws at any time too great a strain on the external finances of the United Kingdom, she will, through Her Government in the United Kingdom of Great Britain and Northern Ireland, invite the North Atlantic Council to review the financial conditions on which the United Kingdom formations are maintained.

In witness whereof, the above-mentioned Plenipotentiaries have signed the present Protocol, being one of the Protocols listed in Article I of the Protocol Modifying and Completing the Treaty, and have affixed thereto their seals.

Done at Paris this twenty-third day of October, 1954, in two texts, in the English and French languages, each text being equally authoritative, in a single copy, which shall remain deposited in the archives of the Belgian Government and of which certified copies shall be transmitted by that Government to each of the other Signatories.

4. Protocol on the Control of Armaments
Paris, 23 October, 1954

His Majesty the King of the Belgians, the President of the French Republic, President of the French Union, the President of the Federal Republic of Germany, the President of the Italian Republic, Her Royal Highness the Grand Duchess of Luxembourg, Her Majesty the Queen of the Netherlands, Her Majesty the Queen of the United Kingdom of Great Britain and Northern Ireland and of Her other Realms and Territories, Head of the Commonwealth, Signatories of the Protocol Modifying and Completing the Brussels Treaty, Have agreed as follows:

Part I. Armaments not to be manufactured

Article I

The High Contracting Parties, members of Western European Union, take note of and record their agreement with the Declaration of the Chancellor of the Federal Republic of Germany (made in London on 3 October, 1954, and annexed hereto as Annex I(a)) in which the Federal

Republic of Germany undertook not to manufacture in its territory atomic, biological and chemical weapons. The types of armaments referred to in this Article are defined in Annex II(a). These armaments shall be more closely defined and the definitions brought up to date by the Council of Western European Union.

Article II

The High Contracting Parties, members of Western European Union, also take note of and record their agreement with the undertaking given by the Chancellor of the Federal Republic of Germany in the same Declaration that certain further types of armaments will not be manufactured in the territory of the Federal Republic of Germany, except that if in accordance with the needs of the armed forces a recommendation for an amendment to, or cancellation of, the content of the list of these armaments is made by the competent Supreme Commander of the North Atlantic Treaty Organization, and if the Government of the Federal Republic of Germany submits a request accordingly, such an amendment or cancellation may be made by a resolution of the Council of Western European Union passed by a two-thirds majority. The types of armaments referred to in this Article are listed in Annex III.

Part II. Armaments to be controlled

Article III

When the development of atomic, biological and chemical weapons in the territory on the mainland of Europe of the High Contracting Parties who have not given up the right to produce them has passed the experimental stage and effective production of them has started there, the level of stocks that the High Contracting Parties concerned will be allowed to hold on the mainland of Europe shall be decided by a majority vote of the Council of Western European Union.

Article IV

Without prejudice to the foregoing Articles, the types of armaments listed in Annex IV(a) will be controlled to the extent and in the manner laid down in Protocol No. IV(a). [*(a) not included.*]

Article V

The Council of Western European Union may vary the list in Annex IV by unanimous decision.

In witness whereof, the above-mentioned Plenipotentiaries have signed the present Protocol, being one of the Protocols listed in Article I of the Protocol Modifying and Completing the Treaty, and have affixed thereto their seals.

Done at Paris on the twenty-third day of October, 1954, in two texts, in the English and French languages, each text being equally authoritative, in a single copy, which shall remain deposited in the archives of the Belgian Government and of which certified copies shall be transmitted by that Government to each of the other Signatories.

Resolution of Association: The North Atlantic Council 22 October 1954

Welcoming the declaration made in London by the Government of the Federal Republic of Germany on 3 October, 1954 (Annex A), and the related declaration made on the same occasion by the Governments of the United States of America, the United Kingdom of Great Britain and Northern Ireland and the French Republic (Annex B), Notes with satisfaction that the representatives of the other Parties to the North Atlantic Treaty have, on behalf of their Governments, today associated themselves with the aforesaid declaration of the Three Powers.

Declaration by the Government of the Federal Republic of Germany

The German Federal Republic has agreed to conduct its policy in accordance with the principles of the Charter of the United Nations and accepts the obligations set forth in Article II of the Charter.

Upon her accession to the North Atlantic Treaty and the Brussels Treaty, the German Federal Republic declares that she will refrain from any action inconsistent with the strictly defensive character of the two treaties. In particular the German Federal Republic undertakes never to have recourse to force to achieve the reunification of Germany or the modification of the present boundaries of the German Federal Republic, and to resolve by peaceful means any disputes which may arise between the Federal Republic and other States.

Declaration by the Governments of the United States of America, the United Kingdom and France

The Governments of the United States of America, the United Kingdom of Great Britain and Northern Ireland and the French Republic,
Being resolved to devote their efforts to the strengthening of peace in accordance with the Charter of the United Nations and in particular with the obligations set forth in Article II of the Charter:

(i)   to settle their international disputes by peaceful means in such a manner that international peace and security and justice are not endangered;
(ii) to refrain in their international relations from the threat or use of force against the territorial integrity of political independence of any State, or in any other manner inconsistent with the purposes of the United Nations;
(iii) to give the United Nations every assistance in any action it takes in accordance with the Charter, and to refrain from giving assistance to any State against which the United Nations take preventive or enforcement action;

(iv) to ensure that States which are not Members of the United Nations act in accordance with the principles of the Charter so far as may be necessary for the maintenance of international peace and security.

Having regard to the purely defensive character of the Atlantic Alliance which is manifest in the North Atlantic Treaty, wherein they reaffirm their faith in the purposes and principles of the Charter of the United Nations and their desire to live in peace with all peoples and all Governments, and undertake to settle their international disputes by peaceful means in accordance with the principles of the Charter and to refrain, in accordance with those principles, from the threat or use of force in their international relations.

Take note that the German Federal Republic has by a Declaration dated 3rd October accepted the obligations set forth in Article II of the Charter of the United Nations and has undertaken never to have recourse to force to achieve the reunification of Germany or the modification of the present boundaries of the German Federal Republic, and to resolve by peaceful means any disputes which may arise between the Federal Republic and other States;

Declare that:

1. They consider the Government of the Federal Republic as the only German Government freely and legitimately constituted and therefore entitled to speak for Germany as the representative of the German people in international affairs.
2. In their relations with the Federal Republic they will follow the principles set out in Article II of the United Nations Charter.
3. A peace settlement for the whole of Germany, freely negotiated between Germany and her former enemies, which should lay the foundation of a lasting peace, remains an essential aim of their policy. The final determination of the boundaries of Germany must await such a settlement.
4. The achievement through peaceful means of a fully free and unified Germany remains a fundamental goal of their policy.
5. The security and welfare of Berlin and the maintenance of the position of the Three Powers there are regarded by the Three Powers as essential elements of the peace of the free world in the present international situation. Accordingly they will maintain armed forces within the territory of Berlin as long as their responsibilities require it. They therefore reaffirm that they will treat any attack against Berlin from any quarter as an attack upon their forces and themselves.
6. They will regard as a threat to their own peace and safety any recourse to force which in violation of the principles of the United Nations Charter threatens the integrity and unity of the Atlantic Alliance or its defensive purposes. In the event of any such action, the three Governments, for their part, will consider the offending

Government as having forfeited its rights to any guarantee and any military assistance provided for in the North Atlantic Treaty and its protocols. They will act in accordance with Article IV of the North Atlantic Treaty with a view to taking other measures which may be appropriate.

7.   They will invite the association of other member States of the North Atlantic Treaty Organization with this Declaration.

Source: NATO

THE WARSAW TREATY OF FRIENDSHIP, COOPERATION AND MUTUAL ASSISTANCE

Between the People's Republic of Albania, the People's Republic of Bulgaria, the Hungarian People's Republic, the German Democratic Republic, the Polish People's Republic, the Rumanian People's Republic, the Union of Soviet Socialist Republics, and the Czechoslovak Republic
14 May 1955

The contracting parties,

Reaffirming their desire for the organization of a system of collective security in Europe, with the participation of all the European states, irrespective of their social and state systems, which would make it possible to combine their efforts in the interests of securing peace in Europe,

Taking into consideration at the same time the situation obtaining in Europe, as the result of ratification of the Paris agreements, which provide for the formation of a new military grouping in the shape of 'Western European Union' together with a remilitarized Western Germany and for the integration of Western Germany in the North Atlantic bloc, which increases the threat of another war and creates a menace to the national security of the peace-loving states,

Convinced that, under these circumstances, the peace-loving states of Europe should take the necessary measures for safe-guarding their security, and in the interests of maintaining peace in Europe,

Guided by the purposes and principles of the United Nations Charter,

In the interests of further strengthening and promoting friendship, co-operation and mutual assistance, in accordance with the principles of respect for the independence and sovereignty of states, and also with the principle of non-interference in their internal affairs.

Have resolved to conclude this Treaty of Friendship, Cooperation and Mutual Assistance and have appointed their authorized representatives . . . who, having presented their credentials, found to be executed in due form and in complete order, have agreed on the following:

Article 1

The contracting parties undertake, in accordance with the Charter of the United Nations Organization, to refrain in their international relations from the threat or use of force, and to settle their international disputes by peaceful means so as not to endanger international peace and security.

Article 2

The contracting parties declare their readiness to take part, in the spirit of sincere co-operation, in all international undertakings intended to safeguard international peace and security and they shall use all their energies for the realization of these aims.

Moreover, the contracting parties shall work for the adoption, in agreement with other states desiring to co-operate in this matter, of effective measures towards a general reduction of armaments and prohibition of atomic, hydrogen and other weapons of mass destruction.

Article 3

The contracting parties shall take council among themselves on all important international questions relating to their common interests, guided by the interests of strengthening international peace and security.

They shall take council among themselves immediately, whenever, in the opinion of any of them, there has arisen the threat of an armed attack on one or several states that are signatories of the treaty, in the interests of organizing their joint defence and of upholding peace and security.

Article 4

In the event of an armed attack in Europe on one or several states that are signatories of the treaty by any state or group of states, each state that is a party to this treaty shall in the exercise of the right to individual or collective self-defence in accordance with Article 51 of the Charter of the United Nations Organization, render the state or states so attacked immediate assistance, individually and in agreement with other states that are parties to this treaty, by all the means it may consider necessary, including the use of armed force. The states that are parties to this treaty shall immediately take council among themselves concerning the necessary joint measures to be adopted for the purpose of restoring and upholding international peace and security.

In accordance with the principles of the Charter of the United Nations Organization, the Security Council shall be advised of the measures taken on the basis of the present article. These measures shall be adopted as soon as the Security Council has taken the necessary measures for restoring and upholding international peace and security.

Article 5

The contracting parties have agreed on the establishment of a joint command for their armed forces, which shall be placed, by agreement among these parties, under this command, which shall function on the basis of jointly defined principles. They shall also take other concerted measures necessary for strengthening their defence capacity, in order to safeguard the peaceful labour of their peoples, to guarantee the inviolability of their frontiers and territories and to provide safeguards against possible aggression.

Article 6

For the purpose of holding the consultations provided for in the present treaty among the states that are parties to the treaty, and for the purpose of considering problems arising in connection with the implementation of this treaty, a political consultative committee shall be formed in which each state that is a party to this treaty shall be represented by a member of the government, or any other specially appointed representative.

The committee may form the auxiliary organs for which the need may arise.

Article 7

The contracting parties undertake not to participate in any coalition and alliances, and not to conclude any agreements the purposes of which would be at variance with those of the present treaty.

The contracting parties declare that their obligation under existing international treaties are not at variance with the provisions of this treaty.

Article 8

The contracting parties declare that they will act in the spirit of friendship and co-operation with the object of furthering the development of and strengthening the economic and cultural relations between them, adhering to the principles of mutual respect for their independence and sovereignty, and of non-interference in their internal affairs.

Article 9

The present Treaty is open to the accession of other states – irrespective of their social and state systems – which may express their readiness to assist, through participation in the present Treaty, in combining the efforts of the peace-loving states for safeguarding the peace and security of the peoples. This act of acceding to the Treaty shall become effective with the consent of the states which are party to the Treaty, after the instrument of accession has been deposited with the Government of the Polish People's Republic.

Article 10

The present Treaty is subject to ratification, and the instruments of ratification shall be deposited with the Government of the Polish People's Republic.

The Treaty shall take effect on the date on which the last ratification instrument is deposited. The Government of the Polish People's Republic shall advise the other states that are party to the Treaty of each ratification instrument deposited with it.

Article 11

The present Treaty shall remain in force for twenty years. For the contracting parties which will not have submitted to the Government of the Polish People's Republic a statement denouncing the Treaty a year before the expiration of its term, it shall remain in force throughout the following ten years.

In the event of the organization of a system of collective security in Europe, and the conclusion of a general European Treaty of collective security to that end, which the contracting parties shall unceasingly seek to bring about, the present Treaty shall cease to be effective on the date the general European Treaty comes into force.

Source: Malcolm Mackintosh, *The Evolution of the Warsaw Pact*, (London, Adelphi Paper No. 58, June 1969)

STATEMENT ON THE FORMATION OF A JOINT COMMAND OF THE ARMED FORCES OF THE WARSAW TREATY STATES

14 May 1955

Under the Treaty of Friendship, Cooperation and Mutual Assistance between the People's Republic of Albania, the People's Republic of Bulgaria, the Hungarian People's Republic, the German Democratic Republic, the Polish People's Republic, the Rumanian People's Republic, the Union of Soviet Socialist Republics and the Czechoslovak Republic, the states that are parties to the treaty have taken the decision to form a joint command of their armed forces.

This decision envisages that general questions pertaining to the strengthening of the defence capacity and to the organization of the joint armed forces of the states that are parties to the treaty will be examined by the Political Consultative Committee, which will take appropriate decisions.

I.S. Koniev, Marshal of the Soviet Union, has been appointed commander-in-chief of the joint armed forces allotted by the states that are signatories to the treaty.

The assistants appointed for the commander-in-chief of the joint armed forces are the Ministers of Defence and other military leaders of the states that are parties to the treaty, who are vested with the command of the armed forces of each state that is a party to the treaty, allotted to the joint armed forces.

The question of participation of the German Democratic Republic in measures pertaining to the armed forces of the joint command will be examined later. (*This was done at the Prague Conference of 27–28 January 1956 when an East German contribution was incorporated in the military forces of the Warsaw Pact.*)

A staff of the joint armed forces of the states that are parties to the treaty will be set up under the commander-in-chief of the joint armed forces and this staff will include permanent representatives of the general staffs of the states that are parties to the treaty.

The headquarters of the staff will be in Moscow.

Distribution of the joint armed forces on the territories of states that are parties to the treaty will be carried out in accordance with the requirements of mutual defence, in agreement among these states.

Source: Documents on International Affairs

TREATY CONCERNING RELATIONS BETWEEN THE UNION OF SOVIET SOCIALIST REPUBLICS AND THE GERMAN DEMOCRATIC REPUBLIC, SIGNED AT MOSCOW, ON 20 SEPTEMBER 1955

Came into force on 6 October 1955, upon the exchange of the instruments of ratification at Berlin, in accordance with Article 7.

The Presidium of the Supreme Soviet of the Union of Soviet Socialist Republics and the President of the German Democratic Republic,

Desirous of promoting close cooperation and further strengthening the friendly relations between the Union of Soviet Socialist Republics and the German Democratic Republic on a basis of equality, respect for each other's sovereignty and non-intervention in each other's domestic affairs,

Mindful of the new situation created by the entry into force of the Paris Agreements of 1954,

Convinced that by combining their efforts towards the maintenance and strengthening of international peace and European security, the reunification of Germany as a peaceful and democratic State, and a settlement by peace treaty with Germany, the Soviet Union and the German Democratic Republic will be serving the interests both of the Soviet and German peoples and of the other peoples of Europe,

Having regard to the obligations of the Soviet Union and of the German Democratic Republic under existing international agreements relating to Germany as a whole,

Have decided to conclude the present Treaty and have appointed their plenipotentiaries ... who, having exchanged their full powers, found in good and due form, have agreed as follows:

Article 1

The Contracting Parties solemnly reaffirm that the relations between them are based on full equality, respect for each other's sovereignty and non-intervention in each other's domestic affairs.

The German Democratic Republic is accordingly free to take decisions on all questions pertaining to its domestic and foreign policy, including its relations with the Federal Republic of Germany and the development of relations with other States.

Article 2

The Contracting Parties declare their readiness to participate, in a spirit of sincere cooperation, in all international actions designed to ensure peace and security in Europe and throughout the world in conformity with the principles of the United Nations Charter.

To this end they shall consult with each other on all major international questions affecting the interests of the two States and shall adopt all measures within their power to prevent any breach of the peace.

Article 3

In accordance with the interests of the two countries and guided by the principles of friendship, the Contracting Parties agree to develop and strengthen the existing ties between the Union of Soviet Socialist Republics and the German Democratic Republic in economic, scientific, technical and cultural matters, to extend to each other all possible economic assistance, and to cooperate, wherever necessary, in the economic, scientific and technical fields.

Article 4

The Soviet forces now stationed in the territory of the German Democratic Republic in accordance with existing international agreements shall temporarily remain in the German Democratic Republic, with the consent of its Government and subject to conditions which shall be defined in a supplementary agreement between the Government of the Soviet Union and the Government of the German Democratic Republic.

The Soviet forces temporarily stationed in the territory of the German Democratic Republic shall not intervene in the domestic affairs or the social and political life of the German Democratic Republic.

Article 5

The Contracting Parties agree that their fundamental aim is to achieve, through appropriate negotiation, a peaceful settlement for the whole of Germany. They will accordingly make the necessary efforts to achieve a settlement by peace treaty and the reunification of Germany on a peaceful and democratic basis.

Article 6

This Treaty shall remain in force until Germany is reunited as a peaceful and democratic State, or until the Contracting Parties agree that the Treaty should be amended or terminated.

Article 7

This Treaty shall be ratified and shall enter into force on the date of the exchange of the instruments of ratification, which shall take place at Berlin as soon as possible.

DONE in duplicate, at Moscow, on 20 September 1955, in the Russian and German languages, both texts being equally authentic.

By authorization of the Presidium of the Supreme Soviet of the USSR: N. BULGANIN
By authorization of the President of the German Democratic Republic: O. GROTEWOHL

Source: UN Treaty Series

TREATY BETWEEN THE GOVERNMENT OF THE UNION OF SOVIET SOCIALIST REPUBLICS AND THE GOVERNMENT OF THE POLISH PEOPLE'S REPUBLIC CONCERNING THE LEGAL STATUS OF SOVIET FORCES TEMPORARILY STATIONED IN POLAND, SIGNED AT WARSAW, ON 17 DECEMBER 1956.

Came into force on 27 February 1957, as from the date of the exchange of the instruments of ratification at Moscow, in accordance with Article 20.

The Government of the Union of Soviet Socialist Republics and the Government of the Polish People's Republic, in conformity with the Joint Statement signed at Moscow on 18 November 1956, have resolved to conclude this Treaty and have appointed their plenipotentiaries for this purpose who, having communicated their full powers, found in good and due form, have agreed as follows:

Article 1

The temporary presence of Soviet forces in Poland shall in no way affect the sovereignty of the Polish State and shall not lead to any intervention by such forces in the domestic affairs of the Polish People's Republic.

Article 2

1. The strength and duty stations of Soviet forces temporarily stationed in the territory of the Polish People's Republic shall be determined by special agreements between the Government of the Union of Soviet Socialist Republics and the Government of the Polish People's Republic.

2. The movement outside their duty stations of Soviet forces in the territory of the Polish People's Republic shall be subject in each case to the consent of the Government of the Polish People's Republic or of the Polish authorities appointed by that Government.

3. The training and manoeuvres of Soviet forces outside their duty stations shall be carried out either on the basis of plans agreed upon with the Polish authorities or with the consent in each case of the Government of the Polish People's Republic or of the Polish authorities appointed by that Government.

Article 3

Soviet forces stationed in the territory of the Polish People's Republic, individuals serving with those forces and members of their families shall be under a duty to respect and comply with the provisions of Polish law.

Article 4

1. Military personnel of the Soviet forces stationed in the territory of the Polish People's Republic shall wear the appropriate uniform and shall possess and carry arms in accordance with the rules laid down by the Soviet Army.

2. The motor vehicles and motorcycles of Soviet military units shall bear a registration number and a clearly visible distinguishing mark. Such registration numbers and marks shall be determined by the command of the Soviet forces and facsimiles thereof shall be transmitted to the competent Polish authorities.

3. The competent Polish authorities shall recognize as valid, without a test or fee, driving licences issued by the competent Soviet authorities to individuals serving with the Soviet forces stationed in the territory of the Polish People's Republic.

Article 5

The procedure governing the entry into and departure from Poland of Soviet military units, of individuals serving with the Soviet forces and of members of their families, administrative questions relating to their presence in the territory of the Polish People's Republic, and the types of documents required in respect of them shall be settled by a special agreement between the Contracting Parties.

Article 6

The procedure and conditions for the use by Soviet forces of barracks, airfields, training grounds, artillery ranges with equipment and installations, buildings, transport and communications, electric power, communal services and commercial facilities, including the terms of payment therefor, shall be determined by special agreements between the competent authorities of the Contracting Parties.

Article 7

The construction at the duty stations of Soviet forces of buildings, airfields, roads, bridges and permanent radio-communications installations and the determination of the frequency and strength of such communications shall be subject to the consent of the competent Polish authorities. The organization outside the duty stations of Soviet forces of permanent service establishments for individuals serving with the Soviet forces shall likewise be subject to such consent.

Article 8

Any barracks, airfield, training ground or range with fixed equipment and installations which is released from use by Soviet armed forces shall be returned to the Polish authorities in good condition.

Such questions as may arise in connexion with the transfer to the Polish authorities of installations released by Soviet forces in the territory of the Polish People's Republic, including installations constructed by Soviet forces, shall be settled by special agreements.

Article 9

Questions of jurisdiction relating to the presence of Soviet forces in the territory of the Polish People's Republic shall be settled as follows:

1. Any individual serving with the Soviet forces or any member of the family of such individual who commits a serious or lesser offence in the territory of the Polish People's Republic shall as a general rule be subject to Polish law and to the jurisdiction of the Polish courts, the procurator's office and other Polish organs having competence in matters relating to the prosecution of persons who have committed serious and lesser offences.

Serious offences committed by Soviet military personnel shall be investigated by the military legal authorities and tried by the military tribunals of the Polish People's Republic.

2. The provisions of paragraph 1 of this article shall not apply:

(a) In the event that an individual serving with the Soviet armed forces or a member of the family of such individual commits a serious or lesser offence solely against the Soviet Union or against an individual serving with the Soviet forces or a member of the family of such an individual;

(b) In the event that an individual serving with the Soviet forces commits a serious or lesser offence in the performance of his official duties.

The cases referred to in sub-paragraphs (a) and (b) shall be subject to the jurisdiction of the Soviet courts and other agencies administering Soviet law.

3. The competent Soviet and Polish authorities may request one another to transfer or accept jurisdiction in specific cases covered by this article. Such requests shall receive sympathetic consideration.

Article 10

Any person convicted of a serious offence against the Soviet forces stationed in the territory of the Polish People's Republic or against military personnel thereof shall be liable to the same penalty as if the offence had been committed against Polish armed forces or Polish military personnel.

Article 11

1. The competent Soviet and Polish authorities shall render each other every assistance, including legal assistance, in matters relating to the prosecution of persons who have committed the serious and lesser offences referred to in articles 9 and 10 of this Treaty.

2. The principles and procedure governing the provision of the assistance referred to in paragraph 1 of this article shall be determined by a special agreement between the Contracting Parties.

Article 12

At the request of the competent Polish authorities, any individual serving with the Soviet forces who is convicted of an offence under Polish law shall be withdrawn from the territory of the Polish People's Republic.

Article 13

1. The Government of the Union of Soviet Socialist Republics agrees to compensate the Government of the Polish People's Republic for any material damage which may be caused to the Polish State by any act or omission of Soviet military units or individuals serving therewith and for any damage which may be caused to Polish institutions or citizens or to citizens of any third State in the territory of the Polish People's Republic by Soviet military units or individuals serving therewith in the performance of their official duties. The amount of such compensation shall be determined in either case by a Mixed Commission established under article 19 of this Treaty, on the basis of the claims filed and in conformity with the provisions of Polish law.

Any disputes arising out of the obligations of Soviet military units shall likewise be examined by the Mixed Commission in accordance with the same principles.

2. The Government of the Union of Soviet Socialist Republics likewise agrees to compensate the Government of the Polish People's Republic for any damage caused to Polish institutions or citizens or to citizens of any third State in the territory of the Polish People's Republic by any act or omission done by individuals serving with the Soviet forces otherwise than in the performance of their official duties or by any act or omission of members of the families of such individuals. The amount of such compensation shall be determined in either case by the competent Polish court, on the basis of the claims filed against the persons who have caused the damage.

3. Compensation for damage shall be payable by the Soviet party within three months after a decision has been taken by the Mixed Commission or after the judgement of the court has entered into force.

The sums awarded by the Mixed Commission or the court shall be paid to the injured persons and institutions by the competent Polish authorities.

4. Any claims for compensation in respect of damage which have

not been settled before the entry into force of this Treaty shall be examined by the Mixed Commission.

Article 14

1. The Government of the Polish People's Republic agrees to compensate the Government of the Union of Soviet Socialist Republics for any damage caused to the property of the Soviet military units stationed in the territory of the Polish People's Republic or to individuals serving with the Soviet forces by any act or omission of Polish State institutions. The amount of such compensation shall be determined by the Mixed Commission established under article 19 of this Treaty, on the basis of the claims filed and in conformity with the provisions of Polish law.

Any dispute arising out of the obligations of Polish state institutions to Soviet military units shall likewise be examined by the Mixed Commission in accordance with the same principles.

2. The Government of the Polish People's Republic likewise agrees to compensate the Government of the Union of Soviet Socialist Republics for any damage caused to Soviet military units stationed in the territory of the Polish People's Republic, to individuals serving with the Soviet forces and to members of the families of such individuals by any act or omission of Polish citizens. The amount of such compensation shall be determined by the Polish court on the basis of the claims filed against the persons who have caused the damage.

Article 15

1. The routes, dates, procedure and terms of payment for the transportation of Soviet forces and military equipment in transit through the territory of the Polish People's Republic and military freight movements within the territory of the Polish People's Republic shall be settled by special agreements.

2. The provisions of this Treaty and, in particular, the provisions relating to jurisdiction and liability for damage, shall be applicable, where appropriate, to Soviet forces in transit through the territory of the Polish People's Republic.

Article 16

Questions concerning the application to the Soviet forces stationed in the territory of the Polish People's Republic, to individuals serving in those forces and to members of their families of the fiscal, customs and foreign exchange regulations in force in Poland and the regulations relating to entry and exit shall be settled by special agreements.

Article 17

The Government of the Union of Soviet Socialist Republics and the Government of the Polish People's Republic, with a view to the due settlement of questions arising from day to day in connexion with the presence of Soviet armed forces in Poland, shall appoint pleni-potentiaries for matters relating to the presence of Soviet armed forces in Poland.

Article 18

For the purposes of this Treaty:

The expression 'individual serving with the Soviet forces' shall mean:

(a) A person in military service in the Soviet Army,

(b) A civilian who is a Soviet national and who is employed in a unit of the Soviet armed forces in the Polish People's Republic;

The expression 'duty station' shall mean an area placed at the disposal of Soviet forces, including places where military units are quartered together with training grounds, rifle and artillery ranges and other installations used by such units.

Article 19

A Soviet-Polish Mixed Commission, to which each Contracting Party shall appoint three representatives, shall be established in order to settle questions relating to the interpretation or application of this Treaty and of the agreements provided for herein.

The Mixed Commission shall adopt its own rules of procedure.

The headquarters of the Mixed Commission shall be Warsaw.

In the event that the Mixed Commission is unable to settle a question referred to it, the said question shall be settled through the diplomatic channel as soon as possible.

Article 20

This Treaty shall be ratified and shall enter into force on the date of the exchange of the instruments of ratification, which shall take place at Moscow.

Article 21

This Treaty shall remain in force for so long as Soviet forces remain in the territory of the Polish People's Republic and may be amended by agreement between the Contracting Parties.

DONE at Warsaw on 17 December 1956 in two copies, each in the Russian and Polish languages, both texts being equally authentic.

Source: UN Treaty Series

★   ★   ★

Similar agreements, although with variations in the preambles and ordering of provisions, were signed with the GDR on 12 March 1957, Hungary on 27 May 1957 and Czechoslovakia on 16 October 1968.

THE FRANCO-GERMAN TREATY ON ORGANIZATION AND PRINCIPLES OF COOPERATION, SIGNED AT PARIS, 22 JANUARY 1963

Following the Joint Declaration of the Chancellor of the Federal Republic of Germany and the President of the French Republic dated 22 January 1963 on organization and principles of cooperation between the two countries, the following provisions have been agreed upon:

I. Organization

(1) The Heads of State and Government shall give the necessary directives as required and shall follow regularly the execution of the program hereafter laid down. For this purpose, they shall meet as often as necessary and, in principle, at least twice a year.

(2) The Foreign Ministers shall supervise the execution of the program as a whole. They shall meet at least every three months. Without prejudice to contacts normally established through the Embassies, high officials of the two Foreign Ministries – charged respectively with political, economic, and cultural affairs – shall meet every month alternately in Bonn and Paris to assess the state of current problems and to prepare the meeting of the Ministers. Furthermore, the diplomatic missions and consulates of the two countries as well as their permanent representatives in international organizations shall establish the necessary contacts on problems of common interest.

(3) Regular meetings shall take place between the appropriate authorities of the two countries in the fields of defense, education, and youth. These meetings shall in no way affect the functioning of already existing organisms – the German-French Cultural Commission and the Permanent Group of the General staffs – whose activities shall, on the contrary, be developed. The Foreign Ministers shall be represented in these meetings to insure the overall coordination of cooperation.

(a) The Ministers of Defense and of the Army shall meet at least once every three months. Furthermore, in the same intervals, the French Minister of Education shall meet the personality who will be designated on the German side to follow up the execution of the program of cooperation in the cultural field.

(b) The chiefs of staff of the two countries shall meet at least once every two months. Should they be unable to attend, they shall be replaced by their responsible deputies.

(c) The Federal Minister for Family and Youth Affairs or his deputy shall meet the French High Commissioner for Youth and Sports at least once every two months.

(4) In each of the two countries an Interministerial Commission shall be charged with following up the problems of cooperation. This Commission shall comprise representatives of all ministries concerned and shall be presided over by a high official of the Foreign Ministry. Its task shall be to coordinate the action of the Ministries concerned and to report at regular intervals to its Government on the state of German-French cooperation. The Commission shall also be responsible for making appropriate suggestions for implementing the program of cooperation and its possible extension to other fields.

II. Programme

A. Foreign affairs

(1) The Two Governments shall consult before any decision on all important questions of foreign policy and primarily on questions of common interest with a view to reaching as far as possible parallel positions. This consultation shall apply, among others, to the following subjects:

Problems relating to the European Communities and European political cooperation;

East-West relations both in the political and economic fields;

Matters dealt with in the North Atlantic Treaty Organization and in the various international organizations in which the two Governments are interested, notably the Council of Europe, the Western European Union, the Organization for Economic Cooperation and Development, and the United Nations and its specialized agencies.

(2) The cooperation already established in the field of information shall be continued and developed between the appropriate agencies in Bonn and Paris and between the missions in third countries.

(3) With respect to development aid, the two Governments shall systematically compare their programs to maintain continuous and close coordination and to enable the joint undertaking of new projects. Since both on the German and the French side several ministries are responsible for this matter, it shall be the concern of the two Foreign ministries to determine jointly the practical bases of this cooperation.

(4) The two Governments shall study jointly the ways and means of strengthening their cooperation within the framework of the Common Market and in other important sectors of economic policy, such as agricultural and forestry policy, energy, the problems of traffic and transport and industrial development, as well as the policy of export credits.

B. Defense

I. The objects pursued in this field shall be the following:

(1) In the field of strategy and tactics, the competent authorities of the two countries shall endeavour to bring their doctrines closer together in order to arrive at joint concepts. German-French institutes for operational research shall be set up.

(2) Exchanges of personnel between the armed forces shall be increased. This shall apply in particular to instructors and students of the general staff colleges. The exchanges may extend to the temporary detachment of entire units. In order to facilitate these exchanges, both sides shall endeavor to promote practical instruction in the languages for the personnel concerned.

(3) In the armament field, the two Governments shall endeavour to organize work in common from the stage of formulating appropriate armament projects and of preparing plans to finance them. To this end, Mixed Commissions shall study, and shall examine on a comparative basis, current research on these projects in the two countries. They shall present proposals to the Ministers who shall examine them at their quarterly meetings and shall give the necessary directives for application.

II. The Governments shall institute a study of the conditions in which German-French cooperation can be established in the field of civil defense.

III. Concluding Provisions

(1) The necessary directives shall be issued in both countries to implement immediately the above provisions. The Foreign Ministers shall ascertain at each of their meetings what progress has been made.

(2) The two Governments shall keep the Governments of the other members of the European Communities continuously informed of the development of German-French cooperation.

(3) With the exception of the provisions regarding defense, the present Treaty shall also apply to Land Berlin, unless the Government of the Federal Republic of Germany shall make, within three months after the entry into force of the present Treaty, a statement to the contrary to the Government of the French Republic.

(4) The two Governments may make those adjustments which may prove desirable for the implementation of the present Treaty.

(5) The present Treaty shall enter into force as soon as each of the two Contracting Parties has informed the other that the conditions of domestic law required for this purpose have been fulfilled.

Done at Paris on the twenty-second of January, 1963, in duplicate in German and French, each text being equally authentic.

Source: US Dept. of State. Documents on Germany, 1944–1985

THE FRUITS OF DÉTENTE

TREATY OF FRIENDSHIP, COOPERATION AND MUTUAL AID BETWEEN THE UNION OF SOVIET SOCIALIST REPUBLICS AND THE CZECHOSLOVAK SOCIALIST REPUBLIC, PRAGUE, 6 MAY 1970

The Union of Soviet Socialist Republics and the Czechoslovak Socialist Republic,

Affirming their fidelity to the aims and principles of the Soviet-Czechoslovak Treaty of Friendship, Mutual Aid and Post-War Cooperation, concluded on December 12, 1943, and extended on November 27, 1963, a treaty that played a historic role in the development of friendly relations between the peoples of the two States and laid a solid foundation for the further strengthening of fraternal friendship and all-round cooperation between them;

Profoundly convinced that the indestructible friendship between the Union of Soviet Socialist Republics and the Czechoslovak Socialist Republic, which was cemented in the joint struggle against Fascism and has received further deepening in the years of the construction of socialism and communism, as well as the fraternal mutual assistance and all-round cooperation between them, based on the teachings of Marxism-Leninism and the immutable principles of socialist inter-nationalism, correspond to the fundamental interests of the peoples of both countries and of the entire socialist commonwealth;

Affirming that the support, strengthening and defence of the socialist gains achieved at the cost of the heroic efforts and selfless labour of each people are the common internationalist duty of the socialist countries;

Consistently and steadfastly favouring the strengthening of the unity and solidarity of all countries of the socialist commonwealth, based on the community of their social systems and ultimate goals;

Firmly resolved strictly to observe the obligations stemming from the May 14, 1955, Warsaw Treaty of Friendship, Cooperation and Mutual Aid;

Stating the economic cooperation between the two States facilitates their development, as well as the further improvement of the inter-

61

national socialist division of labour and socialist economic integration within the framework of the Council for Mutual Economic Aid;

Expressing the firm intention to promote the cause of strengthening peace and security in Europe and throughout the world, to oppose imperialism, revanchism and militarism;

Guided by the goals and principles proclaimed in the United Nations Charter;

Taking into account the achievements of socialist and communist construction in the two countries, the present situation and the prospects for all-round cooperation, as well as the changes that have taken place in Europe and throughout the world since the conclusion of the Treaty of December 12, 1943;

Have agreed on the following:

Article 1

In accordance with the principles of socialist internationalism, the High Contracting Parties will continue to strengthen the eternal, indestructible friendship between the peoples of the Union of Soviet Socialist Republics and the Czechoslovak Socialist Republic, to develop all-round cooperation between the two countries and to give each other fraternal assistance and support, basing their actions on mutual respect for State sovereignty and independence, on equal rights and non-interference in one another's internal affairs.

Article 2

The High Contracting Parties will continue, proceeding from the principles of friendly mutual assistance and the international socialist division of labour, to develop and deepen mutually advantageous bilateral and multilateral economic, scientific and technical cooperation with the aim of developing their national economies, achieving the highest possible scientific and technical level and efficiency of social production, and increasing the material well-being of the working people of their countries.

The two sides will promote the further development of economic ties and cooperation and the socialist economic integration of the member countries of the Council for Mutual Economic Aid.

Article 3

The High Contracting Parties will continue to develop and expand cooperation between the two countries in the fields of science and culture, education, literature and the arts, the press, radio, motion pictures, television, public health, tourism and physical culture and in other fields.

Article 4

The High Contracting Parties will continue to facilitate the expansion of cooperation and direct ties between the bodies of State authority and the public organizations of the working people, with the aim of achieving a deeper mutual familiarization and a closer drawing together between the peoples of the two States.

Article 5
The High Contracting Parties, expressing their unswerving determination to proceed along the path of the construction of socialism and communism, will take the necessary steps to defend the socialist gains of the peoples and the security and independence of the two countries, will strive to develop all-round relations among the States of the socialist commonwealth, and will act in a spirit of the consolidation of the unity, friendship and fraternity of these States.

Article 6
The High Contracting Parties proceed from the assumption that the Munich Pact of September 29, 1938, was signed under the threat of aggressive war and the use of force against Czechoslovakia, that it was a component part of Hitler Germany's criminal conspiracy against peace and was a flagrant violation of the basic norms of international law, and hence was invalid from the very outset, with all the consequences stemming therefrom.

Article 7
The High Contracting Parties, consistently pursuing a policy of the peaceful coexistence of States with different social systems, will exert every effort for the defence of international peace and the security of the peoples against encroachments by the aggressive forces of imperialism and reaction, for the relaxation of international tension, the cessation of the arms race and the achievement of general and complete disarmament, the final liquidation of colonialism in all its forms and manifestations, and the giving of support to countries that have been liberated from colonial domination and are marching along the path of strengthening national independence and sovereignty.

Article 8
The High Contracting Parties will jointly strive to improve the situation and to ensure peace in Europe, to strengthen and develop cooperation among the European States, to establish good-neighbour relations among them and to create an effective system of European security on the basis of the collective efforts of all European States.

Article 9
The High Contracting Parties declare that one of the main preconditions for ensuring European security is the immutability of the State borders that were formed in Europe after the Second World War. They express their firm resolve, jointly with the other Member States of the May 14, 1955, Warsaw Treaty of Friendship, Cooperation and Mutual

Aid and in accordance with this Treaty, to ensure the inviolability of the borders of the Member States of this Treaty and to take all necessary steps to prevent aggression on the part of any forces of militarism and revanchism and to rebuff the aggressor.

Article 10

In the event that one of the High Contracting Parties is subjected to an armed attack by any States or group of States, the other Contracting Party, regarding this as an attack against itself, will immediately give the first party all possible assistance, including military aid, and will also give it support with all means at its disposal, by way of implementing the right to individual or collective self-defence in accordance with Article 51 of the United Nations Charter.

The High Contracting Parties will without delay inform the United Nations Security Council of steps taken on the basis of this Article, and they will act in accordance with the provisions of the United Nations Charter.

Article 11

The High Contracting Parties will inform each other and consult on all important international questions affecting their interests and will act on the basis of common positions agreed upon in accordance with the interests of both States.

Article 12

The High Contracting Parties declare that their obligations under existing international treaties are not at variance with the provisions of this Treaty.

Article 13

This Treaty is subject to ratification and will enter into force on the day of the exchange of instruments of ratification, which will be conducted in Moscow in a very short time.

Article 14

This Treaty is concluded for a period of twenty years and will be automatically extended every five years thereafter, if neither of the High Contracting Parties gives notice that it is denouncing the Treaty twelve months before the expiration of the current period.

[Signed] L. BREZHNEV and A. KOSYGIN; G. HUSAK and L. STROUGAL.

Source: The Major International Treaties since 1945

TREATY BETWEEN THE FEDERAL REPUBLIC OF GERMANY AND THE SOVIET UNION, MOSCOW, 12 AUGUST 1970

The High Contracting Parties

Anxious to contribute to strengthening peace and security in Europe and the world.

Convinced that peaceful cooperation among States on the basis of the purposes and principles of the Charter of the United Nations complies with the ardent desire of nations and the general interests of international peace.

Appreciating the fact that the agreed measures previously implemented by them, in particular the conclusion of the Agreement of 13 September 1955 on the Establishment of Diplomatic Relations have created favourable conditions for new important steps destined to develop further and to strengthen their mutual relations.

Desiring to lend expression, in the form of a treaty, to their determination to improve and extend cooperation between them, including economic relations as well as scientific, technological and cultural contacts, in the interest of both States

Have agreed as follows:

Article 1

The Federal Republic of Germany and the Union of Soviet Socialist Republics consider it an important objective of their policies to maintain international peace and achieve detente.

They affirm their endeavour to further the normalization of the situation in Europe and the development of peaceful relations among all European States, and in so doing proceed from the actual situation existing in this region.

Article 2

The Federal Republic of Germany and the Union of Soviet Socialist Republics shall in their mutual relations as well as in matters of ensuring European and international security be guided by the purposes and principles embodied in the Charter of the United Nations. Accordingly they shall settle their disputes exclusively by peaceful means and undertake to refrain from the threat or use of force, pursuant to Article 2 of the Charter of the United Nations, in any matters affecting security in Europe or international security, as well as in their mutual relations.

Article 3

In accordance with the foregoing purposes and principles the Federal Republic of Germany and the Union of Soviet Socialist Republics share the realization that peace can only be maintained in Europe if nobody disturbs the present frontiers.

— They undertake to respect without restriction the territorial integrity of all States in Europe within their present frontiers;
— They declare that they have no territorial claims against anybody nor will assert such claims in the future;
— They regard today and shall in future regard the frontiers of all States in Europe as inviolable such as they are on the date of signature of the present Treaty, including the Oder-Neisse line which forms the western frontier of the People's Republic of Poland and the frontier between the Federal Republic of Germany and the German Democratic Republic.

Article 4

The present Treaty between the Federal Republic of Germany and the Union of Soviet Socialist Republics shall not affect any bilateral or multilateral treaties or arrangements previously concluded by them.

Article 5

The present Treaty is subject to ratification and shall enter into force on the date of exchange of the instruments of ratification which shall take place in Bonn.

The Government of the Federal Republic of Germany to the Government of the Soviet Union, 12 August 1970

In connection with today's signature of the Treaty between the Federal Republic of Germany and the Union of Soviet Socialist Republics the Government of the Federal Republic of Germany has the honour to state that this Treaty does not conflict with the political objective of the Federal Republic of Germany to work for a state of peace in Europe in which the German nation will recover its unity in free self-determination.

Source: US Dept. of State, Documents on Germany, 1944–1985

TREATY BETWEEN THE FEDERAL REPUBLIC OF GERMANY AND THE PEOPLE'S REPUBLIC OF POLAND, WARSAW

Initialled 18 November 1970 and signed 7 December 1970

The Governments of the Federal Republic of Germany and the People's Republic of Poland,

1. Considering the fact that more than 25 years have passed since the end of the Second World War in which Poland was the first victim and which brought great misfortune upon the people of Europe:

2. Bearing in mind that, in the meantime, a new generation has grown up in both countries for whom a peaceful future should be assured;

3. Wishing to create a durable basis for a peaceful coexistence and the development of good and normal relations between them;

4. In the endeavour to fortify peace and security in Europe;

5. Conscious that the inviolability of frontiers and respect for territorial integrity and the sovereignty of all states in Europe, within their present frontiers, is a fundamental condition for peace, have agreed as follows:

Article One

(i) The Federal Republic of Germany and the People's Republic of Poland declare in agreement that the existing border line, the course of which was determined in Chapter IX of the decisions of the Potsdam conference of 2 August 1945 as from the Baltic Sea immediately west of Swinemunde, thence along the Oder to the confluence of the Lausitzer Neisse, and along the Lausitzer Neisse to the frontier with Czechoslovakia, forms the western state frontier of the People's Republic of Poland.

(ii) They affirm the inviolability of their existing frontiers, now and in the future, and mutually commit themselves to unrestricted respect for their territorial integrity.

(iii) They declare that they have no territorial claims against one another, and will not raise such claims in the future.

Article Two

(i) The Federal Republic of Germany and the People's Republic of Poland will be guided in their mutual relations, as well as in questions

67

concerning the safeguarding of security in Europe and in the world, by the purposes and principles laid down in the Charter of the United Nations.

(ii) Therefore they will, in accordance with Articles 1 and 2 of the Charter of the United Nations, settle all their disputes exclusively by peaceful means and will refrain from the threat of force or use of force in questions which affect European and international security, as well as in their mutual relations.

Article Three

(i) The Federal Republic of Germany and the People's Republic of Poland will undertake further steps towards full normalization and comprehensive development of their mutual relations of which this treaty forms the firm foundation.

(ii) They are agreed that an expansion of their cooperation in the area of economic, scientific, scientific-technical, cultural and other relations lies in their common interest.

Article Four

This treaty does not affect bilateral or multilateral international agreements previously concluded by, or affecting the parties.

Article Five

This treaty requires ratification. It will come into force on the day the instruments of ratification are exchanged. This shall be done in Bonn.

Source: US Dept. of State, Documents on Germany, 1944–1985

AGREEMENT ON BERLIN BY THE GOVERNMENTS OF FRANCE, GREAT BRITAIN, THE UNITED STATES AND THE SOVIET UNION, 3 SEPTEMBER 1971, WITH ANNEXES AND RELATED DOCUMENTS

The Governments of the United States of America, the French Republic, the Union of Soviet Socialist Republics and the United Kingdom of Great Britain and Northern Ireland.

Represented by their Ambassadors, who held a series of meetings in the building formerly occupied by the Allied Control Council in the American Sector of Berlin.

Acting on the basis of their quadripartite rights and responsibilities, and of the corresponding wartime and postwar agreements and decisions of the Four Powers, which are not affected.

Taking into account the existing situation in the relevant area,

Guided by the desire to contribute to practical improvements of the situation,

Without prejudice to their legal positions,

Have agreed on the following:

Part I
General Provisions

1. The four Governments will strive to promote the elimination of tension and the prevention of complications in the relevant area.

2. The four Governments, taking into account their obligations under the Charter of the United Nations, agree that there shall be no use or threat of force in the area and that disputes shall be settled solely by peaceful means.

3. The four Governments will mutually respect their individual and joint rights and responsibilities, which remain unchanged.

4. The four Governments agree that, irrespective of the differences in legal views, the situation which has developed in the area, and as it is defined in this Agreement as well as in the other agreements referred to in this Agreement, shall not be changed unilaterally.

Part II
Provisions Relating to the Western Sectors of Berlin

A. The Government of the Union of Soviet Socialist Republics declares that transit traffic by road, rail and waterways through the territory of the German Democratic Republic of civilian persons and goods between the Western Sectors of Berlin and the Federal Republic of Germany will be unimpeded; that such traffic will be facilitated so as to take place in the most simple and expeditious manner; and that it will receive preferential treatment.

Detailed arrangements concerning this civilian traffic, as set forth in Annex I, will be agreed by the competent German authorities.

B. The Governments of the French Republic, the United Kingdom and the United States of America declare that the ties between the Western Sectors of Berlin and the Federal Republic of Germany will be maintained and developed, taking into account that these Sectors continue not to be a constituent part of the Federal Republic of Germany and not to be governed by it.

Detailed arrangements concerning the relationship between the Western Sectors of Berlin and the Federal Republic of Germany are set forth in Annex II.

C. The Government of the Union of Soviet Socialist Republics declares that communications between the Western Sectors of Berlin and areas bordering on these Sectors and those areas of the German Democratic Republic which do not border on these Sectors will be improved. Permanent residents of the Western Sectors of Berlin will be able to travel to and visit such areas for compassionate, family, religious, cultural or commercial reasons, or as tourists, under conditions comparable to those applying to other persons entering these areas.

The problems of small enclaves, including Steinstuecken, and of other small areas may be solved by exchange of territory.

Detailed arrangements concerning travel, communications and the exchange of territory, as set forth in Annex III, will be agreed by the competent German authorities.

D. Representation abroad of the interests of the Western Sectors of Berlin and consular activities of the Union of Soviet Socialist Republics in the Western Sectors of Berlin can be exercised as set forth in Annex IV.

Part III
Final Provisions

This Quadripartite Agreement will enter into force on the date specified in a Final Quadripartite Protocol to be concluded when the measures envisaged in Part II of this Quadripartite Agreement and in its Annexes have been agreed.

Annex I

Communications From the Government of the Union of Soviet Socialist Republics to the Governments of the French Republic, the United Kingdom and the United States of America

The Government of the Union of Soviet Socialist Republics, with reference to Part II(A) of the Quadripartite Agreement of this date and after consultation and agreement with the Government of the German Democratic Republic, has the honor to inform the Governments of the French Republic, the United Kingdom and the United States of America that:

1. Transit traffic by road, rail and waterways through the territory of the German Democratic Republic of civilian persons and goods between the Western Sectors of Berlin and the Federal Republic of Germany will be facilitated and unimpeded. It will receive the most simple, expeditious and preferential treatment provided by international practice.

2. Accordingly,

(a) Conveyances sealed before departure may be used for the transport of civilian goods by road, rail and waterways between the Western Sectors of Berlin and the Federal Republic of Germany. Inspection procedures will be limited to the inspection of seals and accompanying documents.

(b) With regard to conveyances which cannot be sealed, such as open trucks, inspection procedures will be limited to the inspection of accompanying documents. In special cases where there is sufficient reason to suspect that unsealed conveyances contain either material intended for dissemination along the designated routes or persons or material put on board along these routes, the content of unsealed conveyances may be inspected. Procedures for dealing with such cases will be agreed by the competent German authorities.

(c) Through trains and buses may be used for travel between the Western Sectors of Berlin and the Federal Republic of Germany. Inspection procedures will not include any formalities other than identification of persons.

(d) Persons identified as through travellers using individual vehicles between the Western Sectors of Berlin and the Federal Republic of Germany on routes designated for through traffic will be able to proceed to their destinations without paying individual tolls and the fees for the use of the transit routes. Procedures applied for such travellers shall not involve delay. The travellers, their vehicles and personal baggage will not be subject to search, detention or exclusion from use of the designated routes, except in special cases, as may be agreed by the competent German authorities, where there is sufficient reason to suspect that misuse of the transit routes is intended for purposes not related to direct travel to and from the Western Sectors of

Berlin and is contrary to generally applicable regulations concerning public order.

(e) Appropriate compensation for fees and tolls and for other costs related to traffic on the communication routes between the Western Sectors of Berlin and the Federal Republic of Germany, including the maintenance of adequate routes, facilities and installations used for such traffic, may be made in the form of an annual lump sum paid to the German Democratic Republic by the Federal Republic of Germany.

3. Arrangements implementing and supplementing the provisions of paragraphs 1 and 2 above will be agreed by the competent German authorities.

Annex II

Communication From the Governments of the French Republic, the United Kingdom and the United States of America to the Government of the Union of Soviet Socialist Republics

The Governments of the French Republic, the United Kingdom and the United States of America, with reference to Part II(B) of the Quadripartite Agreement of this date and after consultation with the Government of the Federal Republic of Germany, have the honor to inform the Government of the Union of Soviet Socialist Republics that:

1. They declare, in the exercise of their rights and responsibilities, that the ties between the Western Sectors of Berlin and the Federal Republic of Germany will be maintained and developed, taking into account that these Sectors continue not to be a constituent part of the Federal Republic of Germany and not to be governed by it. The provisions of the Basic Law of the Federal Republic of Germany and of the Constitution operative in the Western Sectors of Berlin which contradict the above have been suspended and continue not to be in effect.

2. The Federal President, the Federal Government, the Bundesversammlung, the Bundesrat and the Bundestag, including their Committees and Fraktionen, as well as other state bodies of the Federal Republic of Germany will not perform in the Western Sectors of Berlin constitutional or official acts which contradict the provisions of paragraph 1.

3. The Government of the Federal Republic of Germany will be represented in the Western Sectors of Berlin to the authorities of the three Governments and to the Senat by a permanent liaison agency.

Annex III

Communication From the Government of the Union of Soviet Socialist Republics to the Governments of the French Republic, the United Kingdom and the United States of America

The Government of the Union of Soviet Socialist Republics, with reference to Part II(C) of the Quadripartite Agreement of this date and after consultation and agreement with the Government of the German Democratic Republic, has the honor to inform the Governments of the French Republic, the United Kingdom and the United States of America that:

1. Communications between the Western Sectors of Berlin and areas bordering on these Sectors and those areas of the German Democratic Republic which do not border on these Sectors will be improved.

2. Permanent residents of the Western Sectors of Berlin will be able to travel to and visit such areas for compassionate, family, religious, cultural or commercial reasons, or as tourists, under conditions comparable to those applying to other persons entering these areas. In order to facilitate visits and travel, as described above by permanent residents of the Western Sectors of Berlin, additional crossing points will be opened.

3. The problems of the small enclaves, including Steinstuecken, and of other small areas may be solved by exchange of territory.

4. Telephonic, telegraphic, transport and other external communications of the Western Sectors of Berlin will be expanded.

5. Arrangements implementing and supplementing the provisions of paragraphs 1 to 4 above will be agreed by the competent German authorities.

Annex IV

A. Communication From the Governments of the French Republic, the United Kingdom and the United States of America to the Government of the Union of Soviet Socialist Republics

The Governments of the French Republic, the United Kingdom and the United States of America, with reference to Part II(D) of the Quadripartite Agreement of this date and after consultation with the Government of the Federal Republic of Germany, have the honor to inform the Government of the Union of Soviet Socialist Republics that:

1. The Governments of the French Republic, the United Kingdom and the United States of America maintain their rights and responsibilities relating to the representation abroad of the interests of the Western Sectors of Berlin and their permanent residents, including those rights and responsibilities concerning matters of security and status, both in international organizations and in relations with other countries.

2. Without prejudice to the above and provided that matters of security and status are not affected, they have agreed that:

(a) The Federal Republic of Germany may perform consular services for permanent residents of the Western Sectors of Berlin.

(b) In accordance with established procedures, international agreements and arrangements entered into by the Federal Republic of Germany may be extended to the Western Sectors of Berlin provided that the extension of such agreements and arrangements is specified in each case.

(c) The Federal Republic of Germany may represent the interests of the Western Sectors of Berlin in international organizations and international conferences.

(d) Permanent residents of the Western Sectors of Berlin may participate jointly with participants from the Federal Republic of Germany in international exchanges and exhibitions. Meetings of international organizations and international conferences as well as exhibitions with international participation may be held in the Western Sectors of Berlin. Invitations will be issued by the Senat or jointly by the Federal Republic of Germany and the Senat.

3. The three Governments authorize the establishment of a Consulate General of the USSR in the Western Sectors of Berlin accredited to the appropriate authorities of the three Governments in accordance with the usual procedures applied in those Sectors, for the purpose of performing consular services, subject to provisions set forth in a separate document of this date.

B. Communication From the Government of the Union of Soviet Socialist Republics to the Governments of the French Republic, the United Kingdom and the United States of America

The Government of the Union of Soviet Socialist Republics, with reference to Part II(D) of the Quadripartite Agreement of this date and to the communication of the Governments of the French Republic, the United Kingdom and the United States of America with regard to the representation abroad of the interests of the Western Sectors of Berlin and their permanent residents, has the honor to inform the Governments of the French Republic, the United Kingdom and the United States of America that:

1. The Government of the Union of Soviet Socialist Republics takes note of the fact that the three Governments maintain their rights and responsibilities relating to the representation abroad of the interests of the Western Sectors of Berlin and their permanent residents, including those rights and responsibilities concerning matters of security and status, both in international organizations and in relations with other countries.

2. Provided that matters of security and status are not affected, for its part it will raise no objection to:

(a) the performance by the Federal Republic of Germany of consular services for permanent residents of the Western Sectors of Berlin;

(b) in accordance with established procedures, the extension to the Western Sectors of Berlin of international agreements and arrangements entered into by the Federal Republic of Germany provided that the extension of such agreements and arrangements is specified in each case;

(c) the representation of the interests of the Western Sectors of Berlin by the Federal Republic of Germany in international organizations and international conferences;

(d) the participation jointly with participants from the Federal Republic of Germany of permanent residents of the Western Sectors of Berlin in international exchanges and exhibitions, or the holding in those Sectors of meetings of international organizations and international conferences as well as exhibitions with international participation, taking into account that invitations will be issued by the Senat or jointly by the Federal Republic of Germany and the Senat.

3. The Government of the Union of Soviet Socialist Republics takes note of the fact that the three Governments have given their consent to the establishment of a Consulate General of the USSR in the Western Sectors of Berlin. It will be accredited to the appropriate authorities of the three Governments, for purposes and subject to provisions described in their communication and as set forth in a separate document of this date.

Related Documents

Agreed Minute I

It is understood that permanent residents of the Western Sectors of Berlin shall, in order to receive at appropriate Soviet offices visas for entry into the Union of Soviet Socialist Republics, present:

(a) a passport stamped 'Issued in accordance with the Quadripartite Agreement of September 3, 1971';

(b) an identity card or other appropriately drawn up document confirming that the person requesting the visa is a permanent resident of the Western Sectors of Berlin and containing the bearer's full address and a personal photograph.

During his stay in the Union of Soviet Socialist Republics, a permanent resident of the Western Sectors of Berlin who has received a visa in this way may carry both documents or either of them, as he chooses. The visa issued by a Soviet office will serve as the basis for entry into the Union of Soviet Socialist Republics, and the passport or identity card will serve as the basis for consular services in accordance with the Quadripartite Agreement during the stay of that person in the territory of the Union of Soviet Socialist Republics.

The above-mentioned stamp will appear in all passports used by permanent residents of the Western Sectors of Berlin for journeys to such countries as may require it.

Agreed Minute II

Provision is hereby made for the establishment of a Consulate General of the USSR in the Western Sectors of Berlin. It is understood that the details concerning this Consulate General will include the following. The Consulate General will be accredited to the appropriate authorities of the three Governments in accordance with the usual procedures applying in those Sectors. Applicable Allied and German legislation and regulations will apply to the Consulate General. The activities of the Consulate General will be of a consular character and will not include political functions or any matters related to quadripartite rights or responsibilities.

The three Governments are willing to authorize an increase in Soviet commercial activities in the Western Sectors of Berlin as described below. It is understood that pertinent Allied and German legislation and regulations will apply to these activities. This authorization will be extended indefinitely, subject to compliance with the provisions outlined herein. Adequate provision for consultation will be made. This increase will include establishment of an 'Office of Soviet Foreign Trade Associations in the Western Sectors of Berlin', with commercial status, authorized to buy and sell on behalf of foreign trade associations of the Union of Soviet Socialist Republics. Soyuzpushnina, Prodintorg and Novoexport may each establish a bonded warehouse in the Western Sectors of Berlin to provide storage and display for their goods. The activities of the Intourist office in the British Sector of Berlin may be expanded to include the sale of tickets and vouchers for travel and tours in the Union of Soviet Socialist Republics and other countries. An office of Aeroflot may be established for the sale of passenger tickets and air freight services.

The assignment of personnel to the Consulate General and to permitted Soviet commercial organizations will be subject to agreement with the appropriate authorities of the three Governments. The number of such personnel will not exceed twenty Soviet nationals in the Consulate General; twenty in the office of the Soviet Foreign Trade Associations: one each in the bonded warehouses; six in the Intourist office; and five in the Aeroflot office. The personnel of the Consulate General and of permitted Soviet commercial organizations and their dependents may reside in the Western Sectors of Berlin upon individual authorization.

The property of the Union of Soviet Socialist Republics at Lietzenburgerstrasse 11 and at Am Sandwerder 1 may be used for purposes to be agreed between appropriate representatives of the three Governments and of the Government of the Union of Soviet Socialist Republics.

Details of implementation of the measures above and a time schedule for carrying them out will be agreed between the four Ambassadors in the period between the signature of the Quadripartite Agreement and the signature of the Final Quadripartite Protocol envisaged in that Agreement.

The Ambassadors of France, Great Britain and the United States to the Ambassador of the Soviet Union

The Ambassadors of the French Republic, the United Kingdom of Great Britain and Northern Ireland and the United States of America have the honor, with reference to the statements contained in Annex II of the Quadripartite Agreement to be signed on this date concerning the relationship between the Federal Republic of Germany and the Western Sectors of Berlin, to inform the Ambassador of the Union of Soviet Socialist Republics of their intention to send to the Chancellor of the Federal Republic of Germany immediately following signature of the Quadripartite Agreement a letter containing clarifications and interpretations which represent the understanding of their Governments of the statements contained in Annex II of the Quadripartite Agreement. A copy of the letter to be sent to the Chancellor of the Federal Republic of Germany is attached to this Note.

The Ambassadors avail themselves of this opportunity to renew to the Ambassador of the Union of Soviet Socialist Republics the assurances of their highest consideration.

The Governments of France, Great Britain and the United States to the Federal German Chancellor

With reference to the Quadripartite Agreement signed on 3 September 1971, our Governments wish by this letter to inform the Government of the Federal Republic of Germany of the following clarifications and interpretations of the statements contained in Annex II, which was the subject of consultation with the Government of the Federal Republic of Germany during the quadripartite negotiations.

These clarifications and interpretations represent the understanding of our Governments of this part of the Quadripartite Agreement, as follows:

a. The phrase in Paragraph 2 of Annex II of the Quadripartite Agreement which reads '. . . will not perform in the Western Sectors of Berlin constitutional or official acts which contradict the provisions of Paragraph 1' shall be interpreted to mean acts in exercise of direct state authority over the Western Sectors of Berlin.

b. Meetings of the Bundesversammlung will not take place and plenary sessions of the Bundesrat and the Bundestag will continue not to take place in the Western Sectors of Berlin. Single committees of the Bundesrat and the Bundestag may meet in the Western Sectors of Berlin in connection with maintaining and developing the ties between those Sectors and the Federal Republic of Germany. In the case of Fraktionen, meetings will not be held simultaneously.

c. The liaison agency of the Federal Government in the Western Sectors of Berlin includes departments charged with liaison functions in their respective fields.

d. Established procedures concerning the applicability to the Western Sectors of Berlin of legislation of the Federal Republic of Germany shall remain unchanged.

e. The term 'state bodies' in Paragraph 2 of Annex II shall be interpreted to mean: the Federal President, the Federal Chancellor, the Federal Cabinet, the Federal Ministers and Ministries, and the branch offices of those Ministries, the Bundesrat and the Bundestag, and all Federal courts.

Accept, Excellency, the renewed assurance of our highest esteem.

The Governments of France, Great Britain and the United States to the Federal German Chancellor

We have the honor by means of this letter to convey to the Government of the Federal Republic of Germany the text of the Quadripartite Agreement signed this day in Berlin. The Quadripartite Agreement was concluded by the Four Powers in the exercise of their rights and responsibilities with respect to Berlin.

We note that, pursuant to the terms of the Agreement and of the Final Quadripartite Protocol which ultimately will bring it into force, the text of which has been agreed, these rights and responsibilities are not affected and remain unchanged. Our Governments will continue, as heretofore, to exercise supreme authority in the Western Sectors of Berlin, within the framework of the Four Power responsibility which we share for Berlin as a whole.

In accordance with Part II(A) of the Quadripartite Agreement, arrangements implementing and supplementing the provisions relating to civilian traffic will be agreed by the competent German authorities. Part III of the Quadripartite Agreement provides that the Agreement will enter into force on a date to be specified in a Final Quadripartite Protocol which will be concluded when the arrangements envisaged between the competent German authorities have been agreed. It is the request of our Governments that the envisaged negotiations now take place between authorities of the Federal Republic of Germany, also acting on behalf of the Senat, and authorities of the German Democratic Republic.

Part II(B) and (D) and Annexes II and IV of the Quadripartite Agreement relate to the relationship between the Western Sectors of Berlin and the Federal Republic. In this connection, the following are recalled inter alia:

— the communications of the three Western Military Governors to the Parliamentary Council of 2 March, 22 April and 12 May 1949.

— the letter of the three High Commissioners to the Federal Chancellor concerning the exercise of the reserved Allied rights relating to

Berlin of 26 May 1952 in the version of the letter X of 23 October 1954.
- the Aide Memoire of the three Governments of 18 April 1967 concerning the decision of the Federal Constitutional Court of 20 January 1966 in the Niekisch case.

Our Governments take this occasion to state, in exercise of the rights and responsibilities relating to Berlin, which they retained in Article 2 of the Convention on Relations between the Three Powers and the Federal Republic of Germany of 26 May 1952 as amended October 23 1954, that Part II(B) and (D) and Annexes II and IV of the Quadripartite Agreement concerning the relationship between the Federal Republic of Germany and the Western Sectors of Berlin accord with the position in the above mentioned documents, which remains unchanged.

With regard to the existing ties between the Federal Republic and the Western Sectors of Berlin, it is the firm intention of our Governments that, as stated in Part II(B)(1) of the Quadripartite Agreement, these ties will be maintained and developed in accordance with the letter from the three High Commissioners to the Federal Chancellor on the exercise of the reserved rights relating to Berlin of 26 May 1952, in the version of letter X of October 23 1954, and with pertinent decisions of the Allied Kommandatura of Berlin.

Accept, Excellency, the renewed assurance of our highest esteem.

Communication from Allied Kommandatura to the Governing Mayor of Berlin

The Allied Kommandatura refers to the Quadripartite Agreement signed on September 3 in Berlin.

Part II(C) and Annex III, Paragraph 5, of the Quadripartite Agreement provide that arrangements implementing and supplementing the provisions relating to travel, communications and the exchange of territory will be agreed by the competent German authorities. Part IV of the Quadripartite Agreement provides that the Agreement will enter into force on a date to be specified in a Final Quadripartite Protocol which will be concluded when the arrangements envisaged between the competent German authorities have been agreed.

The Senat of Berlin is hereby authorized and requested to conduct appropriate negotiations on the subjects covered in Paragraphs 1, 2 and 3 in Annex III.

Source: DSB 27 September 1971

TREATY ON THE BASIS OF RELATIONS BETWEEN THE FEDERAL REPUBLIC OF GERMANY AND THE GERMAN DEMOCRATIC REPUBLIC

East Berlin, 21 December 1972

The High Contracting Parties,

Conscious of their responsibility for the preservation of peace,

Anxious to render a contribution to détente and security in Europe,

Aware that the inviolability of frontiers and respect for the territorial integrity and sovereignty of all States in Europe within their present frontiers are a basic condition for peace,

Recognizing that therefore the two German States have to refrain from the threat or use of force in their relations,

Proceeding from the historical facts and without prejudice to the different views of the Federal Republic of Germany and the German Democratic Republic on fundamental questions, including the national question,

Desirous to create the conditions for cooperation between the Federal Republic of Germany and the German Democratic Republic for the benefit of the people in the two German States,

Have agreed as follows:

Article 1
The Federal Republic of Germany and the German Democratic Republic shall develop normal, good-neighbourly relations with each other on the basis of equal rights.

Article 2
The Federal Republic of Germany and the German Democratic Republic will be guided by the aims and principles laid down in the United Nations Charter, especially those of the sovereign equality of all States, respect for their independence, autonomy and territorial integrity, the right of self-determination, the protection of human rights, and non-discrimination.

Article 3
In conformity with the United Nations Charter the Federal Republic of Germany and the German Democratic Republic shall settle any

disputes between them exclusively by peaceful means and refrain from the threat or use of force.

They reaffirm the inviolability now and in the future of the frontier existing between them and undertake fully to respect each other's territorial integrity.

Article 4

The Federal Republic of Germany and the German Democratic Republic proceed on the assumption that neither of the two States can represent the other in the international sphere or act on its behalf.

Article 5

The Federal Republic of Germany and the German Democratic Republic shall promote peaceful relations between the European States and contribute to security and cooperation in Europe.

They shall support efforts to reduce forces and arms in Europe, without allowing disadvantages to arise for the security of those concerned.

The Federal Republic of Germany and the German Democratic Republic shall support, with the aim of general and complete disarmament under effective international control, efforts serving international security to achieve armaments limitation and disarmament, especially with regard to nuclear weapons and other weapons of mass destruction.

Article 6

The Federal Republic of Germany and the German Democratic Republic proceed on the principle that the sovereign jurisdiction of each of the two States is confined to its own territory. They respect each other's independence and autonomy in their internal and external affairs.

Article 7

The Federal Republic of Germany and the German Democratic Republic declare their readiness to regulate practical and humanitarian questions in the process of the normalization of their relations. They shall conclude agreements with a view to developing and promoting on the basis of the present Treaty and for their mutual benefit cooperation in the fields of economics, science and technology, transport, judicial relations, posts and telecommunications, health, culture, sport, environmental protection, and in other fields. The details have been agreed in the Supplementary Protocol.

Article 8

The Federal Republic of Germany and the German Democratic Republic shall exchange Permanent Missions. They shall be established at the respective Government's seat.

Practical questions relating to the establishment of the Missions shall be dealt with separately.

★   ★   ★

[A number of documents were exchanged at the same time as the treaty. These included the supplementary protocol which dealt with the detailed application of Articles 3 and 7 of the treaty. The other documents included correspondence concerning the applications by the two states for membership of the United Nations, correspondence on the reunification of families, and exchanges concerning the improvement of travel and communications facilities between East and West Germany.]

Source: The Major International Treaties Since 1945

TREATY ESTABLISHING NORMAL RELATIONS BETWEEN THE FEDERAL REPUBLIC OF GERMANY AND CZECHOSLOVAKIA

Prague, 11 December 1973

Preamble. The Federal of Republic of Germany and the Czechoslovak Socialist Republic,

In the historic awareness that the harmonious coexistence of the nations in Europe is a necessity for peace,

Determined to put an end once and for all to the disastrous past in their relations, especially in connection with the Second World War which has inflicted immeasurable suffering on the peoples of Europe,

Recognizing that the Munich Agreement of 29 September 1938 was imposed on the Czechoslovak Republic by the National Socialist régime under the threat of force,

Considering the fact that a new generation has grown up in both countries which has a right to a secure and peaceful future,

Intending to create lasting foundations for the development of good-neighbourly relations.

Anxious to strengthen peace and security in Europe,

Convinced that peaceful cooperation on the basis of the purposes and principles of the United Nations Charter complies with the wishes of nations and the interests of peace in the world,

Have agreed as follows:

Article I

The Federal Republic of Germany and the Czechoslovak Socialist Republic, under the present Treaty, deem the Munich Agreement of 29 September 1938 void with regard to their mutual relations.

Article II

1. The present Treaty shall not affect the legal effects on natural or legal persons of the law as applied in the period between 30 September 1938 and 9 May 1945.

This provision shall exclude the effects of measures which both Contracting Parties deem to be void owing to their incompatibility with the fundamental principles of justice.

2. The present Treaty shall not affect the nationality of living or

deceased persons ensuing from the legal system of either of the two Contracting Parties.

3. The present Treaty, together with its declarations on the Munich Agreement, shall not constitute any legal basis for material claims by the Czechoslovak Socialist Republic and its natural and legal persons.

Article III

1. The Federal Republic of Germany and the Czechoslovak Socialist Republic shall in their mutual relations as well as in matters of ensuring European and international security be guided by the purposes and principles embodied in the United Nations Charter.

2. Accordingly they shall, pursuant to Articles 1 and 2 of the United Nations Charter, settle all their disputes exclusively by peaceful means and shall refrain from any threat or use of force in matters affecting European and international security, and in their mutual relations.

Article IV

1. In conformity with the said purposes and principles, the Federal Republic of Germany and the Czechoslovak Socialist Republic reaffirm the inviolability of their common frontier now and in the future and undertake to respect each other's territorial integrity without restriction.

2. They declare that they have no territorial claims whatsoever against each other and that they will not assert any such claims in the future.

Article V

1. The Federal Republic of Germany and the Czechoslovak Socialist Republic will undertake further steps for the comprehensive development of their mutual relations.

2. They agree that an extension of their neighbourly cooperation in the economic and scientific fields, in their scientific and technological relations, and in the fields of culture, environmental protection, sport, transport and in other sectors of their relations, is in their mutual interest.

Source: The Major International Treaties since 1945

FINAL ACT OF THE CONFERENCE ON SECURITY AND COOPERATION IN EUROPE

Helsinki, 1 August 1975

The Conference on Security and Cooperation in Europe, which opened at Helsinki on 3 July 1973 and continued at Geneva from 18 September 1973 to 21 July 1975, was concluded at Helsinki on 1 August 1975 by the High Representatives of Austria, Belgium, Bulgaria, Canada, Cyprus, Czechoslovakia, Denmark, Finland, France, the German Democratic Republic, the Federal Republic of Germany, Greece, the Holy See, Hungary, Iceland, Ireland, Italy, Liechtenstein, Luxembourg, Malta, Monaco, the Netherlands, Norway, Poland, Portugal, Romania, San Marino, Spain, Sweden, Switzerland, Turkey, the Union of Soviet Socialist Republics, the United Kingdom, the United States of America and Yugoslavia . . .

Motivated by the political will, in the interest of peoples, to improve and intensify their relations and to contribute in Europe to peace, security, justice and cooperation as well as to rapprochement among themselves and with the other States of the world.

Determined, in consequence, to give full effect to the results of the Conference and to assure, among their States and throughout Europe, the benefits deriving from those results and thus to broaden, deepen and make continuing and lasting the process of detente.

The High Representatives of the participating States have solemnly adopted the following:

Questions Relating to Security in Europe

The States participating in the Conference on Security and Cooperation in Europe,

Reaffirming their objective of promoting better relations among themselves and ensuring conditions in which their people can live in true and lasting peace free from any threat to or attempt against their security;

Convinced of the need to exert efforts to make detente both a continuing and an increasingly viable and comprehensive process, universal in scope, and that the implementation of the results of the Conference on Security and Cooperation in Europe will be a major contribution to this process;

Considering that solidarity among peoples, as well as the common purpose of the participating States in achieving the aims as set forth by the Conference on Security and Cooperation in Europe, should lead to the development of better and closer relations among them in all fields and thus to overcoming the confrontation stemming from the character of their past relations, and to better mutual understanding;

Mindful of their common history and recognising that the existence of elements common to their traditions and values can assist them in developing their relations, and desiring to search, fully taking into account the individuality and diversity of their positions and views for possibilities of joining their efforts with a view to overcoming distrust and increasing confidence, solving the problems that separate them and cooperating in the interest of mankind;

Recognising the indivisibility of security in Europe as well as their common interest in the development of cooperation throughout Europe and among themselves and expressing their intentions to pursue efforts accordingly;

Recognising the close link between peace and security in Europe and in the world as a whole and conscious of the need for each of them to make its contribution to the strengthening of world peace and security and to the promotion of fundamental rights, economic and social progress and well-being for all peoples;

Have adopted the following:

1.
(a) Declaration on Principles Guiding Relations between Participating States

The participating States,

Reaffirming their commitment to peace, security and justice and the continuing development of friendly relations and cooperation;

Recognising that this commitment, which reflects the interest and aspirations of peoples, constitutes for each participating State a present and future responsibility, heightened by experience of the past;

Reaffirming, in conformity with their membership in the United Nations and in accordance with the purposes and principles of the United Nations, their full and active support of the United Nations and for the enhancement of its role and effectiveness in strengthening international peace, security and justice, and in promoting the solution of international problems, as well as the development of friendly relations and cooperation among States;

Expressing their common adherence to the principles which are set forth below and are in conformity with the Charter of United Nations, as well as their common will to act, in the application of these principles, in conformity with the purposes and principles of the Charter of the United Nations;

Declare their determination to respect and put into practice, each of them in its relations with all other participating States, irrespective of their political, economic or social systems as well as of their size, geographical location or level of economic development, the following principles, which are all of primary significance, guiding their mutual relations:

I. Sovereign equality, respect for the rights inherent in sovereignty

The participating States will respect each other's sovereign equality and individuality as well as all the rights inherent in and encompassed by its sovereignty, including in particular the right of every State to juridical equality, to territorial integrity and to freedom and political independence. They will also respect each other's right freely to choose and develop its political, social, economic and cultural systems as well as its right to determine its laws and regulations.

Within the framework of international law, all the participating States have equal rights and duties. They will respect each other's right to define and conduct as it wishes its relations with other States in accordance with international law and in the spirit of the present Declaration. They consider that their frontiers can be changed, in accordance with international law, by peaceful means and by agreement. They also have the right to belong or not to belong to international organisations, to be or not to be a party to bilateral or multilateral treaties including the right to be or not to be a party to treaties of alliance; they also have the right to neutrality.

II. Refraining from the threat or use of force

The participating States will refrain in their mutual relations, as well as in their international relations in general, from the threat or use of force against the territorial integrity or political independence of any State, or in any other manner inconsistent with the purposes of the United Nations and with the present Declaration. No consideration may be invoked to serve to warrant resort to the threat or use of force in contravention of this principle.

Accordingly, the participating States will refrain from any acts constituting a threat of force or direct or indirect use of force against another participating State. Likewise they will refrain from any manifestation of force for the purpose of inducing another participating State to renounce the full exercise of its sovereign rights. Likewise they will also refrain in their mutual relations from any act of reprisal by force.

No such threat or use of force will be employed as a means of settling disputes, or questions likely to give rise to disputes, between them.

III. Inviolability of frontiers

The participating States regard as inviolable all one another's frontiers as well as the frontiers of all States in Europe and therefore they will refrain now and in the future from assaulting these frontiers.

Accordingly, they will also refrain from any demand for, or act of, seizure and usurpation of part or all of the territory of any participating State.

IV. Territorial integrity of States

The participating States will respect the territorial integrity of each of the participating States.

Accordingly, they will refrain from any action inconsistent with the purposes and principles of the Charter of the United Nations against the territorial integrity, political independence or the unity of any participating State, and in particular from any such action constituting a threat or use of force.

The participating States will likewise refrain from making each other's territory the object of military occupation or other direct or indirect measures of force in contravention of international law, or the object of acquisition by means of such measures or the threat of them. No such occupation or acquisition will be recognised as legal.

V. Peaceful settlement of disputes

The participating States will settle disputes among them by peaceful means in such a manner as not to endanger international peace and security, and justice.

They will endeavour in good faith and a spirit of cooperation to reach a rapid and equitable solution on the basis of international law.

For this purpose they will use such means as negotiation, enquiry, mediation, conciliation, arbitration, judicial settlement or other peaceful means of their own choice including any settlement procedure agreed to in advance of disputes to which they are parties.

In the event of failure to reach a solution by any of the above peaceful means, the parties to a dispute will continue to seek a mutually agreed way to settle the dispute peacefully.

Participating States, parties to a dispute among them, as well as other participating States, will refrain from any action which might aggravate the situation to such a degree as to endanger the maintenance of international peace and security and thereby make a peaceful settlement of the dispute more difficult.

VI. Non-intervention in internal affairs

The participating States will refrain from any intervention, direct or indirect, individual or collective, in the internal or external affairs falling within the domestic jurisdiction of another participating State, regardless of their mutual relations.

They will accordingly refrain from any form of armed intervention or threat of such intervention against another participating State.

They will likewise in all circumstances refrain from any other act of military, or of political, economic or other coercion designed to subordinate to their own interest the exercise by another participating State of the rights inherent in its sovereignty and thus to secure advantages of any kind.

Accordingly, they will, *inter alia*, refrain from direct or indirect assistance to terrorist activities, or to subversive or other activities directed towards the violent overthrow of the regime of another participating State.

VII. Respect for human rights and fundamental freedoms, including the freedom of thought, conscience, religion or belief

The participating States will respect human rights and fundamental freedoms, including the freedom of thought, conscience, religion or belief, for all without distinction as to race, sex, language or religion.

They will promote and encourage the effective exercise of civil, political, economic, social, cultural and other rights and freedoms all of which derive from the inherent dignity of the human person and are essential for his free and full development.

Within this framework the participating States will recognise and respect the freedom of the individual to profess and practise, alone or in community with others, religion or belief acting in accordance with the dictates of his own conscience.

The participating States on whose territory national minorities exist will respect the right of persons belonging to such minorities to equality before the law, will afford them the full opportunity for the actual enjoyment of human rights and fundamental freedoms and will, in this manner, protect their legitimate interests in this sphere.

The participating States recognise the universal significance of human rights and fundamental freedoms, respect for which is an essential factor for the peace, justice and well-being necessary to ensure the development of friendly relations and cooperation among themselves as among all States.

They will constantly respect these rights and freedoms in their mutual relations and will endeavour jointly and separately, including in cooperation with the United Nations, to promote universal and effective respect for them.

They confirm the right of the individual to know and act upon his rights and duties in this field.

In the field of human rights and fundamental freedoms, the participating States will act in conformity with the purposes and principles of the Charter of the United Nations and with the Universal Declaration of Human Rights. They will also fulfil their obligations as set forth in the international declarations and agreements in this field, including *inter alia* the International Covenants on Human Rights, by which they may be bound.

VIII. Equal rights and self-determination of peoples

The participating States will respect the equal rights of peoples and their right to self-determination, acting at all times in conformity with the purposes and principles of the Charter of the United Nations and with the relevant norms of international law, including those relating to territorial integrity of States.

By virtue of the principle of equal rights and self-determination of peoples, all peoples always have the right, in full freedom, to determine, when and as they wish their internal and external political status, without external interference, and to pursue as they wish their political, economic, social and cultural development.

The participating States reaffirm the universal significance of respect for and effective exercise of equal rights and self-determination of peoples for the development of friendly relations among themselves as among all States; they also recall the importance of the elimination of any form of violation of this principle.

IX. Cooperation among States

The participating States will develop their cooperation with one another and with all States in all fields in accordance with the purposes and principles of the Charter of the United Nations. In developing their cooperation the participating States will place special emphasis on the fields as set forth within the framework of the Conference on Security and Cooperation in Europe, with each of them making its contribution in conditions of full equality.

They will endeavour, in developing their cooperation as equals, to promote mutual understanding and confidence, friendly and good-neighbourly relations among themselves, international peace, security and justice. They will equally endeavour, in developing their cooperation, to improve the well-being of peoples and contribute to the fulfilment of their aspirations through, *inter alia*, the benefits resulting from increased mutual knowledge and from progress and achievement in the economic, scientific, technological, social, cultural and humanitarian fields. They will take steps to promote conditions favourable to making these benefits available to all, they will take into account the interest of all in the narrowing of differences in the levels of economic development, and in particular the interest of developing countries throughout the world.

They confirm that governments, institutions, organisations and persons have a relevant and positive role to play in contributing toward the achievement of these aims of their cooperation.

They will strive, in increasing their cooperation as set forth above, to develop closer relations among themselves on an improved and more enduring basis for the benefit of peoples.

X. Fulfilment in good faith of obligations under international law

The participating States will fulfil in good faith their obligations under international law, both those obligations arising from the generally recognised principles and rules of international law and those obligations arising from treaties or other agreements, in conformity with international law, to which they are parties.

In exercising their sovereign rights, including the right to determine their laws and regulations, they will conform with their legal obligations under international law; they will furthermore pay due regard to and implement the provisions in the Final Act of the Conference on Security and Cooperation in Europe.

The participating States confirm that in the event of a conflict between the obligations of the members of the United Nations under the Charter of the United Nations and their obligations under any treaty or other international agreement, their obligations under the Charter will prevail, in accordance with Article 103 of the Charter of the United Nations.

All the principles set forth above are of primary significance and, accordingly, they will be equally and unreservedly applied, each of them being interpreted taking into account the others.

The participating States express their determination fully to respect and apply these principles, as set forth in the present Declaration, in all aspects, to their mutual relations and cooperation in order to ensure to each participating State the benefits resulting from the respect and application of these principles by all.

The participating States, paying due regard to the principles above and, in particular, to the first sentence of the tenth principle, 'Fulfilment in good faith of obligations under international law', note that the present Declaration does not affect their rights and obligations, nor the corresponding treaties and other agreements and arrangements.

The participating States express the conviction that respect for these principles will encourage the development of normal and friendly relations and the progress of cooperation among them in all fields. They also express the conviction that respect for these principles will encourage the development of political contacts among them which in turn would contribute to better mutual understanding of their position and views.

The participating States declare their intention to conduct their relations with all other States in the spirit of the principles contained in the present Declaration.

(b) Matters related to giving effect to certain of the above Principles

(i) The participating States,

Reaffirming that they will respect and give effect to refraining from the threat or use of force and convinced of the necessity to make it an effective norm of international life,

Declare that they are resolved to respect and carry out, in their relations with one another, *inter alia*, the following provisions which are in conformity with the Declaration on Principles Guiding Relations between Participating States;

To give effect and expression, by all the ways and forms which they consider appropriate, to the duty to refrain from the threat or use of force in their relations with one another.

To refrain from any use of armed forces inconsistent with the purposes and principles of the Charter of the United Nations and the provisions of the Declaration on Principles Guiding Relations between Participating States, against another participating State, in particular from invasion of or attack on its territory.

To refrain from any manifestation of force for the purpose of inducing another participating State to renounce the full exercise of its sovereign rights.

To refrain from any act of economic coercion designed to subordinate to their own interest the exercise by another participating State of the rights inherent in its sovereignty and thus to secure advantages of any kind.

To take effective measures which by their scope and by their nature constitute steps towards the ultimate achievement of general and complete disarmament under strict and effective international control.

To promote, by all means which each of them considers appropriate, a climate of confidence and respect among peoples consonant with their duty to refrain from propaganda for wars of aggression or for any threat or use of force inconsistent with the purposes of the United Nations and with the Declaration on Principles Guiding Relations between Participating States, against another participating State.

To make every effort to settle exclusively by peaceful means any dispute between them, the continuance of which is likely to endanger the maintenance of international peace and security in Europe, and to seek, first of all, a solution through the peaceful means set forth in Article 33 of the United Nations Charter.

To refrain from any action which could hinder the peaceful settlement of disputes between the participating States.

(ii) The participating States,

Reaffirming their determination to settle their disputes as set forth in the Principle of Peaceful Settlement of Disputes;

Convinced that the peaceful settlement of disputes is a complement to refraining from the threat or use of force, both being essential though not exclusive factors for the maintenance and consolidation of peace and security;

Desiring to reinforce and to improve the methods at their disposal for the peaceful settlement of disputes;

1. Are resolved to pursue the examination and elaboration of a generally acceptable method for the peaceful settlement of disputes aimed at complementing existing methods, and to continue to this end to work upon the 'Draft Convention on a European System for the Peaceful Settlement of Disputes' submitted by Switzerland during the second stage of the Conference on Security and Cooperation in Europe, as well as the other proposals relating to it and directed towards the elaboration of such a method.

2. Decide that, on the invitation of Switzerland, a meeting of experts of all the participating States will be convoked in order to fulfil the mandate described in paragraph 1 above within the framework and under the procedures of the follow-up to the Conference laid down in the chapter 'Follow-up to the Conference'.

3. This meeting of experts will take place after the meeting of the representatives appointed by the Ministers of Foreign Affairs of the participating States, scheduled according to the chapter 'Follow-up to the Conference' for 1977, the results of the work of this meeting of experts will be submitted to Governments.

2.
Document on confidence-building measures and certain aspects of security and disarmament

The participating States,

Desirous of eliminating the causes of tension that may exist among them and thus of contributing to the strengthening of peace and security in the world;

Determined to strengthen confidence among them and thus to contribute to increasing stability and security in Europe;

Determined further to refrain in their mutual relations, as well as in their interntional relations in general, from the threat or use of force against the territorial integrity or political independence of any State, or in any other manner inconsistent with the purposes of the United Nations and with the Declaration on Principles Guiding Relations between Participating States as adopted in this Final Act,

Recognising the need to contribute to reducing the dangers of armed conflict and of misunderstanding or miscalculation of military activities which could give rise to apprehension, particularly in a situation where the participating States lack clear and timely information about the nature of such activities;

Taking into account considerations relevant to efforts aimed at lessening tension and promoting disarmament;

Recognising that the exchange of observers by invitation at military manoeuvres will help to promote contacts and mutual understanding;

Having studied the question of prior notification of major military movements in the context of confidence-building;

Recognising that there are other ways in which individual States can contribute further to their common objectives;

Convinced of the political importance of prior notification of major military manoeuvres for the promotion of mutual understanding and the strengthening of confidence, stability and security;

Accepting the responsibility of each of them to promote these objectives and to implement this measure, in accordance with the accepted criteria and modalities, as essentials for the realisation of these objectives,

Recognising that this measure deriving from political decision rests upon a voluntary basis;

Have adopted the following:

I

Prior notification of major military manoeuvres

They will notify their major military manoeuvres to all other participating States through usual diplomatic channels in accordance with the following provisions:

Notification will be given of major military manoeuvres exceeding a total of 25,000 troops, independently or combined with any possible air or naval components (in this context the word 'troops' includes amphibious and airborne troops). In the case of independent manoeuvres of amphibious or airborne troops, or of combined manoeuvres involving them, these troops will be included in this total. Furthermore, in the case of combined manoeuvres which do not reach the above total but which involve land forces together with significant numbers of either amphibious or airborne troops, or both, notification can also be given.

Notification will be given of major military manoeuvres which take place on the territory, in Europe, of any participating State as well as, if applicable, in the adjoining sea area and air space.

In the case of a participating State whose territory extends beyond Europe, prior notification need be given only of manoeuvres which take place in an area within 250 kilometres from its frontier facing or shared with any other European participating State; the participating State need not, however, give notification in cases in which that area is also contiguous to the participating State's frontier facing or shared with a non-European non-participating State.

Notification will be given 21 days or more in advance of the start of the manoeuvre or in the case of a manoeuvre arranged at shorter notice at the earliest possible opportunity prior to its starting date.

Notification will contain information of the designation, if any, the general purpose of and the States involved in the manoeuvre, the type or types and numerical strength of the forces engaged, the area and estimated time-frame of its conduct. The participating States will also, if possible, provide additional relevant information, particularly that related to the components of the forces engaged and the period of involvement of these forces.

Prior notification of other military manoeuvres

The participating States recognise that they can contribute further to strengthening confidence and increasing security and stability, and to this end may also notify smaller-scale military manoeuvres to other participating States, with special regard for those near the area of such manoeuvres.

To the same end, the participating States also recognise that they may notify other military manoeuvres conducted by them.

Exchange of observers

The participating States will invite other participating States, voluntarily and on a bilateral basis, in a spirit of reciprocity and goodwill towards all participating States, to send observers to attend military manoeuvres.

The inviting State will determine in each case the number of observers, the procedures and conditions of their participation, and give other information which it may consider useful. It will provide appropriate facilities and hospitality.

The invitation will be given as far ahead as is conveniently possible through usual diplomatic channels.

Prior notification of major military movements

In accordance with the Final Recommendations of the Helsinki Consultations the participating States studied the question of prior notification of major military movements as a measure to strengthen confidence.

Accordingly, the participating States recognise that they may, at their own discretion and with a view to contributing to confidence-building, notify their major military movements.

In the same spirit, further consideration will be given by the States participating in the Conference on Security and Cooperation in Europe to the question of prior notification of major military movements, bearing in mind, in particular, the experience gained by the implementation of the measures which are set forth in this document.

Other confidence-building measures

The participating States recognise that there are other means by which their common objectives can be promoted.

In particular, they will, with due regard to reciprocity and with a view to better mutual understanding, promote exchanges by invitation among their military personnel, including visits by military delegations.

In order to make a fuller contribution to their common objective of confidence-building, the participating States, when conducting their military activities in the area covered by the provisions for the prior notification of major military manoeuvres, will duly take into account and respect this objective.

They also recognise that the experience gained by the implementation of the provisions set forth above, together with further efforts, could lead to developing and enlarging measures aimed at strengthening confidence.

II

Questions relating to disarmament

The participating States recognise the interest of all of them in efforts aimed at lessening military confrontation and promoting disarmament which are designed to complement political detente in Europe and to strengthen their security. They are convinced of the necessity to take effective measures in these fields which by their scope and by their nature constitute steps towards the ultimate achievement of general and complete disarmament under strict and effective international control, and which should result in strengthening peace and security throughout the world.

III

General considerations

Having considered the views expressed on various subjects related to the strengthening of security in Europe through joint efforts aimed at promoting detente and disarmament, the participating States, when engaged in such efforts, will, in this context, proceed, in particular, from the following essential considerations:

The complementary nature of the political and military aspects of security;
The interrelation between the security of each participating State and security in Europe as a whole and the relationship which exists, in the broader context of world security, between security in Europe and security in the Mediterranean area;

Respect for the security interests of all States participating in the Conference on Security and Cooperation in Europe inherent in their sovereign equality;

The importance that participants in negotiating fora see to it that information above relevant documents, progress and results is provided on an appropriate basis to other States participating in the Conference on Security and Cooperation in Europe and, in return, the justified interest of any of those States in having their views considered.

Cooperation in the Field of Economics, Science and Technology and of the Environment

The participating States,

Convinced that their efforts to develop cooperation in the fields of trade, industry, science and technology, the environment and other areas of economic activity contribute to the reinforcement of peace and security in Europe and in the world as a whole,

Recognising that cooperation in these fields would promote economic and social progress and the improvement of the conditions of life,

Aware of the diversity of their economic and social systems,

Reaffirming their will to intensify such cooperation between one another, irrespective of their systems.

Recognising that such cooperation, with due regard for the different levels of economic development, can be developed, on the basis of equality and mutual satisfaction of the partners, and of reciprocity permitting, as a whole, an equitable distribution of advantages and obligations of comparable scale, with respect for bilateral and multilateral agreements,

Taking into account the interests of the developing countries throughout the world, including those among the participating countries as long as they are developing from the economic point of view; reaffirming their will to cooperate for the achievement of the aims and objectives established by the appropriate bodies of the United Nations in the pertinent documents concerning the development, it being understood that each participating State maintains the positions it has taken on them; giving special attention to the least developed countries,

Convinced that the growing world-wide economic interdependence calls for increasing common and effective efforts towards the solution of major world economic problems such as food, energy, commodities, monetary and financial problems, and therefore emphasises the need for promoting stable and equitable international economic relations, thus contributing to the continuous and diversified economic development of all countries,

Having taken into account the work already undertaken by relevant international organisations and wishing to take advantage of the possibilities offered by these organisations, in particular by the United Nations Economic Commission for Europe, for giving effect to the provisions of the final documents of the Conference,

Considering that the guidelines and concrete recommendations contained in the following texts are aimed at promoting further development of their mutual economic relations, and convinced that their cooperation in this field should take place in full respect for the principles guiding relations among participating States as set forth in the relevant document,

Have adopted the following:

[There then follow provisions relating to industrial cooperation, trade, science and technology, environment and cooperation in other areas]

Questions Relating to Security and Cooperation in the Mediterranean

The participating States,

Conscious of the geographical, historical, cultural, economic and political aspects of their relationship with the non-participating Mediterranean States,

Convinced that security in Europe is to be considered in the broader context of world security and is closely linked with security in the Mediterranean area as a whole, and that accordingly the process of improving security should not be confined to Europe but should extend to other parts of the world, and in particular to the Mediterranean area,

Believing that the strengthening of security and the intensification of cooperation in Europe would stimulate positive processes in the Mediterranean region, and expressing their intention to contribute towards peace, security and justice in the region, in which ends the participating States and the non-participating Mediterranean States have a common interest,

Recognising the importance of their mutual economic relations with the non-participating Mediterranean States, and conscious of their common interest in the further development of cooperation,

Noting with appreciation the interest expressed by the non-participating Mediterranean States in the Conference since its inception, and having duly taken their contributions into account,

Declare their intention:

to promote the development of good neighbourly relations with the non-participating Mediterranean States in conformity with the purposes and principles of the Charter of the United Nations, on which their relations are based, and with the United Nations Declaration on Principles of International Law concerning Friendly Relations and Cooperation among States and accordingly, in this context, to conduct their relations with the non-participating Mediterranean States in the spirit of the principles set forth in the Declaration on Principles Guiding Relations between Participating States;

to seek, by further improving their relations with the non-participating Mediterranean States, to increase mutual confidence, so as to promote security and stablity in the Mediterranean area as a whole;

to encourage with the non-participating Mediterranean States the development of mutually beneficial cooperation in the various fields of economic activity, especially by expanding commercial exchanges, on the basis of a common awareness of the necessity for stability and progress in trade relations, of their mutual economic interests, and of differences in the levels of economic development, thereby promoting their economic advancement and well-being;

to contribute to a diversified development of the economies of the non-participating Mediterranean countries, whilst taking due account of their national development objectives, and to cooperate with them, especially in the sectors of industry, science and technology, in their efforts to achieve a better utilisation of their resources, thus promoting a more harmonious development of economic relations;

to intensify their efforts and their cooperation on a bilateral and multilateral basis with the non-participating Mediterranean States directed towards the improvement of the environment of the Mediterranean, especially the safeguarding of the biological resources and ecological balance of the sea, by appropriate measures including the prevention and control of pollution; to this end, and in view of the present situation, to cooperate through competent international organisations and in particular within the United Nations Environment Programme (UNEP);

to promote further contacts and cooperation with the non-participating Mediterranean States in other relevant fields.

In order to advance the objectives set forth above, the participating States also declare their intention of maintaining and amplifying the contacts and dialogue as initiated by the CSCE with the non-participating Mediterranean States to include all the States of the Mediterranean, with the purpose of contributing to peace, reducing armed forces in the region, strengthening security, lessening tensions in the region, and widening the scope of cooperation, ends in which all share a common interest, as well as with the purpose of defining further common objectives.

The participating States would seek, in the framework of their multilateral efforts, to encourage progress and appropriate initiatives and to proceed to an exchange of views on the attainment of the above purposes.

Cooperation in Humanitarian and Other Fields

The participating States,

Desiring to contribute to the strengthening of peace and understanding among peoples and to the spiritual enrichment of the human personality without distinction as to race, sex, language or religion,

Conscious that increased cultural and educational exchanges, broader dissemination of information, contacts between people, and the solution of humanitarian problems will contribute to the attainment of these aims,

Determined therefore to cooperate among themselves, irrespective of their political, economic and social systems, in order to create better conditions in the above fields, to develop and strengthen existing forms of cooperation and to work out new ways and means appropriate to these aims,

Convinced that this cooperation should take place in full respect for the principles guiding relations among participating States as set forth in the relevant document,

Have adopted the following:

1. Human Contacts

The participating States,

Considering the development of contacts to be an important element in the strengthening of friendly relations and trust among peoples,

Affirming, in relation to their present effort to improve conditions in this area, the importance they attach to humanitarian considerations,

Desiring in this spirit to develop, with the continuance of detente, further efforts to achieve continuing progress in this field,

And conscious that the questions relevant hereto must be settled by the States concerned under mutually acceptable conditions,

Make it their aim to facilitate freer movements and contacts, individually and collectively, whether privately or officially, among persons, institutions and organisations of the participating States, and to contribute to the solution of the humanitarian problems that arise in that connection,

Declare their readiness to these ends to take measures which they consider appropriate and to conclude agreements or arrangements among themselves, as may be needed, and

Express their intention now to proceed to the implementation of the following:

(a) Contacts and Regular Meetings on the Basis of Family Ties

In order to promote further development of contacts on the basis of family ties the participating States will favourably consider applications for travel with the purpose of allowing persons to enter or leave their territory temporarily, and on a regular basis if desired, in order to visit members of their families.

Applications for temporary visits to meet members of their families will be dealt with without distinction as to the country of origin or destination: existing requirements for travel documents and visas will be applied in this spirit. The preparation and issue of such documents and visas will be effected within reasonable time limits; cases of urgent necessity – such as serious illness or death will be given priority . . .

Source: HM Stationery Office Cmnd. 6198

WESTERN EUROPEAN UNION, ROME DECLARATION

27 October 1984

1. At the invitation of the Italian Government, the Foreign and Defence Ministers of the seven member States of Western European Union met in extraordinary session in Rome on 26–27 October 1984 to mark the 30th anniversary of the modified Brussels Treaty.

2. The Ministers stressed the importance of the Treaty and their attachment to its goals:
— to strengthen peace and security;
— to promote the unity and to encourage the progressive integration of Europe;
— to cooperate more closely both among member States and with other European organisations.

3. Conscious of the continuing necessity to strengthen western security and of the specifically Western European geographical, political, psychological and military dimensions, the Ministers underlined their determination to make better use of the WEU framework in order to increase cooperation between the member States in the field of security policy and to encourage consensus. In this context, they called for continued efforts to preserve peace, strengthen deterrence and defence and thus consolidate stability through dialogue and cooperation.

4. The Ministers recalled that the Atlantic Alliance, which remains the foundation of western security, had preserved peace on the Continent for 35 years. This permitted the construction of Europe. The Ministers are convinced that a better utilisation of WEU would not only contribute to the security of Western Europe but also to an improvement in the common defence of all the countries of the Atlantic Alliance and to greater solidarity among its members.

5. The Ministers emphasised the indivisibility of security within the North Atlantic Treaty area. They recalled in particular the vital and substantial contribution of all the European allies, and underlined the crucial importance of the contribution to common security of their allies who are not members of WEU. They stressed the necessity, as a complement to their joint efforts, of the closest possible concertation with them.

6. The Ministers are convinced that increased cooperation within WEU will also contribute to the maintenance of adequate military

strength and political solidarity and, on that basis, to the pursuit of a more stable relationship between the countries of East and West by fostering dialogue and cooperation.

7. The Ministers called attention to the need to make the best use of existing resources through increased cooperation, and through WEU to provide a political impetus to institutions of cooperation in the field of armaments.

8. The Ministers therefore decided to hold comprehensive discussions and to seek to harmonise their views on the specific conditions of security in Europe, in particular:
— defence questions;
— arms control and disarmament;
— the effects of developments in East-West relations on the security of Europe;
— Europe's contribution to the strengthening of the Atlantic Alliance, bearing in mind the importance of transatlantic relations;
— the development of European cooperation in the field of armaments in respect of which WEU can provide a political impetus.
They may also consider the implications for Europe of crises in other regions of the world.

9. The Ministers recalled the importance of the WEU Assembly which, as the only European parliamentary body mandated by treaty to discuss defence matters, is called upon to play a growing role.

They stressed the major contribution which the Assembly has already made to the revitalisation of WEU and called upon it to pursue its efforts to strengthen the solidarity among the member States, and to strive to consolidate the consensus among public opinion on their security and defence needs.

10. In pursuance of these goals, the Ministers have decided on a number of specific measures with regard to the better functioning of the WEU structure and organisation, which are set out in a separate document.

Institutional Reform of WEU

At their meeting in Rome on 26 and 27 October 1984 to mark the 30th anniversary of the modified Brussels Treaty of 1954, the Foreign and Defence Ministers of the signatory States decided to make fuller use of the institutions of WEU and, accordingly, to bring the existing institutions into line with the changed tasks of the Organisation.

I. Activation of the Council

The Ministers regard activation of the Council as a central element in the efforts to make greater use of Western European Union. In conformity with Article VIII of the modified Brussels Treaty, which allows the Council to decide on the organisation of its work and to consult or set up subsidiary bodies, the Ministers decided the following:

1. The Council would in future normally meet twice a year at ministerial level. One of these sessions could take place in a small group with no formal agenda. These meetings would bring together the Foreign Ministers and Defence Ministers. Separate meetings of the Foreign Ministers and/or Defence Ministers could also take place, if the member States considered it necessary, to discuss matters lying within their respective area of responsibility.

2. The Presidency of the Council will be held by each member State for a one year term. Meetings of the Council will in principle take place in the country holding the Presidency.

3. The work of the Permanent Council will have to be intensified in line with the increased activities of the Council of Ministers. The Permanent Council, mandated to discuss in greater detail the views expressed by the Ministers and to follow up their decisions, will, pursuant to the second paragraph of the above-mentioned Article VIII, make the necessary arrangements for this purpose, including as appropriate the setting-up of working groups.

4. The Secretariat-General should be adapted to take account of the enhanced activities of the Council of Ministers and the Permanent Council.

5. The Ministers have asked the Secretariat-General to submit, as soon as possible, a report on the work done by the Secretariat and to consider what measures might be necessary to strengthen its activities. In this connection, the Ministers stated that any reorganisation in the staffing of the Secretariat-General should take account of the adjustments made elsewhere in the other WEU institutions. They stressed that any proposed adjustments should not result in an overall increase in the Organisation's establishment.

II. Relations Between Council and Assembly

The Ministers supported the idea of greater contact between the Council and the Assembly.

Recalling that, under Article IX of the Treaty, the Assembly is expressly required to discuss the reports submitted to it by the Council of Ministers on matters concerning the security and defence of the member States, and considering that the practice adopted has enabled the Assembly to widen the topics of its discussions, the Ministers wish to see the Assembly playing an increasing role, particularly by contributing even more to associating public opinion in the member States with the policy statements of the Council, which expresses the political will of the individual governments. Accordingly, the Ministers submit the following proposals to the Assembly:

1. In order to improve the contacts between the Council and the Assembly, the Ministers believe there are a number of options, noteworthy among which are:

— A substantial improvement in the existing procedures for giving written replies to Assembly Recommendations and questions. On this point, the Ministers consider that a leading role should be given to the Presidency, making the best use of the services of the Secretariat-General.

— The development of informal contacts between government representatives and the representatives of the Assembly.

— If appropriate, a colloquium involving the Presidency of the Council and the Committees of the Assembly.

— The improvement of the contacts that traditionally take place after the ministerial meetings of the Council, and more generally, the improvement of the procedures under which the Assembly is kept informed by the Presidency, whose representatives could – between the Assembly sessions – keep the various committees up to date with the work of the Council and even take part in their decisions.

— The possibility that the Assembly might make use of contributions from the technical institutions of WEU.

2. Convinced that greater cooperation between the Council and the Assembly is a key factor in the enhanced utilisation of WEU, the Ministers underscored the importance they attach to the Recommendations and the work of the Assembly.

3. Without wishing to preempt the decision of the members of the Assembly, the Ministers also stress the value, in their eyes, of developing a dialogue between the Assembly and other parliaments or parliamentary institutions.

4. The Ministers also stated that the member States were always ready to inform their national delegations of their governments' attitude to questions dealt with in Assembly reports and were prepared to offer information to their rapporteurs.

III. Agency for the Control of Armaments and the Standing Armaments Committee
The Ministers also considered the activity of the Agency for the Control of Armaments (ACA) and the Standing Armaments Committee (SAC).

1. In connection with the Agency, which was set up in 1954 to monitor compliance with the voluntary arms limitations agreed by the contracting parties, the Ministers underlined the exemplary nature of these commitments, which had instilled confidence among the signatory States and for this reason they acclaimed the work that the Agency had done.

Noting the value of the experience thus gained, the Ministers emphasised the interest that they attached to the development by the WEU member States of reflection on arms control and disarmament questions.

2. As regards the SAC, the Ministers recalled the importance of the tasks defined in the decision of the Council of 7 May 1955 which established this body.

In this connection, they emphasised that the existence of an effective and competitive European armaments industry was a fundamental aspect of Europe's contribution to the Atlantic Alliance. In this context, it seemed very important to them that the seven member States of WEU should be able to harmonise their positions in this sphere and coordinate their efforts with a view to increasing the effectiveness of cooperative activity in the various multilateral fora.

3. With the aim of better adapting the institutions of WEU to present and future requirements, the Ministers reached the following decisions.

(a) Noting that the control functions originally assigned to the ACA have now become, for the most part, superfluous, the Ministers decided, in accordance with Article V of Protocol No. III, which allows the Council to make changes to the ACA's control activity, to abolish gradually the remaining quantitative controls on conventional weapons. The Ministers agreed that these controls should be substantially reduced by 1 January 1985 and entirely lifted by 1 January 1986.

The commitments and controls concerning ABC weapons would be maintained at the existing level and in accordance with the procedures agreed up to the present time.

(b) The Ministers have instructed the Permanent Council to define, in consultation with the directors of the ACA and the SAC, the precise modalities of an overall reorganisation affecting both the ACA, the International Secretariat of the SAC and the SAC which could be structured in such a way as to fulfil a threefold task:
— to study questions relating to arms control and disarmament whilst carrying out the remaining control functions;
— undertake the function of studying security and defence problems;
— to contribute actively to the development of European armaments cooperation.

(c) As regards the first two functions indicated above, the intention would be to have available a common basis of analysis which could form a useful point of reference for the work of both the Council and the Assembly and also for informing public opinion.

This reorganisation will have to be carried out taking into account, on the one hand, changes in duties resulting first from the reduction and then from the abolition of the control tasks and, on the other hand, the need to have the appropriate experts available.

(d) As regards armaments cooperation, WEU should be in a position to play an active role in providing political impetus:
— by supporting all cooperative efforts including those of the IEPG and the CNAD;
— by encouraging in particular the activity of the IEPG as a forum whose main objective is to promote European cooperation and also to contribute to the development of balanced cooperation within the Atlantic Alliance;
— by developing continuing concertation with the various existing bodies.

(e) In this general context, the Permanent Council will also take into account the existence of the FINABEL framework.

(f) In carrying out this overall reorganisation the Permanent Council will have to:
— propose a precise organisation table which will make it possible to define and give a breakdown of the posts required for carrying out the three functions referred to above;
— ensure that the various arrangements proposed remain within the present limits in terms of staff and the Organisation's budget, without weakening WEU's ability to play its role;

The Ministers asked the Permanent Council to complete its work before their next session. They expressed the wish, however, that in the meantime a start should be made on all or part of the new tasks as soon as possible.

IV. Contacts with Non-Member States

1. The Ministers also attached great importance to liaison with those States in the Alliance which are not members of WEU.

2. Invoking the relevant provisions of the modified Brussels Treaty, and in particular Article IV, the Ministers pointed out that it was the responsibility of the Presidency of WEU to inform those countries on either a bilateral or multilateral basis.

Source: Western European Union

SECTION II
Arms Control

Arms control agreements have covered the military relationship between the United States and the Soviet Union, and also among other nuclear powers, for some years. However until recently there were no agreements specifically geared to Europe. Negotiations on a treaty for mutual force reductions in central Europe were conducted for much of the 1970s and 1980s in Vienna but failed to reach a conclusion and were disbanded when new talks on conventional forces in Europe (CFE) were agreed.

These began in early 1989 – also in Vienna – and cover an area from the Atlantic to the Urals. The draft treaties submitted by NATO and the Warsaw Pact included here still contain a number of gaps but significant convergence on the major issues can be detected and since late 1989 there has been further progress on detail as well as on the extent of the reductions in US and Soviet manpower. Reference is made to this process in a number of the speeches and statements contained in Section III.

For the moment the two key treaties in place are the 1986 Stockholm Agreement on Confidence- and Security-Building Measures (CSBMs), which builds on earlier provisions in the 1975 CSCE Final Act, and the 1987 US-Soviet Treaty on Intermediate Nuclear Forces (INF), which involves the removal of a whole category of weapons, and not just from Europe.

Although the Strategic Arms Reduction Talks (START) are not directly related to developments in Europe, the overall nuclear balance has been critical to the structure of European security. The likely form of an eventual START Treaty is indicated in the American briefing paper included here.

CSCE – CONFERENCE ON DISARMAMENT IN EUROPE 19 SEPTEMBER 1986

[Preambular form – includes 'manifestation of force' concept – forbids use or threat of force – refers to human rights and fundamental freedoms – necessity to combat terrorism]

I. Prior Notification Of Certain Military Activities

The participating States will give notification in writing through diplomatic channels in an agreed form of content, to all other participating States 42 days or more in advance of the start of notifiable military activities in the zone of application for CSBMs.

Notification will be given by the participating State on whose territory the activity in question is planned to take place even if the forces of that State are not engaged in the activity or their strength is below the notifiable level. This will not relieve other participating States of their obligation to give notification, if their involvement in the planned military activity reaches the notifiable level.

Each of the following military activities in the field conducted as a single activity in the zone of application for CSBMs at or above the levels defined below, will be notified:

The engagement of formations of land forces of the participating States in the same exercise activity conducted under a single operational command independently or in combination with any possible air or naval components.

This military activity will be subject to notification whenever it involves at any time durir.g the activity:

- at least 13,000 troops, including support troops, or
- at least 300 battle tanks

if organised into a divisional structure or at least two brigades/regiments, not necessarily subordinate to the same division.

The participation of air forces of the participating States will be included in the notification if it is foreseen that in the course of the activity 200 or more sorties by aircraft, excluding helicopters, will be flown.

The engagement of military forces either in an amphibious landing or in a parachute assault by airborne forces in the zone of application for CSBMs.

These military activities will be subject to notification whenever the amphibious landing involves at least 8,000 troops or whenever the parachute drop involves at least 3,000 troops.

The engagement of formations of land forces of the participating States in a transfer from outside the zone of application for CSBMs to arrival points in the zone, or from inside the zone of application for CSBMs to points of concentration in the zone, to participate in a notifiable exercise activity or to be concentrated.

The arrival or concentration of these forces will be subject to notification whenever it involves, at any time during the activity:

- at least 13,000 troops, including support troops, or
- at least 300 battle tanks

if organised into a divisional structure or at least two brigades/regiments, not necessarily subordinate to the same division.

Forces which have been transferred into the zone will be subject to all provisions of agreed CSBMs when they depart their arrival points to participate in a notifiable exercise activity or to be concentrated within the zone of application for CSBMs.

Notifiable military activities carried out without advance notice to the troops involved, are exceptions to the requirement for prior notification to be made 42 days in advance.

Notification of such activities, above the agreed thresholds, will be given at the time the troops involved commence such activities.

Notification will be given in writing of each notifiable military activity in the following agreed form:

General Information
The designation of the military activity;
The general purpose of the military activity;
The names of the States involved in the military activity;
The level of command, organising and commanding the military activity;
The start and end dates of the military activity.

Information on Different Types of Notifiable Military Activities
The engagement of land forces of the participating States in the same exercise activity conducted under a single operational command independently or in combination with any possible air or naval components;

The total number of troops taking part in the military activity (i.e., ground troops, amphibious troops, airmobile and airborne troops) and the number of troops participating for each State involved, if applicable;

Number and type of divisions participating for each State;

The total number of battle tanks for each State and the total number of anti-tank guided missile launchers mounted on armoured vehicles;

The total number of artillery pieces and multiple rocket launchers (100 mm calibre or above);

The total number of helicopters, by category;

Envisaged number of sorties by aircraft, excluding helicopters;

Purpose of air missions;

Categories of aircraft involved;

The level of command, organizing and commanding the air force participation;

Naval ship-to-shore gunfire;

Indication of other naval ship-to-shore support;

The level of command, organizing and commanding the naval force participation.

The engagement of military forces either in an amphibious landing or in a parachute assault by airborne forces in the zone of application for CSBMs;

The total number of amphibious troops involved in notifiable amphibious landings, and/or the total number of airborne troops involved in notifiable parachute assaults;

In the case of a notifiable amphibious landing, the point or points of embarkation, if in the zone of application for CSBMs.

The engagement of formations of land forces of the participating States in a transfer from outside the zone of application for CSBMs to arrival points in the zone, or from inside the zone of application for CSBMs to points of concentration in the zone to participate in a notifiable exercise activity or to be concentrated.

The total number of troops transferred;

Number and type of divisions participating in the transfer;

The total number of battle tanks participating in a notifiable arrival or concentration;

Geographical coordinates for the points of arrival and for the points of concentration.

The Envisaged Area and Timeframe of the Activity

The area of the military activity delimited by geographic features together with geographic coordinates, as appropriate;

The start and end dates of each phase (transfers, deployment, concentration of forces, active exercise phase, recovery phase) of activities in the zone of application for CSBMs of participating formations, the tactical purpose and corresponding geographical areas (delimited by geographical coordinates) for each phase;

Other Information

Changes, if any, in relation to information provided in the annual calendar regarding the activity;

Relationship of the activity to other notifiable activities.

II. Observation of Certain Military Activities

The participating States will invite observers from all other participating States to the following notifiable military activities:

- The engagement of formations of land forces of the participating States in the same exercise activity conducted under a single operational command independently or in combination with any possible air or naval components.
- The engagement of military forces either in an amphibious landing or in a parachute assault by airborne forces in the zone of application for CSBMs.
- In the case of the engagement of formations of land forces of the participating States in a transfer from outside the zone of application for CSBMs to arrival points in the zone, or from inside the zone of application for CSBMs to points of concentration in the zone, to participate in a notifiable exercise activity or to be concentrated, the concentration of these forces. Forces which have been transferred into the zone will be subject to all provisions of agreed confidence- and security-building measures when they depart their arrival points to participate in a notifiable exercise activity or to be concentrated within the zone of application for CSBMs.

The above-mentioned activities will be subject to observation whenever the number of troops engaged meets or exceeds 17,000 troops, except in the case of either an amphibious landing or a parachute assault by airborne forces, which will be subject to observation whenever the number of troops engaged meets or exceeds 5,000 troops.

The host State will extend the invitations in writing through diplomatic channels to all other participating States at the time of notification. The host State will be the participating State on whose territory the notified activity will take place.

The host State may delegate some of its responsibilities as host to another participating State engaged in the military activity on the territory of the host State. In such cases, the host State will specify the allocation of responsibilities in its invitation to observe the activity.

Each participating State may send up to two observers to the military activity to be observed.

The invited State may decide whether to send military and/or civilian observers, including members of its personnel accredited to the host State. Military observers will, normally, wear their uniforms and insignia while performing their tasks.

Replies to the invitation will be given in writing not later than 21 days after the issue of the invitation.

The participating States accepting an invitation will provide the names and ranks of their observers in their reply to the invitation. If the invitation is not accepted in time, it will be assumed that no observers will be sent.

Together with the invitation the host State will provide a general observation program, including the following information:

- the date, time and place of assembly of observers;
- planned duration of the observation program;
- languages to be used in interpretation and/or translation;
- arrangements for board, lodging and transportation of the observers;
- arrangements for observation equipment which will be issued to the observers by the host State;
- possible authorization by the host State of the use of special equipment that the observers may bring with them;

The host state may delegate some of its responsibilities as host to another participating State engaged in the military activity on the territory of the host State. In such cases, the host State will specify the allocation of responsibilities in its invitation to observe the activity.

Each participating State may send up to two observers to the military activity to be observed.

The invited State may decide whether to send military and/or civilian observers, including members of its personnel accredited to the host State. Military observers will, normally, wear their uniforms and insignia while performing their tasks.

Replies to the invitation will be given in writing not later than 21 days after the issue of the invitation.

The participating States accepting an invitation will provide the names and ranks of their observers in their reply to the invitation. If the invitation is not accepted in time, it will be assumed that no observers will be sent.

Together with the invitation the host State will provide a general observation programme, including the following information:

- the date, time and place of assembly of observers;
- planned duration of the observation program;
- languages to be used in interpretation and/or translation;
- arrangements for board, lodging and transportation of the observers;
- arrangements for observation equipment which will be issued to the observers by the host State;
- possible authorization by the host State of the use of special equipment that the observers may bring with them;
- arrangements for special clothing to be issued to the observers because of weather or environmental factors.

The observers may make requests with regard to the observation program. The host State will, if possible, accede to them.

The host State will determine a duration of observation which permits the observers to observe a notifiable military activity from the time that agreed . . . thresholds are met or exceeded until, for the last time during the activity, the . . . thresholds are no longer met.

The host State will provide the observers with transportation to the area of the notified activity and back. This transportation will be provided from either the capital or another suitable location to be announced in the invitation, so that the observers are in position before the start of the observation program.

The invited State will cover the travel expenses for its observers to the capital, or another suitable location specified in the invitation, of the host State, and back.

The observers will be provided equal treatment and offered equal opportunities to carry out their functions.

The observers will be granted, during their mission, the privileges and immunities accorded to diplomatic agents in the Vienna Convention on Diplomatic Relations.

The host State will not be required to permit observation of restricted locations, installations or defence sites.

In order to allow the observers to confirm that the notified activity is non-threatening in character and that it is carried out in conformity with the appropriate provisions of the notification, the host State will:

- at the commencement of the observation program give a briefing on the purpose, the basic situation, the phases of the activity and possible changes as compared with the notification and provide the observers with a map of the area of the military activity with a scale of 1 to not more than 500,000 and an observation program with a daily schedule as well as a sketch indicating the basic situation;
- provide the observers with appropriate observation equipment; however, the observers will be allowed to use their personal binoculars, which will be subject to examination and approval by the host State;
- in the course of the observation program give the observers daily briefings with the help of maps on the various phases of the military activity and their development and inform the observers about their positions geographically; in the case of a land force activity conducted in combination with air or naval components, briefings will be given by representatives of these forces;
- provide opportunities to observe directly forces of the State/States engaged in the military activity so that the observers get an impression of the flow of the activity; to this end, the observers will be given the opportunity to observe major combat units of the participating formations of a divisional or equivalent level and, whenever possible, to visit some units and communicate with commanders and troops; commanders or other senior personnel of participating formations as well as of the visited units will inform the observers of the mission of their respective units;

- guide the observers in the area of the military activity; the observers will follow the instructions issued by the host State in accordance with the provisions set out in this document;
- provide the observers with appropriate means of transportation in the area of the military activity;
- provide the observers with opportunities for timely communication with their embassies or other official missions and consular posts; the host State is not obligated to cover the communication expenses of the observers;
- provide the observers with appropriate board and lodging in a location suitable for carrying out the observation program and, when necessary, medical care.

The participating States need not invite observers to notifiable military activities which are carried out without advance warning to the troops involved unless these notifiable activities have a duration of more than 72 hours. The continuation of these activities beyond this time will be subject to observation while the agreed thresholds are met or exceeded. The observation programme will follow as closely as practically possible all the provisions for observation set out in this document.

III. Annual Calendars

Each participating State will exchange, with all other participating States, an annual calendar of its military activities subject to prior notification, within the zone of application for CSBMs, forecast for the subsequent calendar year. It will be transmitted every year, in writing, through diplomatic channels, not later than 15 November for the following year.

Each participating State will list the above-mentioned activities chronologically and will provide information on each activity in accordance with the following model:

- type of military activity and its designation;
- general characteristics and purpose of the military activity;
- States involved in the military activity;
- area of the military activity, indicated by appropriate geographic features and/or defined by geographic coordinates;
- planned duration of the military activity and the 14-day period, indicated by dates, within which it is envisaged to start;
- the envisaged total number of troops engaged in the military activity;
- the types of armed forces involved in the military activity;
- the envisaged level of command under which the military activity will take place;
- the number and type of divisions whose participation in the military activity is envisaged;

- any additional information concerning, inter alia, components of forces, which the participating State planning the military activity considers relevant.

Should changes regarding the military activities in the annual calendar prove necessary, they will be communicated to all other participating States no later than in the appropriate notification.

Information on military activities subject to prior notification not included in an annual calendar will be communicated to all participating States as soon as possible, in accordance with the model provided in the annual calendar.

IV. Constraining Provisions

Each participating State will communicate, in writing, to all other participating States, by 15 November each year, information concerning military activities subject to prior notification involving more than 40,000 troops, which it plans to carry out in the second subsequent calendar year. Such communication will include preliminary information on each activity, as to its general purpose, timeframe and duration, area size and States involved.

Participating States will not carry out military activities subject to prior notification involving more than 75,000 troops, unless they have been the object of communication as defined above. Participating States will not carry out military activities subject to prior notification involving more than 40,000 troops unless they have been included in the annual calendar, not later than 15 November each year.

If military activities subject to prior notification are carried out in addition to those contained in the annual calendar, they should be as few as possible.

V. Compliance and Verification

According to the Madrid Mandate, the confidence- and security-building measures to be agreed upon 'will be provided with adequate forms of verification which correspond to their content.'

The participating States recognise that national technical means can play a role in monitoring compliance with agreed CSBMs.

In accordance with the provisions contained in this document each participating State has the right to conduct inspections on the territory of any other participating State within the zone of application for CSBMs.

Any participating State will be allowed to address a request for inspection to another participating State on whose territory, within the zone of application for CSBMs, compliance with the agreed CSBMs is in doubt.

No participating State will be obliged to accept, on its territory within the zone of application for CSBMs, more than three inspection per calendar year.

No participating State will be obliged to accept more than one inspection per calendar year from the same participating State.

An inspection will not be counted if, due to force majeure, it cannot be carried out.

The participating State which requests an inspection will state the reasons for such a request.

The participating State which has received such a request will reply in the affirmative to the request within the agreed period of time, subject to the provisions contained in paragraphs (5 and 6 of this working document).

Any possible dispute as to the validity of the reasons for a request will not prevent or delay the conduct of an inspection.

The participating State which requests an inspection will be permitted to designate for inspection, on the territory of another State within the zone of application for CSBMs, a specific area. Such an area will be referred to as the 'specified area.' The specified area will comprise terrain where notifiable military activities are conducted or where another participating State believes a notifiable military activity is taking place. The specified area will be defined and limited by the scope and scale of notifiable military activities but will not exceed that required for an army level military activity.

In the specified area the representatives of the inspecting State accompanied by representatives of the receiving State will be permitted access, entry and unobstructed survey, except for areas or sensitive points to which access is normally denied or restricted, military and other defense installations, as well as naval vessels, military vehicles and aircraft. The number and extent of the restricted areas should be as limited as possible. Areas where notifiable military activities can take place will not be declared restricted areas, except for certain permanent or temporary military installation which, in territorial terms, should be as small as possible, and consequently those areas will not be used to prevent inspection of notifiable military activities. Restricted areas will not be employed in a way inconsistent with the agreed provisions on inspection.

Within the specified area, the forces of participating States other than the receiving State will also be subject to the inspection conducted by the inspecting State.

Inspection will be permitted on the ground, from the air, or both.

The representatives of the receiving State will accompany the inspection team, including when it is in land vehicles and on aircraft from the time of their first employment until the time they are no longer in use for the purposes of inspection.

In its request, the inspecting State will notify the receiving State of:

(a) the reasons for the request;

(b) the location of the specified area defined by geographical coordinates;

(c) the preferred point(s) of entry for the inspection team;

(d) mode of transport to and from the point(s) of entry and, if applicable, to and from the specified area;

(e) where in the specified area the inspection will begin;

(f) whether the inspection will be conducted from the ground, from the air, or both simultaneously;

(g) whether aerial inspection will be conducted using an airplane, a helicopter, or both;

(h) whether the inspection team will use land vehicles provided by the receiving State or, if mutually agreed, its own vehicles;

(i) information for the issuance of diplomatic visas to inspectors entering the receiving State.

The reply to the request will be given in the shortest possible of time, but within not more than 24 hours. Within 36 hours after the issuance of the request, the inspection team will be permitted to enter the territory of the receiving State.

Any request for inspection as well as the reply thereto will be communicated to all participating States without delay.

The receiving State should designate the point(s) of entry as close as possible to the specified area. The receiving State will insure that the inspection team will be able to reach the specified area without delay from the point(s) of entry.

All participating States will facilitate the passage of the inspection teams through their territory.

Within 48 hours after the arrival of the inspection team at the specified area, the inspection will be terminated.

There will be no more than four inspectors in an inspection team. While conducting the inspection the inspection team may divide into two parts.

The inspectors and, if applicable, auxiliary personnel, will be granted during their mission the privileges and immunities in accordance with the Vienna Convention on diplomatic relations.

The receiving State will provide the inspection team with appropriate board and lodging in a location suitable for carrying out the inspection, and, when necessary, medical care; however, this does not exclude the use by the inspection team of its own tents and rations.

The inspection team will have use of its own maps, own photo cameras, own binoculars and own Dictaphones, as well as own aeronautical charts.

The inspection team will have access to appropriate telecommunications equipment of the receiving State, including the opportunity for continuous communication between the members of an inspection team in an aircraft and those in a land vehicle employed in the inspection.

The inspecting State will specify whether aerial inspection will be conducted using an airplane, a helicopter or both. Aircraft for inspection will be chosen by mutual agreement between the inspecting and receiving States. Aircraft will be chosen which provide the inspection team a continuous view of the ground during the inspection.

After the flight plan, specifying inter alia, the inspection team's choice of flight path, speed and altitude in the specified area, has been filed with the competent air traffic control authority the inspection aircraft will be permitted to enter the specified area without delay. Within the specified area, the inspection team will, at its request, be permitted to deviate from the approved flight plan to make specific observations provided such deviation is consistent with paragraph (12 of this working paper) as well as flight safety and air traffic requirements. Directions to the crew will be given through a representative of the receiving State on board the aircraft involved in the inspection.

One member of the inspection team will be permitted, if such a request is made, at any time to observe data on navigational equipment of the aircraft and to have access to maps and charts used by the flight crew for the purpose of determining the exact location of the aircraft during the inspection flight.

Aerial and ground inspectors may return to the specified area as often as desired within the 48-hour inspection period.

The receiving State will provide for inspection purposes land vehicles with cross country capability. Whenever mutually agreed, taking into account the specific geography relating to the area to be inspected, the inspecting State will be permitted to use its own vehicles.

If land vehicles or aircraft are provided by the inspecting State, there will be one accompanying driver for each land vehicle, or accompanying aircraft crew.

The inspecting State will prepare a report of its inspection and will provide a copy of that report to all participating States without delay.

The inspection expenses will be incurred by the receiving State except when the inspecting State used its own aircraft and/or land vehicles. The travel expenses to and from the point(s) of entry will be borne by the inspecting State.

Diplomatic channels will be used for communications concerning compliance and verification.

Each participating State will be entitled to obtain timely clarification from any other participating State concerning the application of agreed CSBMs. Communications in this context will, if appropriate, be transmitted to all other participating States.

The participating States stress that these CSBMs are designed to reduce the dangers of armed conflict and of misunderstanding or miscalculation of military activities and emphasize that their implementation will contribute to these objectives.

Reaffirming the relevant objectives of the Final Act, the participating

States are determined to continue building confidence, to lessen military confrontation and to enhance security for all. They are also determined to achieve progress in disarmament.

The measures adopted in this document are politically binding and will come into force on 1 January 1987.

The Government of Sweden is requested to transmit the present document to the follow-up meeting of the CSCE in Vienna and to the Secretary General of the United Nations. The Government of Sweden is also requested to transmit the present document to the Governments of the non-participating Mediterranean States. The text of this document will be published in each participating State, which will disseminate it and make it known as widely as possible.

The representatives of the participating States express their profound gratitude to the Government and people of Sweden for the excellent arrangements made for the Stockholm Conference and the warm hospitality extended to the delegations which participated in the Conference.

Source: *Arms Control Reporter* Brookline, US

TREATY BETWEEN THE UNITED STATES OF AMERICA AND THE UNION OF SOVIET SOCIALIST REPUBLICS ON THE ELIMINATION OF THEIR INTERMEDIATE-RANGE AND SHORTER-RANGE MISSILES

10 December 1987

The United States of America and the Union of Soviet Socialist Republics, hereinafter referred to as the Parties,

Conscious that nuclear war would have devastating consequences for all mankind,

Guided by the objective of strengthening strategic stability,

Convinced that the measures set forth in this Treaty will help to reduce the risk of outbreak of war and strengthen international peace and security, and

Mindful of their obligations under Article VI of the Treaty on the Non-Proliferation of Nuclear Weapons,

Have agreed as follows:

Article I

In accordance with the provisions of this Treaty which includes the Memorandum of Understanding and Protocols which form an integral part thereof, each Party shall eliminate its intermediate-range and shorter-range missiles, not have such systems thereafter, and carry out the other obligations set forth in this Treaty.

Article II

For the purposes of this Treaty:

1. The term 'ballistic missile' means a missile that has a ballistic trajectory over most of its flight path. The term 'ground-launched ballistic missile (GLBM)' means a ground-launched ballistic missile that is a weapon-delivery vehicle.

2. The term 'cruise missile' means an unmanned, self-propelled vehicle that sustains flight through the use of aerodynamic lift over most of its flight path. The term 'ground-launched cruise missile (GLCM)' means a ground-launched cruise missile that is a weapon-delivery vehicle.

3. The term 'GLBM launcher' means a fixed launcher or a mobile land-based transporter-erector-launcher mechanism for launching a GLBM.

4. The term 'GLCM launcher' means a fixed launcher or a mobile land-based transporter-erector-launcher mechanism for launching a GLCM.

5. The term 'intermediate-range missile' means a GLBM or a GLCM having a range capability in excess of 1000 kilometers but not in excess of 5500 kilometers.

6. The term 'shorter-range missile' means a GLBM or a GLCM having a range capability equal to or in excess of 500 kilometers but not in excess of 1000 kilometers.

7. The term 'deployment area' means a designated area within which intermediate-range missiles and launchers of such missiles may operate and within which one or more missile operating bases are located.

8. The term 'missile operating base' means:

(a) in the case of intermediate-range missiles, a complex of facilities, located within a deployment area, at which intermediate-range missiles and launchers of such missiles normally operate, in which support structures associated with such missiles and launchers are also located and in which support equipment associated with such missiles and launchers is normally located; and

(b) in the case of shorter-range missiles, a complex of facilities, located any place, at which shorter-range missiles and launchers of such missiles normally operate and in which support equipment associated with such missiles and launchers is normally located.

9. The term 'missile support facility,' as regards intermediate-range or shorter-range missiles and launchers of such missiles, means a missile production facility or a launcher production facility, a missile repair facility or a launcher repair facility, a training facility, a missile storage facility or a launcher storage facility, a test range, or an elimination facility as those terms are defined in the Memorandum of Understanding.

10. The term 'transit' means movement, notified in accordance with paragraph 5(f) of Article IX of this Treaty, of an intermediate-range missile or a launcher of such a missile between missile support facilities, between such a facility and a deployment area or between deployment areas, or of a shorter-range missile or a launcher of such a missile from a missile support facility or a missile operating base to an elimination facility.

11. The term 'deployed missile' means an intermediate-range missile located within a deployment area or a shorter-range missile located at a missile operating base.

12. The term 'non-deployed missile' means an intermediate-range missile located outside a deployment area or a shorter-range missile located outside a missile operating base.

13. The term 'deployed launcher' means a launcher of an intermediate-range missile located within a deployment area or a launcher of a shorter-range missile located at a missile operating base.

14. The term 'non-deployed launcher' means a launcher of an intermediate-range missile located outside a deployment area or a launcher of a shorter-range missile located outside a missile operating base.

15. The term 'basing country' means a country other than the United States of America or the Union of Soviet Socialist Republics on whose territory intermediate-range or shorter-range missiles of the Parties, launchers of such missiles or support structures associated with such missiles and launchers were located at any time after November 1, 1987. Missiles or launchers in transit are not considered to be 'located'.

Article III

1. For the purposes of this Treaty, existing types of intermediate-range missiles are:

(a) for the United States of America, missiles of the types designated by the United States of America as the Pershing II and the BGM-109G, which are known to the Union of Soviet Socialist Republics by the same designations; and

(b) for the Union of Soviet Socialist Republics, missiles of the types designated by the Union of Soviet Socialist Republics as the RSD-10, the R-12 and the R-14, which are known to the United States of America as the SS-20, the SS-4 and the SS-5, respectively.

2. For the purposes of this Treaty, existing types of shorter-range missiles are:

(a) for the United States of America, missiles of the type designated by the United States of America as the Pershing IA, which is known to the Union of Soviet Socialist Republics by the same designation; and

(b) for the Union of Soviet Socialist Republics, missiles of the types designated by the Union of Soviet Socialist Republics as the OTR-22 and the OTR-23, which are known to the United States of America as the SS-12 and the SS-23, respectively.

Article IV

1. Each Party shall eliminate all its intermediate-range missiles and launchers of such missiles, and all support structures and support equipment of the categories listed in the Memorandum of Understanding associated with such missiles and launchers, so that no later than three years after entry into force of this Treaty and thereafter no such missiles, launchers, support structures or support equipment shall be possessed by either Party.

2. To implement paragraph 1 of this Article, upon entry into force of this Treaty, both Parties shall begin and continue throughout the

duration of each phase, the reduction of all types of their deployed and non-deployed intermediate-range missiles and deployed and non-deployed launchers of such missiles and support structures and support equipment associated with such missiles and launchers in accordance with the provisions of this Treaty. These reductions shall be implemented in two phases so that:

(a) by the end of the first phase, that is, no later than 29 months after entry into force of this Treaty:

(i) the number of deployed launchers of intermediate-range missiles for each Party shall not exceed the number of launchers that are capable of carrying or containing at one time missiles considered by the Parties to carry 171 warheads;

(ii) the number of deployed intermediate-range missiles for each Party shall not exceed the number of such missiles considered by the Parties to carry 180 warheads;

(iii) the aggregate number of deployed and non-deployed launchers of intermediate-range missiles for each Party shall not exceed the number of launchers that are capable of carrying or containing at one time missiles considered by the Parties to carry 200 warheads;

(iv) the aggregate number of deployed and non-deployed intermediate-range missiles for each Party shall not exceed the number of such missiles considered by the Parties to carry 200 warheads; and

(v) the ratio of the aggregate number of deployed and non-deployed intermediate-range GLBMs of existing types for each Party to the aggregate number of deployed and non-deployed intermediate-range missiles of existing types possessed by that Party shall not exceed the ratio of such intermediate-range GLBMs to such intermediate-range missiles for that Party as of November 1, 1987, as set forth in the Memorandum of Understanding; and

(b) by the end of the second phase, that is, no later than three years after entry into force of this Treaty, all intermediate-range missiles of each Party, launchers of such missiles and all support structures and support equipment of the categories listed in the Memorandum of Understanding associated with such missiles and launchers, shall be eliminated.

Article V

1. Each Party shall eliminate all its shorter-range missiles and launchers of such missiles, and all support equipment of the categories listed in the Memorandum of Understanding associated with such missiles and launchers, so that no later than 18 months after entry into force of this Treaty and thereafter no such missiles, launchers or support equipment shall be possessed by either Party.

2. No later than 90 days after entry into force of this Treaty, each Party shall complete the removal of all its deployed shorter-range missiles and deployed and non-deployed launchers of such missiles to elimination facilities and shall retain them at those locations until they

are eliminated in accordance with the procedures set forth in the Protocol on Elimination. No later than 12 months after entry into force of this Treaty, each Party shall complete the removal of all its non-deployed shorter-range missiles to elimination facilities and shall retain them at those locations until they are eliminated in accordance with the procedures set forth in the Protocol on Elimination.

3. Shorter-range missiles and launchers of such missiles shall not be located at the same elimination facility. Such facilities shall be separated by no less than 1000 kilometers.

Article VI

1. Upon entry into force of this Treaty and thereafter, neither Party shall:

(a) produce or flight-test any intermediate-range missiles or produce any stages of such missiles or any launchers of such missiles; or

(b) produce, flight-test or launch any shorter-range missiles or produce any stages of such missiles or any launchers or such missiles.

2. Notwithstanding paragraph 1 of this Article, each Party shall have the right to produce a type of GLBM not limited by this Treaty which uses a stage which is outwardly similar to, but not interchangeable with, a stage of an existing type of intermediate-range GLBM having more than one stage, providing that that Party does not produce any other stage which is outwardly similar to, but not interchangeable with, any other stage of an existing type of intermediate-range GLBM.

Article VII

For the purposes of this Treaty:

1. If a ballistic missile or a cruise missile has been flight-tested or deployed for weapon delivery, all missiles of that type shall be considered to be weapon-delivery vehicles.

2. If a GLBM or GLCM is an intermediate-range missile, all GLBMs or GLCMs of that type shall be considered to be intermediate-range missiles. If a GLBM or GLCM is a shorter-range missile, all GLBMs or GLCMs of that type shall be considered to be shorter-range missiles.

3. If a GLBM is of a type developed and tested solely to intercept and counter objects not located on the surface of the earth, it shall not be considered to be a missile to which the limitations of this Treaty apply.

4. The range capability of a GLBM not listed in Article III of this Treaty shall be considered to be the maximum range to which it has been tested. The range capability of a GLCM not listed in Article III of this Treaty shall be considered to be the maximum distance which can be covered by the missile in its standard design mode flying until fuel exhaustion, determined by projecting its flight path onto the earth's sphere from the point of launch to the point of impact. GLBMs or GLCMs that have a range capability equal to or in excess of 500 kilometers but not in excess of 1000 kilometers shall be considered to be shorter-range missiles. GLBMs or GLCMs that have a range capability

in excess of 1000 kilometers but not in excess of 5000 kilometers shall be considered to be intermediate-range missiles.

5. The maximum number of warheads an existing type of intermediate-range missile or shorter-range missile carries shall be considered to be the number listed for missiles of that type in the Memorandum of Understanding.

6. Each GLBM or GLCM shall be considered to carry the maximum number of warheads listed for a GLBM or GLCM of that type in the Memorandum of Understanding.

7. If a launcher has been tested for launching a GLBM or a GLCM, all launchers of that type shall be considered to have been tested for launching GLBMs or GLCMs.

8. If a launcher has contained or launched a particular type of GLBM or GLCM, all launchers of that type shall be considered to be launchers of that type of GLBM or GLCM.

9. The number of missiles each launcher of an existing type of intermediate-range missile or shorter-range missile shall be considered to be capable of carrying or containing at one time is the number listed for launchers of missiles of that type in the Memorandum of Understanding.

10. Except in the case of elimination in accordance with the procedures set forth in the Protocol on Elimination, the following shall apply:

(a) for GLBMs which are stored or moved in separate stages, the longest stage of an intermediate-range or shorter-range GLBM shall be counted as a complete missile;

(b) for GLBMs which are not stored or moved in separate stages, a canister of the type used in the launch of an intermediate-range GLBM, unless a Party proves to the satisfaction of the other Party that it does not contain such a missile, or an assembled intermediate-range or shorter-range GLBM, shall be counted as a complete missile; and

(c) for GLCMs, the airframe of an intermediate-range or shorter-range GLCM shall be counted as a complete missile.

11. A ballistic missile which is not a missile to be used in a ground-based mode shall not be considered to be a GLBM if it is test-launched at a test site from a fixed land-based launcher which is used solely for test purposes and which is distinguishable from GLBM launchers. A cruise missile which is not a missile to be used in a ground-based mode shall not be considered to be a GLCM if it is test-launched at a test site from a fixed land-based launcher which is used solely for test purposes and which is distinguishable from GLCM launchers.

12. Each Party shall have the right to produce and use for booster systems, which might otherwise be considered to be intermediate-range or shorter-range missiles, only existing types of booster stages for such booster systems. Launches of such booster systems shall not be considered to be flight-testing of intermediate-range or shorter-range missiles provided that:

(a) stages used in such booster systems are different from stages used in those missiles listed as existing types of intermediate-range or shorter-range missiles in Article III of this Treaty;

(b) such booster systems are used only for research and development purposes to test objects other than the booster systems themselves;

(c) the aggregate number of launchers for such booster systems shall not exceed 35 for each Party at any one time; and

(d) the launchers for such booster systems are fixed, emplaced above ground and located only at research and development launch sites which are specified in the Memorandum of Understanding.

Research and development launch sites shall not be subject to inspection pursuant to Article XI of this Treaty.

Article VIII

1. All intermediate-range missiles and launchers of such missiles shall be located in deployment areas, at missile support facilities or shall be in transit. Intermediate-range missiles or launchers of such missiles shall not be located elsewhere.

2. Stages of intermediate-range missiles shall be located in deployment areas, at missile support facilities or moving between deployment areas, between missile support facilities or between missile support facilities and deployment areas.

3. Until their removal to elimination facilities as required by paragraph 2 of Article V of this Treaty, all shorter-range missiles and launchers of such missiles shall be located at missile operating bases, at missile support facilities or shall be in transit. Shorter-range missiles or launchers of such missiles shall not be located elsewhere.

4. Transit of a missile or launcher subject to the provisions of this Treaty shall be completed within 25 days.

5. All deployment areas, missile operating bases and missile support facilities are specified in the Memorandum of Understanding or in subsequent updates of data pursuant to paragraphs 3, 5(a) or 5(b) of Article IX of this Treaty. Neither Party shall increase the number of, or change the location or boundaries of, deployment areas, missile operating bases or missile support facilities, except for elimination facilities, from those set forth in the Memorandum of Understanding. A missile support facility shall not be considered to be part of a deployment area even though it may be located within the geographic boundaries of a deployment area.

6. Beginning 30 days after entry into force of this Treaty, neither Party shall locate intermediate-range or shorter-range missiles, including stages of such missiles, or launchers of such missiles at missile production facilities, launcher production facilities or test ranges listed in the Memorandum of Understanding.

7. Neither Party shall locate any intermediate-range or shorter-range missiles at training facilities.

8. A non-deployed intermediate-range or shorter-range missile shall not be carried on or contained within a launcher of such a type of missile, except as required for maintenance conducted at repair facilities or for elimination by means of launching conducted at elimination facilities.

9. Training missiles and training launchers for intermediate-range or shorter-range missiles shall be subject to the same locational restrictions as are set forth for intermediate-range and shorter-range missiles and launchers of such missiles in paragraphs 1 and 3 of this Article.

Article IX

1. The Memorandum of Understanding contains categories of data relevant to obligations undertaken with regard to this Treaty and lists all intermediate-range and shorter-range missiles, launchers of such missiles, and support structures and support equipment associated with such missiles and launchers, possessed by the Parties as of November 1, 1987. Updates of that data and notifications required by this Article shall be provided according to the categories of data contained in the Memorandum of Understanding.

2. The Parties shall update that data and provide the notifications required by this Treaty through the Nuclear Risk Reduction Centers, established pursuant to the Agreement Between the United States of America and the Union of Soviet Socialist Republics on the Establishment of Nuclear Risk Reduction Centers of September 15, 1987.

3. No later than 30 days after entry into force of this Treaty, each Party shall provide the other Party with updated data, as of the date of entry into force of this Treaty, for all categories of data contained in the Memorandum of Understanding.

4. No later than 30 days after the end of each six-month interval following the entry into force of this Treaty, each Party shall provide updated data for all categories of data contained in the Memorandum of Understanding by informing the other Party of all changes, completed and in process, in that data, which have occurred during the six-month interval since the preceding data exchange, and the net effect of those changes.

5. Upon entry into force of this Treaty and thereafter, each Party shall provide the following notifications to the other Party:

(a) notification, no less than 30 days in advance, of the scheduled date of the elimination of a specific deployment area, missile operating base or missile support facility;

(b) notification, no less than 30 days in advance, of changes in the number or location of elimination facilities, including the location and scheduled date of each change;

(c) notification, except with respect to launches of intermediate-range missiles for the purpose of their elimination, no less than 30 days in advance, of the scheduled date of the initiation of the elimination of intermediate-range and shorter-range missiles, and stages of such missiles, and launchers of such missiles and support structures and support equipment associated with such missiles and launchers, including:

    (i) the number and type of items of missile systems to be eliminated;

    (ii) the elimination site;

    (iii) for intermediate-range missiles, the location from which such missiles, launchers of such missiles and support equipment associated with such missiles and launchers are moved to the elimination facility; and

    (iv) except in the case of support structures, the point of entry to be used by an inspection team conducting an inspection pursuant to paragraph 7 of Article XI of this Treaty and the estimated time of departure of an inspection team from the point of entry to the elimination facility;

(d) notification, no less than 10 days in advance, of the scheduled date of the launch, or the scheduled date of the initiation of a series of launches, of intermediate-range missiles for the purpose of their elimination, including:

    (i) the type of missiles to be eliminated;

    (ii) the location of the launch, or, if elimination is by a series of launches, the location of such launches and the number of launches in the series;

    (iii) the point of entry to be used by an inspection team conducting an inspection pursuant to paragraph 7 of Article XI of this Treaty; and

    (iv) the estimated time of departure of an inspection team from the point of entry to the elimination facility;

(e) notification, no later than 48 hours after they occur, of changes in the number of intermediate-range and shorter-range missiles, launchers of such missiles and support structures and support equipment associated with such missiles and launchers resulting from elimination as described in the Protocol on Elimination, including:

    (i) the number and type of items of a missile system which were eliminated; and

    (ii) the date and location of such elimination; and

(f) notification of transit of intermediate-range or shorter-range missiles or launchers of such missiles, or the movement of training missiles or training launchers for such intermediate-range and shorter-range missiles, no later than 48 hours after it has been completed, including:

    (i) the number of missiles or launchers;

    (ii) the points, dates and times of departure and arrival;

    (iii) the mode of transport; and

    (iv) the location and time at that location at least once every four days during the period of transit.

    6. Upon entry into force of this Treaty and thereafter, each Party shall

notify the other Party, no less than 10 days in advance, of the scheduled date and location of the launch of a research and development booster system as described in paragraph 12 of Article VII of this Treaty.

Article X

1. Each Party shall eliminate its intermediate-range and shorter-range missiles and launchers of such missiles and support structures and support equipment associated with such missiles and launchers in accordance with the procedures set forth in the Protocol on Elimination.

2. Verification by on-site inspection of the elimination of items of missile systems specified in the Protocol on Elimination shall be carried out in accordance with Article XI of this Treaty, the Protocol on Elimination and the Protocol on Inspection.

3. When a Party removes its intermediate-range missiles, launchers of such missiles and support equipment associated with such missiles and launchers from deployment areas to elimination facilities for the purpose of their elimination, it shall do so in complete deployed organizational units. For the United States of America, these units shall be Pershing II batteries and BGM-109G flights. For the Union of Soviet Socialist Republics, these units shall be SS-20 regiments composed of two or three battalions.

4. Elimination of intermediate-range and shorter-range missiles and launchers of such missiles and support equipment associated with such missiles and launchers shall be carried out at the facilities that are specified in the Memorandum of Understanding or notified in accordance with paragraph 5(b) of Article IX of this Treaty, unless eliminated in accordance with Sections IV or V of the Protocol on Elimination. Support structures, associated with the missiles and launchers subject to this Treaty, that are subject to elimination shall be eliminated *in situ*.

5. Each Party shall have the right, during the first six months after entry into force of this Treaty, to eliminate by means of launching no more than 100 of its intermediate-range missiles.

6. Intermediate-range and shorter-range missiles which have been tested prior to entry into force of this Treaty, but never deployed, and which are not existing types of intermediate-range or shorter-range missiles listed in Article III of this Treaty, and launchers of such missiles, shall be eliminated within six months after entry into force of this Treaty in accordance with the procedures set forth in the Protocol on Elimination. Such missiles are:

(a) for the United States of America, missiles of the type designated by the United States of America as the Pershing IB, which is known to the Union of Soviet Socialist Republics by the same designation; and

(b) for the Union of Soviet Socialist Republics, missiles of the type designated by the Union of Soviet Socialist Republics as the RK-55, which is known to the United States of America as the SSC-X-4.

7. Intermediate-range and shorter-range missiles and launchers of such missiles and support structures and support equipment associated with such missiles and launchers shall be considered to be eliminated after completion of the procedures set forth in the Protocol on Elimination and upon the notification provided for in paragraph 5(e) of Article IX of this Treaty.

8. Each Party shall eliminate its deployment areas, missile operating bases and missile support facilities. A Party shall notify the other Party pursuant to paragraph 5(a) of Article IX of this Treaty once the conditions set forth below are fulfilled:

(a) all intermediate-range and shorter-range missiles, launchers of such missiles and support equipment associated with such missiles and launchers located there have been removed;

(b) all support structures associated with such missiles and launchers located there have been eliminated; and

(c) all activity related to production, flight-testing, training, repair, storage or deployment of such missiles and launchers has ceased there.

Such deployment areas, missile operating bases and missile support facilities shall be considered to be eliminated either when they have been inspected pursuant to paragraph 4 of Article XI of this Treaty or when 60 days have elapsed since the date of the scheduled elimination which was notified pursuant to paragraph 5(a) of Article IX of this Treaty. A deployment area, missile operating base or missile support facility listed in the Memorandum of Understanding that met the above conditions prior to entry into force of this Treaty, and is not included in the initial data exchange pursuant to paragraph 3 of Article IX of this Treaty, shall be considered to be eliminated.

9. If a Party intends to convert a missile operating base listed in the Memorandum of Understanding for use as a base associated with GLBM or GLCM systems not subject to this Treaty, then that Party shall notify the other Party, no less than 30 days in advance of the scheduled date of the initiation of the conversion, of the scheduled date and the purpose for which the base will be converted.

Article XI

1. For the purpose of ensuring verification of compliance with the provisions of this Treaty, each Party shall have the right to conduct on-site inspections. The Parties shall implement on-site inspections in accordance with this Article, the Protocol on Inspection and the Protocol on Elimination.

2. Each Party shall have the right to conduct inspections provided for by this Article both within the territory of the other Party and within the territories of basing countries.

3. Beginning 30 days after entry into force of this Treaty, each Party shall have the right to conduct inspections at all missile operating bases and missile support facilities specified in the Memorandum of

Understanding other than missile production facilities, and at all elimination facilities included in the initial data update required by paragraph 3 of Article IX of this Treaty. These inspections shall be completed no later than 90 days after entry into force of this Treaty. The purpose of these inspections shall be to verify the number of missiles, launchers, support structures and support equipment and other data, as of the date of entry into force of this Treaty, provided pursuant to paragraph 3 of Article IX of this Treaty.

4. Each Party shall have the right to conduct inspections to verify the elimination, notified pursuant to paragraph 5(a) of Article IX of this Treaty, of missile operating bases and missile support facilities other than missile production facilities, which are thus no longer subject to inspections pursuant to paragraph 5(a) of this Article. Such an inspection shall be carried out within 60 days after the scheduled date of the elimination of that facility. If a Party conducts an inspection at a particular facility pursuant to paragraph 3 of this Article after the scheduled date of the elimination of that facility, then no additional inspection of that facility pursuant to this paragraph shall be permitted.

5. Each Party shall have the right to conduct inspections pursuant to this paragraph for 13 years after entry into force of this Treaty. Each Party shall have the right to conduct 20 such inspections per calendar year during the first three years after entry into force of this Treaty, 15 such inspections per calendar year during the subsequent five years, and 10 such inspections per calendar year during the last five years. Neither Party shall use more than half of its total number of these inspections per calendar year within the territory of any one basing country. Each Party shall have the right to conduct:

(a) inspections, beginning 90 days after entry into force of this Treaty, of missile operating bases and missile support facilities other than elimination facilities and missile production facilities, to ascertain, according to the categories of data specified in the Memorandum of Understanding, the numbers of missiles, launchers, support structures and support equipment located at each missile operating base or missile support facility at the time of the inspection; and

(b) inspections of former missile operating bases and former missile support facilities eliminated pursuant to paragraph 8 of Article X of this Treaty other than former missile production facilities.

6. Beginning 30 days after entry into force of this Treaty, each Party shall have the right, for 13 years after entry into force of this Treaty, to inspect by means of continuous monitoring:

(a) the portals of any facility of the other Party at which the final assembly of a GLBM using stages, any of which is outwardly similar to a stage of a solid-propellant GLBM listed in Article III of this Treaty, is accomplished; or

(b) if a Party has no such facility, the portals of an agreed former missile production facility at which existing types of intermediate-range or shorter-range GLBMs were produced.

The Party whose facility is to be inspected pursuant to this paragraph shall ensure that the other Party is able to establish a permanent continuous monitoring system at that facility within six months after entry into force of this Treaty or within six months of initiation of the process of final assembly described in subparagraph (a). If, after the end of the second year after entry into force of this Treaty, neither Party conducts the process of final assembly described in subparagraph (a) for a period of 12 consecutive months, then neither Party shall have the right to inspect by means of continuous monitoring any missile production facility of the other Party unless the process of final assembly as described in subparagraph (a) is initiated again. Upon entry into force of this Treaty, the facilities to be inspected by continuous monitoring shall be: in accordance with subparagraph (b), for the United States of America, Hercules Plant Number 1, at Magna, Utah; in accordance with subparagraph (a), for the Union of Soviet Socialist Republics, the Votkinsk Machine Building Plant, Udmurt Autonomous Soviet Socialist Republic, Russian Soviet Federative Socialist Republic.

7. Each Party shall conduct inspections of the process of elimination, including elimination of intermediate-range missiles by means of launching, of intermediate-range and shorter-range missiles and launchers of such missiles and support equipment associated with such missiles and launchers carried out at elimination facilities in accordance with Article X of this Treaty and the Protocol on Elimination. Inspectors conducting inspections provided for in this paragraph shall determine that the processes specified for the elimination of the missiles, launchers and support equipment have been completed.

8. Each Party shall have the right to conduct inspections to confirm the completion of the process of elimination of intermediate-range and shorter-range missiles and launchers of such missiles and support equipment associated with such missiles and launchers eliminated pursuant to Section V of the Protocol on Elimination, and of training missiles, training missile stages, training launch canisters and training launchers eliminated pursuant to Sections II, IV and V of the Protocol on Elimination.

Article XII

1. For the purpose of ensuring verification of compliance with the provisions of this Treaty, each Party shall use national technical means of verification at its disposal in a manner consistent with generally recognized principles of international law.

2. Neither Party shall:

(a) interfere with national technical means of verification of the other Party operating in accordance with paragraph 1 of this Article; or

(b) use concealment measures which impede verification of compliance with the provisions of this Treaty by national technical means of verification carried out in accordance with paragraph 1 of this Article. This obligation does not apply to cover or concealment practices, within a deployment area, associated with normal training, maintenance and operations, including the use of environmental shelters to protect missiles and launchers.

3. To enhance observation by national technical means of verification, each Party shall have the right until a treaty between the Parties reducing and limiting strategic offensive arms enters into force, but in any event for no more than three years after entry into force of this Treaty, to request the implementation of cooperative measures at deployment bases for road-mobile GLBMs with a range capability in excess of 5500 kilometers, which are not former missile operating bases eliminated pursuant to paragraph 8 of Article X of this Treaty. The Party making such a request shall inform the other Party of the deployment base at which cooperative measures shall be implemented. The Party whose base is to be observed shall carry out the following cooperative measures:

(a) no later than six hours after such a request, the Party shall have opened the roofs of all fixed structures for launchers located at the base, removed completely all missiles on launchers from such fixed structures for launchers and displayed such missiles on launchers in the open without using concealment measures; and

(b) the Party shall leave the roofs open and the missiles on launchers in place until 12 hours have elapsed from the time of the receipt of a request for such an observation.

Each Party shall have the right to make six such requests per calendar year. Only one deployment base shall be subject to these cooperative measures at any one time.

Article XIII

1. To promote the objectives and implementation of the provisions of this Treaty, the Parties hereby establish the Special Verification Commission. The Parties agree that, if either Party so requests, they shall meet within the framework of the Special Verification Commission to:

(a) resolve questions relating to compliance with the obligations assumed; and

(b) agree upon such measures as may be necessary to improve the viability and effectiveness of this Treaty.

2. The Parties shall use the Nuclear Risk Reduction Centers, which provide for continuous communication between the Parties, to:

(a) exchange data and provide notifications as required by paragraphs 3, 4, 5 and 6 of Article IX of this Treaty and the Protocol on Elimination;

(b) provide and receive the information required by paragraph 9 of Article X of this Treaty;

(c) provide and receive notification of inspections as required by Article XI of this Treaty and the Protocol on Inspection; and

(d) provide and receive requests for cooperative measures as provided for in paragraph 3 of Article XII of this Treaty.

Article XIV

The Parties shall comply with this Treaty and shall not assume any international obligations or undertakings which would conflict with its provisions.

Article XV

1. This Treaty shall be of unlimited duration.

2. Each Party shall, in exercising its national sovereignty, have the right to withdraw from this Treaty if it decides that extraordinary events related to the subject matter of this Treaty have jeopardized its supreme interests. It shall give notice of its decision to withdraw to the other Party six months prior to withdrawal from this Treaty. Such notice shall include a statement of the extraordinary events the notifying Party regards as having jeopardized its supreme interests.

Article XVI

Each Party may propose amendments to this Treaty. Agreed amendments shall enter into force in accordance with the procedures set forth in Article XVII governing the entry into force of this Treaty.

Article XVII

1. This Treaty, including the Memorandum of Understanding and Protocols, which form an integral part thereof, shall be subject to ratification in accordance with the constitutional procedures of each Party. This Treaty shall enter into force on the date of the exchange of instruments of ratification.

2. This Treaty shall be registered pursuant to Article 102 of the Charter of the United Nations.

DONE at Washington on December 8, 1987, in two copies, each in the English and Russian languages, both texts being equally authentic. For the U.S.A.: President of the U.S.A. For the U.S.S.R.: General Secretary of the Central Committee of the CPSU.

Source: Arms Control Today January/February 1988

CSCE: MANDATE FOR NEGOTIATION ON CONVENTIONAL ARMED FORCES* IN EUROPE

10 January 1989

The representatives of Belgium, Bulgaria, Canada, Czechoslovakia, Denmark, France, the German Democratic Republic, the Federal Republic of Germany, Greece, Hungary, Iceland, Italy, Luxembourg, the Netherlands, Norway, Poland, Portugal, Romania, Spain, Turkey, the Union of Soviet Socialist Republics, the United Kingdom and the United States of America, held consultations in Vienna from 17 February 1987 to 10 January 1989.

These States,

Conscious of the common responsibility which they all have for seeking to achieve greater stability and security in Europe;

Acknowledging that it is their armed forces which bear most immediately on the essential security relationship in Europe, in particular, as they are signatories of the Treaties of Brussels (1948), Washington (1949) or Warsaw (1955), and accordingly are members of the North Atlantic Alliance or parties to the Warsaw Treaty;

Recalling that they are all participants in the CSCE process; Recalling that, as reaffirmed in the Helsinki Final Act, they have the right to belong or not to belong to international organisations, to be or not to be a party to bilateral or multilateral treaties including the right to be or not to be a party to treaties of alliance;

Determined that a Negotiation on Conventional Armed Forces in Europe should take place in the framework of the CSCE process;

Reaffirming also that they participate in negotiations as sovereign and independent States and on the basis of full equality;

Have agreed on the following provisions:

Participants

The participants in this negotiation shall be the 23 above-listed States hereinafter referred to as 'the participants'.

Objectives and Methods

The objectives of the negotiation shall be to strengthen stability and security in Europe through the establishment of a stable and secure balance of conventional armed forces, which include conventional

armaments and equipment, at lower levels; the elimination of disparities prejudicial to stability and security; and the elimination, as a matter
of priority, of the capability for launching surprise attack and for
initiating large-scale offensive action. Each and every participant
undertakes to contribute to the attainment of these objectives.

These objectives shall be achieved by the application of militarily
significant measures such as reductions, limitations, redeployment
provisions, equal ceilings, and related measures, among others.

In order to achieve the above objectives, measures should be
pursued for the whole area of application with provisions, if and where
appropriate, for regional differentiation to redress disparities within the
area of application and in a way which precludes circumvention.

The process of strengthening stability and security should proceed
step-by-step, in a manner which will ensure that the security of each
participant is not affected adversely at any stage.

Scope and Area of Application

The subject of the negotiation shall be the conventional armed forces,
which include conventional armaments and equipment, of the participants based on land within the territory of the participants in Europe
from the Atlantic to the Urals.

The existence of multiple capabilities will not be a criterion for
modifying the scope of the negotiation:

- No conventional armaments or equipment will be excluded from the
  subject of the negotiation because they may have other capabilities
  in addition to conventional ones. Such armaments or equipment
  will not be singled out in a separate category;
- Nuclear weapons will not be a subject of this negotiation. Particular
  emphasis will initially be placed on those forces directly related to
  the achievement of the objectives of the negotiation set out above.

Naval forces and chemical weapons will not be addressed. The area
of application† shall be the entire land territory of the participants in
Europe from the Atlantic to the Urals, which includes all the European
island territories of the participants. In the case of the Soviet Union the
area of application includes all the territory lying west of the Ural River
and the Caspian Sea. In the case of Turkey, the area of application
includes the territory of Turkey north and west of the following line: the
point of intersection of the border with the 39th parallel, Muradiye,
Patnos, Karayazi, Tekman, Kemaliye, Feke, Ceyhan, Dogankent, Gozne,
and thence to the sea.

Exchange of Information and Verification

Compliance with the provisions of any agreement shall be verified
through an effective and strict verification regime which, among other

things, will include on-site inspections as a matter of right and exchanges of information.

Information shall be exchanged in sufficient detail so as to allow a meaningful comparison of the capabilities of the forces involved. Information shall also be exchanged in sufficient detail so as to provide a basis for the verification of compliance.

The specific modalities for verification and the exchange of information, including the degree of detail of the information and the order of its exchange, shall be agreed at the negotiation proper.

Procedures and Other Arrangements

The procedures for the negotiation, including the agenda, work programme and timetable, working methods, financial issues and other organisational modalities, as agreed by the participants themselves, are set out in Annex 1 of this mandate (*not included here*). They can be changed only by consensus of the participants.

The participants decided to take part in meetings of the States signatories of the Helsinki Final Act to be held at least twice during each round of the Negotiation on Conventional Armed Forces in Europe in order to exchange views and substantive information concerning the course of the Negotiation on Conventional Armed Forces in Europe. Detailed modalities for these meetings are contained in Annex 2 to this mandate.

The participants will take into consideration the views expressed in such meetings by other CSCE participating States concerning their own security.

Participants will also provide information bilaterally.

The participants undertake to inform the next CSCE Follow-up Meeting of their work and possible results and to exchange views, at that meeting, with the other CSCE participating States on progress achieved in the negotiation.

The participants foresee that, in the light of circumstances at the time, they will provide in their timetable for a temporary suspension to permit this exchange of views. The appropriate time and duration of this suspension is their sole responsibility.

Any modification of this mandate is the sole responsibility of the participants, whether they modify it themselves or concur in its modification at a future CSCE Follow-up Meeting.

The results of the negotiation will be determined only by the participants.

Character of Agreements

Agreements reached shall be internationally binding. Modalities for their entry into force will be decided at the negotiation.

Venue

The negotiation shall commence in Vienna no later than in the seventh week following the closure of the Vienna CSCE Follow-up Meeting.

The representatives of the 23 participants, whose initials appear below, have concluded the foregoing mandate, which is equally authentic in the English, French, German, Italian, Russian and Spanish languages.

The representatives, recalling the commitment of their States to the achievement of a balanced outcome at the Vienna CSCE Meeting, have decided to transmit it to that Meeting with the recommendation that it be attached to its Concluding Document.

(Initialed by the representatives of the 23 States at the Palais Liechtenstein Vienna, Austria, the 10th day of January 1989)

Source: Arms Control Reporter Brookline, US

---

* Conventional Armed Forces include conventional armaments and equipment.
† The participants will be guided by the language on non-circumvention as set out in the section on Objectives and Methods.

CSCE STOCKHOLM CONFERENCE: CONFIDENCE- AND SECURITY-BUILDING MEASURES AND CERTAIN ASPECTS OF SECURITY AND DISARMAMENT IN EUROPE

15 January 1989

The participating States,

In accordance with the relevant provisions of the Madrid Concluding Document, assessed progress achieved during the Conference on Confidence- and Security-building Measures and Disarmament in Europe, which met in Stockholm from 17 January 1984 to 19 September 1986.

They welcomed the adoption at Stockholm of a set of mutually complementary confidence- and security-building measures (CSBMS).

They noted that these measures are in accordance with the criteria of the Madrid mandate and constitute a substantial improvement and extension of the confidence-building measures adopted in the Final Act.

They noted that the adoption of the Stockholm Document was a politically significant achievement and that its measures are an important step in efforts aimed at reducing the risk of military confrontation in Europe. They agreed that the extent to which the measures will in practice contribute to greater confidence and security will depend on the record of implementation. They were encouraged by initial implementation and noted that further experience and detailed review will be required. They reaffirmed their determination to comply strictly with and apply in good faith all the provisions of the Document of the Stockholm Conference.

They reaffirmed their commitment to the provisions of the Madrid Concluding Document relating to the Conference on Confidence- and Security-building Measures and Disarmament in Europe and agreed to resume the work of the Conference with a view to achieving further progress towards it aim.

New Efforts for Security and Disarmament in Europe

The participating States,

Recalling the relevant provisions of the Final Act and of the Madrid Concluding Document according to which they recognize the interest of all of them in efforts aimed at lessening military confrontation and promoting disarmament,

Reaffirming their determination expressed in the Final Act to strengthen confidence among them and thus to contribute to increasing stability and security in Europe,

Stressing the complementary nature of the efforts within the framework of the CSCE process aimed at building confidence and security and establishing stability and achieving progress in disarmament in order to lessen military confrontation and to enhance security for all,

Stressing that in undertaking such efforts they will respect the security interests of all CSCE participating States inherent in their sovereign equality,

Having also considered ways and appropriate means to continue their efforts for security and disarmament in Europe,

Have reached the understanding that these efforts should be structured as set forth below:

Negotiations on Confidence- and Security-building Measures

The participating States have agreed that Negotiations on Confidence- and Security-building Measures will take place in order to build upon and expand the results already achieved at the Stockholm Conference with the aim of elaborating and adopting a new set of mutually complementary confidence- and security-building measures designed to reduce the risk of military confrontation in Europe. These negotiations will take place in accordance with the Madrid mandate. The decisions of the Preparatory Meeting held in Helsinki from 25 October to 11 November 1983 will be applied *mutatis mutandis* (see Annex II). (a)

These negotiations will take place in Vienna, commencing in the week beginning on 6 March 1989.

The next Follow-up Meeting of the participating States of the CSCE, to be held in Helsinki, commencing on 24 March 1992, will assess the progress achieved in these negotiations.

Negotiation on Conventional Armed Forces in Europe

The Negotiation on Conventional Armed Forces in Europe will take place as agreed by those States named in the mandate contained in the Chairman's statement in Annex III of this document, (a) who among themselves have determined the agenda, the rules of procedure and the organizational modalities of these negotiations, and will determine their timetable and results. These negotiations will be conducted within the framework of the CSCE process.

These negotiations will take place in Vienna, commencing in the week beginning on 6 March 1989.

The next Follow-up Meeting of the participating States of the CSCE, to be held in Helsinki, commencing on 24 March 1992, will exchange views on the progress achieved in these negotiations.

Meetings on the Course of the Negotiation on Conventional Armed Forces in Europe

It has been agreed that the participating States will hold meetings in order to exchange views and information concerning the course of the Negotiation on Conventional Armed Forces in Europe.

These meetings will be held at least twice during each session of the Negotiation on Conventional Armed Forces in Europe.

Provisions on practical modalities relating to these meetings are contained in Annex IV of this document.

At these meetings, substantive information will be provided by the participants in the Negotiation on Conventional Armed Forces in Europe on developments, progress and results in the negotiations with the aim of enabling each participating State to appraise their course.

The participants in these negotiations have undertaken to take into consideration, in the course of their negotiations, the views expressed at such meetings by other participating States concerning their own security.

Information will also be provided on a bilateral basis.

The next Follow-up Meeting of the participating States of the CSCE, to be held in Helsinki, commencing on 24 March 1992, will consider the functioning of these arrangements.

Taking into account the relevant provisions of the Final Act and of the Madrid Concluding Document, and having considered the results achieved in the two negotiations, and also in the light of other relevant negotiations on security and disarmament affecting Europe, a future CSCE follow-up meeting will consider ways and appropriate means for the participating States to continue their efforts for security and disarmament in Europe, including the question of supplementing the Madrid mandate for the next stage of the Conference on Confidence- and Security-building Measures and Disarmament in Europe.

Source: USIA, 15 January 1989

(a) not included

NEGOTIATIONS ON CONFIDENCE-
AND SECURITY-BUILDING IN EUROPE

*Proposal submitted by the delegations of Bulgaria, Czechoslovakia,
the German Democratic Republic and Hungary, on 9 March 1989, in Vienna*

The role of CSBMs in reducing international tensions is significantly increasing today when a movement away from confrontation to broad international cooperation is taking place in Europe and in the rest of the world.

The system of such measures established by the Stockholm Agreements has been effective for some years now, thus helping to improve the situation in Europe and make it more stable and predictable. These measures have a visible effect in terms of removing the risk of surprise attack and achieving real disarmament. All this creates good preconditions for the elaboration of a set of new-generation confidence-building measures.

At issue is a set of mutually complementary measures that would enable the negotiators ot make further headway towards reducing the risk of military confrontation.

Increased openness about and predictability of all military activities are becoming a key element of a future agreement. Openness must be viewed as a natural and integral rule in relations among States and as the basis for a real and verifiable disarmament process.

It is equally important to progress from CSBMs in particular areas of military activities to large-scale policies of confidence covering those activities in their totality. Air and naval activities must cease to be zones 'closed' to *glasnost* and openness. New steps will also be required in verification, exchange of information and consultations.

Appropriate measures taken on a bilateral basis could also play an important role in confidence- and security-building in Europe.

Specifically, to develop confidence- and security-building measures the following areas are proposed:

I. Constraining measures

The continuing trend of building up the scale of military activities on the European continent is clearly at variance with the current political realities in Europe. Training and exercising activities of the armed forces are no longer distinguishable in scale and numbers of troops and equipment involved from their deployment for the start of combat activities.

To counter that tendency and erect barriers against the unbridled growth of military activities it is necessary to limit the scale, number and duration of major military exercises.

1. To limit the scale of notifiable military activities of the participating States (exercises, transfers and concentrations of troops and equipment), including activities carried out without advance notice to the troops involved to a level of 40,000 troops.

2. Not to carry out simultaneously on the territory of each participating State in the zone of application for confidence- and security-building measures more than three activities that are subject to prior notification. The total number of troops involved concurrently in those activities must not at any time exceed 40,000 troops.

3. Not to carry out on the territory of any participating State more than two notifiable activities annually if each of them involves more than 25,000 troops.

4. To place an overall limit of 40,000 on the number of troops engaged in a series of exercises, including those carried out without advance notice to the troops involved, which take place in close proximity to each other, even in the absence of a formal link between them if they could nevertheless share a common purpose.

5. To place a time limit not exceeding 15 days on the duration of the conduct of military activities that are subject to prior notification.

II. CSBMs covering naval and air activities

Activities of air and naval forces of the participating States in Europe and the adjoining sea (ocean) area and air space can be a source of serious threat to the security of States. The absence of timely information about them and possible misjudgement or misunderstanding may lead to the risk of an outbreak of armed conflict. All this makes it essential, in accordance with the mandate of the conference, to extend measures of notification, observation and limitation to cover air and naval activities carried out in the zone of application for CSBMs.

The following measures are proposed:

Measures covering air forces

1. Notification within an agreed period of time of air exercises involving 150 or more combat aircraft, or when it is envisaged that more than 130 combat aircraft will be simultaneously in the air in the declared exercise area, or more than 500 sorties will be flown during the exercise;

2. notification within an agreed period of time of air force transfers to the zone of application for CSBMs and inside the zone from the level of 70 combat aircraft or more;

3. invitation of observers to air exercises whenever they involve 300 or more combat aircraft or 600 or more sorties are flown during the exercise;

4. limitation of the scale of air exercises to a ceiling of 600 combat aircraft involved or 1,800 sorties flown during the exercises;

5. inclusion in the annual calendars of notifiable military activities of information on notifiable air activities to the extent determined by the relevant provisions of the Document of the Stockholm Conference.

Measures covering naval forces

1. Notification within an agreed period of time of naval exercises involving 20 or more combat ships (1,500 or more tons displacement each); or 5 or more ships of which at least one has a displacement of 5,000 or more tons and is equipped with cruise missiles or aircraft; or over 80 naval aviation (including carrier-based) combat aircraft;

2. notification of transfers of naval forces involving entry into or movement for agreed distances within the zone of application for CSBMs of groups consisting of 10 or more combat ships (1,500 or more tons displacement each); or 5 or more ships of which at least one has a displacement of 5,000 tons or more and is equipped with cruise missiles or aircraft;

3. notification of marine force transfers (by sea or by air) to the territory of another State starting from a level of 3,000 men;

4. notification of naval aviation transfers to the territory of another State starting from a level of 30 combat aircraft;

5. invitation of observers to naval exercises involving 25 or more combat ships (1,500 or more tons displacement each) or 100 or more combat aircraft;

6. limitation of major naval exercises to a level of 50 combat ships;

7. limitation of the duration of naval exercises to 10–14 days;

8. limitation of notifiable exercises conducted by each State (including cases of its participation in joint exercises) to a level of six to eight exercises in a calendar year;

9. prohibition of notifiable naval exercises in zones of intensive shipping and fishing as well as in straits of international significance;

10. inclusion of information on notifiable naval activities in annual calendars of notifiable military activities to the extent determined by the relevant provisions of the Document of the Stockholm Conference;

11. conclusion of an agreement on measures to prevent incidents in the sea area and air space adjoining Europe.

III. Development and amplification of the provisions of the Document of the Stockholm Conference

Taking into account the implementation of the agreements achieved at the Stockholm Conference it is necessary to take steps aimed at the development and expansion of the previously agreed measures.

— to lower, under certain conditions, parameters of land force military activities subject to notification and observation;

— to include in the annual calendars of notifiable military activities and in the notifications additional information on the activities in question;
— to improve observers' opportunities (inclusion in the observation programme of observation from helicopters and aerial survey of the exercise area).

IV. Measures relating to the establishment of confidence and security zones in Europe

Establishing zones of confidence and security could become a reliable factor of confidence-building in Europe, above all in its central part. Lowering the levels of offensive armaments in such zones and introducing more rigorous limitations on the various military activities carried out therein would contribute to reducing to a minimum the risk of military confrontation in the region and preclude the possibility of surprise attack.

The main criteria for such zones could be as follows:

— changing the structure of military formations deployed in the zones to give them a purely defensive character;
— lower notification and observation levels for military activities conducted in the zones;
— stricter limitation or prohibition of certain military activities, for example transfer and concentration of troops and bringing groups of troops into combat readiness.

The geographical boundaries of confidence and security zones could be determined by the participating States at the negotiations themselves. For example, for Central Europe the zone could include the territories of the Federal Republic of Germany, Belgium, the Netherlands, Luxembourg, Denmark, the German Democratic Republic, Czechoslovakia, Poland and Hungary.

For the purpose of verifying compliance with the status of such zones, observation posts in agreed locations (points) could be envisaged along with other measures.

V. Measures to improve openness and predictability of military activities, exchange of information and consultations; verification and control measures

A new generation of CSBMs that would meet the increased requirements of *glasnost* and openness in the field of military activities cannot be envisaged without the inclusion therein of measures relating to the exchange of information, mutual consultation as well as improved forms of verification and control. They should be based on reciprocity and should not be in any way prejudicial to the security of the participating States.

As *glasnost*, openness and predictability in the military field are growing the significance of verification and control forms is not diminishing. Their development and improvement should ensure stricter compliance by States with agreed confidence- and security-building measures and promote progress in the negotiation on conventional armed forces.

The negotiations could consider, as measures of information, verification and control, the following:

1. Regular (no less than once a year) exchange of information including data on the number, structure and deployment of land, naval and air forces, disaggregated down to brigade/regiment or equivalent formations (down to regiment/squadron for air forces, down to brigade/operational-tactical group for naval forces).

2. Provision, on a goodwill basis, of other additional information on armed forces components and military activities not covered by agreed CSBMs.

3. Periodic discussion and comparison at various forums (conferences, symposia, seminars) of political and technico-military aspects of military doctrine as well as other issues of military policies of the participating States and their military-political alliances.

4. Development and improvement of the practice of mutual visits of military delegations and individual military officials, exchanges of military personnel including military diplomatic representatives of the participating States.

5. Holding on a regular basis (or at the request of any participating State) of bilateral and multilateral consultations on matters under consideration within the context of the objectives and purposes of the negotiations on confidence- and security-building measures.

6. Making use of modern technology for automatic (remote) control (automatic recording systems) in the interests of verifying compliance with adopted CSBMs.

7. Establishment of a centre for the reduction of the risk of war and prevention of surprise attack in Europe which could have an informational and consultative character.

8. Development of a special communications system for the mutual clarification of situations giving rise to doubts or apprehensions on any side.

Source: Arms Control Reporter, Brookline, US

NEGOTIATIONS ON CONFIDENCE-
AND SECURITY-BUILDING MEASURES
IN EUROPE

*Proposal submitted by the delegations of Belgium, Canada,
Denmark, France, The Federal Republic of Germany, greece, Iceland, Italy,
Luxembourg, The Netherlands, Norway, Portugal, Spain, Turkey,
The United Kingdom and the United States of America,
9 March 1989, Vienna*

The delegations of Belgium, Canada, Demark, France, the Federal
Republic of Germany, Greece, Iceland, Italy, Luxembourg, the Nether-
lands, Norway, Portugal, Spain, Turkey, the United Kingdom and the
United States of America,

Recalling that the adoption of the Stockholm Document in September 1986 was a politically significant achievement and that its measures
are an important step in efforts aimed at reducing the risk of military
confrontation in Europe,

Encouraged by the satisfactory implementation of these measures
thus far,

Determined to build upon and expand the results achieved at the
Stockholm Conference and to carry forward the dynamic process of
confidence building,

Stressing the complementary nature within the framework of the
CSCE process of negotiations on further confidence- and security-
building measures and negotiations on conventional armed forces in
Europe,

Determined

— to create greater transparency about military organization;
— to create greater transparency and predictability about military
activities;
— to improve contacts and communications between the participating
States;

And determined, in the forthcoming negotiations, to promote an
exchange of views on military policy,

150

In conformity with the Madrid Mandate 1983 as confirmed by the CSCE Review Meeting in Vienna 1989, propose confidence- and security-building measures including the following:

I. Transparency about Military Organization

These measures are designed to create more openness and confidence about the military force disposition of each participating State. This will be achieved by regular exchanges of information on forces on land in the zone and on major weapons deployment programmes. The information exchanged will be subject to evaluation.

Measure 1: Exchange of military information

Participating states will exchange information concerning military organization, manpower and equipment in the zone. This will include annual information on:

— land forces command organization in the zone;
— the designation of major ground units, down to and below divisional level;
— the normal peacetime locations of these units;
— the personnel strength of these units;
— the major weapons systems and equipment belonging to these units;
— land-based air units and their aircraft strength.

It will also include immediate notification of:

— the relocation in the zone of major ground units as specified above from one normal peacetime location to another;
— the calling up of a significant number of reservists.

Measure 2: Information exchange on major conventional weapon deployment programmes

Each participating State will inform the others of those major conventional weapon systems and equipment specified in measure 1 which it intends to introduce into service with its armed forces in the CDE zone in a specified period.

Measure 3: Establishment of a random evaluation system

In order to evaluate the information provided under measures 1 and 2, participating States will establish a random evaluation system in which:

— they will have the right to conduct a number of pre-announced visits to normal peacetime locations specified under measure 1;
— these visits, of a limited duration, will be carried out by personnel already accredited to the host State or designated by the visiting State;

— evaluators will be allowed to observe major weapon systems and equipment;
— appropriate arrangements for the evaluation visit will be made by the host State, whose representatives will accompany the evaluation teams at all times.

II. Transparency and Predictability of Military Activities

These measures will build upon those agreed in Stockholm by refining them in order to enhance openness and produce greater predictability of military activities.

Measure 4: Enhanced information in the annual calendar
Participating States will provide in their annual calendars more information, and in greater detail, about future military activities. This will include the designation, number and type of ground units down to divisional level scheduled to take part in notifiable military activities in the zone.

Measure 5: Enhanced information in notification
To improve the notification concerning military activities, participating States will communicate more information, and in greater detail, about the engagement of their armed forces as well as their major weapon systems and equipment in such ground-force activities.

Measure 6: Improvements to observation modalities
Participating States will facilitate observation by organizing more detailed briefings, providing better maps and allowing more observation equipment to be used. Furthermore, in order to improve the observers' opportunities to assess the scope and scale of the activity, the participating States are encouraged to provide an aerial survey of the area of the activity. Moreover, the duration of the observation programme will be improved.

Measure 7: Lowering of the observation threshold
Participating States will invite observers to notified activities whenever the number of troops engaged meets or exceeds 13,000 or if more than 300 tanks participate in it.

Measure 8: Improvement to inspection modalities
Participating States will adopt measures for a substantial improvement of the inspection which include:

— increasing the number of passive inspections;
— shortening the period between the inspection request and access of the inspectors to the specified area;
— permitting, on request by inspectors, an aerial survey before the commencement of the inspection;

— improving the equipment and communications facilities that the inspecting team will be permitted to use;
— improving the briefings to inspectors.

Measure 9: Lowering the thresholds for
longer notice of larger-scale activities

Participating States will not carry out military activities subject to prior notification involving more than 50,000 troops unless they have been the object of communication stipulated in the Stockholm Document.

III. Contacts and Communication

These measures are designed to increase the knowledge about the military capabilities of the participating States by developing communications and military contacts.

Measure 10: Improved access for accredited
personnel dealing with military matters

In order to implement the principle of greater openness in military matters and to enhance mutual confidence, the participating States will facilitate the traval arrangements of accredited personnel dealing with military matters and assist them in obtaining access to government officials. Restrictions on the activities of accredited personnel in the CDE zone should be reduced.

Measure 11: Development of means of communication

Participating States, while using diplomatic channels for transmitting communications related to agreed measures (calendars, notifications etc.) are encouraged to consider additional arrangements to ensure the speediest possible exchange of information.

Measure 12: Equal treatment of media representatives

Participating States will be encouraged to permit media representatives to attend observed military activities; if media representatives are invited, the host State will admit such representatives from all participating States and treat them without discrimination.

Exchanges of Views on Military Policy

Confidence-building is a dynamic process which is enhanced by the free and frank interchange of ideas designed to reduce misunderstanding and misrepresentation of military capabilities. To this end, participating States will, in the forthcoming negotiations, avail themselves of the following opportunities:

— to discuss issues concerning the implementation of the provisions of the Stockholm Document;

— to discuss, in a seminar setting, military doctrine in relation to the posture and structure of conventional forces in the zone, including *inter alia*;
— exchanging information on their annual military spending;
— exchanging information on the training of their armed forces, including references to military manuals;
— seeking clarification of developments giving rise to uncertainty, such as changes in the number and pattern of notified military activities.

Source: *Arms Control Reporter* Brookline, US

DRAFT TREATY ON CONVENTIONAL ARMED FORCES IN EUROPE

*Proposal submitted by the delegations of
People's Republic of Bulgaria, The Republic of Hungary,
The German Democratic Republic, The Polish People's Republic,
The Socialist Republic of Romania, The Union of Soviet Socialist Republics,
and the Czechoslovak Socialist Republic, 14 December 1989*

The Kingdom of Belgium, the People's Republic of Bulgaria, Canada, the Czechoslovak Socialist Republic, the Kingdom of Denmark, the French Republic, the German Democratic Republic, the Federal Republic of Germany, the Hellenic Republic, the Republic of Hungary, the Republic of Iceland, the Italian Republic, the Grand Duchy of Luxembourg, the Kingdom of the Netherlands, the Kingdom of Norway, the Polish People's Republic, the Portuguese Republic, the Socialist Republic of Romania, the Kingdom of Spain, the Republic of Turkey, the Union of Soviet Socialist Republics, the United Kingdom of Great Britain and Northern Ireland, and the United States of America, hereinafter referred to as the 'States Parties',

Acting in accordance with the objectives and purposes of the Conference on Security and Cooperation in Europe,

Recalling their obligation to refrain, in their mutual relations as well as in their international relations in general, from the threat or use of force against the territorial integrity or political independence of any State, or in any other manner inconsistent with the purposes and principles of the charter of the United Nations,

Proceeding from the inadmissibility of any military conflict in Europe,

Guided by the Mandate for Negotiation on Conventional Armed Forces in Europe of January 19, 1989,

Committed to the objectives of establishing a secure and stable balance of conventional armed forces in Europe at lower levels than heretofore, of eliminating disparities prejudicial to stability and security, and of climinating, as a matter of high priority, the capability for launching surprise attack and for initiating large-scale offensive action in Europe,

Proceeding from the premise that the subject of this Treaty shall be the conventional armed forces of the States Parties which include conventional armaments and equipment based on land within the territory of the States Parties in Europe from the Atlantic to the Urals,

Conscious of the common responsibility which they all have for seeking to achieve greater stability and security in Europe,

Acknowledging that they are signatories of the Treaties of Brussels (1948), Washington (1949) or Warsaw (1955), and accordingly, at the time of signature of this Treaty are members of the North Atlantic Alliance or parties to the Warsaw Treaty,

Confirming their desire to reduce the level of military confrontation in Europe and with a view, eventually, to a simultaneous dissolution of the military-political alliances,

Recalling that they are all participants in the CSCE process,

Recalling that, as reaffirmed in the Helsinki Final Act, they have the right to belong or not to belong to international organizations, to be or not to be a party to bilateral or multilateral treaties including the right to be or not to be a party to treaties of alliance,

Reaffirming also that they participate in negotiations as sovereign and independent States and on the basis of full equality,

Have agreed as follows:

Article I

1. The States Parties shall reduce to ceilings as well as shall not exceed the ceilings established in Articles VI–X of this Treaty for the following Treaty-limited categories of conventional armed forces:

- personnel;
- combat aircraft of front/tactical aviation;
- combat helicopters;
- battle tanks;
- armoured combat vehicles;
- artillery.

2. The States Parties shall also take other measures designed to ensure security both during the period of reduction of the Treaty-limited categories of conventional armed forces and after its completion as provided for in Article XIII of this Treaty.

3. This Treaty includes an Annex on the types of the Treaty-Limited Categories of Conventional Armaments, an Agreed Format of Data Provided in Relation to the Treaty on Conventional Armed Forces in Europe, a Protocol on Information and Verification, a Protocol on Reduction of the Treaty-Limited Categories of Conventional Armed Forces . . . These documents constitute an integral part of the Treaty.

Article II

For the purposes of this Treaty:

1. The term 'group' of States Parties' means the group of States which signed the Warsaw Treaty (1955), consisting of the People's Republic of Bulgaria, the Czechoslovak Socialist Republic, the German Democratic Republic, the Republic of Hungary, the Polish People's Republic, the

Socialist Republic of Romania and the Union of Soviet Socialist Republics, or the group of States which signed the Treaties of Brussels (1948), Washington (1949) consisting of the Kingdom of Belgium, Canada, the Kingdom of Denmark, the French Republic, the Federal Republic of Germany, the Hellenic Republic, the Republic of Iceland, the Italian Republic, the Grand Duchy of Luxembourg, the Kingdom of the Netherlands, the Kingdom of Norway, the Portuguese Republic, the Kingdom of Spain, the Republic of Turkey, the United Kingdom of Great Britain and Northern Ireland, and the United States of America;

2. The term 'personnel' means all active duty military personnel wearing uniform, listed in agreed armed services and arms, units and other formations subordinated to the Ministries of Defence and/or to the joint commands of the armed forces of the States Parties to Warsaw Treaty or the North Atlantic Alliance. It comprises the personnel of combat, combat support and combat service support forces and command and control elements of the land forces and of front/tactical aviation.

3. The term 'combat aircraft of front/tactical aviation' means a fixed-wing or swing-wing aircraft, constructed, armed and equipped to engage ground targets or ground and air targets by employing missiles and rockets, bombs, guns/cannons or any other means of destruction.

Combat aircraft of front/tactical aviation currently in the armed forces of the States Parties are front bombers, fighter-bombers, ground attack aircraft, front/tactical fighters, reconnaissance aircraft, electronic warfare aircraft.

4. The term 'combat helicopter' means a rotary-wing aircraft constructed, armed and equipped to engage ground and air targets by employing missiles and rockets, bombs, guns/cannons or other means of destruction.

5. The term 'battle tank' means a self-propelled armoured combat vehicle capable of high firepower and cross-country mobility, providing protection and armed to engage armoured and other targets mainly by employing its main gun.

Such armoured vehicles serve as an asset to tank and other land force formations.

6. The term 'armoured combat vehicle' means a self-propelled vehicle with light armour, high cross-country mobility and organic mounted armament. It is normally armed with a cannon and/or machine gun, and sometimes an anti-tank missile launcher. Armoured combat vehicles are designed to provide the capability for the crew/troops to deliver fire from under armoured protection, transportation of personnel (troops) as well as performance of other combat missions.

7. The term 'artillery' means large calibre systems capable of engaging ground targets primarily by delivering indirect fire, namely guns, howitzers, artillery pieces combining the characteristics of guns and howitzers, mortars and multiple launch rocket systems. Such artillery systems provide the essential indirect fire support to combined arms

formations. In addition, any future large calibre direct fire system which has a secondary effective indirect fire capability will be counted against the artillery ceilings.

Large calibre artillery systems are considered to be artillery systems with a caliber of 100 mm and above.

(Further definitions to be submitted additionally).

Lists of types of combat aircraft of front/tactical aviation, combat helicopters, battle tanks, armoured combat vehicles and artillery in the armed forces are contained in the Annex on the Types of the Treaty-Limited Categories of Conventional Armaments. These lists shall be updated as regards the inclusion in them of new types of Treaty-limited categories of conventional armaments and their modifications. Such changes in the lists shall not be deemed amendments to this Treaty.

Article III

Personnel of land forces and front/tactical aviation, combat aircraft of front/tactical aviation, combat helicopters, battle tanks, armoured combat vehicles and artillery shall be counted in accordance with the following rules:

1. Personnel _____ (to be submitted additionally).
2. Combat aircraft of front/tactical aviation:

— in formations and units;
— in permanent storage in all storage sites and storage bases.

3. Combat helicopters, battle tanks, armoured combat vehicles and artillery:

— in formations and units;
— in permanent storage in all depots and storage bases;
— in military educational establishments of the land forces.

4. Combat aircraft of front/tactical aviation, combat helicopters, battle tanks, armoured combat vehicles and artillery rendered incapable of combat in accordance with the provisions of the Protocol on the Reduction of Treaty-Limited Categories of the Conventional Armed Forces and placed in temporary storage for the period until their final elimination under permanent monitoring by inspectors of the States Parties belonging to the other group of States Parties, in accordance with Article XV of this Treaty shall not be counted against the levels established by Articles VI–X of this Treaty.

Article IV

New Types of combat aircraft of front/tactical aviation, combat helicopters, battle tanks, armoured combat vehicles and artillery and their modifications capable of carrying out the missions performed by the types of the Treaty-limited categories of conventional armaments, listed in the Annex on the Types of the Treaty-Limited Categories of Conventional Armaments, adopted for service by the States Parties and located in the area of application shall be subject to limitations provided for in Articles VI–X of this Treaty.

Article V

Area of Application

Article VI

In the area of application the aggregate ceilings for the Treaty-limited categories of conventional armed forces of the States Parties to this Treaty shall not exceed:

– for personnel strength	2,700,000
– for combat aircraft of front/tactical aviation	9,400
– for combat helicopters	3,800
– for battle tanks	40,000
– for armoured combat vehicles	56,000
– for artillery	48,000

Article VII

In the area of application the collective ceilings for the Treaty-limited categories of conventional armed forces for each of the two groups of States Parties shall not exceed:

– for personnel strength	1,350,000
– for combat aircraft of front/tactical aviation	4,700
– for combat helicopters	1,900
– for battle tanks	20,000
– for armoured combat vehicles	28,000
– for artillery	24,000

Article VIII

In the area of application the ceilings for the Treaty-limited categories of conventional armed forces of any State Party shall not exceed:

– for personnel strength	920,000
– for combat aircraft of front/tactical aviation	3,400
– for combat helicopters	1,500
– for battle tanks	14,000
– for armoured combat vehicles	18,000
– for artillery	17,000

Article IX

In the area of application the collective ceilings for the Treaty-limited categories of conventional armed forces stationed outside of the national territories for each of the two groups of States Parties shall not exceed:

– for personnel strength	300,000
– for combat aircraft of front/tactical aviation	1,200
– for combat fhelicopters	600
– for battle tanks	4,500
– for armoured combat vehicles	7,500
– for artillery	4,000

Article X

Regional Ceilings

In the area of application the collective ceilings for the Treaty-limited categories of conventional armed forces located in the following regions for each of the two groups of States Parties shall not exceed:

(Further text to be submitted additionally)

Article XI

National Levels of Holdings

The States Parties at the time of signature of the Treaty shall declare their national levels of holdings of the Treaty-limited categories of conventional armed forces, related to the implementation of the provisions of Articles VI–X of this Treaty.

(Additional clarifications and considerations concerning the practical implementation of this Article to be submitted additionally)

Article XII

Temporarily Exceeding the Ceilings

(Text to be submitted additionally)

Article XIII

In addition to the measures of reduction of the Treaty-limited categories of conventional armed forces, in order to contribute to the achievement of a more stable and secure balance of forces in Europe, to increased openness and predictability of military activities, the States Parties shall implement the stabilizing measure listed below.

1. They shall limit the scope and the number of military exercises. Thus:

a) a State Party or several States Parties belonging to the same group of States Parties shall not conduct military exercises exceeding at least one of the following levels:

– for personnel	40,000
– for combat aircraft of front/tactical aviation	400
– for combat helicopters	150
– for battle tanks	800

- for armoured combat vehicles   1,500
- for artillery   800

b) a State Party or several States Parties belonging to the same group of States Parties may conduct as an exception a military exercise involving not more than 75 thousand troops not more than once in three calendar years, provided that notification of such an exercise is given not later than two calendar years prior to its beginning;

c) a State Party may conduct not more than two military exercises in a calendar year exceeding at least one of the following levels:

- for personnel   25,000
- for combat aircraft of front/tactical aviation   200
- for combat helicopters   100
- for battle tanks   400
- for armoured combat vehicles   750
- for artillery   400

d) the States Parties belonging to the same group of States Parties shall not conduct simultaneously more than three exercises specified in paragraph c) in a calendar year;

e) the States Parties belonging to the same group of States Parties may conduct not more than six military exercises specified in paragraph c) in a calendar year;

2. They shall limit the call-up of reservists. Thus:

a) a State Party within the framework of military exercises may call-up simultaneously more than _____ thousand reservists not more than once in two calendar years with prior notification thereof;

b) the States Parties belonging to the same group of States Parties within the framework of military exercises shall not call-up more than _____ thousand reservists simultaneously;

c) a State Party shall notify of the call-up of reservists within the framework of exercises whenever the total number of the called-up reservists exceeds _____ thousand men.

3. (Text to be submitted additionally)

4. They shall establish limits on transfers of the Treaty-limited categories of conventional armed forces into the area of application or through it. Thus:

a) a State Party or several States Parties belonging to the same group of States Parties shall not transfer into the area of application or through it personnel, combat aircraft of front/tactical aviation, combat helicopters, battle tanks, armoured combat vehicles and artillery the number of which exceeds at least one of the following levels for _____ days:

- for personnel _____
- for combat aircraft of
  front/tactical aviation _____
- for combat helicopters _____
- for battle tanks _____
- for armoured combat vehicles _____
- for artillery _____

b) a State Party or several States Parties belonging to the same group of States Parties, in accordance with the Protocol on Information and Verification, shall notify not later than 42 days in advance of planned transfers of personnel, combat aircraft of front/tactical aviation, combat helicopters, battle tanks, armoured combat vehicles and artillery into the area of application or through it, if their number exceeds at least one of the following levels:

- for personnel _____
- for combat aircraft of
  front/tactical aviation _____
- for combat helicopters _____
- for battle tanks _____
- for armoured combat vehicles _____
- for artillery _____

c) transfers of the Treaty-limited categories of conventional armed forces into the area of application or through it shall be conducted via permanent or temporary entry/exit points specified in _____ or in subsequent data and notifications.

5. They shall limit the number of armoured vehicle launched bridges. Thus:

a) the States Parties belonging to the same group of States Parties shall hold no more than 700 armoured vehicle launched bridges in active units in the area of application. Armoured vehicle launched bridges exceeding this level shall be placed at permanent storage sites;

b) a State Party shall not remove from permanent storage sites simultaneously more than _____ armoured vehicle launched bridges;

c) a State Party shall not remove from permanent storage sites simultaneously more than _____ armoured vehicle launched bridges if it did not notify thereof at least 42 days in advance.

6. They shall provide information on the volume and structure of military spending. Thus:

a) the States Parties shall annually provide information on the volume and structure of military spending taking into account the scheme worked out under the auspices of the United Nations;

b) the States Parties shall provide information on the relevant changes in military spending caused by reductions of the Treaty-limited conventional armed forces in the area of application.

7. They shall conduct restructuring of the Treaty-limited conventional armed forces. Thus:

a) the States Parties shall implement measures to restructure their Treaty-limited conventional armed forces and to reduce their offensive capabilities. As priority measures in this direction the States Parties shall:

(i) limit military activities and the number of highly mobile, attack formations and units (aviation, tank, airborne, air assault and air mobile) in forward-deployed groupings;

(ii) withdraw bridging equipment from forward-deployed groupings;

(iii) change accordingly the permanent location of land force units equipped with attack weapons (combat helicopters, tanks, artillery with a calibre of 100 mm and above, including multiple launch rocket systems);

b) the States Parties shall refrain from establishing new and expanding the existing military bases (large military installations) outside of their national territories in the area of application.

8. Military activities covered by the provisions of this Article shall be subject to notification and verification in accordance with the Protocol on Information and Verification.

(Provisions of this Article to be specified)

Article XIV

1. The States Parties acting within their respective groups of States Parties shall reduce the Treaty-limited categories of conventional armed forces in such a manner that at all stages of the reductions the overall military equilibrium between the groups of States Parties shall not be upset and security of any State Party shall not be undermined.

2. The States Parties shall reduce the Treaty-limited categories of conventional armed forces to the ceilings specified in Articles VI–X of this Treaty in accordance with the Protocol on Reduction within three years from the time of entry into force of this Treaty.

3. The reduction of personnel shall be implemented through:

a) demobilization;

b) relocation from the area of application.

4. The reduction of the Treaty-limited categories of conventional armaments shall be implemented through:

a) elimination;

b) conversion.

5. The reduction of personnel shall be implemented:

a) at permanent locations of formations and units;

b) at temporary disbandment points;

c) at points of exit from the area of application.

6. The reduction of the Treaty-limited categories of conventional armaments shall be implemented:

a) at   sites of elimination;

b) at   sites of conversion;

7. Sites of reduction of the Treaty-limited categories of conventional armed forces shall be listed when providing data and/or in subsequent notifications.

8. Personnel and conventional armaments listed in Article I of this Treaty shall be deemed reduced after the implementation of the procedures envisaged by the Protocol on Reduction.

(Further provisions to be submitted additionally)

Article XV
Temporary Storage
(To be submitted additionally)

Article XVI

1. The States Parties shall provide data and notifications in accordance with the provisions of this Article and of the Protocol on Information and Verification. A State Party shall be responsible for its own data. Receipt of this data and subsequent notifications shall not imply validation or acceptance of the data provided.

2. The States Parties shall provide data on the Treaty-limited categories of their conventional armed forces in the area of application by types of data contained in the Agreed Format of Data, effective as of the date of signature of this Treaty.

3. The States Parties shall provide data on the Treaty-limited categories of their conventional armed forces in the area of application by the types of data contained in the Agreed Format of Data, effective as of _____ (day after entry into force of this Treaty).

4. The States Parties shall provide data on the Treaty-limited categories of their conventional armed forces in the area of application by the types of data contained in the Agreed format of Data, effective as of the date of achieving of the ceilings established in Articles VI–X of this Treaty.

5. The States Parties after entry into force of this Treaty on the 15th day of December annually shall provide data on the Treaty-limited categories of their conventional armed forces in the area of application by the types of data contained in the Agreed Format of Data, effective as of the 1st day of January of the following year.

6. After the achieving of the ceilings established in Articles VI–X of this Treaty a State Party in case of a planned change in the organizational structure of its formations in the area of application, including addition or withdrawal of regiments and units equivalent to them as well as larger formations, shall notify thereof 42 days in advance.

7. Beside the regular provision of data envisaged in paragraph 5 of this Article, the States Parties shall provide notifications of changes of _____ per cent and more of the authorized peacetime strength of personnel, of combat aircraft of front/tactical aviation, combat helicopters, battle tanks, armoured combat vehicles and artillery in combat, combat support and combat service support units down to the

level of regiment or equivalent unit in the area of application, occurred since the last annual exchange of data. Such notifications shall be provided not later than 5 days after such changes occur.

8. The States Parties shall provide time-tables of reduction of the Treaty-limited conventional armed forces.

9. The States Parties shall provide:

a) notifications of reduction of the Treaty-limited conventional armed forces in the area of application, including their relocation from the area of application;

b) notifications of national levels of holdings defined in accordance with Article XI and related to the implementation of the provisions of Articles VI–X of this Treaty;

c) notifications of temporarily exceeding the ceilings specified in Articles VI–X which is envisaged in Article XII of this Treaty.

d) notifications related to the implementation of measures to verify compliance with the provisions of this Treaty, envisaged by the provisions of Article XVII of this Treaty and the Protocol on Information and Verification;

e) notifications envisaged by Article XIII of this Treaty and related to the implementation of stabilizing measures.

(Timeframes for providing data and notifications envisaged by this Article as well as the volume of information included in such data and notifications shall be governed by the provisions of the Protocol on Information and Verification)

Article XVII
Inspections and Monitoring
(Text to be submitted additionally)

Article XVIII

1. The States Parties shall settle all disputes or ambiguous situations arising in the course of implementation of this Treaty by conducting consultations between the States Parties concerned in accordance with the provisions of the Protocol on Consultations.

2. To ensure the viability of this Treaty and to promote its implementation, the States Parties shall establish a Joint Consultative Body. Regulations of the Joint Consultative Body shall be contained in Annex _____ to this Treaty. The States Parties agree that meetings of the Joint Consultative Body shall be convened at the request of any one of them for the purposes of:

a) the settling of disputes which have not been resolved in accordance with the procedure envisaged in paragraph 1 of this Article as well as solving other questions relating to compliance with the obligations assumed under this Treaty;

b) agreeing upon measures as may be necessary to improve the viability and effectiveness of this Treaty.

3. The Depositary(ies) of this Treaty shall convene a conference of

duly authorized representatives of the States Parties in order to review the operation of this Treaty.

4. In case a situation arises substantially affecting the stability and security in Europe and influencing the compliance with the provisions of this Treaty, the Depositary(ies) shall, at the request of any State Party; convene not later than ＿＿＿ days after the receipt of such a request, a conference of States Parties in order to review the operation of this Treaty and, if necessary, to revise it.

5. Any State Party may propose amendments to this Treaty. The text of each amendment shall be submitted to the Depositary(ies) which shall circulate it to all States Parties and, if necessary, convene a conference for discussing and approving it. Amendments approved by all States Parties shall enter into force in accordance with the procedures governing the entry into force of this Treaty.

Article XIX
Arrangements for Providing Data and Notifications
(To be submitted additionally)

Article XX

1. For the purposes of ensuring the viability and effectiveness of this Treaty the States Parties shall not perform any actions leading to a disruption of the stable and secure balance of conventional armed forces between the two groups of States Parties in the area of application, which would constitute circumvention of this Treaty.

2. The States Parties shall not adopt any international obligations and shall not resort to any actions that would be contrary to the provisions of this Treaty.

Article XXI
Nothing in this Treaty affects any States which are not Parties to it and their security interests or shall be interpreted as prejudicial to other international treaties previously concluded by the States Parties.

DRAFT TREATY ON CONVENTIONAL ARMED FORCES IN EUROPE

Proposal submitted by the delegations of Belgium, Canada, Denmark, France, Federal Republic of Germany, Greece, Iceland, Italy, Luxembourg, Netherlands, Norway, Portugal, Spain, Turkey, United Kingdom, and United States, 14 December 1989

The Kingdom of Belgium, the People's Republic of Bulgaria, Canada, the Czechoslovak Socialist Republic, the Kingdom of Denmark, France, the German Democratic Republic, the Federal Republic of Germany, the Hellenic Republic, the Republic of Hungary, the Republic of Iceland, the Italian Republic, the Grand Duchy of Luxembourg, the Kingdom of the Netherlands, the Kingdom of Norway, the Polish People's Republic, the Portuguese Republic, the Socialist Republic of Romania, the Kingdom of Spain, the Republic of Turkey, the Union of Soviet Socialist Republics, the United Kingdom of Great Britain and Northern Ireland, and the United States of America, hereinafter referred to as the Parties,

Striving to establish a new pattern of relations among the Parties in which military confrontation is replaced by co-operation and peaceful competition, and to contribute thereby to overcoming the division of Europe,

Recalling that their negotiation of this Treaty has been conducted within the framework of the CSCE (Conference on Security and Co-operation in Europe) process,

Guided by the Mandate for Negotiation on Conventional Armed Forces in Europe of January 1989,

Committed to the objectives of establishing a secure and stable balance of conventional armed forces in Europe at lower levels than heretofore, of eliminating disparities prejudicial to stability and security, and of eliminating, as a matter of high priority, the capability for launching surprise attack and for initiating large-scale offensive action in Europe,

Seeking in pursuit of these objectives to ensure that, within the area of application of this Treaty, the Parties' aggregate conventional armaments in key weapons categories are reduced to and thereafter do not exceed, except as permitted by the treaty, the limits of 40,000 main battle tanks, 33,000 artillery pieces, 56,000 armoured troop carriers, 11,400 combat aircraft and 3,800 combat helicopters, and also to ensure that these limitations are reinforced by appropriate verification, notification, consultation, and related measures designed to strengthen stability and security in Europe,

Willing in the longer term, and in light of the implementation of this Treaty, to contemplate further steps to enhance stability and security in Europe, such as further reductions or limitations of conventional armaments and equipment, and the restructuring of armed forces to enhance defensive capabilities and further to reduce offensive capabilities,

Recalling their obligation to refrain in their mutual relations, as well as in their international relations in general, from the threat or use of force against the territorial integrity or political independence of any state or in any other manner inconsistent with the purposes of the United Nations,

Have agreed as follows:

Article I

The Parties shall carry out the obligations set forth in this Treaty in accordance with its provisions. This Treaty includes an Annex on existing types of conventional armaments, an Annex with maps of the area of application, a Protocol establishing and maintaining a data base, a Protocol on inspection with an Annex on privileges and immunities, and a Protocol on destruction, all of which form an integral part of the Treaty.

Article II

1. For the purposes of this Treaty:

(a) The term 'each group of Parties' means two groups of states, one group consisting of the Kingdom of Belgium, Canada, the Kingdom of Denmark, France, the Federal Republic of Germany, the Hellenic Republic, the Republic of Iceland, the Italian Republic, the Grand Duchy of Luxembourg, the Kingdom of the Netherlands, the Kingdom of Norway, the Portuguese Republic, the Kingdom of Spain, the Republic of Turkey, the United Kingdom of Great Britain and Northern Ireland, and the United States of America; and the other group consisting of the People's Republic of Bulgaria, the Czechoslovak Socialist Republic, the German Democratic Republic, the Republic of Hungary, the Polish People's Republic, the Socialist Republic of Romania, and the Union of Soviet Socialist Republics.

(b) The term 'area of application' means the European land area from the Atlantic Ocean to the Ural Mountains which includes the territory of the Kingdom of Belgium; the People's Republic of Bulgaria; the Czechoslovak Socialist Republic; the Kingdom of Denmark including the Faroe Islands; France; the German Democratic Republic; the Federal Republic of Germany; the Hellenic Republic; the Republic of Hungary; the Republic of Iceland; the Italian Republic; the Grand Duchy of Luxembourg; the Kingdom of the Netherlands; the Kingdom of Norway including Svalbard; the Polish People's Republic; the Portuguese Republic including the islands of the Azores and Madeira; the Socialist Republic of Romania; the Kingdom of Spain including the Canary Islands; that part of the Republic of Turkey comprising the territory north and west of a line extending from the point of intersection of the Turkish border with the 39th Parallel to Muradiye, Patnos, Karayazi, Tekman, Kemaliye, Feke, Ceyham, Dogankent, and Gozne, and thence to the sea; the United Kingdom of Great Britain and Northern Ireland; and that part of the territory of the Union of Soviet Socialist Republics west of the Ural Mountains, the Ural River, and the Caspian Sea, as well as Franz Josef Land and Novaya Zemlya.

(c) The term 'conventional armed forces' means . . .

(d) The term 'conventional armaments' means . . .

(e) The term 'active units' means . . .

(f) The term 'main battle tank' means a self-propelled armoured combat vehicle capable of heavy firepower, primarily of a high muzzle velocity . . . main gun necessary to engage armoured and other targets and high cross-country mobility, and providing a high level of self-protection. Such armoured vehicles serve as the principal weapon system of ground-force tank formations. Main battle tanks currently in the armed forces of the participants include armoured all-tracked combat vehicles weighing at least . . . metric tonnes.

(g) The term 'artillery' comprises large calibre systems capable of engaging ground targets by delivering primarily indirect fire, namely guns, howitzers, artillery pieces combining the characteristics of guns and howitzers, mortars, and multiple launch rocket systems. Such artillery systems provide the essential indirect fire support to combined arms formations. In addition, any future large calibre direct fire system which has a secondary effective indirect fire capability will be counted against the artillery ceilings. Large calibre artillery systems are considered to be artillery systems with a calibre of 100mm and above.

(h) The term 'armoured troop carrier' (ATC) means a self-propelled vehicle with light armour and cross-country capability, designed for the transportation of combat troops. It is normally armed with an organic, mounted cannon or machine gun, and sometimes an anti-tank missile launcher. ATCs include Armoured Infantry Fighting Vehicles. An Armoured Infantry Fighting Vehicle (AIFV) is an ATC with an organic cannon and is designed to provide the capability for troops to deliver fire from inside the vehicle under armoured protection. Such AIFVs serve as the principal weapon system of armoured infantry or mechanized formations.

(i) The term 'combat aircraft' means a fixed-wing or swing-wing aircraft, permanently land-based, of a type initially constructed or later converted to drop bombs, deliver air-to-air or air-to-surface missiles, fire guns/cannons, or employ any other weapons of destruction.

(j) The term 'combat helicopter' means a permanently land-based, rotary-wing aircraft constructed or later converted to employ air-to-air or air-to-surface ordnance such as guns, cannons, rockets, bombs, missiles, or any other weapons of destruction.

[Further definitions to be developed.]

2. The existing types of conventional armaments subject to this Treaty are listed in the Annex to this Treaty on existing types of conventional armaments. This list shall be periodically updated.

Article III
[Counting Rules]

[To be developed.]

Article IV

Each Party shall limit and, as necessary, reduce its main battle tanks, artillery pieces, armoured troop carriers, combat aircraft, and combat helicopters so that, . . . years after entry into force of this Treaty and thereafter, the numbers within the area of application for each Party do not exceed:

  (a) 12,000 main battle tanks;
  (b) 10,000 artillery pieces;
  (c) 16,000 armoured troop carriers;
  (d) 3,420 combat aircraft; and
  (e) 1,140 combat helicopters.

Article V

Each Party shall limit, and, as necessary, reduce its main battle tanks, artillery pieces, and armoured troop carriers so that, . . . years after entry into force of this Treaty and thereafter, for the group of Parties to which it belongs the aggregate numbers in active units stationed outside of the respective national territories of those units and stationed within the area of application do not exceed:

  (a) 3,200 main battle tanks;
  (b) 1,700 artillery pieces; and
  (c) 6,000 armoured troop carriers.

Article VI

1. Each Party shall limit and, as necessary, reduce its main battle tanks, artillery pieces, armoured troop carriers, combat aircraft, and combat helicopters so that, . . . years after entry into force of this Treaty and thereafter, for the group of Parties to which it belongs the aggregate numbers within the area of application do not exceed:

  (a) 20,000 main battle tanks;
  (b) 16,500 artillery pieces;
  (c) 28,000 armoured troop carriers, of which no more than 12,000 shall be armoured infantry fighting vehicles;
  (d) 5,700 combat aircraft; and
  (e) 1,900 combat helicopters.

2. Each Party shall limit and, as necessary, reduce its main battle tanks, artillery pieces, and armoured troop carriers so that, . . . years after entry into force of this Treaty and thereafter, for the group of Parties to which it belongs the aggregate numbers in active units in the area consisting of the Kingdom of Belgium, the Czechoslovak Socialist Republic, the Kingdom of Denmark including the Faroe Islands, France, the German Democratic Republic, the Federal Republic of Germany, the Republic of Hungary, the Italian Republic, the Grand Duchy of Luxembourg, the Kingdom of the Netherlands, the Polish People's Republic, the Portuguese Republic including the islands of the Azores and Madeira, the Kingdom of Spain including the Canary Islands, the United Kingdom of Great Britain and Northern Ireland, and that part of the territory of the Union of Soviet Socialist Republics west of the Ural Mountains comprising the Baltic, Byelorussian, Carpathian, Moscow, and Volga-Ural military districts do not exceed:

  (a) 11,300 main battle tanks;
  (b) 9,000 artillery pieces; and
  (c) 20,000 armoured troop carriers.

3. Each Party shall limit and, as necessary, reduce its main battle tanks, artillery pieces, and armoured troop carriers so that, . . . years after entry into force of this Treaty and thereafter, for the group of Parties to which it belongs the aggregate numbers in active units in the area consisting of the Kingdom of Belgium, the Czechoslovak Socialist Republic, the Kingdom of Denmark including the Faroe Islands, France, the German Democratic Republic, the Federal Republic of Germany, the Republic of Hungary, the Italian Republic, the Grand Duchy of Luxembourg, the Kingdom of the Netherlands, the Polish People's Republic, the United Kingdom of Great Britain and Northern Ireland, and that part of the territory of the Union of Soviet Socialist Republics comprising the Baltic, Byelorussian, and Carpathian military districts do not exceed:

  (a) 10,300 main battle tanks;
  (b) 7,600 artillery pieces; and
  (c) 18,000 armoured troop carriers.

4. Each Party shall limit and, as necessary, reduce its main battle tanks, artillery pieces, and armoured troop carriers, so that, . . . years after entry into force of this Treaty and thereafter, for the group of Parties to which it belongs the aggregate numbers in active units in the area consisting of the Kingdom of Belgium, the Czechoslovak Socialist Republic, the German Democratic Republic, the Federal Republic of Germany, the Grand Duchy of Luxembourg, the Kingdom of the Netherlands, and the Polish People's Republic do not exceed:

  (a) 8,000 main battle tanks;
  (b) 4,500 artillery pieces; and
  (c) 11,000 armoured troop carriers.

[5. Placeholder for: possible provisions for safeguarding against destabilization as a result of redeployments in any sub-region under the regional differentiation scheme in order to ensure that the security of each Party is not affected adversely at any stage.]

Article VII

1. The United States of America and the Union of Soviet Socialist Republics shall limit their ground personnel and air force personnel stationed outside of their national territory and within the area of application so that, . . . years after entry into force of this Treaty and thereafter, the aggregate number of such personnel for each of them does not exceed 275,000.

2. The reductions provided for in paragraph 1 of this Article shall be implemented by demobilizing personnel.

Article VIII

[Placeholder for: provision for temporarily exceeding the numerical limitations under this Treaty, for example for military exercises.]

Article IX

1. In order to ensure that the limits under Articles V and VI are complied with, each Party shall not exceed the maximum levels which it has previously agreed within its group for its holdings in treaty-limited equipment in accordance with paragraphs 2 or 4, as appropriate, of this Article and which it has notified under paragraphs 3 or 4 of this Article.

2. It shall be the responsibility solely of the Parties belonging to the same group to ensure that the maximum levels of holdings notified under paragraphs 3 and 4 of this Article, taken together as appropriate, do not exceed the limits under Articles V and VI.

3. Upon signature of the Treaty, each Party shall notify to all other Parties the maximum levels which shall apply to its holdings of main battle tanks, armoured troop carriers, artillery pieces, combat aircraft and combat helicopters. In respect of each such items, the aggregate maximum levels of holdings of each group resulting from the individual notifications of all the Parties belonging to that group shall not exceed the limits set out in Articles V and VI. A notification under this paragraph shall be binding on the notifying Party until a new notification is made under paragraph 4 of this Article.

4. Any Party may notify a change in the maximum levels which apply to its holdings of any or all of the types of conventional armament limited by this Treaty. But if such a change would, on the basis of the maximum levels of holdings notified under this paragraph or paragraph 3 of this Article by other Parties belonging to the same group, result in the limits for each group of Parties in Articles V and VI being exceeded, then it must be accompanied by the notification of a change in the maximum levels of holdings applying to one or more other Parties belonging to the same group so as to ensure continued respect for the limits set out in Articles V and VI.

Article X
[Stabilizing Measures]
[To be developed.]

Article XI
1. The Parties shall provide the notification required by this Article according to the categories of data contained in the Protocol establishing and maintaining a data base.
2. The Parties shall provide the notifications required by this Article in accordance with the procedures set forth in Article XVII of this Treaty.
3. Upon entry into force of this Treaty and thereafter, each Party shall provide the following notifications to the other Parties:
[Details to be developed for data exchange as well as further details to be developed for notifications.]

Article XII
1. The reductions to achieve the numerical limitations set forth in Articles V, VI and VII of this Treaty shall be accomplished by means of destruction. The conventional armaments subject to destruction in accordance with the obligations of this Treaty are main battle tanks, artillery pieces, armoured troop carriers, combat aircraft, and combat helicopters.
2. All destruction of equipment above agreed limits shall be notified and be subject to on-site monitorings without quotas or right of refusal and to other measures to be specified.

Article XIII
[Verification Provisions]
[To be developed.]

Article XIV
1. For the purpose of ensuring verification of compliance with the provisions of this Treaty, each Party shall have the right to use, in addition to the procedures included in Article XIII, national technical means of verification at its disposal in a manner consistent with generally recognized principles of international law.
2. A Party shall not interfere with the carrying out of any inspection or monitoring activity provided for in Article XIII of this Treaty, with the national technical means of verification of another Party operating in accordance with paragraph 1 of this Article, or with any other agreed measure of verification.
3. A Party shall not use concealment measures that impede verification of compliance with the provisions of this Treaty by any inspection or monitoring activity provided for in Article XIII of this Treaty or by national technical means of verification. The obligation not to use

concealment measures does not apply to cover or concealment practices associated with normal training, maintenance, or operations.

4. For the purpose of enhancing observation by national technical
means of verification, each Party shall implement co-operative
measures. Such measures shall include: [To be developed].

Article XV

1. Subject to the provisions of this Treaty, main battle tanks, artillery
pieces, armoured troop carriers, combat aircraft and combat helicopters may be replaced within the area of application.

2. Subject to the provisions of this Treaty, such equipment may be
modernized within the area of application.

3. [To be considered: provision concerning new technologies.]

Article XVI

To promote the objectives and implementation of the provisions of this
Treaty, the Parties establish a Joint Consultative Group in the framework of which they will resolve ambiguities, address questions
of compliance as well as promote the Treaty's viability. [To be
developed.]

Article XVII

The Parties shall use . . . to:

(a) exchange data and provide notifications as required by paragraphs . . . of Articles . . . of this Treaty;

[Further details to be developed.]

Article XVIII

1. This Treaty shall be of unlimited duration.

2. Each Party shall, in exercising its national sovereignty, have the
right to withdraw from this Treaty if it decides that extraordinary events
related to the subject matter of this Treaty have jeopardized its supreme
interests. A Party intending to withdraw shall give notice of its decision
to withdraw to the depositary(ies), as well as to all other Parties, three
months in advance of its withdrawal. Such notice shall include a
statement of the extraordinary events the Party regards as having
jeopardized its supreme interests.

3. Each Party shall, in particular, in exercising its national sovereignty, have the right to withdraw from this Treaty if another Party were
to increase its holdings in main battle tanks, artillery pieces, armoured
troop carriers, combat aircraft, or combat helicopters, as defined in
Article II of this Treaty, which are outside the scope of the limitations of
this Treaty, in such proportions as to pose an obvious threat to the
balance of forces within the zone of application.

4. In the event that a Party gives notice of its decision to withdraw
from this Treaty, a conference of all of the other Parties shall be
convened not more than . . . days after receipt of such notice by the

depositary(ies) in order to consider the effect of the withdrawal on this Treaty.

Article XIX

1. Any Party may propose amendments to this Treaty or to its Annexes or Protocols. The text of proposed amendments shall be submitted to the depositary(ies), which shall circulate them to all Parties. Thereupon, if requested to do so by five or more of the Parties, the depositary(ies) shall convene a conference to consider such amendments.

2. An amendment to this Treaty must be approved by all Parties to the Treaty. An amendment so approved shall enter into force in accordance with the procedures set forth in Article XX governing entry into force of this Treaty.

3. As provided for in Article XVI, the Joint Consultative Group may agree upon such implementing and other measures as may be necessary to improve the viability and effectiveness of this Treaty. Such measures shall not be deemed amendments to this Treaty.

4. Five years after entry into force of this Treaty, and at five-year intervals thereafter, the Parties shall together conduct a review of the operation of this Treaty, unless requested to do so sooner by five or more of the Parties.

Article XX

1. This Treaty, including the Annexes and Protocols referred to in Article I, all of which form an integral part hereof, shall be subject to ratification in accordance with the constitutional procedures of each Party. Instruments of ratification shall be deposited with . . ., hereby designated the depositary(ies).

2. This Treaty shall enter into force . . . days after instruments of ratification have been deposited by the Kingdom of Belgium, the People's Republic of Bulgaria, Canada, the Czechoslovak Socialist Republic, the Kingdom of Denmark, France, the German Democratic Republic, the Federal Republic of Germany, the Hellenic Republic, the Republic of Hungary, the Republic of Iceland, the Italian Republic, the Grand Duchy of Luxembourg, the Kingdom of the Netherlands, the Kingdom of Norway, the Polish People's Republic, the Portuguese Republic, the Socialist Republic of Romania, the Kingdom of Spain, the Republic of Turkey, the Union of Soviet Socialist Republics, the United Kingdom of Great Britain and Northern Ireland, and the United States of America.

3. The depositary(ies) shall promptly inform all Parties of the date of deposit of each instrument of ratification, the date of entry into force of this Treaty, and the date of receipt of any requests for convening a conference or other notices.

Article XXI

1. This Treaty, of which the English, French, German, Italian, Russian, and Spanish texts are each equally authentic, shall be deposited in the archives of the depositary(ies).

2. This Treaty shall be registered by the depositary(ies) pursuant to Article 102 of the Charter of the United Nations.

NORTH ATLANTIC COUNCIL, OPEN SKIES: THE BASIC ELEMENTS

Agreed in Ministerial Session at NATO Headquarters, Brussels on 14 and 15 December 1989

I. Introduction

1.   On 12 May 1989, President Bush proposed the creation of a so-called 'Open Skies' regime, in which the participants would voluntarily open their airspace on a reciprocal basis, permitting the overflight of their territory in order to strengthen confidence and transparency with respect to their military activities.

This proposal expanded on a concept that had already been proposed during the 1950s but had failed to reach fruition because of the unfavourable international political climate prevailing at the time.

Today, this new initiative has been made in a very different context as openness becomes a central theme of East-West relations and the past few years have been marked by important advances in the areas of confidence-building and arms control.

2.   The provisions for notification and observation of military activities specified in the Helsinki Final Act were strengthened and made obligatory by the Stockholm Document concluded by the CDE in 1986.

With respect to arms control, in 1987, the INF Treaty, apart from its immediate goals, represented a very important precedent because of the extent of its verification provisions.

All this leads one to expect today that even more spectacular advances will be achieved in the near future. In particular, a two-pronged effort is under way in Vienna: on the one hand, to deepen the measures for confidence-building and transparency among the 35 countries of the CSCE, and on the other, to reach an unprecedented agreement between the countries of the Atlantic Alliance and the Warsaw Treaty Organization on the elimination of large numbers of conventional arms.

Furthermore, one awaits important developments in other sectors of disarmament such as chemical weapons and the Soviet-American strategic arms negotiations.

3.   All of these agreements will naturally require their own verification regimes, often of a highly intrusive nature. Moreover, the specific

provisions of each verification treaty will be supplemented by the habitual means by which countries verify compliance with agreements (national technical means).

It seems useful, however, particularly in the prevailing context of improved East-West relations, to reflect on other ways of creating a broadly favourable context for confidence-building and disarmament efforts.

In this context, the Open Skies concept has a very special value. The willingness of a country to be overflown is, in itself, a highly significant political act in that it demonstrates its availability to openness; aerial inspection also represents a particularly effective means of verification, along with the general transparency in military activities discussed above.

This double characteristic of an Open Skies regime would make it a valuable complement to current East-West endeavours, mainly in the context of the Vienna negotiations but also in relation to the other disarmament efforts (START, chemical weapons).

It would seem desirable to focus now on the European region, while also including the entire territories of the Soviet Union, the United States, and Canada. Accordingly, we will be ready to consider at an appropriate time the wish of any other European country to participate in the Open Skies regime. This element could be complementary to their efforts at confidence-building and conventional arms control and would conform to the objectives of those negotiations.

4. To this end, the Open Skies Regime should be based on the following guidelines:

— The commitment of the parties to greater transparency through aerial overflights of their entire national territory, in principle without other limitations than those imposed by flight safety or rules of international law.
— The possibility for the participants to carry out such observation flights on a national basis or jointly with their allies.
— The commitment of all parties to conduct and to receive such observation flights on the basis of national quotas.
— The establishment of agreed procedures designed to ensure both transparency and flight safety.
— The possibility for the parties to employ the result of such overflights to improve openness and transparency of military activities as well as ensuring compliance with current or future arms control measures.

II. Purpose

The basic purpose of Open Skies is to encourage reciprocal openness on the part of the participating states and to allow the observation of military activities and installation on their territories, thus enhancing confidence and security. Open Skies can serve these ends as a complement both to national technical means of data collection and to information exchange and verification arrangements established by current and future arms control agreements.

III. Participation and Scope

Participation in Open Skies is initially open to all members of the Atlantic Alliance and the Warsaw Treaty Organization. All territories of the participants in North America and Asia, as well as in Europe, will be included.

IV. Quotas

1.   Open Skies 'accounting' will be based on quotas which limit the number of overflights. The quotas will be derived from the geographic size of the participating countries. The duration of flights can also be limited in relation to geographic size. For larger countries, the quota should permit several flights a month over their territory. All of the parties will be entitled to participate in such observation flights on a national basis, either individually or jointly in co-operation with their allies.

2.   Effective implementation of a quota system requires agreement that a country will not undertake flights over the territory of any other country belonging to the same alliance.

3.   Quota totals for participating states should be established in such a manner that there is a rough correspondence between totals for NATO and the Warsaw Treaty Organization and, within that total, for the USSR and the North American members of NATO.

4.   Every participant, regardless of size, would be obligated to accept a quota of at least one overflight per quarter.

5.   Smaller nations, that is, those subject to the minimum quota, may group themselves into one unit for the purposes of hosting Open Skies overflights and jointly accept the quota that would apply to the total land mass of the larger unit.

V. Aircraft

The country or countries conducting an observation flight would use unarmed, fixed-wing civilian or military aircraft capable of carrying host country observers.

VI. Sensors

A wide variety of sensors would be allowed, with one significant limitation – devices used for the collection and recording of signals intelligence would be prohibited. A list of prohibited categories and types of sensors will be agreed among the participating states which will be updated every year.

VII. Technical Cooperation among Allies

Multilateral or bilateral arrangements concerning the sharing of aircraft or sensors, as well as the conduct of joint overflights, will be possible among members of the same alliance.

VIII. Mission Operation

1. Aircraft will begin observation flights from agreed, pre-designated points of entry and terminate at pre-designated points of exit; such entry and exit points for each participating state will be designated by that state and listed in an annex to the agreement.

2. The host country will make available the kind of support equipment, servicing and facilities normally provided to commercial air carriers. Provision will be made for refuelling stops during the overflight.

3. An observing state will provide 16 hours notification of arrival at a point of entry. However, if the point of entry is on a coast or at a border and no territory of the receiving state will be overflown prior to arrival at the point of entry, this pre-arrival period could be abbreviated.

4. The crew of the observation aircraft shall file a flight plan within six hours of its arrival at the point of entry.

5. After arrival and the filing of a flight plan, a 24 hour pre-flight period will begin. This period is to allow time to determine that there are no flight safety problems associated with the planned flight route and to provide necessary servicing for the aircraft. During this pre-flight period the aircraft will also be subject to intrusive but non-destructive inspection for prohibited sensors and recorders.

6. Prior to the flight, host-country monitors will be able to board the observation aircraft. During the flight they would ensure that the aircraft is operated in accordance with the flight plan and would monitor operation of the sensors. There would be no restrictions on the movement of the monitors within the aircraft during flight.

7. The flight will be from the agreed point of entry to an agreed point of exit, where the host country observers would depart the aircraft. The points of entry and exit could be the same. Loitering over a single location will not be permitted. Aircraft will not be limited to commercial air corridors. Observation aircraft may in principle only be prohibited from flying through airspace that is publicly announced as closed to other aircraft for valid air safety reasons. Such reasons would include specific hazards posing extreme danger to the aircraft and its occupants. Each country will make arrangements to ensure that public announcements of such hazardous airspace are widely and promptly disseminated; each country will produce for an annex to the agreement

a list of where these public announcements can be found. The minimum altitudes for such flights may vary depending upon air safety considerations. The extent of ground control over aircraft will be determined in advance by agreement among the parties on compatible rules such as those recognized by ICAO. In the application of these considerations and procedures, the presumption shall be on behalf of encouraging the greatest degree of openness consistent with air safety.

8. The operation of the Open Skies regime will be without prejudice to states not participating in it.

IX. Mission Results

The members of the same alliance will determine among themselves how information acquired through Open Skies is to be shared. Each party may decide how it wishes to use this information.

X. Transits

A transit flight over a participating state on the way to the participating state over which an observation flight is to be conducted shall not be counted against the quota of the transitted state, provided the transit flight is conducted exclusively within civilian flight corridors.

XI. Type of Agreement

The Open Skies regime will be established through a multilateral treaty among the parties.

XII. Open Skies Consultative Body

To promote the objectives and implementation of the Open Skies regime, the participating states will establish a body to resolve questions of compliance with the terms of the treaty and to agree upon such measures as may be necessary to improve the effectiveness of the regime.

Source: NATO, 15 December 1989

NUCLEAR AND SPACE TALKS: US–SOVIET PROPOSALS, 22 JANUARY 1990

US Arms Control and Disarmament Agency Issue Brief

START (Strategic Arms Reduction Talks)

General Approach:

United States – Reduction to equal levels in strategic offensive arms, carried out in a phased manner achieving equal intermediate ceilings by agreed dates over seven years from the date the treaty comes into force.

Soviet Union – Reduction to equal levels in strategic offensive arms, carried out in two phases over seven years from the date the treaty enters into force, with equal ceilings after phase 1.

United States – Completion of START not contingent upon the resolution of Defense and Space issues.

Soviet Union – Conclusion of START agreement not contingent upon reaching a Defense and Space agreement. However, Soviets indicate that they claim a right to withdraw from START if they determine that the US has gone beyond the ABM Treaty as they define it.

United States – No further strategic arms control treaties can be concluded with the Soviet Union until it corrects its violation of the ABM Treaty involving the Krasnoyarsk radar in a verifiable manner that meets US criteria.

Soviet Union – Soviets have stated they will completely eliminate the Krasnoyarsk radar station.

Delivery Vehicles:

United States – 1,600 ceiling on the number of strategic nuclear delivery vehicles (SNDVs), which comprise deployed intercontinental ballistic missiles (ICBMs) and their associated launchers, deployed submarine-launched ballistic missiles (SLBMs) and their associated launchers, and heavy bombers.

Soviet Union – Broadly the same as the US position. Differences remain, however, on accountability.

Warheads:

United States – 6,000 warhead ceiling, to include the accountable number of deployed ICBMs and SLMB warheads and long-range, nuclear-armed ALCMs (air-launched cruise missiles) (see ALCMs), and with each heavy bomber equipped only for nuclear-armed gravity bombs and short-range attack missiles (SRAMs) counting as one warhead.

Soviet Union – Same as the US position. Some differences on how to count ALCM warheads (see ALCMs).

Warhead Sublimits:

United States – Sublimits of 4,900 ballistic missile warheads and 3,000–3,300 ICBM warheads.

Soviet Union – Sublimit of 4,900 ballistic missile warheads; if 3,300 sublimit on ICBMs, then must also be 3,300 sublimit on SLBMs. Sublimit of 1,100 on deployed heavy bomber-carried warheads.

Heavy ICBMs:

United States – A limit of 1,540 warheads on 154 deployed heavy ballistic missiles. Ban on production, flight testing or modernization of new or existing types of heavy ICBMs.

Soviet Union – A limit of 1,540 warheads on 154 deployed heavy ICBMs. Production, flight testing or modernization of existing types of heavy ICBMs permitted. Development, testing and deployment of new types of heavy ICBMs banned.

Throw-weight:

United States – The aggregate throw-weight of Soviet ICBMs and SLBMs will be reduced to 50 percent below their throw-weight level as of 31 December 1986. Neither side will exceed this level for the duration of this treaty.

Soviet Union – Same as the US position in principle, but differences remain on how to determine accountable throw-weight. Reductions will be from the throw-weight level existing at treaty signature.

Ballistic Missile Warheads:

United States – Each ballistic missile warhead counts as one warhead under the 6,000 warhead ceiling. For existing types, a quota of on-site inspections to verify that deployed missiles contain no more than the number of warheads declared and agreed for each type at the Washington Summit.

For future types, as well as changes in the number of warheads on existing types, procedures remain to be agreed.

Soviet Union – Same as US position for existing types.

Mobile ICBMs:

United States – US has lifted ban on mobile ICBMs. START negotiators must work out the appropriate details of limits to be applied to mobile ICBMs and effective verification measures.

Soviet Union – Permitted, with numerical limits on launchers and warheads.

Heavy Bombers:

United States – Each heavy bomber counts as one strategic nuclear delivery cehicle (SNDV). Each heavy bomber equipped only for gravity bombs and short-range attack missiles (SRAMs) would count as one warhead under the 6,000 limit. An agreed number of heavy bombers could be removed from accountability under the 1,600 SNDV limit by conversion to a conventional-only capability.

Soviet Union – Same as the US position, except that Soviet agreement on conversion of heavy bombers to a conventional-only capability is contingent on US acceptance of Soviet position on ALCM range and attribution.

ALCMs:

United States – ALCMs defined as air-launched, nuclear-armed cruise missiles with a range in excess of 1,500 kilometers. An agreed number of ALCMs (10) shall be attributed to each type of heavy bomber equipped for ALCMs, for the purpose of counting against the 6,000 warhead limit.

Soviet Union – ALCMs defined as air-launched cruise missiles with a range in excess of 600 kilometers. The number of ALCMs attributed to ALCM heavy bombers shall be the maximum number for which each type is equipped. ALCMs shall be limited under the proposed sublimit of 1,100 for all deployed heavy bomber-carried warheads (see warhead sublimits).

SLCMs:

United States – The sides shall find a mutually acceptable solution to the question of limiting the deployment of long-range, nuclear-armed SLCMs (sea-launched cruise missiles). Such limitations will not involve counting these SLCMs within the 6,000 warhead and 1,600 strategic nuclear delivery vehicle (SNDV) limits. The sides commit themselves to establish ceilings on such missiles, and to seek mutually acceptable and effective methods of verification of such limitations, which could include use of National Technical Means, cooperative measures and on-site inspection. Thus far, the United States has not identified any effective verification approach for SLCMs. In absence of plan for effective verification, US proposed that the sides make non-binding declarations of nuclear SLCM numbers.

Soviet Union – Soviets accept basic principles. Specific force level limitations of 400 on nuclear-armed and of 600 on conventional-armed SLCMs, but the Soviets fail to identify effective verification measures. The Soviet approach would also undermine US policy of neither confirming nor denying the presence of nuclear weapons at any particular location – an important underpinning of deterrence.

United States – US has agreed to study Soviet proposals to move some or all of SLCM issues outside START negotiations. US opposes discussions on naval arms limitations.

Soviet Union – Soviets have proposed either that the entire SLCM issue be removed from START and be dealt with in a broader naval arms context, or that START concentrate on SLCM verification, with the issue of SLCM limits being dealt with in a separate binding agreement outside, but in association with, START. In either case, the Soviets would require binding, verifiable SLCM limits in order to conclude START.

Verification of Compliance:

United States – Provisions, at a minimum, to include: exchange of data both before and after the reductions take place; on-site inspection to verify data and to observe elimination of weapons; continuous on-site monitoring of the perimeter and portals of critical production facilities; and short-notice inspection of sites where treaty-limited systems are located both during and after the reduction period. Inspections requested at sites where a party considers that covert production, storage, repair or deployment may be occurring.

Right to short-notice inspections at certain types of 'suspect sites.' Right to request inspection at other 'suspect sites.' If challenged party refuses inspection, it must make good faith effort to resolve concerns.

Soviet Union – Soviets have accepted much of the US verification position, although many details remain to be resolved, especially in the area of mobile ICBM verification.

United States – US has proposed that the two sides accelerate efforts to agree on, and begin implementing as soon as possible, verification and stability measures to acquire practical experience and speed up resolution of verification issues. Proposed measures include: establishment now of on-site perimeter/portal monitoring of certain missile production facilities, exchange of data on each side's strategic nuclear forces, prohibiting data denial, including encryption of telemetry, on all launches of designated ICBMs and SLBMs, and addressing the problem of short-time-of-flight SLBMs.

Soviet Union – Soviets have accepted the principle of verification and stability measures, have made some proposals of their own, and have been discussing US proposals in detail in Geneva.

United States – Agreement reached with Soviets on: 1) advance notification of one major strategic exercise involving heavy bomber aircraft per calendar year; 2) exhibitions of one type of heavy bomber on each side to demonstrate verification procedures for distinguishing ALCM heavy bombers from non-ALCM heavy bombers; and, 3) demonstration of each side's proposed procedures for on-site inspection of reentry vehicles for each side's ballistic missiles. The sides also exchanged information on missile tagging technologies.

Soviet Union – Agreement reached with US on: 1) advance notification of one major strategic exercise involving heavy bomber aircraft per calendar year; 2) exhibitions of one type of heavy bomber on each side to demonstrate verification procedures for distinguishing ALCM heavy bombers from non-ALCM heavy bombers; and, 3) demonstration of each side's proposed procedures for on-site inspection of reentry vehicles for each side's ballistic missiles. The sides also exchanged information on missile tagging technologies.

D and S (Defense and Space)

General Approach:

United States – The US seeks to facilitate a cooperative transition to a stabilizing balance of offensive and defensive forces, should effective defenses against strategic ballistic missiles prove feasible. The US also seeks to preserve the option to develop and deploy advanced defenses when they are ready, at a measured pace and in a cooperative way. Defense and Space issues should be addressed in a new treaty building upon and clarifying the language in the Washington Summit Joint Statement to ensure unambiguous meaning of commitments made in the future treaty.

Soviet Union – Defense and Space issues should be addressed now in the form of a protocol to the ABM Treaty, not in a new Defense and Space Treaty. The protocol would cover permitted/prohibited activities under the ABM Treaty and predictability measures to ensure compliance with the ABM Treaty. The Soviets have stated that they will table such a draft protocol early in 1990. Issues on which the sides have not been able to reach agreement by the time a START agreement is completed should continue to be addressed in post-START strategic stability talks.

United States – No further strategic arms control treaties can be concluded with the Soviet Union until it corrects its violation of the Anti-Ballistic Missile (ABM) Treaty involving the Krasnoyarsk radar in a verifiable manner that meets US criteria. The US has expressed satisfaction with the Soviet announcement that it will completely eliminate the Krasnoyarsk radar station.

Soviet Union – Soviets have stated that they will completely eliminate the Krasnoyarsk radar station.

Commitment of Non-withdrawal from ABM Treaty:

United States – The sides have agreed to drop the approach of a commitment not to withdraw from the ABM Treaty.

Soviet Union – The sides have agreed to drop the approach of a commitment not to withdraw from the ABM Treaty.

Activities under the ABM Treaty:

United States – US has proposed initiatives to help clarify the meaning of the phrase, 'research, development, and testing as required, which are permitted by the ABM Treaty.'

In order to demonstrate that US testing of space-based components of ABM systems based on 'other physical principles' and capable of substituting for ABM interceptor missiles, which is permitted by the

ABM Treaty, does not represent the deployment of such components, the US is prepared to carry out such permitted testing only from designated ABM test satellites. The US view is that the number of such satellites in orbit simultaneously shall not exceed a number well short of that associated with any realistic deployed capability. The US believes the number 15 falls well below that threshold.

Notification associated with ABM tests in space would be provided for in the predictability protocol (see below).

The US also proposed that each party may develop, test, or deploy space-based sensors without restriction. This proposal is designed to avoid future verification problems and to encourage stabilizing space-based sensors.

Soviet Union – Soviets seek agreement on permitted and prohibited activities under the ABM Treaty, to be in the form of a protocol to the ABM Treaty. The Soviets would constrain activities to an interpretation of the ABM Treaty that is more restrictive than agreed to by the parties in 1972, and possibly even more restrictive than the 'narrow interpretation.'

The Soviets have rejected the US testing in space (ABM test satellite) initiative and the space-based sensors proposal, claiming they are contrary to the ABM Treaty and the Washington Summit Joint Statement.

The Soviets have proposed that intensive discussions of strategic stability take place after the conclusion of a START Treaty.

Duration of Treaty/Linkage:

United States – A D and S Treaty would be of unlimited duration. The ABM Treaty will be observed until either party exercises the right to deploy (See *Transition to Defenses*, below).

The D and S Treaty must stand on its own merits. Completion of a START Treaty and adherence to the Treaty should not be linked to resolution of D and S issues. The US opposes as unnecessary the Soviet-proposed agreed statements giving them the right to withdraw from START if they determine the US has gone beyond the ABM Treaty as they define it.

Soviet Union – The Soviet Union has agreed that completion of a START Treaty is not contingent upon reaching an agreement on Defense and Space Issues. The Soviets have indicated, however, that they claim a right to withdraw from START if they determine that the US has gone beyond the ABM Treaty as they define it, and have proposed agreed US-Soviet statements to that effect.

Transition to Defenses:

United States – The ABM Treaty would remain in force under a Defense and Space Treaty. However, either party would be permitted to give notice of its intent to deploy strategic ballistic missile defenses beyond the limitations in the ABM Treaty. Upon the giving of such notice, the initiating party would propose specific measures for a cooperative transition to a strategic regime which would include defenses, and the parties would begin intensive discussions concerning those specific measures and strategic stability. Three years later, either party could give six months notice of its decision to deploy strategic ballistic missile defenses, after which the sides would be free to deploy unless the parties agreed otherwise.

Soviet Union – The Soviet Union opposes a transition to defenses beyond those permitted under the ABM Treaty.

Intensive discussions of strategic stability shall take place following conclusion of a START Treaty. The Soviets propose that these discussions deal with the 'problems of ABM defenses taking into account the new situation resulting from reductions in strategic offensive arms.' Following these discussions, should the sides not agree otherwise, each side shall determine for itself its further actions with respect to the ABM Treaty and the START Treaty, subject to compliance with the relevant procedures of these treaties. The Soviets argue that the 'right to deploy' was not agreed at the Washington Summit, but that ABM Treaty rights would govern the parties' actions.

Predictability:

United States – The sides shall discuss ways to ensure predictability in the developments of the US-Soviet strategic relationship to reduce the risk of nuclear war. As confidence-building measures to provide predictability in the strategic defense programs of the other nation, the US proposed the following measures in the field of strategic ballistic missile defense, to be implemented on a reciprocal, comparable and voluntary basis: annual exchanges of programmatic data and meetings of experts, briefings, visits to laboratories, and observations of tests. The US has pointed out that Soviet-proposed verification measures are unworkable and could jeopardize US and Allied security.

Soviet Union – The sides shall discuss ways to ensure predictability in the development of the US-Soviet strategic relationship in order to reduce the risk of nuclear war.

The Soviets have accepted some US concepts for confidence-building measures, including exchanges of data, meetings of experts, and observations of tests. (The Soviets have not accepted the US proposal that predictability measures encompass research activities not observable by National Technical Means.) However, the Soviets would make such measures compulsory in order to ensure compliance with the ABM Treaty. Additionally, they propose an exchange of information to clarify ambiguous situations, mandatory on-site inspection of certain sites and facilities which give rise to concerns, and resolution of compliance questions in the Standing Consultative Commission.

United States – In December 1989, at US invitation, Soviet government experts visited two US facilities involved in research on strategic ballistic missile defenses.

Soviet Union – In December 1989, at US invitation, Soviet government experts visited two US facilities involved in research on strategic ballistic missile defenses.

Source: United States Information Service

JOINT NATO–WARSAW PACT COMMUNIQUÉ ON CFE/CSCS

Ottawa, 13 February 1990

The foreign ministers and senior representatives of the governments of Belgium, Bulgaria, Canada, Czechoslovakia, Denmark, France, and Federal Republic of Germany, the German Democratic Republic, Greece, Hungary, Iceland, Italy, Luxembourg, the Netherlands, Norway, Poland, Portugal, Romania, Spain, Turkey, the United Kingdom, the United States of America and the Union of Soviet Socialist Republics, meeting in Ottawa at the invitation of the government of Canada, gathered on the margins of the Open Skies Conference on February 13, 1990 to review progress in the Negotiation on Conventional Armed Forces in Europe.

The ministers welcomed this meeting as an opportunity to review and assess progress in the negotiations and provide impetus to their successful conclusion. They welcomed in particular an agreement in Ottawa between the United States and the USSR on the reduction of their stationed forces in Europe.

Convinced that a CFE agreement would strengthen stability and security in Europe through the establishment of a stable and secure balance of conventional armed forces at lower levels, the ministers agreed that the negotiations in Vienna should proceed as expeditiously as possible. For this purpose, the ministers also agreed that negotiations in Vienna should be encouraged to develop solutions designed to overcome remaining obstacles, especially in those areas where new elements have been put forward recently:

- aircraft
- regional limitations, differentiation and storage
- helicopters
- tanks and armoured combat vehicles.

The ministers recognized that the essential elements for a CFE treaty are now on the table in Vienna, though much remains to be done, in particular to develop an effective verification regime.

The ministers expressed their willingness to give simultaneously impetus to the CSBM negotiations. They emphasized their shared commitment to achieving a CFE agreement as soon as possible in 1990, and agreed on the principle of holding a CSCE summit meeting this year. They stressed the need for timely and thorough preparation for such a meeting through appropriate consultation among the 35 participation states.

They affirmed their interest in continuing the conventional arms control process, taking into account future requirements for European stability and security in the light of political developments in Europe.

Source: NATO

'OPEN SKIES',
COMMUNIQUÉ OF FOREIGN MINISTERS

Ottawa, 14 February 1990

At the invitation of the government of Canada, the foreign ministers and senior representatives of the government of Belgium, Bulgaria, Canada, Czechoslovakia, Denmark, France, the German Democratic Republic, the Federal Republic of Germany, Greece, Hungary, Iceland, Italy, Luxembourg, the Netherlands, Norway, Poland, Portugal, Rumania, Spain, Turkey, the Union of Soviet Socialist Republics, the United Kingdom and the United States of America met in Ottawa February 12–14, 1990 to begin negotiation of 'Open Skies.' Also present at the ministerial session were observers of other CSCE states. (Those present as observers were Austria, Cyprus, Finland, Ireland, Monaco, Sweden, Switzerland and Yugoslavia. Turkey reserves her position on the status and representation of Cyprus.)

The ministers welcomed the accelerating trend toward openness and the reduction of international tensions. In this context, they noted that although an 'Open Skies' regime is neither an arms control nor a verification measure per se its successful implementation would encourage reciprocal openness on the part of participating states. It would strengthen confidence among them, reduce the risk of conflict, and enhance the predictability of military activities of the participating states. Finally it would contribute to the process of arms reduction and limitation along with verification measures under arms limitation and reduction agreements and existing observation capabilities. The ministers notedf further that the establishment of an 'Open Skies' regime may promote greater openness in the future in other spheres.

Believing that an effective 'Open Skies' regime would serve to consolidate improved relations among their countries, the ministers therefore agreed on the following:

– The 'Open Skies' regime will be implemented on a reciprocal and equitable basis which will protect the interests of each participating state, and in accordance with which the participating states will be open to aerial observation. The regime will ensure the maximum possible openness and minimum restrictions for observation flights;

– Each participating state will have the right to conduct, and the obligation to receive, observation flights on the basis of annual quotas which will be determined in negotiations so as to provide for equitable coverage;

– The agreement will have provisions concerning the right to conduct observation flights using unarmed aircraft and equipment capable in all circumstances of fulfilling the goals of the regime;
– The participating states willk favorably consider the possible participator in the regime of other countries, primarily the European countries.

The ministers expressed their gratitude to the government of Canada for organizing this conference and welcomed the invitation of the government of Hungary to a second part of the conference to conclude the negotiation in Budapest this spring.

Source: Communiqué, Foreign Ministers' Meeting, Ottawa.

STATEMENT BY
THE SECRETARY GENERAL OF NATO

14 February 1990

The Alliance very much welcomes the agreement reached at Ottawa on the levels of stationed US and Soviet ground and air force personnel in Europe to be achieved in the CFE negotiations. The agreement is based on the proposal made by President Bush, and subsequently tabled by the Allies in Vienna last week. These limits on US and Soviet manpower will effectively complement the parity in key weapons systems which the Allies are working for in Vienna. By recognizing the US right to station another 30,000 troops in Europe outside of the central zone, the agreement also underlines the essential geographical asymmetry between the two Alliances. The presence of US troops in Europe, voluntarily agreed by free and sovereign democracies, is at the express wish of the Allies. It is necessary due to the geographical distance from the continental US, and as a concrete expression of the American commitment to Europe. It will remain an essential feature of the structure of European security of the future. The Ottawa agreement is an encouraging new step towards the successful conclusion of a CFE Treaty this year.

Source: NATO Press Service, 14 February 1990

SECTION III

Speeches and Statements

This collection can be divided into two. For the period prior to the breaching of the Berlin Wall on 10 November 1989 it contains some landmark speeches and statements from the second half of the 1980s. The start of 1985 saw Ronald Reagan begin his second term as President of the United States and Mikhail Gorbachev take over as General Secretary of the Communist Party of the Soviet Union. In most of the material from this period there is a presumption that the existing alliance framework will endure, but one can also detect attempts to see how, if at all, the division of Europe might be transcended.

This can be seen in the communiqués from the Reagan-Gorbachev summits in Geneva (October 1985), Washington (December 1987) and Moscow (June 1988). The meeting at Reykjavik in October 1986 did not produce a communiqué; nor did the informal Bush-Gorbachev meeting off Malta in December 1989.

During this period Mikhail Gorbachev can generally be seen to be forcing the pace, especially when it comes to arms control and disarmament. NATO found it necessary to restate carefully its established position while at the same time responding to the pressures for change. This is reflected, for example, in the 1989 Comprehensive Concept which was influenced by a sharp intra-alliance debate over the future of short-range nuclear forces. These weapons could be presented as necessary to the integrity of the strategy of flexible response, yet also singling out Germany for nuclear destruction (following the removal of longer-range systems under the INF Treaty) and anachronistic in the light of improved East-West relations.

From November 1989 onwards there has been a growing preoccupation with German unification. It was recognized as a likely outcome of the process set in motion by the movement of population from East to West Germany and the tearing down of the Berlin Wall. From February 1990, with the East German economy in a parlous state, it was recognized as having to come sooner rather than later. The diplomatic process had to run fast to catch up with the drive for unification. In the speeches and statements of this period can be found a clarification of the issues – the German-Polish border, stationing of troops on German territory, neutrality or membership of NATO – and a look forward to a new security system based on the CSCE.

195

JOINT US–USSR STATEMENT

Geneva, 21 November 1985

By mutual agreement, President of the United States Ronald Reagan and General Secretary of the Central Committee of the Communist Party of the Soviet Union Mikhail Gorbachev, met in Geneva, on November 19–21 1985.

Their comprehensive discussions covered the basic questions of US-Soviet relations and the current international situation. The meetings were frank and useful. Serious differences remain on a number of critical issues.

While acknowledging the differences in their systems and approaches to international issues, some greater understanding of each side's view was achieved by the two leaders. They agreed about the need to improve US-Soviet relations and the international situation as a whole.

In this connection, the two sides have confirmed the importance of an ongoing dialogue, reflecting their strong desire to seek common ground on existing problems.

They agreed to meet again in the nearest future. The General Secretary accepted an invitation by the President of the United States to visit the United States of America, and the President of the United States accepted an invitation by the General Secretary of the Central Committee of the CPSU to visit the Soviet Union. Arrangements for and timing of the visits will be agreed upon through diplomatic channels.

In their meetings, agreement was reached on a number of specific issues. Areas of agreement are registered on the following pages.

Security

The sides, having discussed key security issues, and conscious of the special responsibility of the USSR and the US for maintaining peace, have agreed that a nuclear war cannot be won and must never be fought. Recognizing that any conflict between the USSR and the US could have catastrophic consequences, they emphasized the importance of preventing any war between them, whether nuclear or conventional. They will not seek to achieve military superiority.

Nuclear and space talks

The President and the General Secretary discussed the negotiations on nuclear and space arms.

They agreed to accelerate the work at these negotiations, with a view to accomplishing the task set down in the Joint US-Soviet Agreement of 8 January 1985, namely, to prevent an arms race in space and to terminate it on earth, to limit and reduce nuclear arms and enhance strategic stability.

Noting the proposals recently tabled by the US and Soviet Union, they called for early progress, in particular in areas where there is common ground, including the principle of 50% reductions in the nuclear arms of the US and the USSR appropriately applied, as well as the idea of an interim INF agreement.

During the negotiation of these agreements, effective measures for verification of compliance with obligations assumed will be agreed upon.

Risk reduction centers

The sides agreed to study the question at the expert level of centers to reduce nuclear risk, taking into account the issues and developments in the Geneva negotiations. They took satisfaction in such recent steps in this direction as the modernization of the Soviet-US hotline.

Nuclear non-proliferation

General Secretary Gorbachev and President Reagan reaffirmed the commitment of the USSR and the US to the Treaty on the Non-Proliferation of Nuclear Weapons and their interest in strengthening together with other countries the non-proliferation regime, and in further enhancing of the Treaty, *inter alia* by enlarging its membership.

They note with satisfaction the overall positive results of the recent Review Conference of the Treaty on the Non-Proliferation of Nuclear Weapons.

The USSR and the US reaffirm their commitment, assumed by them under the Treaty on the Non-Proliferation of Nuclear Weapons, to pursue negotiations in good faith on matters of nuclear arms limitation and disarmament in accordance with Article VI of the Treaty.

The two sides plan to continue to promote the strengthening of the International Atomic Energy Agency and to support the activities of the Agency in implementing safeguards as well as in promoting the peaceful uses of nuclear energy.

They view positively the practice of regular Soviet-US consultations on non-proliferation of nuclear weapons which have been businesslike and constructive and express their intent to continue this practice in the future.

Chemical weapons

In the context of discussing security problems, the two sides reaffirmed that they are in favor of a general and complete prohibition of chemical weapons and the destruction of existing stockpiles of such weapons. They agreed to accelerate efforts to conclude an effective and verifiable international convention on this matter.

The sides agreed to intensify bilateral discussions on the level of experts on all aspects of such a chemical weapon ban, including the question of verification. They agreed to initiate a dialogue on preventing the proliferation of chemical weapons.

MBFR

The two sides emphasized the importance they attach to the Vienna MBFR [Mutual Balanced Force Reductions] negotiations and expressed their willingness to work for positive results.

CDE

Attaching great importance to the Stockholm Conference on Confidence and Security Building Measures and Disarmament in Europe [CDE] and noting the progress made there, the two sides stated their intention to facilitate, together with the other participating states, an early and successful completion of the work of the conference. To this end, they reaffirmed the need for a document which would include mutually acceptable confidence and security building measures and give concrete expression and effect to the principle of non-use of force.

Process of dialogue

President Reagan and General Secretary Gorbachev agreed on the need to meet on a regular basis and intensify dialogue at various levels. Along with meetings between the leaders of the two countries, this envisages regular meetings between the USSR Minister of Foreign Affairs and the US Secretary of State, as well as between the heads of other ministries and agencies. They agree that the recent visits of the heads of ministries and departments in such fields as agriculture, housing and protection of the environment have been useful.

Recognizing that exchanges of views on regional issues on the expert level have proven useful, they agreed to continue such exchanges on a regular basis.

The sides intend to expand the programs of bilateral cultural, educational and scientific-technical exchanges, and also to develop trade and economic ties. The President of the United States and the General Secretary of the Central Committee of the CPSU attended the signing of the Agreement on Contacts and Exchanges in Scientific, Educational and Cultural Fields.

They agreed on the importance of resolving humanitarian cases in the spirit of cooperation.

They believe that there should be greater understanding among our peoples and that to this end they will encourage greater travel and people-to-people contact.

Northern Pacific air safety

The two leaders also noted with satisfaction that, in cooperation with the Government of Japan, the United States and the Soviet Union have agreed to a set of measures to promote safety on air routes in the North Pacific and have worked out steps to implement them.

Civil aviation/consulates

They acknowledged that delegations from the United States and the Soviet Union have begun negotiations aimed at resumption of air services. The two leaders expressed their desire to reach a mutually beneficial agreement at an early date. In this regard, an agreement was reached on the simultaneous opening of Consulates General in New York and Kiev.

Environmental protection

Both sides agreed to contribute to the preservation of the environment – a global task – through joint research and practical measures. In accordance with the existing US-Soviet agreement in this area, consultations will be held next year in Moscow and Washington on specific programs of cooperation.

Exchange initiatives

The two leaders agreed on the utility of broadening exchanges and contacts including some of their new forms in a number of scientific, educational, medical and sports fields (*inter alia*, cooperation in the development of educational exchanges and software for elementary and secondary school instruction; measures to promote Russian language studies in the United States and English language studies in the USSR; the annual exchange of professors to conduct special courses in history, culture and economics at the relevant departments of Soviet and American institutions of higher education; mutual allocation of scholarships for the best students in the natural sciences, technology, social sciences and humanities for the period of an academic year; holding regular meets in various sports and increased television coverage of sports events). The two sides agreed to resume cooperation in combating cancer diseases.

The relevant agencies in each of the countries are being instructed to develop specific programs for these exchanges. The resulting programs will be reviewed by the leaders at their next meeting.

Fusion research

The two leaders emphasized the potential importance of the work aimed at utilizing controlled thermonuclear fusion for peaceful purposes and, in this connection, advocated the widest practicable development of international cooperation in obtaining this source of energy, which is essentially inexhaustible, for the benefit of all mankind.

Source: *Survival*, vol 28, no 2 (Mar/Apr 1986)

STATEMENT BY MIKHAIL GORBACHEV

15 January 1986

A new year, 1986, has begun. It will be an important year, one might say a turning point in the history of the Soviet state, the year of the 27th Congress of the CPSU. The Congress will chart the guidelines for the political, social, economic and intellectual development of Soviet society in the period up to the next millennium. It will adopt a programme for accelerating our peaceful construction.

All efforts of the CPSU are directed towards ensuring a further improvement of the life of the Soviet people.

A turn for the better is also needed on the international scene. This is the expectation and the demand of the peoples of the Soviet Union and of the peoples throughout the world.

Being aware of this, at the very start of the new year the Political Bureau of the CPSU Central Committee and the Soviet Government have adopted a decision on a number of major foreign policy measures that are of a fundamental nature. They are designed to promote to a maximum degree an improvement of the international situation. They are prompted by the need to overcome the negative confrontational tendencies that have been growing in recent years and to clear the way towards curbing the nuclear arms race on earth and preventing it in outer space, towards an overall reduction of the war danger and towards confidence-building as an integral part of relations among states.

I.

The most important of these measures is a concrete programme aimed at the complete elimination of nuclear weapons throughout the world within a precisely defined period of time.

The Soviet Union proposes that a step-by-step, consistent process of ridding the earth of nuclear weapons be implemented and completed within the next 15 years, before the end of this century.

The 20th century has given mankind the gift of the energy of the atom. However, this great achievement of the human intellect can turn into an instrument of mankind's self-annihilation.

Is it possible to resolve this contradiction? We are convinced that it is possible. Finding effective ways of eliminating nuclear weapons is a feasible task, provided it is tackled without delay.

The Soviet Union proposes that a programme of ridding mankind of the fear of a nuclear catastrophe be carried out beginning in 1986. The fact that this year has been proclaimed by the United Nations the International Year of Peace provides an additional political and moral stimulus for this. What is required here is that we should rise above national selfishness, tactical considerations, differences and disputes, whose significance is nothing compared to the preservation of what is most cherished – peace and a secure future. The energy of the atom should be placed solely at the service of peace, a goal that our socialist state has consistently pursued and continues to pursue.

Our country was the first to raise, back in 1946, the question of prohibiting the production and use of atomic weapons and to make nuclear energy serve peaceful purposes, for the benefit of mankind.

How does the Soviet Union envisage today in practical terms the process of reducing nuclear weapons, both delivery vehicles and warheads, up to their complete elimination? Our proposals on this subject can be summarized as follows.

Stage One. Within the next 5 to 8 years the USSR and the USA will reduce by one half the nuclear weapons that can reach each other's territory. As for the remaining delivery vehicles of this kind, each side will retain no more than 6,000 warheads.

It stands to reason that such a reduction is possible only if both the USSR and the USA renounce the development, testing and deployment of space-strike weapons. As the Soviet Union has repeatedly warned, the development of space-strike weapons will dash the hopes for a reduction of nuclear armaments on earth.

The first stage will include the adoption and implementation of a decision on the complete elimination of medium-range missiles of the USSR and the USA in the European zone – both ballistic and cruise missiles – as a first step towards ridding the European continent of nuclear weapons.

At the same time the United States should undertake not to transfer its strategic and medium-range missiles to other countries, while Britain and France should pledge not to build up their respective nuclear arsenals.

The USSR and the USA should from the very beginning agree to stop all nuclear explosions and call upon other states to join in such a moratorium as soon as possible.

The reason why the first stage of nuclear disarmament should concern the Soviet Union and the United States is that it is they who should set an example for the other nuclear powers. We said that very frankly to President Reagan of the United States during our meeting in Geneva.

Stage Two. At this stage, which should start no later than 1990 and last for 5 to 7 years, the other nuclear powers will begin to join the process of nuclear disarmament. To start with, they would pledge to freeze all their nuclear arms and not to have them on the territories of other countries.

In this period the USSR and the USA will continue to carry out the reductions agreed upon during the first stage and also implement further measures aimed at eliminating their medium-range nuclear weapons and freezing their tactical nuclear systems.

Following the completion by the USSR and the USA of a 50-per-cent reduction of their respective armaments at the second stage, another radical step will be taken: all nuclear powers will eliminate their tactical nuclear weapons, i.e. weapons having a range (or radius of action) of up to 1,000 kilometres.

At this stage the Soviet-US accord on the prohibition of space-strike weapons would become multilateral, with the mandatory participation in it of major industrial powers.

All nuclear powers would stop nuclear weapon tests.

There would be a ban on the development of non-nuclear weapons based on new physical principles, whose destructive power is close to that of nuclear arms or other weapons of mass destruction.

Stage Three will begin no later than 1995. At this stage the elimination of all remaining nuclear weapons will be completed. By the end of 1999 there will be no nuclear weapons on earth. A universal accord will be drawn up that such weapons should never again come into being.

We envisage that special procedures will be worked out for the destruction of nuclear weapons as well as for the dismantling, re-equipment or scrapping of delivery vehicles. In the process, agreement will be reached on the number of weapons to be scrapped at each stage, the sites of their destruction and so on.

Verification of the destruction or limitation of arms should be carried out both by national technical means and through on-site inspections. The USSR is ready to reach agreement on any other additional verification measures.

Adoption of the nuclear disarmament programme that we are proposing would unquestionably have a favourable impact on the negotiations conducted at bilateral and multilateral forums. The programme would envisage clearly-defined routes and reference points, establish a specific time-table for achieving agreements and implementing them and would make the negotiations purposeful and task-oriented. This would stop the dangerous trend whereby the momentum of the arms race is greater than the progress of negotiations.

Thus, we propose that we should enter the third millennium without nuclear weapons, on the basis of mutually acceptable and strictly verifiable agreements. If the United States Administration is indeed committed to the goal of the complete elimination of nuclear weapons everywhere, as it has repeatedly stated, it now has a practical opportunity to carry it out in practice. Instead of spending the next 10 to 15 years in developing new space weapons, which are extremely dangerous for mankind, weapons, allegedly designed to make nuclear arms unnecessary, would it not be more sensible to start eliminating those weapons and finally doing away with them altogether? The Soviet

Union, I repeat, proposes precisely that.

The Soviet Union calls upon all peoples and states, and, naturally, above all nuclear states, to support the programme of eliminating nuclear weapons before the year 2000. It is absolutely clear to any unbiased person that if such a programme is implemented, nobody would lose and all stand to gain. This is a problem common to all mankind and it can and must be solved only through joint efforts. And the sooner this programme is translated into practical deeds, the safer life on our planet will be.

Guided by the same approach, and a desire to take another practical step within the context of the nuclear disarmament programme, the Soviet Union has adopted an important decision.

We are extending by three months our unilateral moratorium on all nuclear explosions, which expired on December 31, 1985. Such a moratorium will remain in force even longer if the United States for its part also stops nuclear tests. We propose once again to the United States that it join this initiative whose significance is evident practically to everyone in the world.

Obviously the adoption of such a decision has by no means been simple for us. The Soviet Union cannot display unilateral restraint with regard to nuclear tests indefinitely. But the stakes are too high and the responsibility too great for us not to try every possibility of influencing the position of others by force of example.

All experts, scientists, politicians and military men agree that the cessation of tests would indeed reliably block the channels of perfecting nuclear weapons. And this is a top-priority task. A reduction of nuclear arsenals alone, without a prohibition of nuclear weapon tests, does not provide a way out of the dilemma of nuclear threat, since the remaining weapons would be modernized and there would still be the possibility of developing increasingly sophisticated and lethal nuclear weapons and appraising their new types at test ranges.

Therefore, the cessation of tests is a practical step towards eliminating nuclear weapons.

I wish to say the following at the outset. Any references to verification as an obstacle to the establishment of a moratorium on nuclear explosions are totally groundless. We declare unequivocally that for us verification is not a problem. Should the United States agree to stop all nuclear explosions on a reciprocal basis, appropriate verification of compliance with the moratorium would be fully ensured by national technical means as well as with the help of international procedures including on-site inspections when necessary. We invite the United States to reach agreement with us to this effect.

The USSR resolutely stands for making the moratorium a bilateral, and later, a multilateral measure. We are also in favour of resuming the tripartite negotiations, involving the USSR, the USA and Great Britain, on the complete and general prohibition of nuclear weapon tests. This could be done immediately, even this month. We are also prepared to begin without delay multilateral test-ban negotiations within the framework of the Geneva Conference on Disarmament, with all nuclear powers taking part.

Non-aligned countries have proposed that consultations be held with the aim of extending the 1963 Moscow Treaty Banning Nuclear Weapon Tests in the Atmosphere, in Outer Space and Under Water to cover also underground tests, whose ban is not envisaged in the Treaty. The Soviet Union agrees to this, too.

Since last summer we have been calling upon the United States to follow our example and stop nuclear explosions. Washington has not yet done that despite protests and demands on the part of the public, and contrary to the will of most states in the world. By carrying out more and more nuclear explosions the US side continues to pursue its elusive dream of achieving military superiority. This policy is futile and dangerous, a policy which is not worthy of the level of civilization that modern society has attained.

In the absence of a positive response from the United States, the Soviet side had every right to resume nuclear tests starting January 1, 1986. If one were to follow the usual 'logic' of the arms race, that, presumably, would have been the thing to do.

But the whole point is that it is precisely that logic, if one can call it that, that has to be resolutely rejected. We are making yet another attempt in this direction. Otherwise the process of military rivalry will assume gigantic proportions and any control over the course of events would be impossible. To yield to the anarchic force of the nuclear arms race is impermissible. This would be acting against reason and the human instinct of self-preservation. What is required are new and bold arroaches, fresh political thinking and a hightened sense of responsibility for the destinies of the peoples.

The US Administration is once again given more time to consider our proposals on stopping nuclear explosions and to give a positive answer to them. It is this kind of response that people everywhere in the world will expect from Washington.

The Soviet Union appeals to the President and Congress of the United States, to the American people: there is an opportunity to halt the process of perfecting nuclear arms and developing new weapons of that kind. The opportunity must not be missed. The Soviet proposals put the USSR and the United States in an equal position. These proposals are not an attempt to outwit or outsmart the other side. We propose embarking on a road of sensible and responsible decisions.

III.

In order to implement the programme of reducing and eliminating nuclear arsenals, it is necessary to activate the entire existing system of negotiations and to ensure the highest possible efficiency of the disarmament mechanism.

In a few days the Soviet-American talks on nuclear and space arms will be resumed in Geneva. When we met with President Reagan last November in Geneva, we had a frank discussion on the whole range of problems which are the subject of those neogtiations, namely on space, strategic offensive armaments and medium-range nuclear systems. It was agreed that the negotiations should be accelerated and this agreement must not remain a mere declaration.

The Soviet delegation in Geneva will be instructed to act in strict compliance with that agreement. We expect the same constructive approach from the US side, above all on the question of space. Space must remain peaceful, strike weapons must not be deployed there. Neither must they be developed. And there must also be introduced very strict control, including the opening of relevant laboratories for inspection.

Mankind is at a crucial stage of the new space age. And it is time to abandon the thinking of the stone age, when the chief concern was to have a bigger stick or a heavier stone. We are against weapons in space. Our material and intellectual capabilities make it possible for the Soviet Union to develop any weapon if we are compelled to do so. But we are fully aware of our responsibility to the present and future generations. It is our profound conviction that we should approach the third millennium not with the Star Wars programme, but with large-scale projects of peaceful space exploration by all mankind. We propose to start practical work in developing and implementing such projects. This is one of the most important ways of ensuring progress on our entire planet and establishing a reliable system of security for all.

To prevent the arms race from spreading to outer space means to remove the obstacle barring the way to drastic reductions in nuclear weapons. On the negotiating table in Geneva is a Soviet proposal to reduce by one half the corresponding nuclear arms of the Soviet Union and the United States, which would be an important step towards the complete elimination of nuclear weapons. To block all possibility of resolving the problem of space, indicates a lack of desire to stop the arms race on earth. This should be stated in clear and straightforward terms. It is not by chance that the proponents of the nuclear arms race are also ardent supporters of the Star Wars programme. These are two sides of the same policy, hostile to the interests of people.

Let me turn to the European aspect of the nuclear problem. It is a matter of extreme concern that in defiance of reason and contrary to the national interests of the European peoples, American first-strike missiles continue to be deployed in certain West European countries. This problem has been under discussion for many years now. Meanwhile the security situation in Europe continues to deteriorate.

It is time to put an end to this course of events and cut this Gordian knot. The Soviet Union has long been proposing that Europe should be freed of both medium-range and tactical nuclear weapons. This proposal remains valid. As a first radical step in this direction we now propose, as I have said, that even at the first stage of our programme all medium-range ballistic and cruise missiles of the USSR and the USA in the European zone should be eliminated.

The achievement of tangible practical results at the Geneva talks would give meaningful material substance to our programme to eliminate nuclear arms completely by the year 2000.

IV.

The Soviet Union considers the task of completely eliminating still in this century such barbaric weapons of mass destruction as chemical weapons fully feasible.

At the talks on chemical weapons within the framework of the Geneva Conference on Disarmament certain signs of progress have recently become evident. However, these talks have been inadmissibly drawn out. We are in favour of intensifying the talks on the conclusion of an effective and justifiable international convention prohibiting chemical weapons and destroying the existing stockpiles of those weapons, as was agreed upon with US President Reagan at Geneva.

In the matter of banning chemical weapons, as in other disarmament matters, all participants in the talks should take a fresh look at things. I would like to make it perfectly clear that the Soviet Union is in favour of prompt and complete elimination of those weapons and of the industrial base for their production. We are prepared to make a timely announcement of the location of enterprises producing chemical weapons and ensure the cessation of their production; we are ready to start developing procedures for destroying the corresponding industrial base and to proceed, soon after the convention enters into force, to eliminate the stockpiles of chemical weapons. All these measures would be carried out under strict control, including international on-site inspections.

A radical solution to this problem would also be facilitated by certain interim steps. For example, agreement could be reached on a multi-lateral basis not to transfer chemical weapons to anyone and not to deploy them in the territories of other states. As for the Soviet Union, it has always strictly abided by these principles in its practical policies. We call upon other states to follow this example and exercise equal restraint.

V.

In addition to eliminating weapons of mass destruction from the arsenals of states, the Soviet Union proposes that conventional weapons and armed forces become subject to agreed-upon reductions.

Reaching an agreement at the Vienna negotiations could signal the beginning of progress in this direction. It now appears that an outline is discernable of a possible decision to reduce Soviet and US troops and subsequently freeze the level of armed forces of the opposing sides in Central Europe. The Soviet Union and our Warsaw Treaty allies are determined to achieve success at the Vienna talks. If the other side also truly wants this, 1986 could become a landmark for the Vienna talks too. We proceed from the understanding that a possible agreement on troop reductions would naturally require reasonable verification. We are prepared for this. As for observing the commitment to freeze the number of troops, in addition to national technical means permanent verification posts could be established to monitor any military contingents entering the reduction zone.

Let me now mention such an important forum as the Stockholm Conference on Confidence- and Security-Building Measures and disarmament in Europe. It is called upon to create barriers against the use of force or covert preparations for war, whether on land, at sea or in the air. The possibilities for this have now become evident.

In our view, especially in the current situation, it is essential to reduce the number of troops participating in major military manoeuvres which are notifiable under the Helsinki Final Act.

It is time to begin dealing effectively with the problems still outstanding at the Conference. The bottleneck there, as we know, is the issue of notifications regarding major ground force, naval and air force exercises. Of course, these are serious problems and they must be addressed in a serious manner in the interests of building confidence in Europe. However, if their comprehensive solution cannot be achieved at this time, why not explore ways for partial solution, for instance reach an agreement now about notifications of major ground force and air force exercises, postponing the question of naval activities until the next stage of the Conference.

It is not by chance that a significant part of the new Soviet initiatives is addressed directly to Europe. Europe could play a special role in bringing about a radical turn towards the policy of peace. That role is to erect a new edifice of detente.

For this Europe has a necessary, often unique historical experience. Suffice it to recall that the joint efforts of the Europeans, the United States and Canada produced the Helsinki Final Act. If there is a need for a specific and vivid example of new thinking and political psychology in approaching the problems of peace, cooperation and international trust, that historic document could in many ways serve as such an example.

VI.

Ensuring security in Asia is of vital importance to the Soviet Union, a major Asian power. The Soviet programme for eliminating nuclear and chemical weapons by the end of the current century is harmonious with the sentiments of the peoples of the Asian continent, for whom the problems of peace and security are no less urgent than for the peoples of Europe. In this context one cannot fail to recall that Japan and its cities of Hiroshima and Nagasaki became the victims of the nuclear bomb and Vietnam – a target for chemical weapons.

We highly appreciate the constructive initiatives put forward by the socialist countries of Asia, by India and other members of the non-aligned movement. We view as very important the fact that the two Asian nuclear powers, the USSR and the People's Republic of China, have undertaken a pledge not to be the first to use nuclear weapons.

The implementation of our programme would fundamentally change the situation in Asia, rid the nations in that part of the globe as well of the fear of nuclear and chemical warfare, bring security in that region to a qualitatively new level.

We see our programme as a contribution to a search, together with all the Asian countries, for an overall comprehensive approach to establishing a system of secure and lasting peace on this continent.

VII.

Our new proposals are addressed to the entire world. Initiating active steps to halt the arms race and reduce weapons is a necessary prerequisite for coping with increasingly acute global problems – those of the deteriorating state of man's environment and of the need to find new energy sources and combat economic backwardness, hunger and disease. The pattern imposed by militarism – arms in place of development – must be replaced by the reverse order of things – disarmament for development. The noose of the trillion-dollar foreign debt, currently strangling dozens of countries and entire continents, is a direct consequence of the arms race. The more than 250,000 million dollars annually siphoned out of the developing countries is practically equal to the size of the mammoth US military budget. Indeed, this is no chance coincidence.

The Soviet Union wants each measure limiting and reducing arms and each step towards eliminating nuclear weapons not only to bring nations greater security but also to make it possible to allocate more funds for improving people's life. It is natural that the peoples seeking to put an end to backwardness and rise to the level of industrially developed countries associate the prospects of freeing themselves from the burden of foreign debt to imperialism, which is draining their economies, with limiting and eliminating weapons, reducing military expenditures and transferring resources to the goals of social and economic development. This subject will undoubtedly figure most prominently at the international conference on disarmament and development to be held in Paris next summer.

The Soviet Union is opposed to making the implementation of disarmament measures dependent on so-called regional conflicts. Behind this lie both an unwillingness to follow the path of disarmament and a desire to impose upon sovereign nations what is alien to them and a system that would make it possible to maintain profoundly unfair conditions whereby some countries live at the expense of others, exploiting their natural, human and intellectual resources for the selfish imperial purposes of individual states or aggressive alliances. The Soviet Union will continue as before to oppose this. It will continue consistently to advocate freedom for the peoples, peace, security, and a stronger international legal order. The Soviet Union's goal is not to whip up regional conflicts but to eliminate them through collective efforts on a just basis, and the sooner the better.

There is no shortage today of statements professing commitment to peace. What is in short supply are concrete actions to strengthen the foundations of peace. All too often peaceful words conceal war preparations and power politics. Moreover, some statements made from high rostrums are in fact intended to eliminate any trace of that new 'spirit of Geneva' which is having a salutary effect on international relations today. It is not only a matter of statements. There are also actions clearly designed to incite animosity and mistrust, to revive confrontation, the antithesis of detente.

We reject such a way of acting and thinking. We want 1986 to be not just a peaceful year but one that will enable us to reach the end of the 20th century under the sign of peace and nuclear disarmament. The set of new foreign policy initiatives we are proposing is intended to make it possible for mankind to approach the year 2000 under peaceful skies and with a peaceful outer space, without fear of nuclear, chemical or any other threat of annihilation and fully confident of its own survival and of the continuation of the human race.

The new resolute measures being taken by the Soviet Union to defend peace and improve the overall international situation give expression to the substance and the spirit of our internal and foreign policies and their organic unity. They reflect the fundamental historic law which was emphasized by Vladimir Lenin. The whole world sees that our country is holding high the banner of peace, freedom and humanism which was raised over our planet by the Great October Revolution.

In questions of preserving peace and saving mankind from the threat of nuclear war, let no one remain indifferent or stand aloof. This concerns all and everyone. Each state, large or small, socialist or capitalist, has an important contribution to make. Every responsible political party, every public organization and every person can also make an important contribution.

No task is more urgent, more noble or humane, than that of uniting all efforts to achieve this lofty goal. This task must be accomplished by our generation, not shifted onto the shoulders of those who will succeed us. This is the imperative of our time. This, I would say, is the burden of historic responsibility for our decisions and actions in the time remaining until the beginning of the third millennium.

The course of peace and disarmament will continue to be pivotal in the foreign policy of the CPSU and the Soviet state. In actively pursuing this course, the Soviet Union is prepared to engage in wide-ranging cooperation with all those who proceed from positions of reason, good will and an awareness of the responsibility to ensure mankind's future – a future without wars or weapons.

Source: Novosti, 1 January 1985

APPEAL BY THE WARSAW TREATY MEMBER STATES TO THE MEMBER STATES OF NATO AND TO ALL EUROPEAN COUNTRIES FOR THE REDUCTION OF ARMED FORCES AND CONVENTIONAL ARMAMENTS IN EUROPE

11 June 1986

The Warsaw Treaty member states, being aware of their responsibility to their respective peoples and to mankind for the peace of Europe and the world at large and seeking a radical change for the better in the current complicated international situation, are of the view that now, more than ever, there is a need for taking resolute action and concrete measures aimed at ending the arms race, proceeding to effective disarmament and averting the danger of war.

They support the programme proposed by the Soviet Union for the complete and comprehensive liquidation of nuclear and other types of weapons of mass destruction by the end of this century. They are convinced that the cessation of nuclear testing, the achievement of nuclear disarmament and the prevention of the arms race in outer space, a ban on and the liquidation of chemical weapons and other disarmament measures would be conducive to bringing about a more secure world for the people of Europe and the entire globe.

The allied states favour an integral approach to disarmament problems and that the liquidation of weapons of mass destruction be supported by significant cuts in armed forces and conventional armaments. With the liberation of Europe from nuclear weapons, the problem of the reduction of armed forces and conventional armaments will acquire an ever greater significance for the present and future of the European continent. It is on this continent that the two largest groupings of armed forces face each other. They are equipped with the most up-to-date armaments with the combat potential of some systems of conventional armaments tending to reach that of mass-destruction weapons. The allied states seek to ensure that concrete nuclear disarmament measures and cuts in conventional armaments and armed forces are followed by appropriate reductions in the military spending of the states.

213

Guided by these considerations, the Warsaw Treaty member states present the following proposals to all the other European states, to the United States of America and Canada. They constitute a significant supplement to the programme for the elimination of weapons of mass destruction. At the same time they bear an independent character. Their realization would substantially reduce the danger of war in Europe.

I.

The Warsaw Treaty member states propose a substantial reduction in the land and tactical air forces of the European states and in the corresponding forces of the United States and Canada stationed in Europe. Simultaneously with conventional armaments, tactical nuclear weapons with a range of up to 1,000 kilometres should also be reduced.

The geographical zone of reduction includes the whole of Europe, from the Atlantic Ocean to the Urals.

The reduction of armed forces and conventional armaments in Europe should be carried out gradually at agreed times, with the military balance maintained at ever lower levels and without jeopardizing the security of any of the parties. Parallel to the units and troops under reduction their armaments and equipment including nuclear means would also be reduced.

As a first step, a single mutual reduction is proposed to be carried out in such a way that the troop strength of the countries belonging to the opposing military-political alliances be cut by 100,000–150,000 troops on each side within one or two years. Cuts in tactical air forces as part of these measures would be of great significance. Immediately afterwards, given the willingness of the NATO countries to act likewise, the Warsaw Treaty member states are ready to carry out further significant reductions, as a result of which the land forces and tactical air forces of both military alliances in Europe would, by the early 1990s, be reduced by some 25% as compared with present levels. Such reductions would amount to more than half a million troops on each side, thus the opposing armed forces in Europe would be reduced by over 1 million troops.

The allied socialist states stand for continuing the process of reductions in the armed forces and armaments of NATO and the Warsaw Treaty. Significant reductions in the armed forces and armaments of the two alliances would make it possible for other European countries to join this process.

The components of armed forces to be reduced should be demobilized in the form of equivalent complete formations and units, together with their arms and equipment. Troops would be discharged in accordance with established procedures in the given state.

Armaments and equipment subject to reduction could be destroyed or stored on national territories in accordance with agreed procedures. Nuclear warheads are to be destroyed. Certain types of military equipment could, subject to agreement, be transferred for peaceful purposes.

Funds becoming available as a result of appropriate reductions in armed forces and conventional armaments must not be allocated to the creation of new types of weapons or to other military purposes; they must be used for economic and social development.

All signatories to a treaty on the reduction of armed forces and armaments would take over the responsibility not to increase their land forces and tactical air forces outside the area of reduction.

II.

The Warsaw Treaty member states propose to work out such a system of reductions in armed forces and conventional armaments under which the process of reduction would result in a lessening of the danger of surprise attack and would consolidate the strategic stability on the European continent. With this end in view, at the very beginning of the process agreement should be reached on a significant reduction in the tactical air forces of the two military political alliances in Europe and on lowering the level of troop concentration along the dividing line between the two alliances.

For the same purpose, supplementary measures should be elaborated and implemented which were suitable for strengthening the conviction of the countries of the Warsaw Treaty and NATO and the other states of Europe that no surprise attacks would be launched against them.

Agreement should be reached on limiting the number and size of larger military exercises, on exchanging more detailed information about them, i.e. the size of forces and equipment regrouped to Europe from other regions for the period of military exercises, and on taking other confidence-building measures.

The implementation of measures like the establishment of nuclear and chemical weapon-free zones on the European continent, gradual reduction in the military activities of the two military alliances, cooperation among their member states on questions of arms reduction and disarmament would facilitate the strengthening of confidence and the creation of more favourable conditions for the reduction of armed forces and armaments in Europe.

III.

The reduction of armed forces and conventional armaments should be accompanied by reliable and effective verification through both national technical means and international procedures including on-site inspection.

Apart from verifying the reduction process the military activities of troops remaining after reductions will be observed.

Appropriate forms of verification should be found concerning measures to strengthen mutual confidence, in keeping with the agreements.

For purposes of verification the parties will exchange, at an agreed date: data on the total troop strengths of their land forces and tactical air forces stationed in the zone of reduction and separately on their components to be reduced and on those not affected by the reduction; information concerning the designation of the formations to be reduced (dismantled), their troops strength, location, and the quantity of their main types of weapons agreed upon. The parties would notify each other of the beginning and completion of the reduction.

For purposes of verification, an international consultative committee will be formed with the participation of representatives of NATO and the Warsaw Treaty as well as of interested neutral and non-aligned and other countries of Europe.

On-site inspections of the reduction of armed forces, the destruction or mothballing of armaments could be carried out, if necessary, with the involvement of representatives of the international consultative committee. For purposes of such supervision posts of control, composed of representatives of the international consultative committee, would be set up at major railway junctions, airports and harbours.

IV.

The present proposals for the reduction of armed forces and conventional armaments in Europe could be the subject of concrete discussion in the second stage of the conference on confidence- and security-building measures and disarmament in Europe.

At the same time, keeping in mind the pressing urgency of taking measures to lower the level of military confrontation in Europe, the Warsaw Treaty member states would consider it possible to proceed without delay to explore the proposals presented here. To this end, they deem it possible to convene a special forum with the participation of the European states as well as the United States and Canada.

They are also prepared to widen the framework of the Vienna negotiations on the mutual reduction of armed forces and armaments in Central Europe through the inclusion of other European States and the corresponding modification of the terms of reference of those negotiations.

While expressing their readiness to make use of all possible channels and forums for mutually lowering the level of military confrontation on an all-European scale, they reaffirm their interest in reducing armaments and armed forces in Central Europe and come out once again for a successful conclusion of the first stage of the Stockholm Conference.

V.

In terms of the assessment of the real intentions of military-political groupings and individual states the question of military doctrines is no less important. The mutual suspicion and distrust accumulated over many years must be dispelled. The two sides must be thoroughly acquainted with their mutual concerns. For the sake of European and world security the military concepts and doctrines of the military alliances must be of a defensive character.

The Warsaw Treaty member states declare with full responsibility that they will never, under any circumstances, initiate military actions against any other state, whether in Europe or in another region of the world, if they themselves are not victims of aggression. Their proposals stem from their consistent policy aimed at the elimination of the war danger and the creation of a stable and secure peace, from the defensive character of their military doctrine which presupposes the maintenance of armed forces at the lowest possible level and the reaction of military capabilities to a level indispensable for defence.

The member states of the Warsaw Treaty were guided by the same peaceful intentions when they presented their proposals for the simultaneous dissolution of the two military alliances.

The member states of NATO also profess the defensive nature of their alliance. Consequently there should be no obstacle to mutual and significant reductions of armed forces and conventional armaments in Europe.

In presenting this Appeal, the Warsaw Treaty member states set no preliminary conditions for starting the objective discussion of the proposals contained therein. They are ready to consider, in a creative spirit, other relevant proposals formulated either by the NATO member states, by neutral and non-aligned or other states of Europe.

Source: *Arms Control Reporter*, Brookline, U.S.

ADDRESS TO THE NATION
BY PRESIDENT RONALD REAGAN

13 October 1986

As most of you know, I have just returned from meetings in Iceland with the leader of the Soviet Union, General Secretary Gorbachev. As I did last year when I returned from the summit conference in Geneva, I want to take a few moments tonight to share with you what took place in these discussions.

The implications of these talks are enormous and only just beginning to be understood. We proposed the most sweeping and generous arms control proposal in history. We offered the complete elimination of all ballistic missiles – Soviet and American – from the face of the Earth by 1996. While we parted company with this American offer still on the table, we are closer than ever before to agreements that could lead to a safer world without nuclear weapons.

But first, let me tell you that, from the start of my meetings with Mr. Gorbachev, I have always regarded you, the American people, as full participants. Believe me, without your support, none of these talks could have been held, nor could the ultimate aims of American foreign policy – world peace and freedom – be pursued. And it is for these aims I went the extra mile to Iceland.

Before I report on our talks though, allow me to set the stage by explaining two things that were very much a part of our talks, one a treaty and the other a defense against nuclear missiles which we are trying to develop. Now you've heard their titles a thousand times – the ABM Treaty and SDI. Those letters stand for, ABM, anti-ballistic missile, SDI, strategic defense initiative.

Some years ago, the United States and the Soviet Union agreed to limit any defense against nuclear missile attacks to the emplacement in one location in each country of a small number of missiles capable of intercepting and shooting down incoming nuclear missiles, thus leaving our real defense – a policy called Mutual Assured Destruction, meaning if one side launched a nuclear attack, the other side could retailiate. And this mutual threat of destruction was believed to be a deterrent against either side striking first.

So here we sit with thousands of nuclear warheads targeted on each other and capable of wiping out both our countries. The Soviets deployed the few anti-ballistic missiles around Moscow as the treaty permitted. Our country didn't bother deploying because the threat of nationwide annihilation made such a limited defense seem useless.

For some years now we have been aware that the Soviets may be developing a nationwide defense. They have installed a large modern radar at Krasnoyarsk which we believe is a critical part of a radar system designed to provide radar guidance for anti-ballistic missiles protecting the entire nation. Now this is a violation of the ABM Treaty.

Now, this policy is now paying dividends – one sign of this in Iceland was the progress on the issue of arms control. For the first time in a long while, Soviet-American negotiations in the area of arms reductions are moving, and moving in the right direction – not just toward arms control, but toward arms reduction.

But for all the progress we made on arms reductions, we must remember there were other issues on the table in Iceland, issues that are fundamental.

As I mentioned, one such issue is human rights. As President Kennedy once said, 'And, is not peace, in the last analysis, basically a matter of human rights?'

I made it plain that the United States would not seek to exploit improvement in these matters for purposes of propaganda. But I also made it plain, once again, that an improvement of the human condition within the Soviet Union is indispensable for an improvement in bilateral relations with the United States. For a government that will break faith with its own people cannot be trusted to keep faith with foreign powers. So, I told Mr. Gorbachev – again in Reykjavik as I had in Geneva – we Americans place far less weight upon the words that are spoken at meetings such as these, than upon the deeds that follow. When it comes to human rights and judging Soviet intentions, we're all from Missouri – you got to show us.

Another subject area we took up in Iceland also lies at the heart of the differences between the Soviet Union and America. This is the issue of regional conflicts. Summit meetings cannot make the American people forget what Soviet actions have meant for the peoples of Afghanistan, Central America, Africa, and Southeast Asia. Until Soviet policies change, we will make sure that our friends in these areas – those who fight for freedom and independence – will have the support they need.

Finally, there was a fourth item. And this area was that of bilateral relations, people-to-people contacts. In Geneva last year, we welcomed several cultural exchange accords; in Iceland, we saw indications of more movement in these areas. But let me say now the United States remains committed to people-to-people programs that could lead to exchanges between not just a few elite but thousands of everyday citizens from both our countries.

So I think, then, that you can see that we did make progress in Iceland on a broad range of topics. We reaffirmed our four-point agenda; we discovered major new grounds of agreement; we probed again some old areas of disagreement.

And let me return again to the SDI issue. I realize some Americans may be asking tonight: Why not accept Mr. Gorbachev's demand? Why not give up SDI for this agreement?

Well, the answer, my friends, is simple. SDI is America's insurance policy that the Soviet Union would keep the commitments made at Reykjavik. SDI is America's security guarantee – if the Soviets should – as they have done too often in the past – fail to comply with their solemn commitments. SDI is what brought the Soviets back to arms control talks at Geneva and Iceland. SDI is the key to a world without nuclear weapons.

The Soviets understand this. They have devoted far more resources for a lot longer time than we, to their own SDI. The world's only operational missile defense today surrounds Moscow, the capital of the Soviet Union.

Secretary Shultz suggested we turn over the notes our note-takers had been making of everything we'd said to our respective teams and let them work through the night to put them together and find just where we were in agreement and what differences separated us. With respect and gratitude, I can inform you those teams worked through the night till 6:30 a.m.

Yesterday, Sunday morning, Mr. Gorbachev and I, with our foreign ministers, came together again and took up the report of our two teams. It was most promising. The Soviets had asked for a 10-year delay in the deployment of SDI programs.

In an effort to see how we could satisfy their concerns while protecting our principles and security, we proposed a 10-year period in which we began with the reduction of all strategic nuclear arms, bombers, air-launched cruise missiles, intercontinental ballistic missiles, submarine launched ballistic missiles and the weapons they carry. They would be reduced 50 percent in the first five years. During the next five years, we would continue by eliminating all remaining offensive ballistic missiles, of all ranges. And during that time we would proceed with research, development and testing of SDI – all done in conformity with ABM provisions. At the 10-year point, with all ballistic missiles eliminated, we could proceed to deploy advanced defenses, at the same time permitting the Soviets to do likewise.

And here the debate began. The General Secretary wanted wording that, in effect, would have kept us from developing the SDI for the entire 10 years. In effect, he was killing SDI. And unless I agreed, all that work toward eliminating nuclear weapons would go down the drain – cancelled.

I told him I had pledged to the American people that I would not trade away SDI – there was no way I could tell our people their government would not protect them against nuclear destruction. I went to Reykjavik determined that everything was negotiable except two things: our freedom and our future.

I'm still optimistic that a way will be found. The door is open and the opportunity to begin eliminating the nuclear threat is within reach.

So you can see, we made progress in Iceland. And we will continue to make progress if we pursue a prudent, deliberate, and, above all, realistic approach with the Soviets. From the earliest days of our administration, this has been our policy. We made it clear we had no illusions about the Soviets or their ultimate intentions. We were publicly candid about the critical moral distinctions between totalitarianism and democracy. We declared the principal objective of American foreign policy to be not just the prevention of war but the extension of freedom. And, we stressed our commitment to the growth of democratic government and democratic institutions around the world. And that's why we assisted freedom fighters who are resisting the imposition of totalitarian rule in Afghanistan, Nicaragua, Angola, Cambodia, and elsewhere. And, finally, we began work on what I believe most spurred the Soviets to negotiate seriously – rebuilding our military strength, reconstructing our strategic deterrence, and, above all, beginning work on the Strategic Defense Initiative.

And yet, at the same time we set out these foreign policy goals and began working toward them, we pursued another of our major objectives: that of seeking means to lessen tensions with the Soviets, and ways to prevent war and keep the peace.

What Mr. Gorbachev was demanding at Reykjavik was that the United States agree to a new version of a 14-year-old ABM Treaty that the Soviet Union has already violated. I told him we don't make those kinds of deals in the United States.

And the American people should reflect on these critical questions.

How does a defense of the United States threaten the Soviet Union or anyone else? Why are the Soviets so adamant that America remain forever vulnerable to Soviet rocket attack? As of today, all free nations are utterly defenseless against Soviet missiles – fired either by accident or design. Why does the Soviet Union insist that we remain so – forever?

So, my fellow Americans, I cannot promise, nor can any President promise, that the talks in Iceland or any future discussions with Mr. Gorbachev will lead inevitably to great breakthroughs or momentous treaty signings.

We will not abandon the guiding principle we took to Reykjavik. We prefer no agreement than to bring home a bad agreement to the United States.

And on this point, I know you're also interested in the question of whether there will be another summit. There was no indication by Mr. Gorbachev as to when or whether he plans to travel to the United States, as we agreed he would last year in Geneva. I repeat tonight that our invitation stands and that we continue to believe additional meetings would be useful. But that's a decision the Soviets must make.

But whatever the immediate prospects, I can tell you that I'm ultimately hopeful about the prospects for progress at the summit and for world peace and freedom. You see, the current summit process is very different from that of previous decades; it's different because the world is different; and the world is different because of the hard work and sacrifice of the American people during the past five and a half years. Your energy has restored and expanded our economic might; your support has restored our military strength. Your courage and sense of national unity in times of crisis have given pause to our adversaries, heartened our friends, and inspired the world. The Western democracies and the NATO alliance are revitalized and all across the world nations are turning to democratic ideas and the principles of the free market. So because the American people stood guard at the critical hour, freedom has gathered its forces, regained its strength, and is on the march.

So, if there's one impression I carry away with me from these October talks, it is that, unlike the past, we're dealing now from a position of strength, and for that reason we have it within our grasp to move speedily with the Soviets towards even more breakthroughs.

Our ideas are out there on the table. They won't go away. We're ready to pick up where we left off. Our negotiators are heading back to Geneva, and we're prepared to go forward whenever and wherever the Soviets are ready. So, there's reason – good reason for hope.

I saw evidence of this in the progress we made in the talks with Mr. Gorbachev. And I saw evidence of it when we left Iceland yesterday, and I spoke to our young men and women at our naval installation at Keflavik – a critically important base far closer to Soviet naval bases than to our own coastline.

As always, I was proud to spend a few moments with them and thank them for their sacrifices and devotion to country. They represent America at her finest: committed to defend not only our own freedom but the freedom of others who would be living in a far more frightening world – were it not for the strength and resolve of the United States.

'Whenever the standard of freedom and independence has been . . . unfurled, there will be America's heart, her benefictions, and her prayers,' John Quincy Adams once said. He spoke well of our destiny as a nation. My fellow Americans, we're honored by history, entrusted by destiny with the oldest dream of humanity – the dream of lasting peace and human freedom.

Another President, Harry Truman, noted that our century had seen two of the most frightful wars in history. And that 'The supreme need of our time is for man to learn to live together in peace and harmony.'

It's in pursuit of that ideal I went to Geneva a year ago and to Iceland last week. And it's in pursuit of that ideal that I thank you now for all the support you've given me, and I again ask for your help and your prayers as we continue our journey toward a world where peace reigns and freedom is enshrined.

Source: White House Press Office

SPEECH BY GENERAL SECRETARY OF THE CPSU CENTRAL COMMITTEE MIKHAIL GORBACHEV ON SOVIET TELEVISION

14 October 1986

As you know, my meeting in Iceland with the President of the United States, Ronald Reagan, concluded the day before yesterday, on Sunday. A press conference on its results has been televised. The text of my statement and my replies to journalists have been published.

Having returned home, I consider it my duty to tell you how the meeting went and how we assess what took place in Reykjavik.

The results of the meeting in the capital of Iceland have just been discussed at a meeting of the Politburo of the CPSU Central Committee. A report will be published tomorrow outlining the opinion our Party's leadership has formed about this major political event, the consequences of which, we are convinced, will be felt in international relations for a long time to come.

Before Reykjavik much was said and written about the forthcoming meeting. As is usually the case in such situations, there was a myriad of conjectures and views. This is normal. And in this case, there was speculation as well.

Now that the meeting is over its results are in the centre of attention of the world public. Everybody wants to know: What happened? What results did it produce? What will the world be like after it?

We strove to give the main questions of world politics – ending the arms race and nuclear disarmament – top priority at the meeting in Reykjavik. And that is how it was.

What are the motives for our persistence in this matter? One often hears conjectures abroad that the reason lies in our domestic difficulties. There is a thesis in Western calculations that the Soviet Union will ultimately be unable to endure the arms race economically, that it will break down and bow to the West. One need only squeeze the Soviet Union harder and step up the position of strength. Incidentally, the US President made a remark to this effect in an address after our meeting.

I have said repeatedly that such plans are not only built on air; they are dangerous as they may result in fatal political decisions. We know our own problems better than anyone else. We do have problems which we openly discuss and resolve. We have our own plans and approaches on this score, and there is a common will of the Party and the people. In general, I would have to say that the Soviet Union's strength today lies in its unity, dynamism, and the political activity of its people. I think that these trends and, consequently, the strength of our society will be growing. The Soviet Union has the capacity to respond to any challenge, should the need arise. The Soviet people know this; the whole world should know this, too. But we are opposed to playing power games, for this is an extremely dangerous thing in the nuclear-missile age.

We are firmly convinced that the protracted feverish state of international relations harbours the threat of a sudden and fatal crisis. We must take practical steps away from the nuclear abyss. We need joint Soviet-American efforts, efforts on the part of the entire international community in order to radically improve international relations.

For the sake of these goals we, the Soviet leadership, carried out extensive preparatory work on the eve of the meeting, even before we received President Reagan's consent to attend it. Taking part in this work, in addition to the Politburo and the Secretariat of the CPSU Central Committee, were the Ministry of Foreign Affairs and the Defence Ministry, plus some other departments, representatives of science, military experts, and specialists from various branches of industry. The positions we worked out for the Reykjavik meeting were the result of wide-scale, repeated discussion with our friends, with the leaderships of the socialist community countries. We sought to make the content of the meeting as meaningful as possible, putting forth far-reaching proposals.

Now about the meeting itself, how events developed there. This should be discussed not only in order to affirm the truth, which is already being distorted by our partners in the Reykjavik talks, but, more importantly, to inform you of what we plan to do next.

The first conversation with President Reagan started on Saturday, at 10.30 a.m. After the greetings necessary on such occasions and a brief conference with journalists, the two of us remained alone; only our interpreters were present. We exchanged views on the general situation, on the way the dialogue between our two countries was developing, and outlined the problems to be discussed.

Then I asked the President to listen to our concrete proposals on the main questions which prompted our meeting. I already spoke at length about them during the press conference. Still, I will recall them here in brief.

A whole **set of major measures** was submitted to the talks. These measures, if accepted, would usher in a new era in the life of mankind – a nuclear-free era. Herein lies the essence of the radical change in the world situation, the possibility of which was obvious and realistic. The talk was no longer about limiting nuclear arms, as was the case with the SALT-1, SALT-2 and other treaties, but about the elimination of nuclear weapons within a comparatively short period of time.

The first proposal concerned strategic offensive weapons. I expressed our readiness to reduce them by fifty per cent within the next five years. The strategic weapons on land, water and in the air would be halved. In order to make it easier to reach accord, we agreed to a major concession by revoking our previous demand that the strategic equation include American medium-range missiles reaching our territory and American forward-based systems. We were also ready to take into account the US concern over our heavy missiles. We regarded the proposal on strategic arms in the context of their total elimination, as we had suggested on January 15 this year.

Our second proposal concerned medium-range missiles. I suggested to the President that both Soviet and American missiles of this class in Europe be completely eliminated. Here, too, we were willing to make a substantial concession: we stated that, contrary to our previous stand, the nuclear-missile weapons of Britain and France need not be taken into account. We proceeded from the necessity to pave the way to detente in Europe, to free the European nations of the fear of a nuclear catastrophe, and then to move further – towards the elimination of all the nuclear weapons. You will agree that this was another bold step on our part.

Anticipating the possible objections, we said we would agree to freeze missiles with a range of under 1,000 km and immediately begin talks on what is to be done with them in the future. As for the medium-range missiles in the Asian part of our country – this issue was invariably present in President Reagan's 'global version' – we suggested that talks be started immediately on this subject as well. As you see, here, too, our proposals were serious and far-reaching, facilitating a radical solution of this problem as well.

The third question I raised during my first talk with the President, one that formed an integral part of our proposal package, was the existing **Anti-Ballistic Missile (ABM) Treaty and the Nuclear Test Ban Treaty**. Our approach is as follows: Since we are entering a totally new situation which will witness the beginning of substantial reductions in nuclear weapons and their complete elimination in the foreseeable future, it is necessary to protect oneself from any unexpected developments. We are speaking of weapons which to this day make up the core of this country's defences. Therefore, it is necessary to exclude everything that could undermine equality in the process of disarmament, to preclude any chance of developing weapons of a new type which would ensure military superiority. We regard this stance as perfectly legitimate and logical.

This being the case, we have firmly stated the need for strict observance of the 1972 ABM Treaty of unlimited duration. Moreover, in order to consolidate its regime, we proposed to the President that a mutual pledge be taken by the US and the Soviet Union to refrain from pulling out of the treaty for at least ten years, during which time strategic weapons would be abolished.

Taking into account the particular difficulties the Administration created for itself on this problem when the President personally committed himself to space weapons, to the so-called SDI, we did not demand termination of work in this field. The implication was, however, that all provisions of the ABM Treaty would be fully honoured – that is, research and testing in this sphere would not go beyond laboratories. This restriction applies equally to the USA and to the USSR.

Listening to us, the President made remarks, asked for clarification on certain points. During the conversation, we presented the question of verification firmly and with resolve, linking it with the post-nuclear situation. This situation demands special responsibility. I told the President that if both countries embark on nuclear disarmament, the Soviet Union will make its position on verification stricter. Verification must be plausible, comprehensive and indisputable. It must create full confidence in reliable compliance with the agreement and include the right to on-site inspection.

I must tell you, comrades, that the President's initial reaction was not entirely negative. He even said: 'What you have just stated is reassuring.' But it did not escape our attention that our American interlocutors (George Shultz as well as Comrade Shevardnadze had joined the conversation on these issues by then) appeared to be somewhat confused. At the same time, immediate doubts and objections cropped up in their separate remarks. Straight away, the President and the Secretary of State started talking about divergencies and disagreement. In their words we clearly discerned the familiar old tones we had heard at the Geneva negotiations for many months: we were reminded of all sorts of sublevels on strategic nuclear armaments, the 'interim proposal' on missiles in Europe, and that we, the Soviet Union, should join the SDI and should replace the existing ABM Treaty with some new agreement, and many other things in the same vein.

I expressed my surprise. How can this be? We propose to accept the American 'zero option' in Europe and take up negotiations on medium-range missiles in Asia while you, Mr. President, are abandoning your previous stand. This is incomprehensible.

As for ABM, we propose to preserve and strengthen this fundamentally important agreement, and you want to give it up and even propose to replace it with some new treaty, and thereby – following renunciation of SALT-2 – to wreck this mechanism standing guard over strategic stability. This, too, is incomprehensible.

We grasped the essence of the SDI plans as well, I said. If the United States creates a three-tiered ABM system in outer space, we shall respond to it. However, we are concerned about another problem: the SDI would mean the transfer of weapons to a new medium, which would destabilize the strategic situation, make it even worse than it is today. If this is the United States' purpose, this should be stated plainly. But if you really want reliable security for your people and for the world in general, then the American stand is totally ungrounded.

I told the President directly: We have put forward major new proposals. However, what we are hearing from you now is precisely what everybody is fed up with and what can lead us nowhere. Mr. President, please, re-examine our proposals carefully and give us an answer point by point. I gave him an English translation of a draft of possible instructions that had been drawn up in Moscow and which, in the event that agreement is reached in principle, could be given to the Foreign Ministers and other departments to draw up **three draft agreements**. They could be signed later during my visit to the USA.

In the afternoon we met again. The President announced the stand that had been drawn up during the break. As soon as he uttered the first phrases, it became clear that they were offering us the same old moth-eaten trash, as I put it at the press conference, from which the Geneva talks are already choking: all sorts of intermediate versions, figures, levels, sublevels and so on. There was not a single new thought, fresh approach or idea which would contain even a hint of a solution, of advance.

It was becoming clear, comrades, that the Americans had come to Reykjavik with nothing at all to offer. The impression was that they had come there empty-handed to gather fruits in their basket.

The situation was taking a dramatic turn.

The American President was not ready to take any radical decisions on questions of principle, to meet the Soviet side halfway so as to give a real impetus to productive and encouraging negotiations. This is precisely what I impressed upon the President in my letter, in which I put forward the idea that an urgent meeting be held in order to give a powerful impetus at the level of the top leaders of the two countries – an impetus to negotiations on nuclear disarmament.

Confident that our proposals were well-balanced and took the partner's interests into account, we decided not to abandon our efforts to bring about a breakthrough at the meeting. A ray of hope on strategic armaments appeared, following many clarifying questions. Clinging to this we took one more great step in search of a compromise. I told the President: We both recognize that there is a triad of strategic offensive armaments: ground-based missiles, strategic submarines and strategic bombers. So let us make a 50-per-cent reduction in each part of the triad. And then there will be no need for all sorts of levels and sublevels, for all sorts of calculations.

After lengthy debate, we managed to reach mutual understanding on that issue.

Then the discussion turned to the problem of medium-range missiles. The Americans stubbornly stuck to the so-called interim proposal which provides for the preservation of a part of their missiles, including Pershing-2 missiles, in Europe, and, naturally, of our corresponding SS-20 missiles. We categorically opposed this, for reasons I have already described. Europe deserves to be free of nuclear weapons, to stop being held nuclear hostage. As for the President, it was difficult for him to fight his own 'zero option', which he had promoted for so long. And still, we sensed the Americans' intention to thwart agreement under the guise of special concern for their allies in Asia.

The American side said much that was ungrounded. It is embarrassing to repeat it here. The talks began to move forward only when on this issue, too, we took one more step to meet the American side and agreed to the following formula: zero missiles in Europe, 100 warheads on medium-range missiles in the eastern part of our country and, accordingly, 100 warheads on medium-range missiles on US territory. Most importantly, we managed to agree on eliminating nuclear weapons on the European continent.

Thus, accord was reached on the problem of medium-range missiles, too, and a major breakthrough was made in this direction of nuclear disarmament. The American Administration failed to hold out against our insistent striving to achieve positive results.

However, there still remained the ABM issue and the ban on nuclear explosions.

Two groups of experts, one from each side, worked through the night before we met on Sunday for our third talk, which was scheduled to be the concluding one. They thoroughly analysed what had been discussed at the two previous meetings with the President and reported the results of their night-time debates respectively to the President and myself.

The result? **A possibility arose of undertaking to work out agreements on strategic offensive armaments and on medium-range missiles**.

The ABM Treaty in this situation acquired key significance; its role was becoming even more important. Could one destroy, I asked, what has made it possible so far to somehow restrain the arms race? If we now begin reducing strategic and medium-range nuclear weapons, both sides should be confident that during that time nobody will develop new systems which would undermine stability and parity. Therefore, in my view, it would be perfectly logical to fix the timeframe – the Americans mentioned seven years, and we proposed ten years – within which nuclear weapons must be eliminated. We proposed ten years during which neither the Soviet nor the American side may avail itself of the right – and they have such a right – to withdraw from the ABM Treaty, and during which research and tests may be conducted in laboratories only.

Thus, I think, you understand why we chose exactly ten years? This was no random choice. The logic is plain and fair. Fifty per cent of strategic armaments is to be reduced in the first five years, the other half – in the next five years. This makes ten years.

In connection with this I proposed that our high-ranking representatives be instructed to start full-scale talks on the discontinuation of nuclear explosions and thus in the end an agreement could at last be worked out completely banning explosions. In the course of working out the agreement – and here again we displayed flexibility and assumed a constructive stand – specific issues connected with nuclear explosions could be resolved.

The reasoning President Reagan used in his response is a familiar one to us in that we have come across it earlier both in Geneva and in his public statements: SDI is a defence system. If we begin eliminating nuclear weapons, how will we protect ourselves from some madman who might get hold of them? And Reagan is ready to share with us the results obtained within the research done on SDI. In answering this last remark, I said: Mr. President, I do not take this idea seriously, your idea about sharing with us the results of research on SDI. You do not even want to share with us oil equipment or equipment for the dairy industry, and still you expect us to believe your promise to share the research developments in the SDI project. That would be something like a 'Second American Revolution', and revolutions do not occur that often. I told President Reagan that we should be realists and pragmatists. This is a more reliable approach for the issues at hand are very serious.

By the way, when trying to justify his position on SDI yesterday, the President said that he needed this program to ensure that America and its allies remain invulnerable to a Soviet missile attack. As you see, he did not even make any mention of madmen. And the 'Soviet threat' was again brought to light.

But this is nothing but a trick. We proposed that not only strategic armaments, but also all the nuclear armaments in the possession of the US and the USSR, be eliminated under strict control.

How can there be a need to protect the 'freedom of America' and its friends from Soviet nuclear misiles if these missiles no longer exist?

If there are no nuclear weapons, why should we need to protect ourselves from them? Thus the entire 'Star Wars' undertaking is purely militaristic in nature and is directed at obtaining military superiority over the Soviet Union.

Let us return, however, to the talks. Although an agreement on strategic arms and medium-range missiles had been reached, it was premature to believe that everything had been completely settled as a result of the two first sessions. An entire day was ahead, nearly eight hours of non-stop and intense discussions in which these issues, which seemed to have been agreed upon already, were to be raised again and again.

The President sought to touch upon ideological issues as well in these discussions and in this way demonstrated, to put it mildly, total ignorance and the inability to understand both the socialist world and what is happening there. I rejected the attempts to link ideological differences to issues of ending the arms race. I persistently drew the President and the Secretary of State back to the subject that had brought us to Reykjavik. It was necessary to remind our interlocutors repeatedly about the third element of our package of proposals, without which it would be impossible to reach accord on the whole. I have in mind the need to comply strictly with the ABM Treaty, to consolidate the regime of this major treaty and to ban nuclear tests.

We had to draw attention again and again to things that seemed to be perfectly clear: having agreed to major reductions in nuclear arms, attempts – both in deed and in thought – to shake strategic stability and to circumvent the agreements should be made to be impossible. That is why we should have confidence in the preservation of the ABM Treaty which has no time-limit. You, Mr. President, I said, ought to agree that if we are beginning to reduce nuclear weapons, there should be the full assurance that the US will not do anything behind the back of the USSR, while the Soviet Union will also not do anything to jeopardize US security, to disvalue the agreement or to create difficulties.

Hence the key task to strengthen the ABM regime: to keep the results of the research under this program in the laboratory and prevent them from being applied in outer space. It is necessary that the right to pull out of the ABM Treaty is not used for ten years in order to create the confidence that in settling the issue of arms reduction at the same time we are ensuring security for both sides and for the world as a whole.

But the Americans obviously had other intentions. We saw that the US actually wants to defeat the ABM Treaty, to revise it so as to develop a large-scale space-based ABM system for its own conceited ends. It would simply be irresponsible of me to agree to this.

As far as nuclear testing is concerned, it was perfectly clear here as well why the American side does not want to conduct serious talks on this issue. It would have preferred to carry these talks on endlessly and thus postpone the settlement of the issue of banning nuclear tests for decades. And once again we had to reject attempts to use the talks as a cover and to get a free hand in the field of nuclear explosions. I said bluntly that I was having doubts about the honesty of the US position and questioned whether there wasn't something in it damaging for the Soviet Union. How can an agreement on the elimination of nuclear arms be reached if the United States continues to perfect these weapons? Still we were under the impression that the SDI was the main snag. If it could have been removed it would have been possible to reach an accord on banning nuclear explosions as well.

At a certain point in the talks, when it became absolutely clear that to continue the discussion would be a waste of time, I reminded the other side that we had proposed a definite package of measures and asked them to consider it as such. If we have worked out a common position on the possibility of making major reductions in nuclear arms and at the same time have failed to reach agreement on the issue of ABM and nuclear testing, then everything we have tried to create here falls apart, I said.

The President and the Secretary of State reacted poorly to our firm position, but I could not pose the question in any other way. This is a matter concerning the security of our country, the security of the entire world, all peoples and all continents.

Our proposals were major, truly large-scale and clearly in the nature of compromise. We made concessions. But we did not see even the slightest desire on the American side to respond in kind or to meet us halfway. We were deadlocked. We began thinking about how to conclude the meeting. And nevertheless we continued our efforts to engage our partners in constructive dialogue.

During the conversation that was supposed to be the concluding one we ran out of time. Instead of going our separate ways – we to Moscow and they to Washington – yet another break was announced to allow the sides to think everything over and meet one more time after dinner. On returning to the house of the city's mayor after the break, we made yet another attempt to end the meeting successfully. We proposed the following text as the basis for summing up the positive results.

Here is the text:

'The Soviet Union and the United States will oblige themselves not to use their right to withdraw from the ABM Treaty, which has no time-limit, for a period of ten years and during this period to ensure strict observance of all of its provisions. All testing on the space elements of the ABM defence in outer space will be prohibited excluding research and testing conducted in laboratories.

'In the first five years of this decade (until 1991 inclusive) the strategic offensive arms of both sides will be reduced by 50 per cent.

'In the next five years of this period the remaining 50 per cent of the strategic offensive arms of both sides will be eliminated.

'Thus, the strategic offensive arms of the USSR and the USA will be completely eliminated by the end of the year 1996.'

Commenting on this text, I made an important addition in reference to the document which had been given to the President at the end of our first conversation. This document is basically a proposal to hold special negotiations after the ten years are up and nuclear weapons no longer exist in order to work out mutually acceptable decisions as to what should be done next.

But this time, too, our attempts to reach an agreement were to no avail. For four hours we again tried to make our interlocutors understand that our approach was well founded, that it was not at all threatening, and did not affect the interests of the genuine security of the United States. But with every hour it became more obvious that the Americans would not agree to keep SDI research and testing in the laboratories. They are bent on going into outer space with weapons.

I said firmly that we would never agree to help undermine the ABM Treaty with our own hands. We consider this an issue of principle, as well as a national security issue.

We were thus literally two or three steps from making possibly historic decisions for the entire nuclear-space era, but we were unable to make those last steps. A turning point in the world's history did not take place, even though, I will say again with full confidence, it could have.

Our conscience is clear, however, and we cannot be reproached. We did everything we could.

The scope of our partners' approach was not broad enough. They did not grasp the uniqueness of the moment and, ultimately, they did not have enough courage, sense of responsibility or political resolve which are all so needed to settle key and pressing issues in world politics. They stuck to old positions which had already eroded with time and did not correspond to the realities of today.

Foreigners in Iceland and my comrades here have asked me what, in my opinion, were the main reasons for the attitude of the American delegation at the Reykjavik meeting? There are a number of reasons, both subjective and objective, but the main one is that the leadership of that great country relies too heavily on the military-industrial complex, on the monopolistic groups which have turned the nuclear and other arms races into a business, into a way of making money, into the object of their existence and the meaning of their activities.

In my opinion, the Americans are making two serious mistakes in their assessment of the situation.

The first is a tactical mistake. They believe that sooner or later the Soviet Union will reconcile itself to the fact that the US is attempting to revive its strategic diktat, that it will agree to the limitation and reduction of only Soviet weapons. It will do so because, so they think, the USSR is more interested in disarmament agreements than the USA. But this is a grave delusion. The sooner the US Administration overcomes it – I repeat perhaps for the hundredth time – the better it will be for them, for our relations and for the world situation in general.

The other mistake is a strategic one. The United States seeks to exhaust the Soviet Union economically with a build-up of sophisticated and costly space arms. It wants to impose hardships of all kinds on the Soviet leadership, to foil its plans, including those in the special sphere and those for improving our people's living standards, and thus spread among the people discontent in regard to their leaders and the country's leadership. Another aim is to restrict the Soviet Union's potential in its economic ties with developing countries which, in such a situation, would all be compelled to bow down before the United States. These are far-reaching designs. The strategic course of the current US Administration also rests on delusions. Washington, it seems, does not wish to burden itself with a thorough analysis of the changes taking place in our country, does not wish to draw the appropriate practical conclusions for itself and for its course, but is rather busy with wishful thinking. It is building its policy toward the USSR on the basis of this delusion. It is, of course, difficult to predict all the long-term consequences of such a policy. One thing is clear to us already now: it will not and it cannot benefit anyone, including the United States.

Before addressing you, I read through the US President's statement on Reykjavik. I noticed that the President gives himself all the credit for all the proposals discussed. Well, it seems as though these proposals are so attractive to the Americans and the peoples throughout the world that it's possible to resort to such a ruse. We are not consumed by vanity, but it is important that people get the true picture of what happened in Reykjavik.

So what is next? I already said at the press conference that the work done before the meeting and that done in Reykjavik was not in vain. We ourselves did a lot of thinking in connection with the meeting and re-examined a great deal. We have now better cleared the way to continue the fight for peace and disarmament. We freed ourselves from obstructions that had developed, from insignificant issues, and from stereotypes which hindered new approaches in the important area of our policies.

We know where we stand and see the possibilities available to us more clearly. The preparations for the Reykjavik meeting helped us to formulate a platform – a new, bold platform which promises greater chances for ultimate success. It meets the interests of our people and society at this new stage of socialist development. This platform also meets the interests of other countries and nations and thereby merits trust. We are confident that it will be received with understanding in many countries of the world and in the most differing political and public circles.

I think that many people around the world, including leaders vested with power, can and must draw weighty conclusions from the Reykjavik meeting. Everyone will have to think again and again about the essence of the matter, and about why such persistent efforts to achieve a breakthrough and start advancing toward a non-nuclear world and toward universal security have thus far failed to produce the needed result.

I would like to hope that the President also has a better insight now into our analysis, the intentions of the Soviet Union, and into the possibilities and limits for adjusting the Soviet stand. And I hope Mr. Reagan understands our analysis more fully and more precisely since receiving first-hand explanations of our constructive measures for stabilising and improving the international situation.

The American leadership will obviously need some time. We are realists and we clearly understand that the issues that have remained unsettled for many years and even decades can hardly be settled at a single sitting. We have a great deal of experience in doing business with the United States. And we are aware that the domestic political climate can change there quickly and that the opponents of peace across the ocean are strong and influential. There is nothing new here for us.

If we do not despair, if we do not slam the door and give vent to our emotions – although there is more than enough reason for this – it is because we are sincerely convinced that new efforts are needed aimed at building normal interstate relations in the nuclear epoch. There is no other alternative.

And another thing: after Reykjavik, the infamous SDI became even more conspicuous as an epitome of obstructing peace, as a strong expression of militaristic designs and an unwillingness to get rid of the nuclear threat looming over mankind. It is impossible to perceive this program in any other way. This is the most important lesson of the Reykjavik meeting.

In summing up these eventful days, I would like to say the following. The meeting was a major event. A reappraisal was made. A qualitatively new situation developed in that no one can continue to act as he acted before. The meeting was useful. It paved the way for a possible step forward, for a real positive shift, should the USA finally adopt realistic positions and abandon delusion in its appraisals.

The meeting has convinced us that the path we have chosen is correct and that a new mode of political thinking in the nuclear age is necessary and constructive.

We are energetic and determined. Having embarked on a program of reorganisation, the country has already traversed a certain path. We have just started this process, but changes have already been made. Growth in industrial production over the past nine months reached 5.2 per cent, labour productivity grew by 4.8 per cent. National production income rose 4.3 per cent as compared to the previous year.

This all is the strongest support for the Party's policies on the part of the people for this is the support by deed.

This shows that under new conditions the people's efforts are helping to accelerate the growth of the country's economic potential and are thus consolidating its defence capabilities.

The Soviet people and the Soviet leadership have unanimously agreed that the policy of socialism can and must be a policy of peace and disarmament. We shall not swerve from the course of the 27th CPSU Congress.

Source: Novosti, 14 October 1986

STATEMENT ON THE MINISTERIAL MEETING OF THE NORTH ATLANTIC COUNCIL AT REYKJAVIK

11–12 June 1987

Serious imbalances in the conventional, chemical and nuclear field, and the persisting build-up of Soviet military power, continue to preoccupy us. We reaffirm that there is no alternative, as far as we can foresee, to the Alliance concept for the prevention of war – the strategy of deterrence, based on an appropriate mix of adequate and effective nuclear and conventional forces, each element being indispensable. This strategy will continue to rest on the linkage of free Europe's security to that of North America since their destinies are inextricably coupled. Thus the US nuclear commitment, the presence of United States nuclear forces in Europe [1] and the deployment of Canadian and United States forces there remain essential.

Arms control and disarmament are integral parts of our security policy; we seek effectively verifiable arms control agreements which can lead to a more stable and secure balance of forces at lower levels.

We reiterate the prime importance we attach to rapid progress towards reductions in the field of strategic nuclear weapons. We thus welcome the fact that the US and the Soviet Union now share the objective of achieving 50% reductions in their strategic arsenals. We strongly endorse the presentation of a US proposal in Geneva to that effect and urge the Soviet Union to respond positively.

We reviewed the current phase of the US-Soviet negotiations in Geneva on defence and space systems which aim to prevent an arms race in space and to strengthen strategic stability. We continue to endorse these efforts.

We note the recent progress achieved at the Geneva Conference on Disarmament towards a total ban on chemical weapons. We remain committed to achieving an early agreement on a comprehensive, worldwide and effectively verifiable treaty embracing the total destruction of existing stockpiles within an agreed timeframe and preventing the future production of such weapons.

Recognising the increasing importance of conventional stability, particularly at a time when significant nuclear reductions appear possible, we reaffirm the initiatives taken in our Halifax Statement and Brussels Declaration aimed at achieving a comprehensive, stable and verifiable balance of conventional forces at lower levels. We recall that negotiations on conventional stability should be accompanied by negotiations between the 35 countries participating in the CSCE, building upon and expanding the confidence and security building measures contained in the Helsinki Final Act and the Stockholm Agreement. We agreed that the two future security negotiations should take place within the framework of the CSCE process, with the conventional stability negotiations retaining autonomy as regards subject matter, participation and procedures. Building on these agreements we took the decisions necessary to enable the High Level Task Force on Conventional Arms Control, which we established at the Halifax Ministerial, to press ahead with its work on the draft mandates to be tabled in the CSCE meeting and in the Conventional Stability mandate talks currently taking place in Vienna.

Having reviewed progress in the negotiations between the United States and the Soviet Union on an INF agreement the Allies concerned call on the Soviet Union to drop its demand to retain a portion of its SS-20 capability and reiterate their wish to see all long-range land-based missiles eliminated in accordance with NATO's long-standing objective.

They support the global and effectively verifiable elimination of all US and Soviet land-based SRINF missiles with a range between 500 and 1,000 km as an integral part of an INF agreement.

They consider that an INF agreement on this basis would be an important element in a coherent and comprehensive concept of arms control and disarmament which, while consistent with NATO's doctrine of flexible response, would include:

- a 50% reduction in the strategic offensive nuclear weapons of the US and the Soviet Union to be achieved during current Geneva negotiations;
- the global elimination of chemical weapons;
- the establishment of a stable and secure level of conventional forces, by the elimination of disparities, in the whole of Europe;
- in conjunction with the establishment of a conventional balance and the global elimination of chemical weapons, tangible and verifiable reductions of American and Soviet land-based nuclear missile systems of shorter range, leading to equal ceilings.

We [2] have directed the North Atlantic Council in Permanent Session, working in conjunction with the appropriate military authorities, to consider the further development of a comprehensive concept of arms control and disarmament. The arms control problems faced by the Alliance raise complex and interrelated issues which must be evaluated together, bearing in mind overall progress in the arms control negotiations enumerated above as well as the requirements of Alliance security and of its strategy of deterrence.

In our endeavour to explore all opportunities for an increasingly broad and constructive dialogue which addresses the concerns of people in both East and West, and in the firm conviction that a stable order of peace and security in Europe cannot be built by military means alone, we attach particular importance to the CSCE process. We are therefore determined to make full use of the CSCE follow-up meeting in Vienna.

The full implementation of all provisions agreed in the CSCE process by the 35 participating states, in particular in the field of human rights and contacts, remains the fundamental objective of the Alliance and is essential for the fruitful development of East-West relations in all fields.

Recalling our constructive proposals, we shall persist in our efforts to persuade the Eastern countries to live up to their commitments.

We will continue to work for a substantive and timely result of the conference.

Those of us participating in the MBFR talks reiterate our desire to achieve a meaningful agreement which provides for reductions, limitations and effective verification, and call upon the Warsaw Pact participants in these talks to respond positively to the very important proposals made by the West in December 1985 and to adopt a more constructive posture in the negotiations.

In Berlin's 750th anniversary year we stress our solidarity with the City, which continues to be an important element in East-West relations. Practical improvements in inner-German relations should in particular be of benefit to Berliners.

It is just 40 years since US Secretary of State Marshall delivered his far-sighted speech at Harvard. The fundamental values he expressed, which we all share, and which were subsequently embodied in the Marshall Plan, remain as vital today as they were then.

We reiterate our condemnation of terrorism in all its forms. Reaffirming our determination to combat it, we believe that close international co-operation is an essential means of eradicating this scourge.

Alliance cohesion is substantially enhanced by the support of freely elected parliamentary representatives and ultimately our publics. We therefore underline the great value of free debate on issues facing the Alliance and welcome the exchanges of views on these issues among the parliamentarians of our countries, including those in the North Atlantic Assembly.

We express our gratitude to the government of Iceland, which makes such a vital contribution to the security of the Alliance's northern maritime approaches, for their warm hospitality.

1   Greece recalls its position on nuclear matters.
2   In this connection France recalled that it had not been a party to the double-track decision of 1979 and that it was not therefore bound by its consequences or implications.

Source: NATO

WESTERN EUROPEAN UNION: PLATFORM ON EUROPEAN SECURITY INTERESTS

The Hague, 27 October 1987

Stressing the dedication of our countries to the principles upon which our democracies are based and resolved to preserve peace in freedom, we, the Foreign and Defence Ministers of the member States of WEU, reaffirm the common destiny which binds our countries.

We recall our commitment to build a European union in accordance with the Single European Act, which we all signed as members of the European Community. We are convinced that the construction of an integrated Europe will remain incomplete as long as it does not include security and defence.

An important means to this end is the modified Brussels Treaty. This Treaty with its far-reaching obligations to collective defence, marked one of the early steps on the road to European unification. It also envisages the progressive association of other States inspired by the same ideals and animated by the like determination. We see the revitalisation of WEU as an important contribution to the broader process of European unification.

We intend therefore to develop a more cohesive European defence identity which will translate more effectively into practice the obligations of solidarity to which we are committed through the modified Brussels and North Atlantic Treaties.

We highly value the continued involvement in this endeavour of the WEU Assembly which is the only European parliamentary body mandated by treaty to discuss all aspects of security including defence.

I. Our starting point is the present conditions of European security

Europe remains at the centre of East-West relations and, forty years after the end of the Second World War, a divided continent. The human consequences of this division remain unacceptable, although certain concrete improvements have been made on a bilateral level and on the basis of the Helsinki Final Act. We owe it to our people to overcome this situation and to exploit in the interest of all Europeans the opportunities for further improvements which may present themselves.

New developments in East-West relations, particularly in arms control and disarmament, and also other developments, for example in the sphere of technology, could have far-reaching implications for European security.

We have not yet witnessed any lessening of the military build-up which the Soviet Union has sustained over so many years. The geostrategic situation of Western Europe makes it particularly vulnerable to the superior conventional, chemical and nuclear forces of the Warsaw Pact. This is the fundamental problem for European security. The Warsaw Pact's superior conventional forces and its capability for surprise attck and large-scale offensive action are of special concern in this context.

Under these conditions the security of the Western European countries can only be ensured in close association with our North American allies. The security of the Alliance is indivisible. The partnership between the two sides of the Atlantic rests on the twin foundations of shared values and interests. Just as the commitment of the North American democracies is vital to Europe's security, a free, independent and increasingly more united Western Europe is vital to the security of North America.

It is our conviction that the balanced policy of the Harmel Report remains valid. Political solidarity and adequate military strength within the Atlantic Alliance, arms control, disarmament and the search for genuine détente continue to be integral parts of this policy. Military security and a policy of détente are not contradictory but complementary.

II. European security should be based on the following criteria:

1)   It remains our primary objective to prevent any kind of war. It is our purpose to preserve our security by maintaining defence readiness and military capabilities adequate to deter aggression and intimidation without seeking military superiority.

2)   In the present circumstances and as far as we can foresee, there is no alternative to the Western strategy for the prevention of war, which has ensured peace in freedom for an unprecedented period of European history. To be credible and effective, the strategy of deterrence and defence must continue to be based on an adequate mix of appropriate nuclear and conventional forces, only the nuclear element of which can confront a potential aggressor with an unacceptable risk.

3)   The substantial presence of US conventional and nuclear forces plays an irreplaceable part in the defence of Europe. They embody the American commitment to the defence of Europe and provide the indispensable linkage with the US strategic deterrent.

4)   European forces play an essential role: the overall credibility of the Western strategy of deterrence and defence cannot be maintained

without a major European contribution, not least because the conventional imbalance affects the security of Western Europe in a very direct way.

The Europeans have a major responsibility both in the field of conventional and nuclear defence. In the conventional field, the forces of the WEU member States represent an essential part of those of the Alliance. As regards nuclear forces, all of which form a part of deterrence, the cooperative arrangements that certain member States maintain with the United States are necessary for the security of Europe. The independent forces of France and the United Kingdom contribute to overall deterrence and security.

5) Arms control and disarmament are an integral part of Western security policy and not an alternative to it. They should lead to a stable balance of forces at the lowest level compatible with our security. Arms control policy should, like our defence policy, take into account the specific European security interests in an evolving situation. It must be consistent with the maintenance of the strategic unity of the Alliance and should not preclude closer European defence cooperation. Arms control agreements have to be effectively verifiable and stand the test of time. East and West have a common interest in achieving this.

III. The Member States of WEU intend to assume fully their responsibilities:

a. In the field of Western defence

We recall the fundamental obligation of Article V of the modified Brussels Treaty to provide all the military and other aid and assistance in our power in the event of armed attack on any one of us. This pledge, which reflects our common destiny, reinforces our commitments under the Atlantic Alliance, to which we all belong, and which we are resolved to preserve.

It is our conviction that a more united Europe will make a stronger contribution to the Alliance, to the benefit of Western security as a whole. This will enhance the European role in the Alliance and ensure the basis for a balanced partnership across the Atlantic. We are resolved to strengthen the European pillar of the Alliance.

We are each determined to carry our share of the common defence in both the conventional and the nuclear field, in accordance with the principles of risk- and burden-sharing which are fundamental to allied cohesion.

- In the conventional field, all of us will continue to play our part in the on-going efforts to improve our defences;
- In the nuclear field also, we shall continue to carry our share: some of us by pursuing appropriate cooperative arrangements with the US; the UK and France by continuing to maintain independent nuclear forces, the credibility of which they are determined to preserve.

We remain determined to pursue European integration including security and defence and make a more effective contribution to the common defence of the West.

To this end we shall:

- ensure that our determination to defend any member country at its borders is made clearly manifest by means of appropriate arrangements,
- improve our consultations and extend our co-ordination in defence and security matters and examine all practical steps to this end,
- make the best possible use of the existing institutional mechanisms to involve the defence ministers and their representatives in the work of WEU,
- see to it that the level of each country's contribution to the common defence adequately reflects its capabilities,
- aim at a more effective use of existing resources, inter alia by expanding bilateral and regional military cooperation, pursue our efforts to maintain in Europe a technologically advanced industrial base and intensify armaments cooperation,
- concert our policies on crises outside Europe in so far as they may affect our security interests.

Emphasizing the vital contribution of the non WEU members of the Alliance to the common security and defence, we will continue to keep them informed of our activities.

b. In the field of arms control and disarmament

1. We shall pursue an active arms control and disarmament policy aimed at influencing future developments in such a way as to enhance security and to foster stability and cooperation in the whole of Europe. The steadfastness and cohesion of the Alliance and close consultations among all the Allies remain essential if concrete results are to be brought about.

2. We are committed to elaborate further our comprehensive concept of arms control and disarmament in accordance with the Alliance's declaration of 12 June 1987 and we will work within the framework of this concept as envisaged particularly in paragraphs 7 and 8 of this declaration. An agreement between the US and the Soviet Union for the global elimination of land-based INF missiles with a range between 500 and 5500 km will constitute an important element of such an approach.

3. In pursuing such an approach we shall exploit all opportunities to make further progress towards arms reductions, compatible with our security and with our priorities, taking into account the fact that work in this area raises complex and interrelated issues. We shall evaluate them together, bearing in mind the political and military requirements of our security and progress in the different negotiations.

c. In the field of East-West dialogue and cooperation

The common responsibility of all Europeans is not only to preserve the peace but to shape it constructively. The Helsinki Final Act continues to serve as our guide to the fulfilment of the objective of gradually overcoming the division of Europe. We shall therefore continue to make full use of the CSCE process in order to promote comprehensive cooperation among all participating states.

The possibilities contained in the Final Act should be fully exploited. We therefore intend:

- to seek to increase the transparency of military potentials and activities and the calculability of behaviour in accordance with the Stockholm Document of 1986 by further confidence-building measures.
- vigorously to pursue our efforts to provide for the full respect of human rights without which no genuine peace is possible.
- to open new mutually beneficial possibilites in the fields of economy, technology, science and the protection of the environment.
- to achieve more opportunities for the people in the whole of Europe to move freely and to exchange opinions and information and to intensify cultural exchanges,

and thus to promote concrete improvements for the benefit of all people in Europe.

It is our objective to further European integration. In this perspective we will continue our efforts towards closer security cooperation, maintaining coupling with the United States and ensuring conditions of equal security in the Alliance as a whole.

We are conscious of the common heritage of our divided continent, all the people of which have an equal right to live in peace and freedom. That is why we are determined to do all in our power to achieve our ultimate goal of a just and lasting peaceful order in Europe.

Source: Western European Union

US–SOVIET SUMMIT STATEMENT

10 December 1987 (excerpts)

... Ronald W. Reagan, President of the United States of America, and Mikhail S. Gorbachev, General Secretary of the Central Committee of the Communist Party of the Soviet Union, met in Washington on 7–10 December, 1987. ...

The President and the General Secretary affirmed the fundamental importance of their meetings in Geneva and Reykjavik, which laid the basis for concrete steps in a process intended to improve strategic stability and reduce the risk of conflict. They will continue to be guided by their solemn conviction that a nuclear war cannot be won and must never be fought. They are determined to prevent any war between the United States and the Soviet Union, whether nuclear or conventional. They will not seek to achieve military superiority. ...

(I) Arms Control

The INF Treaty

The two leaders signed the treaty between the United States of America and the Union of the Soviet Socialist Republics on the Elimination of their Intermediate-Range and Shorter-Range Missiles. This treaty is historic both for its objective – the complete elimination of an entire class of US and Soviet nuclear arms – and for the innovative character and scope of its verification provisions. This mutual accomplishment makes a vital contribution to greater stability.

Nuclear and Space Talks

... They agreed to instruct their negotiators in Geneva to work toward the completion of the Treaty on the Reduction and Limitation of Strategic Offensive Arms and all integral documents at the earliest possible date, preferably in time for signature of the treaty during the next meeting of leaders of state in the first half of 1988. ...

In so doing, the negotiators should build upon the agreements on 50 percent reductions achieved at Reykjavik as subsequently developed and now reflected in the agreed portions of the Joint Draft START Treaty Text being developed in Geneva, including agreement on ceilings of no more than 1,600 strategic offensive delivery systems, 6,000 warheads, 1,540 warheads on 154 heavy missiles; the agreed rule of account for heavy bombers and their nuclear armament; and an agreement that as a result of the reductions the aggregate throw-weight of the Soviet Union's ICBM and SLBM will be reduced to a level approximately 50 percent below the existing level, and this level will not be exceeded by either side. Such an agreement will be recorded in a mutually satisfactory manner.

As priority tasks, they should focus on the following issues:

(a) The additional steps necessary to ensure that the reductions enhance strategic stability. This will include a ceiling of 4,900 on the aggregate number of ICBM and SLBM warheads within the 6,000 total.

(b) The counting rules governing the number of long-range, nuclear-armed air-launched cruise missiles (ALCM) to be attributed to each type of heavy bomber. The delegations shall define concrete rules in this area.

(c) The counting rules with respect to existing ballistic missiles. The sides proceed from the assumption that existing types of ballistic missiles are deployed with the following number of warheads. In the United States: *Peacekeeper* (MX): 10, *Minuteman* III: 3, *Minuteman* II: 1, *Trident* I: 8, *Trident* II: 8, *Poseidon*: 10. In the Soviet Union: SS-17: 4, SS-19: 6, SS-18: 10, SS-24: 10, SS-25: 1, SS-11: 1, SS-13: 1, SS-N-6: 1, SS-N-8: 1, SS-N-17: 1, SS-N-18: 7, SS-N-20: 10 and SS-N-23: 4. Procedures will be developed that enable verification of the number of warheads on deployed ballistic missiles of each specific type. In the event either side changes the number of warheads declared for a type of deployed ballistic missile, the sides shall notify each other in advance. There shall also be agreement on how to account for warheads on future types of ballistic missiles covered by the Treaty on the Reduction and Limitation of Strategic Offensive Arms.

(d) The sides shall find a mutually acceptable solution to the question of limiting the deployment of long-range, nuclear-armed SLCM. Such limitations will not involve counting long-range, nuclear-armed SLCM within the 6,000 warhead and 1,600 strategic offensive delivery systems limits. The sides committed themselves to establish ceilings on such missiles, and to seek mutually acceptable and effective methods of verification of such limitations, which could include the employment of National Technical Means, cooperative measures and on-site inspection.

(e) Building upon the provisions of the Treaty on the Elimination of Their Intermediate-Range and Shorter-Range Missiles, the measures by which the provisions of the Treaty on the Reduction and Limitation of Strategic Offensive Arms can be verified will, at a minimum, include:

(1) Data exchanges, to include declarations by each side of the number and location of weapon systems limited by the Treaty and of facilities at which such systems are located and appropriate notifications. These facilities will include locations and facilities for production and final assembly, storage, testing, and deployment of systems covered by this Treaty. Such declarations will be exchanged between the sides before the Treaty is signed and

updated periodically after entry into force.

(2) Baseline inspection to verify the accuracy of these declarations promptly after entry into force of the Treaty.

(3) On-site observation of the elimination of strategic systems necessary to achieve the agreed limits.

(4) Continuous on-site monitoring of the perimeter and portals of critical production and support facilities to confirm the output of these facilities.

(5) Short-notice on-site inspection of:

(i) declared locations during the process of reducing to agreed limits;

(ii) locations where systems covered by this Treaty remain after achieving the agreed limit; and

(iii) locations where such systems have been located (formerly declared facilities).

(6) The right to implement, in accordance with agreed-upon procedures, short-notice inspections at locations where either side considers covert deployment, production, storage or repair of strategic offensive arms could be occurring.

(7) Provisions prohibiting the use of concealment or other activities which impede verification by National Technical Means. Such provisions would include a ban on telemetry encryption and would allow for full access to all telemetric information broadcast during missile flight.

(8) Measures designed to enhance observation of activities related to reduction and limitation of strategic offensive arms by National Technical Means. These would include open displays of treaty-limited items at missile bases, bomber bases, and submarine ports at locations and times chosen by the inspecting party.

Taking into account the preparation of the Treaty on Strategic Offensive Arms, the leaders of the two countries also instructed their delegations in Geneva to work out an agreement that would commit the sides to observe the ABM Treaty, as signed in 1972, while conducting their research, development, and testing as required, which are permitted by the ABM Treaty, and not to withdrawn from the ABM Treaty, for a specified period of time. Intensive discussions of strategic stability shall begin not later than three years before the end of thje specified period, after which, in the event the sides have not agreed otherwise, each side will be free to decide its course of action. Such an agreement must have the same legal status as the Treaty on Strategic Offensive Arms, the ABM Treaty, and other similar, legally binding agreements. This agreement will be recorded in a mutually satisfactory manner. Therefore, they direct their delegations to address these issues on a priority basis.

The sides shall discuss ways to ensure predictability in the development of the US–Soviet strategic relationship under conditions of strategic stability, to reduce the risk of nuclear war.

Other Arms Control Issues

The President and the General Secretary reviewed a broad range of other issues concerning arms limitation and reduction. . . .

Nuclear Testing

. . . The United States and Soviet sides have agreed to begin before December 1, 1987, full-scale stage-by-stage negotiations which will be conducted in a single forum. In these negotiations the sides as the first step will agree upon effective verification measures which will make it possible to ratify the US–USSR Threshold Test Ban Treaty of 1974 and Peaceful Nuclear Explosions Treaty of 1976, and proceed to negotiating further intermediate limitations on nuclear testing leading to the ultimate objective of the complete cessation of nuclear testing as part of an effective disarmament process. This process, among other things, would pursue, as the first priority, the goal of the reduction of nuclear weapons and, ultimately, their elimination. For the purpose of the elaboration of improved verification measures for the US–USSR Treaties of 1974 and 1976 the sides intend to design and conduct joint verification experiments at each other's test sites. These verification measures will, to the extent appropriate, be used in further nuclear test limitation agreements which may subsequently be reached.

The leaders also welcomed the prompt agreement by the sides to exchange experts' visits to each other's nuclear testing sites in January 1988 and to design and subsequently to conduct a Joint Verification Experiment at each other's test site. . . .

Nuclear Non-Proliferation

The President and the General Secretary reaffirmed the continued commitment of the United States and the Soviet Union to the non-proliferation of nuclear weapons, and in particular to strengthening the Treaty on the Non-Proliferation of Nuclear Weapons. . . .

Nuclear Risk Reduction Centers

The leaders welcomed the signing on September 15, 1987, in Washington of the agreement to establish Nuclear Risk Reduction Centers in their capitals. The agreement will be implemented promptly.

Chemical Weapons

The leaders expressed their commitment to negotiation of a verifiable, comprehensive and effective international convention on the prohibition and destruction of chemical weapons. They welcomed progress to date and reaffirmed the need for intensified negotiations toward conclusion of a truly global and verifiable convention encompassing all chemical weapons-capable states. . . .

Conventional Forces

. . . The two leaders spoke in favor of early completion of the work in Vienna on the mandate for negotiations on this issue, so that substantive negotiations may be started at the earliest time with a view to elaborating concrete measures. They also noted that the implementation of the provisions of the Stockholm Conference on Confidence- and Security-Building Measures and Disarmament in Europe is an important factor in strengthening mutual understanding and enhancing stability, and spoke in favor of continuing and consolidating this process. The President and the General Secretary agreed to instruct their appropriate representatives to intensify efforts to achieve solutions to outstanding issues. . . .

(II) Human Rights and Humanitarian Concerns

The leaders held a thorough and candid discussion of human rights and humanitarian questions and their place in the US–Soviet dialogue.

(III) Regional Issues

The President and the General Secretary engaged in wide-ranging, frank and businesslike discussion of regional questions, including Afghanistan, the Iran–Iraq War, the Middle East, Cambodia, southern Africa, Central America and other issues. They acknowledged serious differences but agreed on the importance of their regular exchange of views. . . .

(IV) Bilateral Affairs

The President and the General Secretary reviewed in detail the state of US–Soviet bilateral relations. . . .

Bilateral Negotiations

. . . the two leaders called for intensified efforts by their representatives, aimed at reaching mutually advantageous agreements on: commercial maritime issues; fishing; marine search and rescue; radio navigational systems; the US–USSR maritime boundary; and cooperation in the field of transportation and other areas. . . .

People-to-People Contacts and Exchanges

The two leaders took note of progress in implementing the US–Soviet General Exchanges Agreement in the areas of education, science, culture and sports, signed at their November 1985 Geneva meeting, and agreed to continue efforts to eliminate obstacles to further progress in these areas. . . .

Global Climate and Environmental Change Initiative

With reference to their November 1985 agreement in Geneva to cooperate in the preservation of the environment, the two leaders approved a bilateral initiative to pursue joint studies in global climate and environmental change through cooperation in areas of mutual concern, such as protection and conservation of stratospheric ozone, and through increased data exchanges. . . .

Cooperative Activities

The President and the General Secretary supported further cooperation among scientists of the United States, the Soviet Union and other countries in utilizing controlled thermonuclear fusion for peaceful purposes. They affirmed the intention of the United States and the USSR to cooperate with the European Atomic Energy Community (EURATO) and Japan, under the auspices of the International Atomic Energy Agency, in the quadripartite conceptual design of a fusion test reactor.

The two leaders noted with satisfaction progress under the bilateral Agreement on Peaceful Uses of Atomic Energy towards establishing a permanent working group in the field of nuclear reactor safety, and expressed their readiness to develop further cooperation in this area.

The President and the General Secretary agreed to develop bilateral cooperation in combatting international narcotics trafficking. They agreed that appropriate initial consultations would be held for these purposes in early 1988.

They also agreed to build on recent contacts to develop more effective cooperation in ensuring the security of air and maritime transportation.

The two leaders exchanged views on means of encouraging expanded contacts and cooperation on issues relating to the Arctic. They expressed support for the development of bilateral and regional cooperation among the Arctic countries on these matters, including coordination of scientific research and protection of the region's environment.

The two leaders welcomed the conclusion of negotiations to institutionalize the COSPAS/SARSAT space-based global search and rescue system, operated jointly by the United States, the Soviet Union, France and Canada.

Trade

The two sides stated their strong support for the expansion of mutually beneficial trade and economic relations. They instructed their trade ministers to convene the US–USSR Joint Commercial Commission in order to develop concrete proposals to achieve that objective. . . .

Diplomatic Missions

Both sides agreed on the importance of adequate, secure facilities for their respective diplomatic and consular establishments, and emphasized the need to approach problems relating to the functioning of Embassies and Consulates General constructively and on the basis of reciprocity.

(V) Further Meetings

The President and the General Secretary agreed that official contacts at all levels should be further expanded and intensified, with the goal of achieving practical and concrete results in all areas of the US–Soviet relationship.

General Secretary Gorbachev renewed the invitation he extended during the Geneva Summit for President Reagan to visit the Soviet Union. The President accepted with pleasure. The visit will take place in the first half of 1988.

Source: *Survival*, vol 130, No. 3 (May/June 1988)

NORTH ATLANTIC COUNCIL: STATEMENT ON CONVENTIONAL ARMS CONTROL: THE WAY AHEAD

Brussels, 3 March 1988

At Halifax in 1986, our governments issued a clear call to strengthen stability in the whole of Europe through conventional arms control negotiations. At Brussels later that year they elaborated the basic purposes and methods for such negotiations.

The military confrontation in Europe is the result, not the cause, of the painful division which burdens this continent. While seeking to overcome this division in other ways, we also seek security and stability in Europe at the lowest possible level of armaments. Both arms control and adequate defence programmes can contribute towards this goal.

A. The Present Realities

1. The Soviet Union's military presence in Europe, at a level far in excess of its needs for self defence, directly challenges our security as well as our hopes for change in the political situation in Europe. Thus the conventional imbalance in Europe remains at the core of Europe's security concerns. The problem is to a large extent a function of the Warsaw Pact's superiority in key conventional weapon systems. But it is not only a matter of numerical imbalances. Other asymmetries are also important, for example:

    - the Warsaw Pact, based on the Soviet Union's forward-deployed forces, has a capability for surprise attack and large-scale offensive action; the Allies neither have, nor aspire to, such a capability;
    - the countries of the Warsaw Pact form a contiguous land mass; those of the Alliance are geographically disconnected;
    - the Warsaw Pact can generate a massive reinforcement potential from distances of only a few hundred kilometres; many Allied reinforcements need to cross the Atlantic;
    - the Warsaw Pact's military posture and activities are still shrouded in secrecy, whereas those of Allied countries are transparent and under permanent public scrutiny.

2. These asymmetries are compounded by the dominant presence in Europe of the conventional armed forces of the Soviet Union. They

represent 50% of all the active divisions in Europe between the Atlantic and the Urals. This Soviet conventional superiority and its military presence in other Eastern European countries serve a political as well as a military function. They cast a shadow over the whole of Europe.

3.   Conventional arms control is not merely a technical corrective to a self-contained problem. It should be seen in a coherent political and security framework.

B. A Political and Security Framework

4.   We reiterate our conviction that military forces should only exist to prevent war and to ensure self defence, not for the purpose of initiating aggression and not for the purposes of political or military intimidation. Our ability to prevent every kind of war, nuclear or conventional, rests on our capacity and determination to deter any form of aggression. All the Allies' military resources are designed to contribute to that objective. This approach is shared alike both by those Allies who belong to the integrated military organisation and by those who do not.

5.   The relationship between nuclear and conventional forces is complex. The existence of a conventional imbalance in favour of the Warsaw Pact is not the only reason for the presence of nuclear weapons in Europe. The countries of the Alliance are, and will remain, under the threat of Soviet nuclear forces of varying ranges. Although conventional parity would bring important benefits for stability, only the nuclear element can confront a potential aggressor with an unacceptable risk; therefore, for the foreseeable future deterrence will continue to require an adequate mix of nuclear as well as conventional forces.

6.   Hence the determination of our nations to ensure defence preparedness as a means of achieving the stability we seek. We will continue to ensure that our military forces are effective and up-to-date, in particular by:

- continued compliance with the principle of shared risks and responsibilities and acceptance of the priorities essential to the strengthening of our defence capabilities;
- provision of adequate defence expenditure, together with efforts to obtain the greatest return on our defence investment;
- closer cooperation designed to remedy key deficiencies and, in this context, support for recent legislative and other initiatives designed to foster cooperation in the area of conventional armaments, especially research, development, production and procurement;
- helping to meet the needs of the less advantaged Allies in strengthening their conventional defences, thus redressing important existing deficiencies.

7. It will be important that defence and arms control policies remain in harmony in order to ensure their complementary contribution to the security of the countries of the Alliance. In framing their negotiating proposals for conventional stability, the Allies will ensure that the continued requirement for deterrence and defence is not prejudiced; accordingly they will neither make nor accept proposals which would involve an erosion of the Allies' nuclear deterrent capability.

8. Security in Europe involves not just military, but also political, economic and, above all, humanitarian factors. We look forward to a Europe undivided, in which people of all states can freely receive ideas and information; enjoy their fundamental human rights; and determine their own future. Allied forces are stationed outside their national territory to protect these values and to uphold the solidarity of our free Alliance. They cannot therefore be equated with Soviet forces stationed in Eastern Europe. A just and lasting peaceful order in Europe requires that all states enjoy relations of confidence with their own citizens; trust them to make political or economic choices of their own; and allow them to receive information from and exchange ideas with citizens of other states.

9. Conventional arms control talks should be guided by a coherent political vision which reflects these values. It was their adherence to this vision which enabled the Allies to secure a successful outcome to the Stockholm Conference. It is these same considerations that have led the Allies to decide that both the negotiations which they have now proposed, on conventional stability, as well as those on confidence and security building measures, will be undertaken within the framework of the CSCE process.

10. Those on confidence and security building will involve all 35 CSCE signatory states and will have as their objective to build upon and expand the results of the Stockholm Conference; the agreement reached there marked a significant step towards reducing the risk of war in Europe. Fully implemented over time, it would create more transparency and contribute to greater confidence and predictability of military activities in the whole of Europe. The momentum generated by Stockholm must be maintained.

11. At the same time we are conscious of the specific responsibility of the 23 members of the two military alliances in Europe whose forces bear most directly on the essential security relationship in Europe. Hence our decision that distinct and autonomous negotiations on conventional stability should take place between the 23 States.

12. The adoption of mandates for both of the negotiations must be part of a balanced outcome to the Vienna CSCE Follow-up Meeting, which necessitates substantial progress in all areas of the Helsinki Final Act.

C. The Allies' Objectives

13. In accordance with the principles of our approach to conventional arms control, as set out in the Brussels Declaration, our objectives in the forthcoming conventional stability negotiations will be:

- the establishment of a secure and stable balance of conventional forces at lower levels;
- the elimination of disparities prejudicial to stability and security;
- and, as a matter of high priority, the elimination of the capability for launching surprise attack and for initiating large-scale offensive action.

14. This latter capability is the most worrying in relation to the seizure of territory by an aggressor. Its essential ingredient is the forward deployment of conventional forces capable of rapid mobility and high firepower. Tanks and artillery are among the most decisive components, though other elements of combat capability could prove to be similarly significant. Manpower is also important. But not all items of equipment are appropriate for limitation, if only for technical reasons, and manpower alone is an imprecise guide to offensive capability.

15. Our aim will be to establish a situation in Europe in which force postures as well as the numbers and deployments of weapon systems no longer make surprise attack and large-scale offensive action a feasible option. We shall pursue this aim on the basis of the following criteria:

- we need to enhance stability in the whole of Europe from the Atlantic to the Urals; and to do so in a way which, while safeguarding the security of all Allies, takes account of the concentrations of Warsaw Pact forces and the particular problems affecting the Central, Southern and Northern regions;
- in seeking to eliminate the ability to conduct large-scale offensive action, we shall focus on the key weapon systems;
- we shall propose provisions dealing with stationed forces, taking account of the weight of forward-deployed Soviet conventional forces; we shall also take into consideration capabilities for force generation and reinforcement;
- equal number or percentage reductions by both sides would not eliminate the disparities which threaten stability in Europe. Our proposals will concentrate instead on results and residual entitlements;
- our goal is to redress the conventional imbalance. This can be achieved through a set of measures including, *inter alia*, reductions, limitations, redeployment provisions and related measures

as well as the establishment of equal ceilings;

- this outcome will require highly asymmetrical reductions by the East and will entail, for example, the elimination from Europe of tens of thousands of Warsaw Pact weapons relevant to surprise attack, among them tanks and artillery pieces;
- reductions of combat-decisive equipment and modification of the Soviet forward deployment posture will only be a part of our approach to reducing the risk of conflict. As a concurrent element in any effort to enhance stability and security, we shall also propose measures to produce greater openness of military activities throughout Europe, safeguard the maintenance of lower force levels, and support a rigorous, effective and reliable monitoring and verification regime;
- this monitoring and verification regime will need to include the exchange of detailed data about forces and deployments; and the right to conduct sufficient on-site inspections to provide confidence that agreed provisions are being complied with.

D. The Way Ahead

16.   Early agreement on a conventional stability mandate, as part of a balanced outcome to the Vienna Follow-up Meeting of the Conference on Security and Cooperation in Europe, would be an important step forward. We seek the elimination of the conventional imbalances which so threaten stability and security in Europe. We also seek enhanced respect for human rights and fundamental freedoms on which lasting security and stability ultimately depend.

Source: NATO

JOINT US–SOVIET SUMMIT STATEMENT

Moscow, 2 June 1988

In accordance with the understanding reached during the Soviet–US summit meeting in Geneva in November 1985, and confirmed at the Washington summit in December 1987, Mikhail S. Gorbachev, General Secretary of the Central Committee of the Communist Party of the Soviet Union, and Ronald W. Reagan, President of the United States of America, met in Moscow 29 May–2 June 1988.

The General Secretary and the President view the Moscow summit as an important step in the process of putting Soviet–US relations on a more productive and sustainable basis. Their comprehensive and detailed discussions covered the full agenda of issues to which the two leaders agreed during their initial meeting in Geneva in November, 1985 – an agenda encompassing arms control, human rights and humanitarian matters, settlement of regional conflicts, and bilateral relations. Serious differences remain on important issues; the frank dialogue which has developed between the two countries remains critical to surmounting these differences.

The talks took place in a constructive atmosphere which provided ample opportunity for candid exchange. As a result, the sides achieved a better understanding of each other's positions. The two leaders welcomed the progress achieved in various areas of Soviet–US relations since their last meeting in Washington, notwithstanding the difficulty and complexity of the issues. They noted with satisfaction numerous concrete agreements which have been achieved, and expressed their determination to redouble efforts in the months ahead in areas where work remains to be done. They praised the creative and intensive efforts made by representatives of both sides in recent months to resolve outstanding differences.

Assessing the state of Soviet–US relations, the General Secretary and the President underscored the historic importance of their meetings in Geneva, Reykjavik, Washington, and Moscow in laying the foundation for a realistic approach to the problems of strengthening stability and reducing the risk of conflict. They reaffirmed their solemn conviction that a nuclear war cannot be won and must never be fought, their determination to prevent any war between the Soviet Union and the United States, whether nuclear or conventional, and their disavowal of any intention to achieve military superiority.

The two leaders are convinced that the expanding political dialogue they have established represents an increasingly effective means of resolving issues of mutual interest and concern. They do not minimize the real differences of history, tradition and ideology which will continue to characterize the Soviet–US relationship. But they believe that the dialogue will endure, because it is based on realism and focused on the achievement of concrete results. It can serve as a constructive basis for addressing not only the problems of the present, but of tomorrow and the next century. It is a process which the General Secretary and the President believe serves the best interests of the peoples of the United States and the Soviet Union, and can contribute to a more stable, more peaceful and safer world.

I. Arms Control

The General Secretary and the President, having expressed the commitment of their two countries to build on progress to date in arms control, determined objectives and next steps on a wide range of issues in this area. These will guide the efforts of the two governments in the months ahead as they work with each other and with other states toward equitable, verifiable agreements that strengthen international stability and security.

INF

The General Secretary and the President signed the protocol on the exchange of instruments of ratification of the Treaty between the Union of Soviet Socialist Republics and the United States of America on the Elimination of Their Intermediate-Range and Shorter-Range Missiles. The two leaders welcomed the entry into force of this historic agreement, which for the first time will eliminate an entire class of Soviet and US nuclear arms, and which sets new standards for arms control. The leaders are determined the achieve the full implementation of all the provisions and understandings of the Treaty, viewing joint and successful work in this respect as an important precedent for future arms control efforts.

Nuclear and Space Talks

The two leaders noted that a Joint Draft Text of a Treaty on Reduction and Limitation of Strategic Offensive Arms has been elaborated. Through this process, the sides have been able to record in the Joint Draft Text extensive and significant areas of agreement and also to detail positions on remaining areas of disagreement. While important additional work is required before this Treaty is ready for signature, many key provisions are recorded in the Joint Draft Text and are considered to be agreed, subject to the completion and ratification of the Treaty.

Taking into account a Treaty on Strategic Offensive Arms, the sides have continued negotiations to achieve a separate agreement concerning the ABM Treaty building on the language of the Washington Summit

Joint Statement dated 10 December 1987. Progress was noted in preparing the Joint Draft Text of an associated Protocol. In connection with their obligations under the Protocol, the sides have agreed in particular to use the Nuclear Risk Reduction Centers for transmission of relevant information. The leaders directed their negotiators to prepare the Joint Draft Text of a separate agreement and to continue work on its associated Protocol.

The Joint Draft Treaty on Reduction and Limitation of Strategic Offensive Arms reflects the earlier understanding on establishing ceilings of no more than 1,600 strategic offensive delivery systems and 6,000 warheads as well as agreement on subceilings of 4,900 on the aggregate of ICBM and SLBM warheads and 1,540 warheads on 154 heavy missiles.

The Draft Treaty also records the sides' agreement that as a result of the reductions the aggregate throw-weight of the Soviet Union's ICBMs and SLBMs will be reduced to a level approximately 50 per cent below the existing level and this level will not be exceeded.

During the negotiations the two sides have also achieved understanding that in future work on the Treaty they will act on the understanding that on deployed ICBMs and SLBMs of existing types the counting rule will include the number of warheads referred to in the Joint Statement of 10 December 1987, and the number of warheads which will be attributed to each new type of ballistic missiles will be subject to negotiation.

In addition, the sides agreed on a counting rule for heavy bomber armaments according to which heavy bombers equipped only for nuclear gravity bombs and SRAMs will count as one delivery vehicle against the 1,600 limit and one warhead against the 6,000 limit.

The delegations have also prepared Joint Draft Texts of an Inspection Protocol, a Conversion or Elimination Protocol, and a Memorandum of Understanding on data, which are integral parts of the Treaty. These documents build on the verification provisions of the INF Treaty, extending and elaborating them as necessary to meet the more demanding requirements of START. The START verification measures will, at a minimum, include:

A.   Data exchanges, to include declarations and appropriate notifications on the number and location of weapons systems limited by START, including locations and facilities for production, final assembly, storage, testing, repair, training, deployment, conversion, and elimination of such systems. Such declarations will be exchanged between the sides before the Treaty is signed and updated periodically.

B.   Baseline inspections to verify the accuracy of these declarations.

C.   On-site observation of elimination of strategic systems necessary to meet the agreed limits.

D.   Continuous on-site monitoring of the perimeter and portals of critical production facilities to confirm the output of weapons to be limited.

E.   Short-notice on-site inspection of:

(i)   declared locations during the process of reducing to agreed limits;

(ii)   locations where systems covered by this Treaty remain after achieving the agreed limits; and

(iii)   locations where such systems have been located (formerly declared facilities).

F.   Short-notice inspection, in accordance with agreed-upon procedures, of locations where either side considers covert deployment, production, storage or repair of strategic offensive arms could be occurring.

G.   Prohibition of the use of concealment or other activities which impeded verification by National Technical Means. Such provisions would include a ban on telemetry encryption and would allow for full access to all telemetric information broadcast during missile flight.

H.   Procedures that enable verification of the number of warheads on deployed ballistic missiles of each specific type, including on-site inspection.

I.   Enhanced observation of activities related to reduction and limitation of strategic offensive arms by National Technical Means. These would include open displays of treaty-limited items at missile bases, bomber bases, and submarine ports at locations and times chosen by the inspecting party.

The two sides have also begun to exchange data on their strategic forces.

During the course of this meeting in Moscow, the exchanges on START resulted in the achievement of substantial additional common ground, particularly in the areas of ALCMs and the attempts to develop and agree, if possible, on a solution to the problem of verification of mobile ICBMs. The details of this additional common ground have been recorded in documents exchanged between the sides. The delegations in Geneva will record these gains in the Joint Draft Text of the START Treaty.

The sides also discussed the question of limiting long-range, nuclear-armed SLCMs.

Mikhail Gorbachev and Ronald Reagan expressed their joint confidence that the extensive work done provides the basis for concluding the Treaty on Reduction and Limitation of Strategic Offensive Arms which will promote strategic stability and strengthen security not only of the peoples of the USSR and the USA, but of all mankind.

Guided by this fundamental agreement, the General Secretary of the Central Committee of the CPSU and the US President agreed to continue their efforts in this area energetically and purposefully. The delegations of the two countries have been instructed to return to Geneva on 12 July 1988. It has been agreed as a matter of principle that, once the remaining problems are solved and the Treaty and its associated documents are agreed, they will be signed without delay.

Ballistic Missile Launch Notifications

The agreement between the USSR and the US on notifications of launches of Intercontinental Ballistic Missiles and Submarine-Launched Ballistic Missiles, signed during the Moscow summit, is a practical new step, reflecting the desire of the sides to reduce the risk of outbreak of nuclear war, in particular as a result of misinterpretation, miscalculation or accident.

Nuclear Testing

The leaders reaffirmed the commitment of the two sides to conduct in a single forum full-scale, stage-by-stage negotiations on the issues relating to nuclear testing. In these negotiations the sides as the first step will agree upon effective verification measures which will make it possible to ratify the USSR–US Threshold Test Ban Treaty of 1974 and Peaceful Nuclear Explosions Treaty of 1976, and proceed to negotiating further intermediate limitations on nuclear testing leading to the ultimate objective of the complete cessation of nuclear testing as part of an effective disarmament process. This process, among other things, would pursue, as the first priority, the goal of the reduction of nuclear weapons and, ultimately, their elimination. In implementing the first objective of these negotiations, agreement upon effective verification measures for the USSR–US Threshold Test Ban Treaty of 1974, the sides agreed to design and conduct a Joint Verification Experiment at each other's test sites.

The leaders therefore noted with satisfaction the signing of the Joint Verification Experiment Agreement, the considerable preparation under way for the Experiment, and the positive cooperation being exhibited in particular by the substantial numbers of personnel now engaged in work at each other's test sites. They also noted the substantial progress on a new Protocol to the Peaceful Nuclear Explosions Treaty and urged continuing constructive negotiations on effective verification measures for the Threshold Test Ban Treaty.

Expressing their conviction that the progress achieved so far forms a solid basis for continuing progress on issues relating to nuclear testing, the leaders instructed their negotiators to complete expeditiously the preparation of a Protocol to the Peaceful Nuclear Explosions Treaty and to complete the preparation of a Protocol to the Threshold Test Ban Treaty as soon as possible after the Joint Verification Experiment has been conducted and analyzed. They confirmed their understanding that verification measures for the TTBT will, to the extent appropriate, be used in further nuclear test limitation agreements which may subsequently be reached. They also declared their mutual intention to seek ratification of both the 1974 and 1976 Treaties when the corresponding protocols to the Threshold Test Ban Treaty and the Peaceful Nuclear Explosions Treaty are completed, and to continue negotiations as agreed in the Washington joint summit statement.

Nuclear Non-Proliferation

The two leaders noted that this year marks the 20th Anniversary of the Nuclear Non-Proliferation Treaty, one of the most important international arms control agreements with over 130 adherents. They reaffirmed their conviction that universal adherence to the NPT is important to international peace and security. They expressed the hope that each state not a party to the Treaty will join it, or make an equally binding commitment under international law to forgo acquisition of nuclear weapons and prevent nuclear weapons proliferation. This will enhance the possibility of progress towards reducing nuclear armaments and reduce the threat of nuclear war.

The two leaders also confirmed their support of the International Atomic Energy Agency, and agreed that they would continue efforts to further strengthen it. They reaffirmed the value of their regular consultations on non-proliferation and agreed that they should continue.

Nuclear Risk Reduction Centers

The leaders expressed satisfaction over the activation of the new communications link between the Nuclear Risk Reduction Centers in Moscow and Washington, established in accordance with the Soviet–US agreement of 15 September 1987. It was agreed that the centers can play an important role in the context of a future Treaty on reducing Soviet and US strategic nuclear arms.

Chemical Weapons

The leaders reviewed the status of on-going multilateral negotiations and bilateral Soviet–US consultations toward a comprehensive, effectively verifiable, and truly global ban on chemical weapons, encompassing all chemical weapons-capable states. They also expressed concern over the growing problem of chemical weapons proliferation and use.

The leaders reaffirmed the importance of efforts to address, as a matter of continuing urgency, the unique challenges of a chemical weapons ban and to achieve an effective convention. While noting the progress already achieved in the talks and the difficult problems with regard to effective monitoring of the global prohibition of chemical weapons and the non-use of dual-capable chemicals for chemical weapons purposes, the leaders underlined the need for concrete solutions to the problems of ensuring effective verification and undiminished security for all convention participants. They gave instructions to their respective delegations to this effect.

Both sides agreed on the vital importance of greater openness by all states as a way to build confidence and strengthen the foundation for an effective convention. The leaders also emphasized the necessity of close coordination on a multilateral basis in order to ensure the participation of all CW-possessing and CW-capable states in the convention.

Both sides strongly condemned the dangerous spread and illegal use of chemical weapons in violation of the 1925 Geneva Protocol. They stressed the importance of both technical and political solutions to this problem and confirmed their support for international investigations of suspected violations. Noting the initial efforts being made to control the export of chemicals used in manufacturing chemical weapons, the leaders called on all nations with the capability of producing such chemicals to institute stringent export controls to inhibit the proliferation of chemical weapons.

Conventional Arms Control

The leaders emphasized the importance of strengthening stability and security in the whole of Europe. They welcomed progress to date on development of a mandate for new negotiations on armed forces and conventional armaments. They expressed their hope for an early and balanced conclusion to the Vienna CSCE Follow-Up Meeting. The President and the General Secretary also noted that full implementation of the provisions of the document of the Stockholm Conference on Confidence- and Security-Building Measures and Disarmament in Europe can significantly increase openness and mutual confidence.

They also discussed the situation in the Mutual and Balanced Force Reduction (MBFR) negotiations in Vienna.

Conference on Security and Cooperation in Europe

They expressed their commitment to further development of the CSCE process. The USSR and the US will continue to work with the other 33 participants to bring the Vienna CSCE follow-up meeting to a successful conclusion, through significant results in all the principal areas of the Helsinki Final Act and Madrid Concluding Document.

Ballistic Missile Technology Proliferation

The leaders agreed to bilateral discussions at the level of experts on the problem of proliferation of ballistic missile technology.

Third Special Session of the UN General Assembly

The General Secretary and the President noted the importance of the ongoing Third Special Session on Disarmament.

II. Human Rights and Humanitarian Concerns

The General Secretary and the President engaged in a detailed discussion of human rights and humanitarian concerns. The leaders reviewed the increasingly broad and detailed Soviet–US dialogue in this area and agreed that it should be conducted at all levels in order to achieve sustained, concrete progress. They noted that this dialogue should seek to maximize assurance of the rights, freedoms and human dignity of individuals; promotion of people-to-people communications and contacts; active sharing of spiritual, cultural, historical and other values; and greater mutual understanding and respect between the two countries. Toward this end, they discussed the possible establishment of a forum which, meeting regularly, would bring together participants from across the range of their two societies. They noted steps already taken to establish the exchange of information and contacts between legislative bodies of both countries, as well as discussions between legal experts, physicians and representatives of other professions directly involved in matters pertaining to human rights, and between representatives of non-governmental organizations.

III. Regional Issues

The General Secretary and the President thoroughly discussed a wide range of regional questions, including the Middle East, the Iran–Iraq war, southern Africa, the Horn of Africa, Central America, Cambodia, the Korean Peninsula, and other issues. They expressed satisfaction with the April 1988 conclusion in Geneva of accords on an Afghanistan settlement. Although the discussions revealed serious differences both in the assessment of the causes of regional tensions and in the means to overcome them, the leaders agreed that these differences need not be an obstacle to constructive interaction between the USSR and the US.

They reaffirmed their intention to continue Soviet–US discussions at all levels aimed at helping parties to regional conflicts find peaceful solutions which advance their independence, freedom and security. They emphasized the importance of enhancing the capacity of the United Nations and other international institutions to contribute to the resolution of regional conflicts.

Source: Novosti, 2 June 1988

REDUCTION OF ARMED FORCES AND CONVENTIONAL ARMAMENTS IN EUROPE

Statement by the Members of the Warsaw Treaty Organisation,
15–16 July 1988

The Warsaw Treaty member states believe that the interests of European and universal security urgently call for sizable cuts in armed forces and conventional armaments in Europe – from the Atlantic to the Urals. They are for talks on this issue to open without delay, in 1988.

The allied states are convinced that the priority objective of these talks is to ensure a radical reduction in the military potentials of both alliances and secure such a situation in the continent in which the NATO and Warsaw Treaty countries would have the forces and armaments needed for defence but insufficient for a surprise attack and offensive operations. This would enhance military-political stability and security in Europe in conditions where the USSR–US Treaty on the Elimination of Their Intermediate-Range and Shorter-Range Missiles is in effect and facilitate further movement along the path of promoting disarmament, strengthening trust and lowering the threat of war.

The Warsaw Treaty member states proceed from the premise that cuts in armed forces and conventional armaments will be accompanied by a corresponding curtailment of military spending.

Acting on the basis of their joint programme for reducing armed forces and conventional armaments in Europe, which they put forward in Budapest in June 1986 and supplemented in Berlin in May 1987, the Warsaw Treaty member states are for the following issues to be resolved during the first phase of the relevant talks.

1. Achieving Equal Lowered Levels

The ultimate goal of the first phase of the talks should be achieving roughly equally (balanced) collective levels as regards troop strength and the amount of conventional armaments for the states members of the two military-political alliances. These levels would be lower than those currently existing on either side.

The process of attaining such levels would be taking place by phases on the European and the regional scale. First of all, it would be expedient to concentrate on the issues of mutually eliminating the imbalances and asymmetries in individual types of conventional arms and in the armed forces of the two military-political alliances in Europe.

The imbalances and asymmetries would be removed by withdrawing forces from the reduction area and subsequently disbanding them or by disbanding them on the spot, as well as by using other possible measures. The arms and military equipment to be reduced would be eliminated on specially assigned sites or be turned over by agreement to be used for peaceful purposes. Provision could be made for storing part of the arms and equipment on a temporary basis. Such storage sites would be kept under constant international control.

The attainment of the final goal of the first phase would lay the groundwork for further significant mutual cuts in troops and armaments. At the second phase the armed forces of each side would be reduced by approximately 25 per cent (by some 500,000 men) with their organic armaments; at the third phase the reduction of the armed forces and conventional armaments would be continued and the armed forces of both sides would acquire a strictly defensive nature.

The Warsaw Treaty member states consider it expedient that all the participants in the talks should not, from the moment they begin and until the agreements achieved at them become effective, take steps running counter to the objectives of the talks, in particular should not build up their armed forces and conventional armaments from the Atlantic to the Urals.

With the agreement's entry into force, all the participants in the negotiations would pledge not to build up their armed forces and conventional armaments in the territory that might be left outside that covered by the initial cuts.

2. Preventing a Surprise Attack

Measures to reduce and eliminate the danger of a surprise attack would be an integral part of the process of reducing armed forces and conventional armaments in Europe.

For this purpose, starting from the first phase, corridors (zones) with a lowered arms level would be created along the line of contact between the two military-political alliances, from which the more dangerous destabilising types of conventional arms would be removed or reduced. As a result, military potentials in these corridors (zones) would be kept at a level ensuring only a defensive capability but ruling out the possibility of a surprise attack.

The depth of the corridors (zones) with a lowered arms level could be agreed on the basis of geostrategic factors, the combat and technical characteristics of the principal types of arms and other criteria.

These steps would be accompanied by agreed confidence-building measures which would limit military activity in the corridors (zones), providing correspondingly a stiffer regime closer to the line of contact. They would cover, in particular, the scale and number of simultaneous exercises, the duration and frequency of exercises, as well as a ban on major exercises, and restrictions on troops movements.

3. Data Exchange and Verification

With a view to determining the correlation of forces between the two military-political alliances and detecting imbalances and asymmetries in the armed forces and conventional armaments on the European and the regional scale early in the talks or, if possible, even before their commencement, relevant initial data essential for conducting the negotiations would be mutually exchanged. Provision would also be made for the possibility of verifying these data with the start of the talks by means of on-site inspections.

An effective system would be created for verifying compliance with the accords to be reached at the talks, by using national technical means and international procedures, including on-site inspections without the right to refuse them. Checkpoints would be set up both along and inside the corridors (zones) with a lowered arms level and in the reduction area (at railway stations and junctions, airfields and ports).

Verification would be effected of the process of reducing, eliminating (dismantling) and storing arms and of disbanding military units, as well as of troop activities and the limit on the number of troops and armaments remaining after the cuts.

An international verification commission would be formed and vested with extensive powers (in terms of monitoring, inspections, dealing with contentious issues, etc.).

* * *

The Warsaw Treaty member states believe that a considerable reduction and subsequent elimination of tactical nuclear weapons, including munitions for dual-capable systems, would be an important measure towards reducing the war danger and creating a more stable situation in Europe. They reaffirm their proposal for an early opening of relevant talks and conducting them with a view to concluding a mutually acceptable agreement.

The Warsaw Treaty member states proceed from the premise that there is a close relationship between the process of reducing armed forces and conventional armaments from the Atlantic to the Urals and the continued development and broadening of confidence- and security-building measures in Europe within the CSCE framework. They maintain that the second phase of the Conference on Confidence- and Security-Building Measures and Disarmament in Europe should continue to examine the issues left unresolved at the Conference's first phase, particularly those concerning the extension of confidence-building measures to cover the activity of air forces and navies, and to agree on new-generation confidence-building measures, including those of a restrictive nature. All these measures would contribute to lowering the risk of a surprise attack and promoting openness and predictability in the military field.

The Warsaw Treaty member states are prepared to discuss other possible measures and proposals for strengthening stability in Europe at ever lower levels of armed forces and armaments, with the principles of equality and equal security being observed and the agreements reached being made effectively verifiable.

Source: Novosti, 19 July 1988

SPEECH BY PRIME MINISTER MARGARET THATCHER AT THE OPENING CEREMONY OF THE 39TH ACADEMIC YEAR OF THE COLLEGE OF EUROPE

Bruges, 20 September 1988 (Excerpts)

Britain and Europe

Mr Chairman, you have invited me to speak on the subject of Britain and Europe. Perhaps I should congratulate you on your courage. If you believe some of the things said and written about my views on Europe, it must seem rather like inviting Genghis Khan to speak on the virtues of peaceful co-existence!

I want to start by disposing of some myths about my country, Britain, and its relationship with Europe. And to do that I must say something about the identity of Europe itself.

Europe is not the creation of the Treaty of Rome. Nor is the European idea the property of any group or institution. We British are as much heirs to the legacy of European culture as any other nation. Our links to the rest of Europe, the continent of Europe, have been *the* dominant factor in our history. For three hundred years we were part of the Roman Empire and our maps still trace the straight lines of the roads the Romans built. Our ancestors – Celts, Saxons and Danes – came from the continent.

Our nation was – in that favourite Community word – 'restructured' under Norman and Angevin rule in the eleventh and twelfth centuries.

This year we celebrate the three hundredth anniversary of the Glorious Revolution in which the British crown passed to Prince William of Holland and Queen Mary.

Visit the great Churches and Cathedrals of Britain, read our literature and listen to our language: all bear witness to the cultural riches which we have drawn from Europe – and Europeans from us.

We in Britain are rightly proud of the way in which, since Magna Carta in 1215, we have pioneered and developed representative institutions to stand as bastions of freedom. And proud too of the way in which for centuries Britain was a home for people from the rest of Europe who sought sanctuary from tyranny.

But we know that without the European legacy of political ideas we could not have achieved as much as we did. From classical and medieval thought we have borrowed that concept of the rule of law which marks out a civilised society from barbarism. And on that concept of Christendom – for long synonomous with Europe – with its recognition of the unique and spiritual nature of the individual, we still base belief in personal liberty and other human rights.

Too often the history of Europe is described as a series of interminable wars and quarrels. Yet from our perspective today surely what strikes us most is our common experience. For instance, the story of how Europeans explored and colonised and – yes, without apology – civilised much of the world is an extraordinary tale of talent and valour.

We British have in a special way contributed to Europe. For over the centuries we have fought and died for her freedom, fought to prevent Europe from falling under the dominance of a single power. Only miles from here lie the bodies of 60,000 British soldiers who died in the First World War. Had it not been for that willingness to fight and die, Europe *would* have been united long before now – but not in liberty and not in justice. It was British help to resistance movements throughout the last War that kept alive the flame of liberty in so many countries until the day of liberation came. Tomorrow, King Baudouin will attend a service in Brussels to commemorate the many brave Belgians who gave their lives in service with the Royal Air Force.

It was from our island fortress that the liberation of Europe itself was mounted. And still today, we station 70,000 British servicemen on the mainland of Europe. All these things alone are proof of our commitment to Europe's future.

The European Community is one manifestation of that European identity. But it is not the only one. We must never forget that East of the Iron Curtain peoples who once enjoyed a full share of European culture, freedom and identity have been cut off from their roots. We shall always look on Warsaw, Prague and Budapest as great European cities.

Nor should we forget that European values have helped to make the United States of America into the dynamic defender of freedom which she has become.

Europe's Future

This is no arid chronicle of obscure historical facts. It is the record of nearly two thousand years of British involvement in Europe and contribution to Europe, a contribution which is today as strong as ever. Yes, we have looked also to wider horizons – and so have others – and thank goodness we did, because Europe would never have prospered and never will prosper as a narrow-minded, inward-looking club.

The European Community belongs to *all* its members, and must reflect the traditions and aspirations of *all* of them in full measure.

And let me be quite clear. Britain does not dream of an alternative to the European Community, of some cosy, isolated existence on its fringes. Our destiny is in Europe, as part of the Community. That is not to say that it lies *only* in Europe. But nor does that of France or Spain or indeed any other members.

The Community is not an end in itself. It is not an institutional device to be constantly modified according to the dictates of some abstract theory. Nor must it be ossified by endless regulation. It is the practical means by which Europe can ensure its future prosperity and security of its people in a world in which there are many other powerful nations and groups.

We Europeans cannot afford to waste our energies on internal disputes or arcane institutional debates. They are no substitute for effective action.

Europe has to be ready both to contribute in full measure to its own *security* and to *compete* – compete in a world in which success goes to the countries which encourage individual initiative and enterprise, rather than to those which attempt to diminish them.

I want this evening to set out some guiding principles for the future which I believe will ensure that Europe *does* succeed, not just in economic and defence terms but in the quality of life and the influence of its people.

Willing cooperation between Sovereign States

My first guideline is this: willing and active cooperation between independent sovereign states is the best way to build a successful European Community.

To try to suppress nationhood and concentrate power at the centre of a European conglomerate would be highly damaging and would jeopardise the objectives we seek to achieve.

Europe will be stronger precisely because it has France as France, Spain as Spain, Britain as Britain, each with its own customs, traditions and identity. It would be folly to try to fit them into some sort of identikit European personality.

Some of the founding fathers of the Community thought that the United States of America might be its model.

But the whole history of America is quite different from Europe. People went there to get away from the intolerance and constraints of life in Europe. They sought liberty and opportunity; and their strong sense of purpose has, over two centuries, helped to create a new unity and pride in being American – just as our pride lies in being British or Belgian or Dutch or German.

I am the first to say that on many great issues the countries of Europe should try to speak with a single voice. I want to see them work more closely on the things we can do better together than alone. Europe is stronger when we do so, whether it be in trade, defence or in our relations with the rest of the world. But working more closely together does *not* require power to be centralised in Brussels or decisions to be taken by an appointed bureaucracy.

Indeed, it is ironic that just when those countries such as the Soviet Union, which have tried to run everything from the centre, are learning that success depends on dispersing power and decisions *away* from the centre, some in the Community seem to want to move in the opposite direction.

We have not successfully rolled back the frontiers of the state in Britain, only to see them reimposed at a European level, with a European super-state exercising a new dominance from Brussels.

Certainly we want to see Europe more united and with a greater sense of common purpose. But it must be in a way which preserves the different traditions, Parliamentary powers and sense of national pride in one's own country, for these have been the source of Europe's vitality through the centuries.

Encouraging Change

My second guiding principle is this. Community policies must tackle present problems in a practical way, however difficult that may be. If we cannot reform those Community policies which are patently wrong or ineffective and which are rightly causing public disquiet, then we shall not get the public's support for the Community's future development.

That is why the achievements of the European Council in Brussels last February are so important.

It wasn't right that half the total Community Budget was being spent on storing and disposing of surplus food. Now those stocks are being sharply reduced.

It was absolutely right to decide that agriculture's share of the budget should be cut in order to free resources for policies, such as helping the less well off regions and training for jobs.

It was right, too, to introduce tighter budgetary discipline to enforce these decisions and to bring total EC spending under better control.

Those who complained that the Community was spending so much time on financial detail missed the point. You cannot build on unsound foundations; and it was the fundamental reforms agreed last winter which paved the way for the remarkable progress which we have since made on the Single Market.

But we cannot rest on what we have achieved so far. For example, the task of reforming the Common Agricultural Policy is far from complete. Certainly, Europe needs a stable and efficient farming industry.

But the CAP has become unwieldy, inefficient and grossly expensive. And production of unwanted surpluses safeguards neither the income nor the future of farmers themselves.

We must continue to pursue policies which relate supply more closely to market requirements, and which will reduce overproduction and limit costs.

Of course, we must protect the villages and rural areas which are such an important part of our national life – but not by the instrument of agricultural prices.

Tackling these problems requires political courage. The Community will only damage itself in the eyes of its own people and the outside world, if that courage is lacking.

Europe open to enterprise

My third guiding principle is the need for Community policies which encourage enterprise if Europe is to flourish and create the jobs of the future. The basic framework is there: the Treaty of Rome itself was intended as a Charter for Economic Liberty. But that is not how it has always been read, still less applied.

The lesson of the economic history of Europe in the 70s and 80s is that central planning and detailed control *don't* work, and that personal endeavour and initiative *do*. That a State-controlled economy is a recipe for low growth; and that free enterprise within a framework of law brings better results.

The aim of a Europe open for enterprise is the moving force behind the creation of the Single European Market by 1992. By getting rid of barriers, by making it possible for companies to operate on a Europe-wide scale, we can best compete with the United States, Japan and the other new economic powers emerging in Asia and elsewhere.

It means action to *free* markets, to *widen* choice and to produce greater economic convergence through *reduced* government inter-vention.

Our aim should *not* be more and more detailed regulation from the centre: it should be to deregulate, to remove the constraints on trade and to open up. Britain has been in the lead in opening its markets to others. The City of London has long welcomed financial institutions from all over the world, which is why it is the biggest and most successful financial centre in Europe.

We have opened our market for telecommunications equipment, introduced competititon into the market for services and even into the network itself – steps which others in Europe are only now beginning to face. In air transport, we have taken the lead in liberalisation and seen the benefits in cheaper fares and wider choice. Our coastal shipping trade is open to the merchant navies of Europe. I wish I could say the same of many other Community members.

Consider monetary matters. The key issue is not whether there should be a European Central Bank. The immediate and practical requirements are:

– to implement the Community's commitment to free movement of capital – we have it;

– and to the abolition throughout the Community of the exchange controls – we abolished them in Britain in 1979, so that people can invest wherever they wish.

– to establish a genuinely free market in financial services, in banking, insurance, investment.

– to make greater use of the ecu. Britain is this autumn issuing ecu-denominated Treasury bills, and hopes to see other Community governments increasingly do the same.

These are the *real* requirements because they are what Community business and industry need, if they are to compete effectively in the wider world. And they are what the European consumer wants, for they will widen his choice and lower his costs.

It is to such basic practical steps that the Community's attention should be devoted. When those have been achieved, and sustained over a period of time, we shall be in a better position to judge the next moves.

It is the same with the frontiers between our countries. Of course we must make it easier for goods to pass through frontiers. Of course we must make it easier for our people to travel throughout the Community. But it is a matter of plain commonsense that we cannot totally abolish frontier controls if we are also to protect our citizens and stop the movement of drugs, of terrorists, of illegal immigrants. That was underlined graphically only three weeks ago, when one brave German customs officer doing his duty on the frontier between Holland and Germany struck a major blow against the terrorists of the IRA.

And before I leave the subject of the Single Market, may I say that we emphatically do not need new regulations which raise the cost of *employment* and make Europe's labour market less flexible and less competitive with overseas suppliers.

If we are to have a European Company Statute, it should contain the minimum regulations. And certainly we in Britain would fight attempts to introduce corporatism at the European level – although what people wish to do in their own countries is a matter for them.

Europe open to the world

My fourth guiding principle is that Europe should not be protectionist. The expansion of the world economy requires us to continue the process of removing barriers to trade, and to do so in the multilateral negotiations in the GATT.

It would be a betrayal if, while breaking down constraints on trade to create the Single Market, the Community were to erect greater external protection. We must ensure that our approach to world trade is consistent with the liberalisation we preach at home.

We have a responsibility to give a lead here, a responsibility which is particularly directed towards the less developed countries. They need not only aid but more than anything they need improved trade opportunities if they are to gain the dignity of growing economic independence and strength.

Europe and Defence

My last guiding principle concerns the most fundamental issue, the European countries' role in defence. Europe must continue to maintain a sure defence through NATO. There can be no question of relaxing our efforts even if it means taking difficult decisions and meeting heavy costs. We are thankful for the peace that NATO has maintained over 40 years. The fact is things are going our way: the democratic model of a free enterprise society has proved itself superior; freedom is on the offensive, a peaceful offensive, the world over for the first time in my life-time.

We must strive to maintain the US commitment to Europe's defence. That means recognising the burden on their resources of the world role they undertake and their point that their Allies should play a full part in the defence of freedom, particularly as Europe grows wealthier. Increasingly they will look to Europe to play a part in out-of-area defence, as we have recently done in the Gulf.

NATO and the WEU have long recognised where the problems with Europe's defence lie and have pointed out the solutions. The time has come when we must give substance to our declarations about a strong defence effort and better value for money.

It's not an institutional problem. It's not a problem of drafting. It's much more simple and more profound: it is a question of political will and political courage, of convincing people in all our countries that we cannot rely for ever on others for our defence but that each member of the Alliance must shoulder a faire share of the burden.

We must keep public support for nuclear deterrence, remembering that obsolete weapons do not deter, hence the need for modernisation.

We must meet the requirements for effective conventional defence in Europe against Soviet forces which are constantly being modernised.

We should develop the WEU, not as an alternative to NATO, but as a means of strengthening Europe's contribution to the common defence of the West.

Above all at a time of change and uncertainty, in the Soviet Union and Eastern Europe, we must preserve Europe's unity and resolve, so that whatever may happen our defence is sure. At the same time, we must negotiate on arms control and keep the door wide open to co-operation on all the other issues covered by the Helsinki Accords.

But our way of life, our vision, and all that we hope to achieve is secured not by the rightness of our cause but by the strength of our defence. On this, we must never falter or fail.

The British Approach

I believe it is not enough just to talk in general terms about a European vision or ideal. If you believe in it, you must chart the way ahead. That's what I have tried to do this evening.

This approach does not require new documents: they are all there, the North Atlantic Treaty, the Revised Brussels Treaty, and the Treaty of Rome, texts written by far-sighted men, a remarkable Belgian – Paul Henri Spaak – among them.

What we need now is to take decisions on the next steps forward rather than let ourselves be distracted by Utopian goals.

However far we may all want to go, the truth is that you can only get there one step at a time.

Let us concentrate on making sure that we get those steps right.

Let Europe be a family of nations, understanding each other better, appreciating each other more, doing more together but relishing our national identity no less than our common European endeavour.

Let us have a Europe which plays its full part in the wider world, which looks outward not inward, and which preserves that Atlantic Community – that Europe on both sides of the Atlantic – which is our greatest inheritance and our greatest strength.

Source: British Embassy, Brussels, 20 September 1988

SPEECH BY SOVIET PRESIDENT MIKHAIL GORBACHEV AT THE UN GENERAL ASSEMBLY

7 December 1988 (Excerpts)

... Profound social changes are taking place. In the East and in the South, in the West and in the North, hundreds of millions of people, new nations and states, new public movements and ideologies have advanced to the foreground of history. The striving for independence, democracy and social justice manifests itself in all its diversity and with all its contradictions, in broad and frequently turbulent popular movements. The idea of democratizating the entire world order has grown into a powerful social and political force.

At the same time, the revolution in science and technology has turned economic, food, energy, ecological, information and demographic problems, which only recently were of national or regional character, into global problems. . . .

The world economy is becoming a single organism, outside which no state can develop normally, regardless of the social system it might belong to or the economic level it has reached.

All this calls for creating an altogether new mechanism for the functioning of the world economy, a new structure of the international division of labour. . . .

Further global progress is now possible only through quest for universal consensus in the movement toward a new world order. . . .

It is evident, in particular, that force and the threat of force neither can nor should be instruments of foreign policy. This mainly refers to nuclear arsenals, but not to them alone. All, the strongest first of all, have to apply self-restraint and renounce the use of force in the international arena. . . .

If we are parts, even if different, of one and the same civilization, if we are aware of the interdependence of the modern world, this understanding should increasingly manifest itself both in politics, and in practical efforts to harmonize international relations. Maybe, the term *perestroika* does not fit in very well in this case, but I express myself for new international relations. . . .

The Soviet Union is ready to establish a long-term (up to one hundred years) moratorium on the repayment of this debt by the least developed countries, and to write it off completely in a whole number of cases.

As for other developing countries, we invite you to consider the following propositions:

- to limit payments on their official debts depending on the economic development figures for each particular country, or to reschedule a considerable share of such payments until much later;
- to support the appeal by the UN Conference for Trade and Development to cut debts to commercial banks;
- to provide government support for market debt relief mechanisms for the Third World, including the establishment of an international debt-takeover agency to buy loans at a discount. . . .

Let us also think about setting up an emergency ecological aid centre within the UN. Its function would be to promptly dispatch international expertise groups to areas that have experienced a sharp deterioration in the ecological situation.

The Soviet Union is also prepared to cooperate in the establishment of an international space laboratory or manned orbiting station that would deal exclusively with control over the state of the environment.

As regards space exploration in general, the outlines of future industry in space are becoming increasingly clear.

The Soviet position on this point is known only too well: any activities in space must exclude any deployment of weapons there. For that, too, we need a legal base which, in fact, already exists, in the 1967 Treaty, and other agreements.

Even so, there is a pressing need to develop a comprehensive regime for peaceful activities in space. As for control over the observance of that regime, that would be a prerogative of a World Space Organization.

We have proposed the establishment of such an organization on many occasions. In fact, we are prepared to include in its network our radar at Krasnoyarsk. The decision to hand that radar over to the USSR Academy of Sciences has already been made. . . .

The Geneva accords, whose essential and practical importance has been appreciated all over the world, offered an opportunity for completing the settlement even before the end of this year. That did not happen. . . .

We will continue to make an active contribution to the healing of the wounds of war, and are also prepared to cooperate in this work both within the UN, and on a bilateral basis.

We are supporting the proposal for the establishment of a UN-sponsored international volunteer peace corps to assist in revitalizing Afghanistan. . . .

A representative of an organization which enjoys the status of a permanent observer in the UN has been banned by the United States authorities from addressing the General Assembly. I am speaking of Yasser Arafat.

Moreover, this has happened at a time when the Palestine Liberation Organization has made a crucial and constructive move to alleviate the quest to solve the Middle East question with the help of the UN Security Council.

This has happened at a time when a positive tendency has emerged towards political settlement of other regional conflicts, in some instances with the help of the USSR and the USA.

We deeply regret what has happened and express our solidarity with the Palestine Liberation Organization. . . .

Let my country join the chorus of voices expressing appreciation and appraisal of the significance of the Universal Declaration of Human Rights adopted forty years ago, on 10 December 1948.

This document remains valid today. It spells out the universal nature of the goals and tasks pursued by the United Nations.

The best way for states to mark the anniversary of the Declaration would be to improve their framework for the observance and protection of the rights of their citizens. . . .

Our country is living amid truly revolutionary enthusiasm. The process of *perestroika* is gathering momentum. We started by elaborating the philosophy of *perestroika*. We had to evaluate the nature and scope of the problems, learn the lessons of the past and translate our findings into political conclusions and programmes. This has been done. . . .

It took genuine democratization to involve society in the drive to accomplish the plans of *perestroika*. Under the banner of democratization, *perestroika* has been projected into the political, economic, cultural and ideological fields.

We have launched a radical economic reform. We have gained some experience and will accomplish a shift of the entire economy to new forms and methods of work from the new year. As part of this effort, we will reorganize production relations and unveil the vast potential inherent in socialist ownership.

While choosing to pursue such bold revolutionary transformations, we knew there would be blunders and resistance to the new, engendering new problems, and we anticipated delays in some areas.

But what makes it certain that the overall process of *perestroika* will proceed steadily ahead and gather momentum is the profound democratic reform of the entire system of government and administration.

As the USSR Supreme Soviet has recently introduced constitutional amendments and adopted a new electoral law, we have completed the first stage of the political reform.

Without pausing, we entered the second stage, whereby the paramount task will be to practise coordination between central authorities and republics, to settle ethnic relations in line with the principles of Leninist internationalism, as bequeathed to us by the Great Revolution, and at the same time to reform the administration of local Soviets. . . .

We have immersed ourselves in constructing a socialist state based on the rule of law. A whole series of new laws have been elaborated or are nearing completion.

Many will enter into force in 1989, and, we believe, comply fully with the highest standards in ensuring human rights.

Soviet democracy will then develop a sound legal basis. The point at issue is to enact the laws on freedom of conscience, on *glasnost*, on public amalgamations and organizations, etc.

No longer are people kept in prisons for their political and religious views.

The draft new laws propose additional guarantees to rule out any forms of persecution on these grounds.

Of course, this would not apply to criminal offenders or those guilty of crimes against the state (spying, subversion, terrorism, etc.), no matter what political views they profess and what their world outlook is. . . .

The problem of emigration and immigration, including the question of emigration for reunification of families, is being resolved in a humane way.

Permission to go, as you all know, is denied to citizens who know state secrets. Stringent time limits are being introduced in relation to knowledge of classified information.

Anyone employed at an office or enterprise with access to classified information will be duly informed about this rule. Disputes shall be appealed in conformity with the law.

This will help to remove the problem of so-called 'refuseniks' from the agenda.

We intend to expand the Soviet Union's participation in the human rights controlling mechanisms under the UN aegis, and within the framework of the European process. We think that the jurisdiction of the International Court in The Hague with regard to interpretation and application of agreements on human rights must be binding on all states.

We see an end to the jamming of broadcasts by all foreign radio stations that transmit programmes to the Soviet Union, also within the context of the Helsinki process. . . .

Today I am able to inform you of the fact that the Soviet Union has decided to reduce its armed forces.

In the next two years their strength will be reduced by 500,000 men, and substantial cuts will be made in conventional armaments. These cuts will be made unilaterally, regardless of the talks on the mandate of the Vienna meeting.

By agreement with our Warsaw Treaty allies, we have decided to withdraw from the German Democratic Republic, Czechoslovakia and Hungary by 1991 six tank divisions, and disband them. In addition, landing-assault and some other units, including landing-crossing units with their armaments and combat materiel, will be withdrawn from Soviet forces stationed in these countries. The Soviet forces stationed in these countries will be reduced by 50,000 men and 5,000 tanks. The Soviet divisions which still remain on the territory of out allies will be restructured, a large number of tanks will be withdrawn, and they will become strictly defensive.

Simultaneously we shall cut troops and armaments in the European part of the USSR.

The total reductions of Soviet armed forces in the European allies will amount to 10,000 tanks, 8,500 artillery systems, and 800 combat aircraft.

During the next two years we shall in addition make considerable reductions in the armed forces in the Asian regions of our country. By agreement with the Mongolian government, a large number of the Soviet troops temporarily stationed there will return home.

The Soviet leadership has taken these historic decisions to meet the wishes of the Soviet people, who are engaged in a radical overhaul of their entire socialist society.

We shall maintain the country's defence capability at a level of reasonable and dependable sufficiency, so that no one is tempted into encroaching upon the security of the USSR or its allies.

By this action and by all our efforts to demilitarize international relations, we want to draw the attention of the international community to yet another urgent matter, the problem of converting the armaments economy into a disarmament economy. Is the conversion of arms production possible? I have already spoken on this score. Our view is that it is possible.

The Soviet Union, for its part, is prepared to do the following:

- draft as part of its economic reform effort and present its own internal conversion plan;
- prepare as an experiment during 1989 plans for the conversion of two or three defence plants;
- make public its experience in re-employing defence personnel and using defence facilities and equipment in civilian production.

We consider it desirable for all countries, especially the great military powers, to submit to the United Nations their national conversion plans. It will also be of benefit if a team of scientists is formed and entrusted with the task of analysing in depth the problem of conversion in general and with regard to individual countries and regions, and reports its findings to the UN Secretary-General. Later, this question should be discussed at a session of the General Assembly. . . .

The relations between the Soviet Union and the United States have a history of five and a half decades. As the world changed, the character, role and place of these relations in world politics changed too.

For too long these relations were characterized by confrontation and sometimes hostility, open or concealed. But in recent years people all over the world have sighed with relief as relations between Moscow and Washington have changed for the better.

I am not underestimating our differences or the complexity of the problems yet to be resolved. However, we have learned the first lessons in mutual understanding and the search for solutions that meet our own and general interest.

The USSR and the United States have built immense nuclear missile arsenals. But they have also managed to realize their responsibility and become the first to conclude an agreement on the reduction and physical elimination of some of those weapons, which threatened our two countries and all the other countries.

Our two countries have the greatest and most sophisticated military secrets. But they also have begun and continue to develop a system of mutually verifying the destruction of armaments, their limitation and the ban on their production.

Our two countries are accumulating experience for future bilateral and multilateral agreements.

We cherish this experience, and we appreciate and value the contribution made by President Ronald Reagan and the members of his administration, especially Mr George Shultz.

All this is capital we have invested in a joint venture of historic significance. It must not be wasted or left idle.

The new US administration, to be led by President-elect George Bush, will find in us a partner prepared, without procrastination or backsliding, to continue the dialogue in the spirit of realism, openness and goodwill, and determined to achieve practical results on the agenda which now embraces key issues of Soviet–American relations and international politics.

I mean, above all, the consistent advance to a treaty on a 50 per cent reduction in strategic offensive arms with simultaneous observance of the ABM Treaty; work to draft a convention to eliminate chemical weapons (we believe that 1989 may become a crucial year in this respect); negotiations on the reduction of conventional arms and armed forces in Europe. . . .

We are not going to oversimplify the situation in the world. . . . The heritage and inertia of the past are still at work and deep contradictions and the root causes of many conflicts have not disappeared. And the fundamental fact remains that the shaping of a period of peace will be accompanied by the existence and rivalry of the different social, economic and political systems.

However, the aim of our efforts in the international arena and one of the key provisions of our concept of new thinking is that we must transform this rivalry into sensible competition on the basis of respect for freedom of choice and balance of interests. In this case, competition may even be useful and beneficial from the point of view of the general development of the world.

Otherwise, if the arms race continues to be its main element, this rivalry will be suicidal. More and more people throughout the world, ordinary people and leaders, are coming to realize this.

Source: *Survival*, vol. 31, No. 2, (Mar/Apl 1989)

SPEECH BY FOREIGN MINISTER, HANS-DIETRICH GENSCHER, TO THE BUNDESTAG

27 April 1989

Our debate is taking place at a time of movement in Europe. It is evident that the people of Europe are separated, but Europe is indivisible. The categorical imperative of the European democracies is: first, to continue resolutely the process of unification within the European Community; second, to overcome the separation in Europe through co-operation, through respect for human rights, through disarmament agreements and through confidence-building; third, never to forget that both the foregoing are only possible on the basis of a secure defence capacity within a Western alliance capable of action.

A peaceful order in Europe in which borders cease to be of a divisive nature, in which nations can live together without mututal fear, in which they can determine their own political and social systems – such a peaceful order is no longer merely a vision. The prospects for realizing it have improved. We must develop further and strengthen the co-operative elements of co-existence. The turn of the tide in European international politics is irreversible and unmistakeable. Nothing is more powerful than an idea whose time has come. This is the idea of eliminating hostility from international relations. It is the idea of demilitarizing East–West relations. It is the idea of de-ideologizing East–West relations. It is the idea of dialogue and co-operation, the idea of developing new peace structures. These are the topics for the forthcoming summit of the Western Alliance.

The central question for the West is whether it regards the democratization and reform in the socialist countries as a danger or as an opportunity that it is willing to make use of. The answer can only be: This is a historic opportunity. We must not let it slip by, nor idly look on from afar, but must seek to exercise creative influence. This is our responsibility! The European Community is the core of Europe's future structure. It is a living model for a peaceful European order, with Franco-German co-operation as its centre-piece. Only with a dynamic European Community can a new and lasting peaceful order emerge in the whole of Europe. The increasing appeal, the attraction and fascination of our liberal model, which has proved successful in social terms, are now evident. There is certainly no cause for us to be faint-hearted or anxious, but to be confident and enterprising. But only with a Western alliance capable of action will we be able to take advantage, without risk, of the new opportunities arising in West–East relations.

Who would deny that the elections in the Soviet Union have shown how deeply the goal of democratization is rooted in the hearts and minds of people in the Soviet Union? The election results were not just a rejection of the opponents to reform in the Soviet Union. They were also a rejection of those in the West who claim that perestroika is merely a game for intellectuals. No, Ladies and Gentlemen, people worldwide want freedom. They make use of the slightest opportunity for gaining it. Nobody has to learn freedom. This is the recognition gained. This process of reform in the Soviet Union is a manifestation of European consciousness. Realistic prospects for fundamentally reshaping international relations and setting up a peaceful order in Europe, as demanded by the Alliance's Harmel Report, are becoming visible.

The INF Treaty showed that disarmament is possible, that it is verifiable and that it leads to greater security. The Vienna negotiations on conventional stability can be assisted by new efforts at the Geneva negotiations for the global prohibition of chemical weapons. The time is ripe for this.

Disarmament must not exclude any class of weapons. The comprehensive concept to be adopted at Brussels in May is called a 'concept of arms control and disarmament', and not a 'concept of armament'. Why should it therefore exclude the demand for negotiations already voiced in 1987 and 1988? I feel we have a great deal to fear in Europe and worldwide, but we certainly need not fear negotiations or a Soviet Union that is willing to negotiate. Whoever seeks disarmament must negotiate on disarmament. Disarmament cannot be obtained by opposing the other side, but only by negotiating with it. And a realistic policy of disarmament requires that disarmament steps be made irreversible through negotiations and treaties so that there is no reversion to a new arms race.

The Federal Republic of Germany renders a significant contribution to common Western security – it makes the main contribution to conventional defence. We owe it to the people of our country and to the members of the Bundeswehr, who serve the cause of peace and freedom, to make actual use of absolutely every opportunity for achieving greater security through disarmament. The great goal of the Western alliance is to prevent war. This is the purpose of our common strategy. We endorse the Alliance's observation that at present there is no foreseeable alternative to the concept of preventing war by deterrence based on a suitable mix of adequate and effective nuclear and conventional forces. In the case of nuclear forces, land, sea and air-based systems are, under the existing circumstances, needed in Europe, too. But we also know that the shorter the ranges, the less nuclear weapons are suited for preventing war.

In accordance with our Alliance's inalienable doctrine, nuclear

weapons serve the political goal of preventing war. Any other interpretation would lead us into a war-fighting scenario, which would
mean the end of all Europe. It is therefore essential to create an
additional network of co-operative security which prevents even more
reliably a conventional or a nuclear war. Nor do we want a so-called
limited nuclear war. In this respect, too, there must be no zones of
differing security – neither in the Alliance nor in Europe. The East's
conventional superiority continues to lie at the heart of the security
problems in Europe.

To replace this by conventional stability with fewer weapons, by
eliminating the capability for surprise attack and for large-scale offensive action, that is the objective of the Vienna negotiations. And that is
why, with regard to the question of whether or not the Federal
Government deems it necessary to have a follow-up system for the
Lance short-range missile in the second half of the 1990s, it is crucial
for us to achieve agreements of that kind as well as the other objectives
mentioned in the policy statement. No-one can today reliably predict
what the political and security situation will be like in 1992. And that
is why it is also not possible today to decide whether a decision must
or not be taken in 1992 for the deployment of such a follow-up system
in 1996.

With its conscripted army, the Bundeswehr, and by virtue of the fact
that our security policy is accepted by the people, the Federal Republic
is rendering an indispensable contribution to the security of all the
allies. And this entitles us to have a big say in the decision-making
process, including Alliance decisions on matters of defence, arms
control and disarmament. Our Alliance of free democracies is capable
of achieving a consensus on all matters on the basis of mutual respect.
That is what we want. It is no sign of weakness when democratic
nations try to agree on a common policy through dialogue. As the
Chancellor has pointed out, we have no need to provide further
evidence of our determination to do everything necessary to maintain
common security. We have done so with the significant decisions we
made in 1979 and 1983.

But at the same time we expect all our partners to stand by our side
as we seek to remove the East's superiority in short-range missiles
through negotiations. And we also expect them to show understanding
when we labour over the decision as to whether or not it is necessary to
deploy new short-range nuclear missiles. In no other category of
weapons is Eastern Europe's superiority so great. It is therefore in the
West's fundamental security interests to remove that superiority by
negotiating equal ceilings as already called for in Reykjavik.

The Federal Republic of Germany shares all, I repeat all, present
security risks with its allies. But the threat emanating from Soviet
short-range missiles affects us in particular. They do not have the range
to reach the territory of most of our partners. So not only is it
understandable that we should want to eliminate the Soviet superiority

in this category of weapons by negotiation, it is in keeping with the Alliance's basic philosophy of creating more stability by removing superiorities.

In making our decision on new short-range nuclear weapons we are talking about systems which can reach the territory of Poland and Czechoslovakia, nations who suffered so terribly during the Second World War. And we are talking about short-range nuclear weapon systems which can reach the other part of our fatherland. Thus, if we are called upon to make such a decision we will not forget this fact, and I state this here on my own personal responsibility. The members of the Federal Government have sworn on oath to dedicate their efforts to the well-being of the German people. The obligation deriving from that oath does not stop at the border cutting through Germany. The responsibility for the nation established by that oath does not exclude my native region, the town where I was born, nor the people in the GDR. Indeed, it includes them. Our sincerity with regard to the German nation is not be judged by what is said in fine-sounding speeches but by our efforts, day in, day out, to strengthen peace and stability and enhance human rights in Europe, and by our efforts to promote co-operation and disarmament. The requirement of our Basic Law to promote peace applies to our relations with all European nations. We have proved our determination to do everything necessary to preserve freedom and security. But we shall seize every opportunity for co-operation, détente and disarmament with the same determination.

I appeal to our American friends, to whom we owe so much, whose airlift to save Berlin we remember so vividly, and whose contribution to Europe's security is indispensable, not to worry about our pausing to think. They would only have cause to worry if we again became unscrupulous. Pausing to think before making decisions on new nuclear weapons is an expression of responsibility. It is anything but a sign of weakness. And it should not be criticized as such. It is a credit to the citizens of our country and it is a credit to all those who are called upon to exercise political responsibility.

We Germans, this we say to all our friends, are not trying to follow our own separate road into the future. By opting for democracy, the Western Alliance and the European Community, we have irrevocably committed ourselves. We are very much aware that any attempt to detach ourselves from that community, to separate Germany's fate from that of the whole of Europe, to 'de-Europeanize' it, would be inimical to the mission prescribed by our constitution: to foster peace in Europe. It would in fact lead to our isolation in both East and West. Through our membership of the community of Western democracies we have used responsibly the freedom we regained on 8 May 1945. By taking that step we entered into the most far-reaching union possible for a state: the union based on fundamental values.

On the other hand we Germans also have neighbours who do not belong to this community of Western democracies but who suffered terribly during the Second World War, neighbours who likewise desire peace. We Germans do not wish to nor can we forget what happened to the Polish people, nor the suffering and sacrifices of the peoples of the Soviet Union. The sorrowful experience of this century makes these nations watch us attentively. And if it is true that East and West need a bridge of trust, then we Germans must build its main support. It is neither presumption nor arrogance on our part but rather a deep awareness of our historical task when we Germans feel we have a special responsibility for confidence-building between East and West, and act accordingly.

This century the Germans have pursued quite different aims from that of good neighbourliness with all Europeans. Today, after two murderous world wars and after decades of confrontation between East and West, Europe has a historic opportunity to embark wholeheartedly on the task of establishing a lasting peaceful order in Europe. We Germans have a special role to play in accomplishing this task. The French diplomat and poet Paul Claudel wrote in 1945: 'Germany is not there to divide nations but to let all the different nations around it feel that they cannot live without one another'. We shall live up to this responsibility for peace.

Source: Embassy of the Federal Republic of Germany, London, 27 April 1989

SPEECH BY PRESIDENT GEORGE BUSH

12 May 1989

We are approaching the conclusion of an historic post-war struggle between two visions – one of tyranny and conflict, and one of democracy and freedom. The review of US–Soviet relations that my administration has just completed outlines a new path toward resolving this struggle.

Our goal is bold – more ambitious than any of my predecessors might have thought possible. Our review indicates that 40 years of perseverance have bought us a precious opportunity. Now it is time to move beyond containment, to a new policy for the 1990s – one that recognises the full scope of change taking place around the world, and in the Soviet Union itself.

In sum, the United States now has as its goal much more than simply containing Soviet expansionism – we seek the integration of the Soviet Union into the community of nations. As the Soviet Union moves towards greater openness and democratisation – as they meet the challenge of responsible international behaviour – we will match their steps with steps of our own. Ultimately our objective is to welcome the Soviet Union back into the world order.

The Soviet Union says it seeks to make peace with the world, and criticises its own post-war policies. These are words we can only applaud. But a new relationship cannot be simply declared by Moscow or bestowed by others. It must be earned. We seek a friendship that knows no season of suspicion, no chill of distrust.

As we seek peace we must also remain strong. The purpose of our military might is not to pressure a weak Soviet economy, or to seek military superiority. It is to deter war. It is to defend ourselves and our allies, and to do something more – to convince the Soviet Union that there can be no reward in pursuing expansionism – to convince the Soviet Union that reward lies in the pursuit of peace.

Western policies must encourage the evolution of the Soviet Union towards an open society. This task will test our strength. It will tax our patience. And it will require a sweeping vision – let me share with you my vision. I see a Western Hemisphere of democratic, prosperous nations, no longer threatened by a Cuba or a Nicaragua armed by Moscow. I see a Soviet Union that pulls away from ties to terrorist nations – like Libya – that threaten the legitimate security of their neighbours. I see a Soviet Union which respects China's integrity, and

286

returns the Northern Territories of Japan; a prelude to the day when all the great nations of Asia will live in harmony. But the fulfilment of this vision requires the Soviet Union to take positive steps, including:

First: Reduce Soviet forces. Although some small steps have already been taken, the Warsaw Pact still possesses more than 30,000 tanks, more than twice as much artillery and hundreds of thousands more troops in Europe than Nato. They should cut their forces to less threatening levels, in proportion to their legitimate security needs.

Second: Adhere to the Soviet obligation – promised in the final days of World War Two – to support self-determination for all the nations of Eastern and Central Europe. This requires specific abandonment of the Brezhnev Doctrine. One day it should be possible to drive from Moscow to Munich without seeing a single guard tower or a strand of barbed wire. In short, tear down the Iron Curtain.

Third: Work with the West in positive, practical – not merely rhetorical – steps towards diplomatic solutions to regional disputes around the world. I welcome the Soviet withdrawal from Afghanistan and the Angola agreement. But there is much more to be done ... We're ready. Let's roll up our sleeves and get to work.

Fourth: Achieve a lasting political pluralism and respect for human rights. Dramatic events have already occurred in Moscow. We are impressed by limited, but freely contested, elections. We are impressed by a greater toleration of dissent. We are impressed by a new frankness about the Stalin era. Mr Gorbachev, don't stop now.

Fifth: Join with us in addressing pressing global problems, including the international drug menace, and dangers of the environment. We can build a better world for our children.

As the Soviet Union moves towards arms reduction and reforms, it will find willing partners in the West. We seek verifiable, stabilising arms control and arms reduction agreements with the Soviet Union and its allies. However, arms control is not an end in itself, but a means of contributing to the security of America, and the peace of the world. I directed Secretary Baker to propose to the Soviets that we resume negotiations on strategic forces in June. And, as you know, the Soviets have agreed.

Our basic approach is clear. In the Strategic Arms Reduction Talks, we wish to reduce the risk of nuclear war. In the companion Defence and Space Talks, our objective will be to preserve our options to deploy advance defences when they are ready. In nuclear testing we will continue to seek the necessary verification improvements in existing treaties to permit them to be brought into force. We will continue to seek a verifiable global ban on chemical weapons. We support Nato efforts to reduce the Soviet offensive threat in the negotiations on Conventional Forces in Europe. And, as I've said, fundamental to all of these objectives is simple openness.

Make no mistake, a new breeze is blowing across the steppes and cities of the Soviet Union. Why not, then, let this spirit of openness grow, let more barriers come down. Open emigration, open debate, open airwaves – let openness come to mean the publication and sale of banned books and newspapers in the Soviet Union. Let the 19,000 Soviet Jews who emigrated last year be followed by any number who wish to emigrate this year. Let openness come to mean nothing less than the free exchange of people, books and ideas between East and West. And let it come to mean one thing more.

Thirty-four years ago, President Eisenhower met in Geneva with Soviet leaders who, after the death of Stalin, promised a new approach toward the West. He proposed a plan called 'Open Skies', which would allow unarmed aircraft from the United States and the Soviet Union to fly over the territory of the other country. This would open up military activities to regular scrutiny and, as President Eisenhower put it, 'convince the world that we are . . . lessening danger and relax tension.'

President Eisenhower's suggestion tested Soviet readiness to open their society. The Kremlin failed the test. Let us again explore that proposal, but on a broader, more intrusive and radical basis – one which I hope would include allies on both sides. We suggest that those countries that wish to examine this proposal meet soon to work out the necessary operational details, separately from other arms control negotiations.

Where there is co-operation, there can be a broader economic relationship. But economic relations have been stifled by Soviet internal policies. They have been injured by Moscow's practice of using the cloak of commerce to steal technology from the West. Ending discriminatory treatment of US firms would be a helpful step. Trade and financial transactions should take place on a normal commercial basis. And should the Soviet Union codify its emigration laws in accord with international standards and implement its new laws faithfully, I am prepared to work with Congress for a temporary waiver of the Jackson-Vannik Amendment, opening the way to extending Most Favoured Nation trade status to the Soviet Union.

Forty-three years ago, a young lieutenant by the name of Albert Kotzebue, Class of 1945 at Texas A&M, was the first American soldier to shake hands with the Soviets at the banks of the Elbe River. Once again, we are ready to extend our hand. Once again, we are ready for a hand in return. Once again, it is a time for peace.

Source: *The Independent*, 13 May 1989

SPEECH BY PRESIDENT GEORGE BUSH

Mainz, West Germany, 31 May 1989

Today, I come to speak, not just of our mutual defense, but of our shared values. I come to speak, not just of the matters of the mind, but of the deeper aspirations of the heart.

Just this morning, Barbara and I were charmed with the experiences we had. I met with a small group of German students, bright young men and women who studied in the United States. Their knowledge of our country and the world was impressive to say the least. But sadly, too many in the West, Americans and Europeans alike, seem to have forgotten the lessons of our common heritage and how the world we know came to be. And that should not be, and that cannot be. We must recall that the generation coming into its own in America and Western Europe is heir to gifts greater than those bestowed to any generation in history – peace, freedom and prosperity.

This inheritance is possible because 40 years ago the nations of the West joined in that noble, common cause called NATO. First there was the vision, the concept of free peoples in North America and Europe working to protect their values. And second, there was the practical sharing of risks and burdens, in a realistic recognition of Soviet expansionism. And finally, there was the determination to look beyond old animosities. The NATO alliance did nothing less than provide a way for Western Europe to heal centuries-old rivalries, to being an era of reconciliation and restoration. It has been, in fact, a second Renaissance of Europe.

As you know best, this is not just the 40th birthday of the alliance. It's also the 40th birthday of the Federal Republic – a republic born in hope, tempered by challenge. At the height of the Berlin crisis in 1948, Ernst Reuter called on Germans to stand firm and confident, and you did – courageously, magnificently.

And the historic genius of the German people has flourished in this age of peace. And your nation has become a leader in technology, the fourth largest economy on Earth. But more important, you've inspired the world by forcefully promoting the principles of human rights, democracy and freedom. The United States and the Federal Republic have always been firm friends and allies. But today we share an added role – partners in leadership.

Of course, leadership has a constant comparison – responsibility. And our responsibility is to look ahead and grasp the promise of the future.

I said recently that we're at the end of one era, and at the beginning of another. And I noted that in regard to the Soviet Union, our policy is to move beyond containment.

For 40 years, the seeds of democracy in Eastern Europe lay dormant, buried under the frozen tundra of the Cold War. And for 40 years, the world has waited for the Cold War to end. And decade after decade, time after time, the flowering human spirit withered from the chill of conflict and oppression. And again, the world waited. But the passion for freedom cannot be denied forever. The world has waited long enough. The time is right. Let Europe be whole and free.

To the founders of the alliance, this aspiration was a distant dream, and now it's the new mission of NATO. If ancient rivals like Britain and France, or France and Germany, can reconcile, then why not the nations of the East and West?

In the East, brave men and women are showing us the way. Look at Poland, where Solidarity – Solidarnosc – and the Catholic Church have won legal status. The forces of freedom are putting the Soviet status quo on the defensive.

In the West, we have succeeded because we've been faithful to our values and our vision. And on the other side of the rusting Iron Curtain, their vision failed.

The Cold War began with the division of Europe. It can only end when Europe is whole. Today, it is this very concept of a divided Europe that is under siege. And that's why our hopes run especially high, because the division of Europe is under seige not by armies, but by the spread of ideas that began here, right here. It was a son of Mainz, Johannes Gutenberg, who liberated the mind of man through the power of the printed word.

And that same liberating power is unleashed today in a hundred new forms. The Voice of America, Deutsche Welle, allow us to enlighten millions deep within Eastern Europe and throughout the world. Television satellites allow us to bear witness from the shipyards of Gdansk to Tiananmen Square. But the momentum for freedom does not just come from the printed word or the transistor or the television screen. It comes from a single powerful idea – democracy.

This one idea is sweeping across Eurasia. This one idea is why the Communist world, from Budapest to Beijing, is in ferment. Of course, for the leaders of the East it's not just freedom for freedom's sake. But whatever their motivation, they are unleashing a force they will find difficult to channel or control – the hunger for liberty of oppressed peoples who have tasted freedom.

Nowhere is this more apparent than in Eastern Europe, the birthplace of the Cold War. In Poland, at the end of World War II, the Soviet army prevented the free elections promised by Stalin at Yalta. And today, Poles are taking the first steps towards real elections, so long promised – so long deferred. And in Hungary, at last we see a chance for multi-party competition at the ballot box.

As president, I will continue to do all I can to help open the closed societies of the East. We seek self-determination for all of Germany and all of Eastern Europe. And we will not relax, and we must not waver. Again, the world has waited long enough.

But democracy's journey east is not easy. Intellectuals like the great Czech playwright, Vaclav Havel, still work under the shadow of coercion. And repression still menaces too many peoples of Eastern Europe. Barriers and barbed wire still fence in nations. So when I visit Poland and Hungary this summer, I will deliver this message: There cannot be a common European home until all within it are free to move from room to room.

And I'll take another message: The path of freedom leads to a larger home – a home where West meets East, a democratic home – the commonwealth of free nations.

And I said that positive steps by the Soviets would be met by steps of our own. And this is why I announced on May 12 a readiness to consider granting to the Soviets a temporary waiver of the Jackson-Vanik trade restriction, if they liberalize emigration. And this is also why I announced on Monday (May 29) that the United States is prepared to drop the 'no exceptions' standard that has guided our approach to controlling the export of technology to the Soviet Union – lifting a sanction enacted in response to their invasion of Afghanistan.

And in this same spirit, I set forth four proposals to heal Europe's tragic division, to help Europe become whole and free.

First, I propose we strengthen and broaden the Helsinki process to promote free elections and political pluralism in Eastern Europe. As the forces of freedom and democracy rise in the East, so should our expectations.

And weaving together the slender threads of freedom in the East will require much from the Western democracies. In particular, the great political parties of the West must assume an historic responsibility – to lend counsel and support to those brave men and women who are trying to form the first truly representative political parties in the East, to advance freedom and democracy, to part the Iron Curtain.

In fact, it's already begun to part. The frontier of barbed wire and minefields between Hungary and Austria is being removed, foot by foot, mile by mile. Just as the barriers are coming down in Hungary, so must they fall throughout all of Eastern Europe. Let Berlin be next. Let Berlin be next!

Nowhere is the division between East and West seen more clearly than in Berlin. And there this brutal wall cuts neighbor from neighbor, brother from brother. And that wall stands as a monument to the failure of communism. It must come down.

Now, *glasnost* may be a Russian word, but openness is a Western concept. West Berlin has always enjoyed the openness of a free city. And our proposal would make all Berlin a center of commerce between East and West – a place of cooperation, not a point of confrontation.

And we rededicate ourselves to the 1987 allied initiative to strengthen freedom and security in that divided city. This, then is my second proposal – bring glasnost to East Berlin.

My generation remembers a Europe ravaged by war. And of course, Europe has long since rebuilt its proud cities and restored its majestic cathedrals. But what a tragedy it would be if your continent was again spoiled, this time by a more subtle and insidious danger – the chancellor referred to it – that of poisoned rivers and acid rain.

America has faced an environmental tragedy in Alaska. Countries from France to Finland suffered after Chernobyl. West Germany is struggling to save the Black Forest today. And throughout, we have all learned a terrible lesson – environmental destruction respects no borders.

So my third proposal is to work together on these environmental problems, with the United States and Western Europe extending a hand to the East. Since much remains to be done in both East and West, we ask Eastern Europe to join us in this common struggle. We can offer technical training, assistance in drafting laws and regulations, and new technologies for tackling these awesome problems. And I invite the environmentalists and engineers of the East to visit the West, to share knowledge so that we can succeed in this great cause.

My fourth proposal, actually, a set of proposals, concerns a less militarized Europe, the most heavily armed continent in the world. Nowhere is this more important than in the two Germanys. And that's why our quest to safely reduce armaments has a special significance for the German people.

To those who are impatient with our measured pace in arms reduction, I respectfully suggest that history teaches us a lesson – that unity and strength are the catalyst and prerequisite to arms control. We've always believed that a strong Western defense is the best road to peace. And 40 years of experience have proven us right.

But we've done more than just keep the peace. By standing together, we have convinced the Soviets that their arms buildup has been costly and pointless. Let us not give them incentives to return to the policies of the past. Let us give them every reason to abandon the arms race for the sake of the human race.

In this era of both negotiation and armed camps, America understands that West Germany bears a special burden. Of course, in this nuclear age, every nation is on the front line. But not all free nations are called to endure the tension of regular military activity, or the constant presence of foreign military forces. We are sensitive to these special conditions that this needed presence imposes.

To significantly ease the burden of armed camps in Europe, we must be aggressive in our pursuit of solid, verifiable agreements between NATO and the Warsaw Pact.

On Monday (May 29), with my NATO colleagues in Brussels, I shared my great hope for the future of conventional arms negotiations in

Europe. I shared with them a proposal for achieving significant reductions in the near future.

And as you know, the Warsaw Pact has now accepted major elements of our Western approach to the new conventional arms negotiations in Vienna. The Eastern bloc acknowledges that a substantial imbalance exists between the conventional forces of the two alliances. And they've moved closer to NATO's position by accepting most elements of our initial conventional arms proposal. These encouraging steps have produced the opportunity for creative and decisive action, and we shall not let that opportunity pass.

Our proposal has several key initiatives.

I propose that we 'lock in' the Eastern agreement to Western-proposed ceilings on tanks and armored troop carriers. We should also seek an agreement on common numerical ceiling for artillery in the range between NATO's and that of the Warsaw Pact, provided these definitional problems can be solved. And the weapons we remove must be destroyed.

We should expand our current offer to include all land-based combat aircraft and helicopters, by proposing that both sides reduce in these categories to a level 15 percent below the current NATO totals. Given the Warsaw Pact's advantage in numbers, the Pact would have to make far-deeper reductions than NATO to establish parity at those lower levels. Again, the weapons we remove must be destroyed.

I propose a 20 percent cut in combat manpower in U.S.-stationed forces, and a resulting ceiling on U.S. and Soviet ground and air forces stationed outside of national territory in the Atlantic-to-the Urals zone, at approximately 275,000 each. This reduction to parity, a fair and balanced level of strength, would compel the Soviets to reduce their 600,000-strong Red Army in Eastern Europe by 325,000. And these withdrawn forces must be demobilized.

And finally, I call on President Gorbachev to accelerate the timetable for reaching these agreements. There is no reason why the five-to-six-year timetable, as suggested by Moscow is necessary. I propose a much more ambitious schedule. And we should aim to reach an agreement within six months to a year, and accomplish reductions by 1992, or 1993 at the latest.

In addition to my conventional arms proposals, I believe that we ought to strive to improve the openness with which we and the Soviets conduct our military activities. And therefore, I want to reiterate my support for greater transparency. I renew my proposal that the Soviet Union and its allies open their skies to reciprocal, unarmed aerial surveillance flights, conducted on short notice, to watch military activities. Satellites are a very important way to verify arms control agreements. But they do not provide constant coverage of the Soviet Union. An Open Skies policy would move both sides closer to a total continuity of coverage, while symbolizing greater openness between East and West.

These are my proposals to achieve a less militarized Europe. A short time ago they would have been too revolutionary to consider. And yet today, we may well be on the verge of a more ambitious agreement in Europe than anyone considered possible.

But we are also challenged by developments outside of NATO's traditional areas of concern. Every Western nation still faces the global proliferation of lethal technologies, including ballistic missiles and chemical weapons. We must collectively control the spread of these growing threats. So we should begin as soon as possible with a worldwide ban on chemical weapons.

Growing political freedom in the East, a Berlin without barriers, a cleaner environment, a less militarized Europe – each is a noble goal, and taken together they are the foundation of our larger vision – a Europe that is free and at peace with itself. And let the Soviets know that our goal is not to undermine their legitimate security interests. Our goal is to convince them, step by step, that their definition of security is obsolete, that their deepest fears are unfounded.

When Western Europe takes its giant step in 1992, it will institutionalize what's been true for years – borders open to people, commerce and ideas. No shadow of suspicion, no sinister fear is cast between you. The very prospect of war within the West is unthinkable to our citizens. But such a peaceful integration of nations into a world community does not mean that any nation must relinquish its culture, much less its sovereignty.

This process of integration, a subtle weaving of shared interests, which is so nearly complete in Western Europe, has now finally begun in the East. We want to help the nations of Eastern Europe realize what we, the nations of Western Euope, learned long ago. The foundation of lasting security comes not from tanks, troops, or barbed wire. It is built on shared values and agreements that link free peoples.

The nations of Eastern Europe are rediscovering the glories of their national heritage. So let the colors and hues of national culture return to these grey societies of the East. Let Europe forego a peace of tension for a peace of trust, one in which the peoples of the East and West can rejoice; a continent that is diverse, yet whole.

Forty years of Cold War have tested Western resolve and the strength of our values. NATO's first mission is now nearly complete. But if we are to fulfill our vision – our European vision – the challenges of the next 40 years will ask no less of us. Together, we shall answer the call. The world has waited long enough.

Source: USIS, London, 1 June 1989

DECLARATION OF
THE HEADS OF STATE AND GOVERNMENT,
NORTH ATLANTIC COUNCIL MEETING

Brussels, 29–30 May 1989

I. NATO'S 40 Years of Success

1.   As our Alliance celebrates its 40th Anniversary, we measure its achievements with pride. Founded in troubled times to safeguard our security, it has withstood the test of four decades, and has allowed our countries to enjoy in freedom one of the longest periods of peace and prosperity in their history. The Alliance has been a fundamental element of stability and co-operation. These are the fruits of a partnership based on enduring common values and interests, and on unity of purpose.

2.   Our meeting takes place at a juncture of unprecedented change and opportunities. This is a time to look ahead, to chart the course of our Alliance and to set our agenda for the future.

A Time of Change

3.   In our rapidly changing world, where ideas transcend borders ever more easily, the strength and accomplishments of democracy and freedom are increasingly apparent. The inherent inability of oppressive systems to fulfil the aspirations of their citizens has become equally evident.

4.   In the Soviet Union, important changes are underway. We welcome the current reforms that have already led to greater openness, improved respect for human rights, active participation of the individual, and new attitudes in foreign policy. But much remains to be done. We still look forward to the full implementation of the announced change in priorities in the allocation of economic resources from the military to the civilian sector. If sustained, the reforms will strengthen prospects for fundamental improvements in East–West relations.

5.   We also welcome the marked progress in some countries of Eastern Europe towards establishing more democratic institutions, freer elections and greater political pluralism and economic choice. However, we deplore the fact that certain Eastern European governments have chosen to ignore this reforming trend and continue all too frequently to violate human rights and basic freedoms.

295

Shaping the Future

6.   Our vision of a just, humane and democratic world has always underpinned the policies of this Alliance. The changes that are now taking place are bringing us closer to the realisation of this vision.

7.   We want to overcome the painful division of Europe, which we have never accepted. We want to move byond the post-war period. Based on today's momentum of increased co-operation and tomorrow's common challenges, we seek to shape a new political order of peace in Europe. We will work as Allies to seize all opportunities to achieve this goal. But ultimate success does not depend on us alone.

Our guiding principles in the pursuit of this course will be the policies of the Harmel Report in their two complementary and mutually reinforcing approaches: adequate military strength and political solidarity and, on that basis, the search for constructive dialogue and co-operation, including arms control, as a means of bringing about a just and lasting peaceful order in Europe.

8.   The Alliance's long-term objectives are:
   – to ensure that wars and intimidation of any kind in Europe and North America are prevented, and that military aggression is an option which no government could rationally contemplate or hope successfully to undertake, and by doing so to lay the foundations for a world where military forces exist solely to preserve the independence and territorial integrity of their countries, as has always been the case for the Allies;
   – to establish a new pattern of relations between the countries of East and West, in which ideological and military antagonism will be replaced with co-operation, trust and peaceful competition; and in which human rights and political freedoms will be fully guaranteed and enjoyed by all individuals.

9.   Within our larger responsibilities as Heads of State or Government, we are also committed
   – to strive for an international community founded on the rule of law, where all nations join together to reduce world tensions, settle disputes peacefully, and search for solutions to those issues of universal concern, including poverty, social injustice and the environment, on which our common fate depends.

II. Maintaining our Defence

10.   Peace must be worked for; it can never be taken for granted. The greatly improved East–West political climate offers prospects for a stable and lasting peace, but experience teaches us that we must remained prepared. We can overlook neither the capabilities of the Warsaw Treaty countries for offensive military action, nor the potential hazards resulting from severe political strain and crisis.

11.   A strong and united Alliance will remain fundamental not only for the security of our countries but also for our policy of supporting

political change. It is the basis for further successful negotiations on arms control and on measures to strengthen mutual confidence through improved transparency and predictability. Military security and policies aimed at reducing tensions as well as resolving underlying political differences are not contradictory but complementary. Credible defence based on the principle of the indivisibility of security for all member countries will thus continue to be essential to our common endeavour.

12.   For the foreseeable future, there is no alternative to the Alliance strategy for the prevention of war. This is a strategy of deterrence based upon an appropriate mix of adequate and effective nuclear and conventional forces which will continue to be kept up-to-date where necessary. We shall ensure the viability and credibility of these forces, while maintaining them at the lowest possible level consistent with our security requirements.

13.   The presence of North American conventional and nuclear forces in Europe remains vital to the security of Europe just as Europe's security is vital to that of North America. Maintenance of this relationship requires that the Allies fulfil their essential commitments in support of the common defence. Each of our countries will accordingly assume its fair share of the risks, rôles and responsibilities of the Atlantic partnership. Growing European political unity can lead to a reinforced European component of our common security effort and its efficiency. It will be essential to the success of these efforts to make the most effective use of resources made available for our security. To this end, we will seek to maximise the efficiency of our defence programmes and pursue solutions to issues in the area of economic and trade policies as they affect our defence. We will also continue to protect our technological capabilities by effective export controls on essential strategic goods.

Initiatives on Arms Control

14.   Arms Control has always been an integral part of the Alliance's security policy and of its overall approach to East–West relations, firmly embedded in the broader political context in which we seek the improvement of those relations.

15.   The Allies have consistently taken the lead in developing the conceptual foundations for arms control, identifying areas in which the negotiating partners share an interest in achieving a mutually satisfactory result while safeguarding the legitimate security interests of all.

16.   Historic progress has been made in recent years, and we now see prospects for further substantial advances. In our determined effort to reduce the excessive weight of the military factor in the East–West relationship and increasingly to replace confrontation by co-operation, we can now exploit fully the potential of arms control as an agent of change.

17.   We challenge the members of the Warsaw Treaty Organization

to join us in accelerating efforts to sign and implement an agreement which will enhance security and stability in Europe by reducing conventional armed forces. To seize the unique opportunity at hand, we intend to present a proposal that will amplify and expand on the position we tabled at the opening of the CFE negotiations on 9 March.[1] We will

- register agreement, based on the ceilings already proposed in Vienna, on tanks, armoured troop carriers and artillery pieces held by members of the two Alliances in Europe, with all of the withdrawn equipment to be destroyed. Ceilings on tanks and armoured troop carriers will be based on proposals already tabled in Vienna; definitional questions on artillery pieces remain to be resolved;
- expand our current proposal to include reductions by each side to equal ceilings at the level 15 per cent below current Alliance holdings of helicopters and of all land-based combat aircraft in the Atlantic-to-the-Urals zone, with all the withdrawn equipment to be destroyed;
- propose a 20 per cent cut in combat manpower in US stationed forces, and a resulting ceiling on US and Soviet ground and air force personnel stationed outside of national territory in the Atlantic-to-the-Urals zone at approximately 275,000. This ceiling would require the Soviet Union to reduce its forces in Eastern Europe by some 325,000. United States and Soviet forces withdrawn will be demobilized;
- seek such an agreement within six months to a year and accomplish the reductions by 1992 or 1993. Accordingly, we have directed the Alliance's High Level Task Force on conventional arms control to complete the further elaboration of this proposal, including its verification elements, so that it may be tabled at the beginning of the third round of the CFE negotiations, which opens on 7 September 1989.

18.   We consider as an important initiative President Bush's call for an 'open skies' regime intended to improve confidence among States through reconnaissance flights, and to contribute to the transparency of military activity, to arms control and to public awareness. It will be the subject of careful study and wide-ranging consultations.

19.   Consistent with the principles and objectives set out in our Comprehensive Concept of Arms Control and Disarmament which we have adopted at this meeting, we will continue to use arms control as a means to enhance security and stability at the lowest possible level of armed forces, and to strengthen confidence by further appropriate measures. We have already demonstrated our commitment to these objectives: both by negotiations and by unilateral action, resulting since 1979 in reductions of over one-third of the nuclear holdings assigned to SACEUR in Europe.

Towards an Enhanced Partnership

20. As the Alliance enters its fifth decade we will meet the challenge of shaping our relationship in a way which corresponds to the new political and economic realities of the 1990s. As we do so, we recognize that the basis of our security and prosperity – and of our hopes for better East–West relations – is and will continue to be the close cohesion between the countries of Europe and of North America, bound together by their common values and democratic institutions as much as by their shared security interests.

21. Ours is a living and developing partnership. The strength and stability derived from our transatlantic bond provide a firm foundation for the achievement of our long-term vision, as well as of our goals for the immediate future. We recognize that our common tasks transcend the resources of either Europe or North America alone.

22. We welcome in this regard the evolution of an increasingly strong and coherent European identity, including in the security area. The process we are witnessing today provides an example of progressive integration, leaving centuries-old conflicts far behind. It opens the way to a more mature and balanced transatlantic partnership and constitutes one of the foundations of Europe's future structure.

23. To ensure the continuing success of our efforts we have agreed to

- strengthen our process of political consultation and, where appropriate, co-ordination, and have instructed the Council in Permanent Session to consider methods for its further improvement;
- expand the scope and intensity of our effort to ensure that our respective approaches to problems affecting our common security are complementary and mutually supportive;
- renew our support for our economically less-favoured partners and to reaffirm our goal of improving the present level of co-operation and assistance;
- continue to work in the appropriate fora for more commercial, monetary and technological co-operation, and to see to it that no obstacles impede such co-operation.

Overcoming the Division of Europe

24. Now, more than ever, our efforts to overcome the division of Europe must address its underlying political causes. Therefore all of us will continue to pursue a comprehensive approach encompassing the many dimensions of the East–West agenda. In keeping with our values, we place primary emphasis on basic freedoms for the people in Eastern Europe. These are also key elements for strengthening the stability and security of all states and for guaranteeing lasting peace on the continent.

25. The CSCE process encompasses our vision of a peaceful and more constructive relationship among all participating states. We

intend to develop it further, in all its dimensions, and to make the fullest use of it.

We recognize progress in the implementation of CSCE commitments by some Eastern countires. But we call upon all of them to recognize and implement fully the commitments which all CSCE states have accepted. We will invoke the CSCE mechanisms as most recently adopted in the Vienna Concluding Document – and the provisions of other international agreement, to bring all Eastern countries to:

- enshrine in law and practice the human rights and freedoms agreed in international covenants and in the CSCE documents, thus fostering progress towards the rule of law;
- tear down the walls that separate us physically and politically, simplify the crossing of borders, increase the number of crossing points and allow the free exchange of persons, information and ideas;
- ensure that people are not prevented by armed force from crossing the frontiers and boundaries which we share with Eastern countries, in exercise of their right to leave any country, including their own;
- respect in law and practice the right of all the people in each country to determine freely and periodically the nature of the government they wish to have;
- see to it that their peoples can decide through their elected authorities what form of relations they wish to have with other countries;
- grant the genuine economic freedoms that are linked inherently to the rights of the individual;
- develop transparency, especially in military matters, in pursuit of greater mutual understanding and reassurance.

26.   The situation in and around Berlin is an essential element in East–West relations. The Alliance declares its commitment to a free and prosperous Berlin and to achieving improvements for the city especially through the Allied Berlin Initiative. The Wall dividing the city is an unacceptable symbol of the division of Europe. We seek a state of peace in Europe in which the German people regains its unity through free self-determination.

Our Design for Co-operation

27.   We, for our part, have today reaffirmed that the Alliance must and will reintensify its own efforts to overcome the division of Europe and to explore all available avenues of co-operation and dialogue. We support the opening of Eastern societies and encourage reforms that aim at positive political, economic and human rights developments. Tangible steps towards genuine political and economic reform improve possibilities for broad co-operation, while a continuing denial of basic freedoms cannot but have a negative effect. Our approach recognizes that each country is unique and must be treated on its own merits. We

also recognize that it is essentially incumbent upon the countries of the East to solve their problems by reforms from within. But we can also play a constructive role within the framework of our Alliance as well as in our respective bilateral relations and in international organizations, as appropriate.

28. To that end, we have agreed the following joint agenda for the future:

- as opportunities develop, we will expand the scope of our contacts and co-operation to cover a broad range of issues which are important to both East and West. Our goal is a sustained effort geared to specific tasks which will help deepen openness and promote democracy within Eastern countries and thus contribute to the establishment of a more stable peace in Europe;

- we will pursue in particular expanded contacts beyond the realm of government among individuals in East and West. These contacts should include all segments of our societies, but in particular young people, who will carry the responsibility for continuing our common endeavour;

- we will seek expanded economic and trade relations with the Eastern countries on the basis of commercially sound terms, mutual interest and reciprocity. Such relations should also serve as incentives for real economic reform and thus ease the way for increased integration of Eastern countries into the international trading system;

- we intend to demonstrate through increased co-operation that democratic institutions and economic choice create the best possible conditions for economic and social progress. The development of such open systems will facilitate co-operation and, consequently, make its benefits more available;

- an important task of our co-operation will be to explore means to extend Western experience and know-how to Eastern countries in a manner which responds to and promotes positive change. Exchanges in technical and managerial fields, establishment of co-operative training programmes, expansion of educational, scientific and cultural changes all offer possibilities which have not yet been exhausted;

- equally important will be to integrate Eastern European countries more fully into efforts to meet the social, environmental and technological challenges of the modern world, where common interests should prevail. In accordance with our concern for global challenges, we will seek to engage Eastern countries in co-operative strategies in areas such as the environment, terrorism, and drugs. Eastern willingness to participate constructively in dealing with such challenges will help further co-operation in other areas as well;

- East–West understanding can be expanded only if our respective societies gain increased knowledge about one another and communicate effectively. To encourage an increase of Soviet and Eastern studies in universities of our countries and of corresponding studies in Eastern countries, we are prepared to establish a Fellowship/Scholarship programme to promote the study of our democratic institutions, with candidates being invited from Eastern as well as Western Europe and North America.

Global Challenges

29.   Worldwide developments which affect our security interests are legitimate matters for consultation and, where appropriate, co-ordination among us. Our security is to be seen in a context broader than the protection from war alone.

30.   Regional conflicts continue to be of major concern. The co-ordinated approach of Alliance members recently has helped toward settling some of the world's most dangerous and long-standing disputes. We hope that the Soviet Union will increasingly work with us in positive and practical steps that continue to preoccupy the international community.

31.   We will seek to contain the newly emerging security threats and destabilizing consequences resulting from the uncontrolled spread and application of modern military technologies.

32.   In the spirit of Article 2 of the Washington Treaty, we will increasingly need to address worldwide problems which have a bearing on our security, particularly environmental degradation, resource conflicts and grave economic disparities. We will seek to do so in the appropriate multilateral fora, in the widest possible co-operation with other States.

33.   We will each futher develop our close co-operation with the other industrial democracies akin to us in their objectives and policies.

34.   We will redouble our efforts in a reinvigorated United Nations, strengthening its role in conflict settlement and peacekeeping, and in its larger endeavours for world peace.

Our 'Third Dimension'

35.   Convinced of the vital need for international co-operation in science and technology, and of its beneficial effect on global security, we have for several decades maintained Alliance programmes of scientific co-operation. Recognizing the importance of safeguarding the environment we have also co-operated, in the Committee on the Challenges of Modern Society, on environmental matters. These activities have demonstrated the broad range of our common pursuits. We intend to give more impact to our programmes with new initiatives in these areas.

The Future of the Alliance

36.   We, the leaders of 16 free and democratic countries, have dedicated ourselves to the goals of the Alliance and are committed to work in unison for their continued fulfilment.

37.   At this time of unprecedented promise in international affairs, we will respond to the hopes that it offers. The Alliance will continue to serve as the cornerstone of our security, peace and freedom. Secure on this foundation, we will reach out to those who are willing to join us in shaping a more stable and peaceful international environment in the service of our societies.

Source: NATO, 30 May 1989

1   France takes this opportunity to recall that, since the mandate for the Vienna negotiations excludes nuclear weapons, it retains complete freedom of judgement and decision regarding the resources contributing to the implementation of its independent nuclear deterrent strategy.

A COMPREHENSIVE CONCEPT
OF ARMS CONTROL AND
DISARMAMENT

Adopted at the North Atlantic Council Meeting
in Brussels, 29 and 30 May 1989

At Reykjavik in June 1987, Ministers stated that the arms control problems facing the Alliance raised complex and interrelated issues that needed to be evaluated together, bearing in mind overall progress in arms control negotiations as well as the requirements of Alliance security and of its strategy of deterrence. They therefore directed the Council in Permanent Session, working in conjunction with the appropriate military authorities, to 'consider the further development of a comprehensive concept of arms control and disarmament'.

The attached report, prepared by the Council in response to that mandate, was adopted by Heads of State and Government at the meeting of the North Atlantic Council in Brussels on 29 and 30 May 1989.

I. Introduction

1.   The overriding objective of the Alliance is to preserve peace in freedom, to prevent war, and to establish a just and lasting peaceful order in Europe. The Allies' policy to this end was set forth in the Harmel Report of 1967. It remains valid. According to the Report, the North Atlantic Alliance's 'first function is to maintain adequate military strength and political solidarity to deter aggression and other forms of pressure and to defend the territory of member countries if aggression should occur'. On that basis, the Alliance can carry out 'its second function, to pursue the search for progress towards a more stable relationship in which the underlying political issues can be solved'. As the Report observed, military security and a policy aimed at reducing tensions are 'not contradictory, but complementary'. Consistent with these principles, Allied Heads of State and Government have agreed that arms control is an integral part of the Alliance's security policy.

2.   The possibilities for fruitful East–West dialogue have significantly improved in recent years. More favourable conditions now exist

for progress towards the achievement of the Alliance's objectives. The Allies are resolved to grasp this opportunity. They will continue to address both the symptoms and the causes of political tension in a manner that respects the legitimate security interests of all states concerned.

3. The achievement of the lasting peaceful order which the Allies seek will require that the unnatural division of Europe, and particularly of Germany, be overcome, and that, as stated in the Helsinki Final Act, the sovereignty and territorial integrity of all states and the right of peoples to self-determination be respected, and that the rights of all individuals, including their right of political choice, be protected. The members of the Alliance accordingly attach central importance to further progress in the Conference on Security and Cooperation in Europe (CSCE) process, which serves as a framework for the promotion of peaceful evolution in Europe.

4. The CSCE process provides a means to encourage stable and constructive East–West relations by increasing contacts between people, by seeking to ensure that basic rights and freedoms are respected in law and practice, by furthering political exchanges and mutually beneficial cooperation across a broad range of endeavours, and by enhancing security and openness in the military sphere. The Allies will continue to demand full implementation of all the principle and provisions of the Helsinki Final Act, the Madrid Concluding Document, the Stockholm Document, and the Concluding Document of the Vienna Meeting. The last document marks a major advance in the CSCE process and should stimulate further beneficial changes in Europe.

5. The basic goal of the Alliance's arms control policy is to enhance security and stability at the lowest balanced level of forces and armaments consistent with the requirements of the strategy of deterrence. The Allies are committed to achieving continuing progress towards all their arms control objectives. The further development of the Comprehensive Concept is designed to assist this by ensuring an integrated approach covering both defence policy and arms control policy: these are complementary and interactive. This work also requires full consideration of the interrelationship between arms control objectives and defence requirements and how various arms control measures, separately and in conjunction with each other, can strengthen Alliance security. The guiding principles and basic objectives which have so far governed the arms control policy of the Alliance remain valid. Progress in achieving these objectives is, of course, affected by a number of factors. These include the overall state of East–West relations, the military requirements of the Allies, the progress of existing and future arms control negotiations, and developments in the CSCE process. The further development and implementation of a comprehensive concept of arms control and disarmament will take place against this background.

II. East–West Relations and Arms Control

6.   The Alliance continues to seek a just and stable peace in Europe in which all states can enjoy undiminished security at the minimum necessary levels of forces and armaments and all individuals can exercise their basic rights and freedoms. Arms control alone cannot resolve longstanding political differences between East and West nor guarantee a stable peace. Nonetheless, achievement of the Alliance's goal will require substantial advances in arms control, as well as more fundamental changes in political relations. Success in arms control, in addition to enhancing military security, can encourage improvements in the East–West political dialogue and thereby contribute to the achievement of broader Alliance objectives.

7.   To increase security and stability in Europe, the Alliance has consistently pursued every opportunity for effective arms control. The Allies are committed to this policy, independent of any changes that may occur in the climate of East–West relations. Success in arms control, however, continues to depend not on our own efforts alone, but also on Eastern and particularly Soviet readiness to work constructively towards mutually beneficial results.

8.   The immediate past has witnessed unprecedented progress in the field of arms control. In 1986 the Stockholm Conference on Disarmament in Europe (CDE) agreement created an innovative system of confidence and security-building measures, designed to promote military transparency and predictability. To date, these have been satisfactorily implemented. The 1987 INF Treaty marked another major step forward because it eliminated a whole class of weapons, it established the principle of asymmetrical reductions, and provided for a stringent verification regime. Other achievements include the establishments in the United States and the Soviet Union of nuclear risk reduction centres, the US/Soviet agreement on prior notification of ballistic missile launches, and the conduct of the Joint Verification Experiment in connection with continued US/Soviet negotiations on nuclear testing.

9.   In addition to agreements already reached, there has been substantial progress in the START negotiations which are intended to reduce radically strategic nuclear arsenals and eliminate destabilising offensive capabilities. The Paris Conference on the Prohibition of Chemical Weapons has reaffirmed the authority of the 1925 Geneva Protocol and given powerful political impetus to the negotiations in Geneva for a global, comprehensive and effectively verifiable ban on chemical weapons. New distinct negotiations within the framework of the CSCE process have now begun in Vienna: one on conventional armed forces in Europe between the 23 members of NATO and the Warsaw Treaty Organization (WTO) and one on confidence- and security-building measures (CSBMs) among all 35 signatories of the Helsinki Final Act.

10. There has also been substantial progress on other matters important to the West. Soviet troops have left Afghanistan. There has been movement toward the resolution of some, although not all, of the remaining regional conflicts in which the Soviet Union is involved. The observance of human rights in the Soviet Union and in some of the other WTO countries has significantly improved, even if serious deficiencies remain. The recent Vienna CSCE Follow-Up meeting succeeded in setting new, higher standards of conduct for participating states and should stimulate further progress in the CSCE process. A new intensity of dialogue, particularly at high level, between East and West opens new opportunities and testifies to the Allies' commitment to resolve the fundamental problems that remain.

11. The Alliance does not claim exclusive responsibility for this favourable evolution in East–West relations. In recent years, the East has become more responsive and flexible. Nonetheless, the Alliance's contribution has clearly been fundamental. Most of the achievements to date, which have been described above, were inspired by initiatives by the Alliance or its members. The Allies' political solidarity, commitment to defence, patience and creativity in negotiations overcame initial obstacles and brought its efforts to fruition. It was the Alliance that drew up the basic blueprints for East–West progress and has since pushed them forward towards realisation. In particular, the concepts of stability, reasonable sufficiency, asymmetrical reductions, concentration on the most offensive equipment, rigorous verification, transparency, a single zone from the Atlantic to the Urals, and the balanced and comprehensive nature of the CSCE process, are Western-inspired.

12. Prospects are now brighter than ever before for lasting, qualitative improvements in the East–West relationship. There continue to be clear signs of change in the internal and external policies of the Soviet Union and some of its Allies. The Soviet leadership has stated that ideological competition should play no part in inter-state relations. Soviet acknowledgement of serious shortcomings in its past approaches to international as well as domestic issues creates opportunities for progress on fundamental political problems.

13. At the same time, serious concerns remain. The ambitious Soviet reform programme, which the Allies welcome, will take many years to complete. Its success cannot be taken for granted given the magnitude of the problems it faces and the resistance generated. In Eastern Europe, progress in constructive reform is still uneven and the extent of these reforms remains to be determined. Basic human rights still need to be firmly anchored in law and practice, though in some Warsaw Pact countries improvements are underway. Although the WTO has recently announced and begun unilateral reductions in some of its forces, the Soviet Union continues to deploy military forces and to maintain a pace of military production in excess of legitimate defensive requirements. Moreover, the geostrategic realities favour the geographically contiguous Soviet-dominated WTO as against the

geographically separate democracies of the North Atlantic Alliance. It has long been an objective of the Soviet Union to weaken the links between the European and North American members of the Alliance.

14.   We face an immediate future that is promising but still uncertain. The Allies and the East face both a challenge and an opportunity to capitalise on present conditions in order to increase mutual security. The progress recently made in East–West relations has given new impetus to the arms control process and has enhanced the possibilities of achieving the Alliance's arms control objectives, which complement the other elements of the Alliance's security policy.

III. Principles of Alliance Security

15.   Alliance security policy aims to preserve peace in freedom by both political means and the maintenance of a military capability sufficient to prevent war and to provide for effective defence. The fact that the Alliance has for forty years safeguarded peace in Europe bears witness to the success of this policy.

16.   Improved political relations and the progressive development of cooperative structures between Eastern and Western countries are important components of Alliance policy. They can enhance mutual confidence, reduce the risk of misunderstanding, ensure that there are in place reliable arrangements for crisis management so that tensions can be defused, render the situation in Europe more open and predictable, and encourage the development of wider cooperation in all fields.

17.   In underlining the importance of these facts for the formulation of Alliance policy, the Allies reaffirm that, as stated in the Harmel Report, the search for constructive dialogue and cooperation with the countries of the East, including arms control and disarmament, is based on political solidarity and adequate military strength.

18.   Solidarity among the Alliance countries is a fundamental principle of their security policy. It reflects the indivisible nature of their security. It is expressed by the willingness of each country to share fairly the risks, burdens and responsibilities of the common effort as well as its benefits. In particular, the presence in Europe of the United States' conventional and nuclear forces and of Canadian forces demonstrates that North American and European security interests are inseparably bound together.

19.   From its inception the Alliance of Western democracies has been defensive in purpose. This will remain so. None of our weapons will ever be used except in self-defence. The Alliance does not seek military superiority nor will it ever do so. Its aim has always been to prevent war and any form of coercion and intimidation.

20.   Consistent with the Alliance's defensive character, its strategy is one of deterrence. Its objective is to convince a potential aggressor before he acts that he is confronted with a risk that outweighs any gain

– however great – he might hope to secure from his aggression. The purpose of this strategy defines the means needed for its implementation.

21. In order to fulfil its strategy, the Alliance must be capable of responding appropriately to any aggression and of meeting its commitment to the defence of the frontiers of its members' territory. For the foreseeable future, deterrence requires an appropriate mix of adequate and effective nuclear and conventional forces which will continue to be kept up to date where necessary; for it is only by their evident and perceived capability for effective us that such forces and weapons deter.

22. Conventional forces make an essential contribution to deterrence. The elimination of asymmetries between the conventional forces of East and West in Europe would be a major breakthrough, bringing significant benefits for stability and security. Conventional defence alone cannot, however, ensure deterrence. Only the nuclear element can confront an aggressor with an unacceptable risk and thus plays an indispensable role in our current strategy of war prevention.

23. The fundamental purpose of nuclear forces – both strategic and sub-strategic – is political: to preserve the peace and to prevent any kind of war. Such forces contribute to deterrence by demonstrating that the Allies have the military capability and the political will to use them, if necessary, in response to aggression. Should aggression occur, the aim would be to restore deterrence by inducing the aggressor to reconsider his decision, to terminate his attack and to withdraw and thereby to restore the territorial integrity of the Alliance.

24. Conventional and nuclear forces, therefore, perform different but complementary and mutually reinforcing roles. Any perceived inadequacy in either of these two elements, or the impression that conventional forces could be separated from nuclear, or sub-strategic from strategic nuclear forces, might lead a potential adversary to conclude that the risks of launching aggression might be calculable and acceptable. No single element can, therefore, be regarded as a substitute compensating for deficiencies in any other.

25. For the foreseeable future, there is no alternative strategy for the prevention of war. The implementation of this strategy will continue to ensure that the security interests of all Alliance members are fully safeguarded. The principles underlying the strategy of deterrence are of enduring validity. Their practical expression in terms of the size, structure and deployment of forces is bound to change. As in the past, these elements will continue to evolve in response to changing international circumstances, technological progress and developments in the scale of the threat – in particular, in the posture and capabilities of the forces of the Warsaw Treaty Organization.

26. Within this overall framework, strategic nuclear forces provide the ultimate guarantee of deterrence for the Allies. They must be capable of inflicting unacceptable damage on an aggressor state even

after it has carried out a first strike. Their number, range, survivability and penetration capability need to ensure that a potential aggressor cannot count on limiting the conflict or regarding his own territory as a sanctuary. The strategic nuclear forces of the United States provide the cornerstone of deterrence for the Alliance as a whole. The independent nuclear forces of the United Kingdom and France fulfil a deterrent role of their own and contribute to the overall deterrence strategy of the Alliance by complicating the planning and risk assessment of a potential aggressor.

27.   Nuclear forces below the strategic level provide an essential political and military linkage between conventional and strategic forces and, together with the presence of Canadian and United States forces in Europe, between the European and North American members of the Alliance. The Allies' sub-strategic nuclear forces are not designed to compensate for conventional imbalances. The levels of such forces in the integrated military structure nevertheless must take into account the threat – both conventional and nuclear – with which the Alliance is faced. Their role is to ensure that there are no circumstances in which a potential aggressor might discount the prospect of nuclear retaliation in response to military action. Nuclear forces below the strategic level thus make an essential contribution in deterrence.

Sub-Strategic Nuclear Forces

42.   The Allies are committed to maintaining only the minimum number of nuclear weapons necessary to support their strategy of deterrence. In line with this commitment, the members of the integrated military structure have already made major unilateral cuts in their sub-strategic nuclear armoury. The number of land-based warheads in Western Europe has been reduced by over one-third since 1979 to its lowest level in over 20 years. Updating where necessary of their sub-strategic systems would result in further reductions.

43.   The Allies continue to face the direct threat posed to Europe by the large numbers of shorter-range nuclear missiles deployed on Warsaw Pact territory and which have been substantially upgraded in recent years. Major reductions in Warsaw Pact systems would be of overall value to Alliance security. One of the ways to achieve this aim would be by tangible and verifiable reductions of American and Soviet land-based nuclear missile systems of shorter range leading to equal ceilings at lower levels.

44.   But the sub-strategic nuclear forces deployed by member countries of the Alliance are not principally a counter to similar systems operated by members of the WTO. As is explained in III above, sub-strategic nuclear forces fulfil an essential role in overall Alliance deterrence strategy by ensuring that there are no circumstances in which a potential aggressor might discount nuclear retaliation in response to his military action.

45.   The Alliance reaffirms its position that for the foreseeable future

there is no alternative to the Alliance's strategy for the prevention of war, which is a strategy of deterrence based upon an appropriate mix of adequate and effective nuclear and conventional forces which will continue to be kept up to date where necessary. Where nuclear forces are concerned, land-, sea-, and air-based systems, including ground-based missiles, in the present circumstances and as far as can be foreseen will be needed in Europe.

46. In view of the huge superiority of the Warsaw Pact in terms of short-range nuclear missiles, the Alliance calls upon the Soviet Union to reduce unilaterally its short-range missile systems to the current levels within the integrated military structure.

47. The Alliance reaffirms that at the negotiations on conventional stability it pursues the objectives of:

- the establishment of a secure and stable balance of conventional forces at lower levels;
- the elimination of disparities prejudicial to stability and security; and
- the elimination as a matter of high priority of the capability for launching surprise attack and for initiating large-scale offensive action.

48. In keeping with its arms control objectives formulated in Reykjavik in 1987 and reaffirmed in Brussels in 1988, the Alliance states that one of its highest priorities in negotiations with the East is reaching an agreement on conventional force reductions which would achieve the objectives above. In this spirit, the allies will make every effort, as evidenced by the outcome of the May 1989 Summit, to bring these conventional negotiations to an early and satisfactory conclusion. The United States has expressed the hope that this could be achieved within six to twelve months. Once implementation of such an agreement is underway, the United States, in consultation with the Allies concerned, is prepared to enter into negotiations to achieve a *partial* reduction of American and Soviet land-based nuclear missile forces of shorter range to equal and verifiable levels. With special reference to the Western proposals on CFE tabled in Vienna, enhanced by the proposals by the United States at the May 1989 Summit, the Allies concerned proceed on the understanding that negotiated reductions leading to a level below the existing level of their SNF missiles will not be carried out until the results of these negotiations have been implemented. Reductions of Warsaw Pact SNF systems should be carried out before that date.

49. As regards the sub-strategic nuclear forces of the members of the integrated military structure, their level and characteristics must be such that they can perform their deterrent role in a credible way across the required spectrum of ranges, taking into account the threat – both conventional and nuclear – with which the Alliance is faced. The question concerning the introduction and deployment of a follow-on

system for the Lance will be dealt with in 1992 in the light of overall security developments. While a decision for national authorities, the Allies concerned recognise the value of the continued funding by the United States of research and development of a follow-on for the existing Lance short-range missile, in order to preserve their options in this respect.

Conventional Forces

50. As set out in the March 1988 Summit statement and in the Alliance's November 1988 data initiative, the Soviet Union's military presence in Europe, at a level far in excess of its needs for self-defence, directly challenges our security as well as our aspirations for a peaceful order in Europe. Such excessive force levels create the risk of political intimidation or threatened aggression. As long as they exist, they present an obstacle to better political relations between all states of Europe. The challenge to security is, moreover, not only a matter of the numerical superiority of WTO forces. WTO tanks, artillery and armoured troop carriers are concentrated in large formations and deployed in such a way as to give the WTO a capability for surprise attack and large-scale offensive action. Despite the recent welcome publication by the WTO of its assessment of the military balance in Europe, there is still considerable secrecy and uncertainty about its actual capabilities and intentions.

51. In addressing these concerns, the Allies' primary objectives are to establish a secure and stable balance of conventional forces in Europe at lower levels, while at the same time creating greater openness about military organisation and activities in Europe.

52. In the Conventional Forces in Europe (CFE) talks between the 23 members of the two alliances, the Western Allies are proposing:

–   reductions to an overall limit on the total holdings of armaments in Europe, concentrating on the total holdings of armaments in Europe, concentrating on the most threatening systems, i.e. those capable of seizing and holding territory;
–   a limit on the proportion of these total holdings belonging to any one country in Europe (since the security and stability of Europe require that no state exceed its legitimate needs for self-defence);
–   a limit on stationed forces (thus restricting the forward deployment and concentration of Soviet forces in Eastern Europe); and,
–   appropriate numerical sub-limits on forces which will apply simultaneously throughout the Atlantic to the Urals area.

These measures, taken together, will necessitate deep cuts in the WTO conventional forces which most threaten the Alliance. The resulting reductions will have to take place in such a way as to prevent circumvention, e.g. by ensuring that the armaments reduced are destroyed or otherwise disposed of. Verification measures will be required to ensure that all states have confidence that entitlements are not exceeded.

53.   These measures alone, however, will not guarantee stability. The regime of reductions will have to be backed up by additional measures which should include measures of transparency, notification and constraint applied to the deployment, storage, movement and levels of readiness and availability of conventional forces.

54.   In the CSBM negotiations, the Allies aim to maintain the momentum created by the successful implementation of the Stockholm Document by proposing a comprehensive package of measures to improve:

- transparency about military organisation,
- transparency and predictabilty of military activities,
- contacts and communication,

and have also proposed an exchange of view on military doctrine in a seminar setting.

55.   The implementation of the Allies' proposals in the CFE negotiations and of their proposals for further confidence – and security – building measures would achieve a quantum improvement in European security. This would have important and positive consequences for Alliance policy both in the field of defence and arms control. The outcome of the CFE negotiations would provide a framework for determining the future Alliance force structure required to perform its fundamental task of preserving peace in freedom. In addition, the Allies would be willing to contemplate further steps to enhance stability and security if the immediate CFE objectives are achieved – for example, further reductions or limitations of conventional armaments and equipment, or the restructuring of armed forces to enhance defensive capabilities and further reduce offensive capabilities.

56.   The Allies welcome the declared readiness of the Soviet Union and other WTO members to reduce their forces and adjust them towards a defensive posture and await implementation of these measures. This would be a step in the direction of redressing the imbalance in force levels existing in Europe and towards reducing the WTO capability for surprise attack. The announced reductions demonstrate the recognition by the Soviet Union and other WTO members of the conventional imbalance, long highlighted by the Allies as a key problem of European security.

Chemical Weapons

57.   The Soviet Union's chemical weapons stockpile poses a massive threat. The Allies are committed to conclude, at the earliest date, a worldwide, comprehensive and effectively verifiable ban on all chemical weapons.

58.   All Alliance states subscribe to the prohibitions contained in the Geneva Protocal for the Use in War of Asphyxiating, Poisonous or Other Gases, and Bacteriological Methods of Warfare. The Paris Conference on the Prohibition of Chemical Weapons reaffirmed the importance of the commitments made under the Geneva Protocol and expressed the unanimous will of the international community to eliminate chemical weapons completely at an early date and thereby to prevent any recourse to their use.

59.   The Allies wish to prohibit not only the use of these abhorrent weapons, but also their development, production, stockpiling and transfer, and to achieve the destruction of existing chemical weapons and production facilities in such a way as to ensure the undiminished security of all participants at each stage in the process. Those objectives are being pursued in the Geneva Conference on Disarmament. Pending agreement on a global ban, the Allies will enforce stringent controls on the export of commodities related to chemical weapons production. They will also attempt to stimulate more openness among states about chemical weapons capabilities in order to promote greater confidence in the effectiveness of a global ban.

V. Conclusions

Arms Control and Defence Interrelationships

60.   The Alliance is committed to pursuing a comprehensive approach to security, embracing both arms control and disarmament, and defence. It is important, therefore, to ensure that interrelationships between arms control issues and defence requirements and amongst the various arms control areas are fully considered. Proposals in any one area of arms control must take account of the implications for Alliance interests in general and for other negotiations. This is a continuing process.

61.   It is essential that defence and arms control objectives remain in harmony in order to ensure their complementary contribution to the goal of maintaining security at the lowest balanced level of forces consistent with the requirements of the Alliance strategy of war prevention, acknowledging that changes in the threat, new technologies, and new political opportunities affect options in both fields. Decisions on arms control matters must fully reflect the requirements of the Allies' strategy of deterrence. Equally, progress in arms control is relevant to military plans, which will have to be developed in the full knowledge of the objectives pursued in arms control negotiations and to reflect, as necessary, the results achieved therein.

62.   In each area of arms control, the Alliance seeks to enhance stability and security. The current negotiations concerning strategic nuclear systems, conventional forces and chemical weapons are, however, independent of one another: the outcome of any one of these negotiations is not contingent on progress in others. However, they can

influence one another: criteria established and agreements achieved in one area of arms control may be relevant in other areas and hence facilitate overall progress. These could affect both arms control possibilities and the forces needed to fulfil Alliance strategy, as well as help to contribute generally to a more predictable military environment.

63. The Allies seek to manage the interaction among different arms control elements by ensuring that the development, pursuit and realisation of their arms control objectives in individual areas are fully consistent both with each other and with the Alliance's guiding principles for effective arms control. For example, the way in which START limits and sub-limits are applied in detail could affect the future flexibility of the sub-strategic nuclear forces of members of the integrated military structure. A CFE agreement would by itself make a major contribution to stability. This would be significantly further enhanced by the achievement of a global chemical weapons ban. The development of confidence- and security-building measures could influence the stabilising measures being considered in connection with the Conventional Forces in Europe negotiations and vice versa. The removal of the imbalance in conventional forces would provide scope for further reductions in the sub-strategic nuclear forces of members of the integrated military structure, though it would not obviate the need for such forces. Similarly, this might make possible further arms control steps in the conventional field.

64. This report establishes the overall conceptual framework within which the Allies will be seeking progress in each area of arms control. In so doing, their fundamental aim will be enhanced security at lower levels of forces and armaments. Taken as a whole, the Allies' arms control agenda constitutes a coherent and comprehensive approach to the enhancement of security and stability. It is ambitious, but we are confident that – with a constructive response from the WTO states – it can be fully achieved in the coming years. In pursuing this goal, the Alliance recognises that it cannot afford to build its security upon arms control results expected in the future. The Allies will be prepared, however, to draw appropriate consequences for their own military posture as they make concrete progress through arms control towards a significant reduction in the scale and quality of the military threat they face. Accomplishment of the Allies' arms control agenda would not only bring great benefits in itself, but could also lead to the expansion of cooperation with the East in other areas. The arms control process itself is, moreover, dynamic; as and when the Alliance reaches agreement in each of the areas set out above, so further prospects for arms control may be opened up and further progress made possible.

65. As noted earlier, the Allies' vision for Europe is that of an undivided continent where military forces only exist to prevent war and to ensure self-defence; a continent which no longer lives in the shadow of overwhelming military forces and from which the threat of war has been removed; a continent where the sovereignty and territorial

integrity of all states are respected and the rights of all individuals, including their right of political choice, are protected. This goal can only be reached by stages: it will require patient and creative endeavour. The Allies are resolved to continue working towards its attainment. The achievement of the Alliance's arms control objectives would be a major contribution towards the realisation of its vision.

Source: NATO, 30 May 1989

JOINT DECLARATION OF THE FEDERAL REPUBLIC OF GERMANY AND THE SOVIET UNION

13 June 1989

I

The Federal Republic of Germany and the Union of Soviet Socialist Republics are agreed that mankind faces historic challenges on the threshold to the third millennium. Problems of vital importance to all can only be resolved jointly by all states and peoples. This calls for new political thinking.

- The individual with his inherent dignity and his rights as well as concern for the survival of mankind must be the central element of politics.
- The vast reservoir of creative energies and abilities of man and modern society must be utilized for the purpose of securing peace and prosperity for all countries and peoples.
- All wars, whether nuclear or conventional, must be prevented, conflicts in various regions of the world settled and peace preserved and shaped.
- The right of all peoples and states to determine freely their destiny and to frame sovereignly their mutual relations on the basis of international law must be guaranteed. The precedence of international law in domestic and international politics must be ensured.
- Modern economic, scientific and technological findings offer unimagined possibilities that should benefit all mankind. The resultant risks and opportunities require common answers. It is therefore important to expand co-operation in all these fields, to dismantle further the trade barriers of all kinds, to seek new forms of collaboration and to make dynamic, mutually beneficial use of them.
- For the sake of present and future generations the natural environment must be saved through resolute action, and hunger and poverty in the world must be overcome.
- New threats, including epidemics and international terrorism, must be vigorously combated.

317

The two sides are determined to live up to their responsibility deriving from this recognition. Persistent differences in values and in political and social systems are not an obstacle to a forward-looking policy across the frontiers between the systems.

II

Europe has a prominent part to play in shaping a peaceful future. Although the continent has been divided for decades, the awareness of Europe's identity and common assets has endured and is becoming ever stronger. This development must be encouraged.

The Federal Republic of Germany and the Soviet Union consider it a paramount objective of their policies to continue Europe's historical traditions and thus contribute towards overcoming the division of Europe. They are resolved to elaborate jointly concepts for attaining this goal through the development of a Europe marked by peace and co-operation – a peaceful European order or a common European home – in which the United States and Canada also have their place. The CSCE Helsinki Final Act in all its parts as well as the Madrid and Vienna concluding documents chart the course for realizing this goal.

Europe, which suffered most from the two World Wars, must set the world an example of stable peace, good-neighbourliness and constructive co-operation which combines the capabilities of all countries, despite their different social systems, for the sake of the common weal. The countries of Europe can and should be able to live together without mutual fear and in peaceful competition.

A Europe of peace and co-operation must include the following:

– Unqualified respect for the integrity and security of every state, which has the right to choose freely its own political and social system, as well as unqualified respect for the norms and principles of international law, especially respect for the right of peoples to self determination.
– Vigorous continuation of the process of disarmament and arms control. In this nuclear age, efforts must be aimed not only at preventing war, but also at shaping peace and making it more secure.
– A close dialogue covering all traditional and new aspects of bilateral and multilateral relations and including regular meetings at the top political level.
– The realization of human rights and the promotion of the exchange of people and ideas. This includes the expansion of town twinning, transport and communication links, cultural contacts, travel and sports meetings, the promotion of language instruction and the favourable treatment of humanitarian matters including the reunification of families and travel abroad.
– The expansion of direct contacts between young people and the commitment of the emerging generations to a peaceful future.

- Comprehensive economic co-operation to the mutual advantage, including new forms of collaboration. The Joint Declaration of 25 June 1988 between the European Community and the Council for Mutual Economic Assistance and the normalization of relations between the European Community and the European members of the Council for Mutual Economic Assistance as well as the political dialogue initiated between the Soviet Union and the twelve members of the European Community open up new prospects for a pan-European development in that direction.
- The progressive advancement of pan-European co-operation in various sectors, particularly transport, energy, health, information and communication.
- Intensive ecological co-operation and the exploitation of new technologies which, for the sake of mankind, prevent above all the emergence of cross-border hazards.
- Respect for and cultivation of the historical cultures of the peoples of Europe. This cultural diversity is one of the great treasures of the continent. National minorities in Europe with their own cultures are part of this wealth. Their legitimate interests deserve protection.

The Federal Republic of Germany and the Soviet Union call upon all CSCE participating states to take part in forming Europe's future architecture.

III

The Federal Republic of Germany and the Soviet Union declare that one's own security must not be obtained at the expense of the security of others. They therefore pursue the goal of eliminating the causes of tension and distrust through a constructive and forward-looking policy so that the feeling of being threatened that still exists today can be replaced gradually by a state of mutual trust.

The two sides acknowledge that every state has legitimate security interests irrespective of its size and its ideological orientation. They condemn any hankering after military superiority. War must no longer be a political instrument. Security policy and armed forces planning must exclusively serve the purpose of reducing and eliminating the danger of war and of safeguarding peace with fewer weapons. This precludes any arms race. The two sides are striving for the elimination of existing asymmetries through binding agreements subject to effective international control and for the reduction of military potentials to a stable balance at a lower level which suffices for defence but not for attack. Above all the two sides consider it necessary to rule out the capability of armed forces for launching surprise attack and initiating large-scale offensive action.

The Federal Republic of Germany and the Soviet Union advocate

- a 50 per cent reduction of the strategic nuclear offensive weapons of the United States and the Soviet Union;
- agreed American–Soviet solutions at the nuclear and space talks; this also applies to observance of the ABM Treaty;
- the establishment of a stable and secure balance of conventional forces at a lower level as well as agreement on further confidence and security-building measures applicable to the whole of Europe;
- a world-wide, comprehensive and effectively verifiable ban on chemical weapons at the earliest possible date;
- agreement as soon as possible on an effectively verifiable nuclear test ban at the Geneva Conference on Disarmament; step-by-step progress towards this goal is desirable in the ongoing talks between the United States and the Soviet Union;
- the creation of further confidence-building measures, greater transparency of military arsenals and budgets as well as effective international mechanisms for managing crises, including ones outside Europe.

IV

The Federal Republic of Germany and the Soviet Union realize, in view of Europe's history and its position in the world as well as the weight which each country carries within its respective alliance, that the positive development of their mutual relations is of central importance to the situation in Europe and to East–West relations as a whole. In the desire to establish a lasting relationship of reliable good-neighbourliness, they intend to take up the good traditions of their centuries-old history. Their common goal is to continue, expand and deepen their fruitful co-operation and give it a new quality.

The Moscow Treaty of 12 August 1970 continues to form the foundation for the relationship between the two countries. The two sides will fully exploit the opportunities afforded by this Treaty and other agreements.

They have decided to expand consistently – on the basis of trust, equal rights and mutual advantage – the contractual foundations of their relations as well as their co-operation conducted in a spirit of partnership in all fields.

Berlin (West) takes part in the development of their co-operation, with the Quadripartite Agreement of 3 September 1971 being strictly observed and fully applied.

V

The Federal Republic of Germany and the Soviet Union, trusting in the long-term predictability of each other's policies, are determined to develop further their relations in all fields. They want to make the upward trend in their relations become stable and lasting.

This policy takes account of each side's treaty and alliance obligations; it is not directed against anyone. It is in line with the deep, long-cherished yearning of the peoples to heal the wounds of the past through understanding and reconciliation and to build jointly a better future.

Bonn, 13 June 1989
Helmut Kohl
Mikhail Gorbachev

Source: Embassy of the Federal Republic of Germany, 13 June 1989

GENERAL SECRETARY MIKHAIL GORBACHEV'S ADDRESS TO THE COUNCIL OF EUROPE

6 July 1989

I thank you for the invitation to take the floor here, one of the epicentres of European politics and European thought. We may assess this meeting as proof that the all-European process is a reality and that it is advancing.

Now that the 20th Century is drawing to a close and the post-war period and the cold war are becoming things of the past, Europeans are beginning to face the unique opportunity of playing their role in building a new world, a role that is worthy of their history and their economic and intellectual potential.

I

The international community is now more subject to profound change than at any time in its history. Many of its integral elements are at the crossroads of destinies. The material basis of life and its spiritual parameters are sharply changing. New, ever more powerful factors of progress are emerging. At the same time, threats connected with this very progress continue to exist and even grow alongside and following these factors.

It is crucial to do everything that is reasonably possible so that man could continue the part he is destined to play on Earth and, probably, in the universe. So that he could adapt himself to the stress-generated novelty of contemporary life and win the struggle for the survival of current and succeeding generations.

This applies to all of mankind, but three times as much to Europe – in the sense of historical responsibility, in the sense of the acuteness and urgency of problems and tasks, and in the sense of potentialities.

The specificity of the situation in Europe is in the fact that it can deal with all that, justify the hopes of its peoples and perform its international duty at the new stage of world history only by recognising its integrity and drawing the appropriate conclusions.

The concept of the 'decline of Europe' was widely in circulation in the 1920s. This subject is still in fashion in some quarters. We do not share this pessimism about the future of Europe.

Europe was the first to have felt the consequences of the internationalisation of economic and then all social life. The interdependence of countries, as a higher stage of the process of internationalisation, had an effect here long before other parts of the world.

Europe has experienced more than once attempts to unite it by force, it has also known the noble dreams about a voluntary democratic community of European peoples. Victor Hugo said: 'A day will come when you, France, you, Russia, you, Italy, you, Britain, and you, Germany, all of you, all nations of the continent will merge tightly without losing your identities and your remarkable originality in some higher society and form a European fraternity . . . A day will come when markets, open to trade, and minds, open to ideas, will become the sole battle-fields.'

It is not enough now to merely state the interdependence and joint destinies of the European states. The idea of European unity should be collectively rethought in the process of the concerted endeavour by all nations – large, medium and small.

Is it realistic to raise this question? I know that many people in the West regard the existence of two social systems as the major difficulty. But the difficulty is rather in the very common conviction (or even a political directive) that overcoming the split of Europe implies the 'overcoming of socialism'. This is a course towards confrontation, if not worse. There will be no European unity along these lines.

The belonging of European states to different social systems is a reality. Recognition of this historical fact and respect for the sovereign right of every nation to choose freely a social system constitute the major prerequisite for a normal European process.

Social and political orders in one or another country changed in the past and may change in the future. But this change is the exclusive affair of the people of that country and is their choice. Any interference in domestic affiars and any attempts to restrict the sovereignty of states, both friends, allies or any others are inadmissible.

Differences among states are not removable. They are, as I have already said on several occasions, even favourable. Provided, of course, that the competition between the different types of society is directed at creating better material and spiritual living conditions for all people.

Due to its restructuring, the USSR will be able fully to take part in this honest, equitable and constructive competition, given all the existing shortcomings and lagging, we well know the intrinsic strengths of our social system. And we are sure that we will be able to put them to use for the benefit of ourselves and for the benefit of Europe.

It is time to deposit in the archives the assumptions of the cold war period when Europe was regarded as an arena of confrontation, divided into 'spheres of influence', and somebody's 'outpost', and as an object of military rivalry, a battlefield. In today's interdependent world, the geo-political notions born of another era turn to be just as useless in real politics as laws of classical mechanics in the quantum theory.

Meanwhile, it is on the basis of outdated stereotypes that the Soviet Union is suspected of planning domination and intending to tear the United States away from Europe. There are some who would like to place the USSR outside Europe from the Atlantic to the Urals, by limiting its expanse 'from Brest to Brest'.

The USSR, it is alleged, is too big for co-existence: others would feel ill at ease with it. The present-day realities and prospects for the foreseeable future are obvious:! the USSR and the United States constitute a natural part of the European international-political structure. And their participation in its evolution is not only justified, but is also historically determined. No other approach is acceptable, nor will it bring forth any results.

In the course of centuries Europe has made an indispensable contribution to world politics, economy and culture, and to the development of the entire civilisation, its world historical role is universally recognised and praised.

Let us not forget, however, that the curse of colonial slavery spread worldwide from Europe. Fascism was born here. The most devastating wars began here. Europe may take legitimate pride in its accomplishments but it has far from paid all its debts to mankind. This is yet to be done. This is to be done by pressing for changes in international relations in the spirit of humanism, equality and justice and setting an example of democracy and social achievements in their own countries.

The Helsinki Process initiated this immense effort of world significance. Vienna and Stockholm have led it to fundamentally new frontiers. The documents adopted there are the most complete expression to date of the political culture and moral traditional of the European peoples.

We all, participants in the European process, are yet to use as fully as possible the prerequisites created by our common effort. This aim is served by our idea of the common European home.

II

It was born of the comprehension of new realities and the understanding of the fact that the linear continuation of the movement along which intra-European relations developed up to the last quarter of the 20th Century no longer matches these realities.

The idea is connected with our domestic economic and political restructuring which was in need of new relationships primarily in that part of the world to which we, the Soviet Union, belong and with which we had been for centuries connected most of all.

We also took into account that the tremendous burden of armaments and the atmosphere of confrontation not only hindered the normal development of Europe but at the same time also prevented our country from joining in the European process economically, politically and psychologically, and deformed our development.

These were the motives from which we decided to revitalise our European policy which in itself, incidentally, had always been of importance to us.

Matters concerning both the architecture of a common home and methods for building it and even its furnishings were touched upon during meetings with European leaders recently. Conversations with President François Mitterrand on this subject in Moscow and Paris were also fruitful and rather wide-ranging.

I do not claim today that I've got a ready-made blueprint for such a home. Instead I shall speak of what, in my view, is the main point, namely, the need for a restructuring of the international order in Europe to bring to the fore all-European values and make it possible to replace the traditional balance of forces by balance of interests.

But what does this involve? Let us first take security issues. Within the framework of new thinking we began with a critical reassessment of our notions of military confrontation in Europe, the scope of outside threats and the importance of the factor of strength in security-building. This was not easy to do and at times the effort was painful. But the endeavour resulted in decisions which make it possible to take East–West relations out of the 'action-counteraction' vicious circle.

The joint Soviet–US efforts in the field of nuclear disarmament have undoubtedly played an initial and considerable role in this respect. The treaty on the elimination of intermediate- and shorter-range missiles was not only endorsed by the Europeans but many also promoted its conclusion.

The Vienna talks opened up a fundamentally new phase in the arms reductions process. The talks already involve 23 countries, and not just two powers. All the 35 participants in the CSCE [Conference on Security and Co-operation in Europe] process continue to work out confidence-building measures in the military field.

And although the two negotiating processes take place at different locations, they are intimately connected with each other. There are and can be no 'strangers' in efforts to build European peace – all are equal partners here, and every country, including neutral and non-aligned ones, bears its share of responsibility to its people and to Europe.

The philosophy of the common European home concept rules out the probability of an armed clash and the very possibility of the use of force or threat of force – alliance against alliance, inside the alliances, wherever. This philosophy suggests that a doctrine of restraint should take the place of the doctrine of deterrence. This is not just a play on words but the logic of European development prompted by life itself.

Our goals at the Vienna talks are well known. We consider it quite attainable – and the US President, too, supports this – to secure a substantially lower level of armaments in Europe in the course of two-three years, with the elimination of all asymmetries and imbalances, of course. And I emphasise – all asymmetries and imbalances. No double standards are admissible here.

We are convinced that it is also time to begin talks on tactical nuclear systems between all countries concerned. The ultimate objective is to fully remove the weapons which threaten only the Europeans who by no means intend to wage war on one another. Who then needs them and what for?

To eliminate nuclear arsenals or to keep them at all costs are the options. Does the strategy of nuclear deterrence strengthen or undermine stability? The positions of NATO and the Warsaw Treaty on these issues look diametrically opposed. However, we do no dramatise the divergences.

We are looking for and invite our partners to look for ways out. We regard the elimination of nuclear weapons as a state-by-stage process. Without abandoning their positions, the Europeans can jointly cover part of the way separating us from the complete elimination of nuclear weapons: the USSR while remaining loyal to non-nuclear ideals, and the West while remaining committed to the concept of 'minimum deterrence'.

It is worthwhile to find out [what] is behind the 'minimum' notion and where is the limit beyond which the potential of nuclear deterrence turns into an attack capability? There is much ambiguity in this respect while the lack of clarity is a source of mistrust.

Why don't the experts of the Soviet Union, the United States, Britain, and France, as well as the countries on whose territories nuclear weapons are stationed discuss these issues in-depth? If they arrive at some common evaluations, the problem would become simpler at the political level as well.

If NATO countries are seen to be ready to enter into negotiations with us on tactical nuclear weapons, we could, upon taking counsel with our allies, of course, make further unilateral cuts in our tactical nuclear missiles in Europe without delay.

The Soviet Union and other Warsaw Treaty countries outside the framework of the Vienna talks, are already unilaterally reducing their armed forces and armaments in Europe. Their structure and fighting strength are changing in line with the defensive doctrine of reasonable sufficiency.

This doctrine, both from the view point of quantities of arms and troops and from the view point of their deployment, training and all military activities – rules out the physical possibility of launching an attack and large-scale offensive operations.

This year we began to slash military spending. As we stated in the USSR Supreme Soviet, we intend, circumstances permitting, to reduce sharply – by 33.4 to 50 per cent – the share of our defence allocations in the national income of the year 1995.

We have begun the conversion of the defence industry in earnest. All countries participating in the CSCE process will encounter this problem in this or that way. We are prepared to exchange opinions and experience.

In our view, United Nations resources can also be utilised and a joint working group can be set up within the framework of the economic commission for Europe to study the problems of conversion.

In the face of European parliamentarians and, it means, the whole of Europe, I would like to speak once again of our simple and clear-cut positions on disarmament issues. They are the result of new thinking and have been legislatively sealed on behalf of all our people in a resolution of the congress of People's Deputies:

– We are categorically against the development of any space weapons whatsoever,

– We are for the elimination of military blocs and the development of a political dialogue between them with this end in view without delay and for the establishment of an atmosphere of trust ruling out any surprises,

– We are for profound, consistent and effective verification of compliance with all treaties and agreements which may be concluded on disarmament issues.

I am convinced that it is high time the Europeans brought their policy and conduct into line with new logic – not to prepare for war, not to intimidate one another, not to compete in the development of weapons, and still less, in attempts to 'make up' for cutbacks, but to learn to jointly lay the foundations for peace.

III

If security is the foundation of the common European home, multifarious co-operation is its superstructure. An intensive inter-state dialogue – bilateral and multilateral – has become a sign of the new situation in Europe and the world in recent years. The range of agreements, treaties and other accords has been considerably extended. Official consultations on diverse issues have become a feature of life.

The first contacts have been formed between NATO and the Warsaw Treaty Organisation, the EEC and the CMEA, not to mention many political and public organisations in both parts of Europe. We were pleased with the decision by the Parliamentary Assembly of the Council of Europe to grant 'Special Guest Status' to the Soviet Union. We are ready to co-operate. But we think that we can go even further.

We could join some international conventions of the Council of Europe, open to other states, on ecology, culture, education, and television broadcasting. We are prepared to co-operate with specialised institutions of the Council of Europe.

The Parliamentary Assembly of the Council of Europe and the European Parliament are based in Strasbourg. If our ties develop and become regular, we, certainly, with the consent of the French

Government, would move toward opening a general consulate there.

Undoubtedly, interparliamentary ties are of immense importance to imparting a greater dynamism to the CSCE process, an important step has already been taken – the first meeting of the heads of parliaments of 35 states was held in Warsaw late last year.

We recognised the value of the visit to the USSR of the delegation of the Parliamentary Assembly of the Council of Europe headed by its President Mr Anders Bjork. They managed to sense firsthand the strong and sharp pulse of Soviet perestroika.

We consider our contacts with the European Parliament to be very important. By the way, we gave special attention to its resolutions on military-political issues, in which, in its own assessment, the nucleus of West European consensus is in the sphere of security. In this regard, I cannot but tell about the West European defence plans. Certainly, any state and any alliance of states has the right to show concern about security and it is important that they are the forms which they consider suitable. It is only important that these forms do not conflict with the positive tendencies of the time – tendencies toward military detente – that they do not provoke the invigoration of confrontational elements in European politics, and, hence, a new arms race.

The need for a second conference of the Helsinki type is becoming increasingly topical. It is time for the present generation of leaders of the European countries, the United States and Canada, to discuss, apart from most pressing issues, how they visualise the subsequent stages in the movement toward the European community of the 21st Century.

As concerns the economic content of the European home, we consider the prospect for forming a vast economic space from the Atlantic to the Urals with a high degree of interdependence between its Eastern and Western parts as real, although not immediate.

The Soviet Union's transition to a more open economy is of fundamental importance in this sense. And not only for ourselves – for enhancing the efficiency of the national economy and meeting consumer requirements. This will enhance inter-dependence of the economies of the East and West and, consequently, have a salutary impact on the entire complex of European relations.

Similarities in the functioning of economic mechanisms, strengthening ties and economic incentives, mutual adaptation, and training respective specialists are long-term factors of co-operation, a pledge of stabilty of the European and international process as a whole.

My contacts with authoritative members of the business community in Britain, the Federal Republic of Germany, France, Italy, and the United States during my foreign trips and in Moscow show that there is enhanced interest in conducting affairs with us in conditions of perestroika. Many do not dramatise our difficulties and take into account the peculiarities of the present period, when reforms discard outdated mechanisms sooner than new ones are put into operation. I have also noticed the determination of experienced businessmen, who think in broad political terms, to take justified risk, display boldness and act while looking ahead. And, by the way, not only in the interests of progress and peace, in the interests of humanity.

Many also understand that if one limits oneself to immediate commercial benefit, the chances of far more advantageous long-term economic co-operation with us, as a component of the CSCE process, will slip away.

I think that this honourable Assembly will agree that economic links without scientific-technical ties are something rather abnormal in our age. But in East–West relations, the latter are bled dry to a considerable extent by the COCOM restrictions. If at the height of the cold war, this practice could be somewhat justified, nowadays many bans look absurd.

Certainly, we have excessive secrecy. But we have begun to deal with it. We have started to eliminate our 'internal COCOM' – the separation of military production from civilian – in the process of conversion.

Perhaps, specialists and representatives of respective governments should get together and sort out all these encrustations generated by the cold war, put secrecy within reasonable frameworks which are really dictated by security, and give a green light to a normal flow of scientific knowledge and technical art?

Such projects as, for instance, a trans-European express railway, a European programme for developing new technologies and equipment, utilising solar energy, processing and disposing of nuclear waste, enhancing the safety of nuclear power stations, additional information transmission channels using light conduits, and European satellite communication systems are equally important to the East and the West.

Developing a television system of a high degree of sharpness is exceptionally interesting. This work is being conducted in several countries and it has a great future also for equipping the European home. Naturally, the more perfect and low-cost variant will be preferable. In Paris in 1985, President Mitterrand and I put forward the idea of developing an international thermo-nuclear experient reactor. This would be an inexhaustible source of ecologically clean energy.

Under the auspices of the International Atomic Energy Agency (IAEA) this project, which is the result of the combining of the research potentials of the Soviet Union, West European countries, the United States, Japan and other states, is entering a stage of practical research.

Scientists forecast that it will be possible to build such a reactor by the turn of the century. This would be the greatest achievement of scientific thought and engineering and would serve the future of Europe and the whole world.

Economic rapprochement between Eastern and Western Europe will be determined, not in a minor degree, by relations between Western regional associations – the European Community (EEC) and the European Free Trade Association (EFTA) – and the Council for Mutual Economic Assistance (CMEA). Each of them has its own development dynamics and its own problems.

We have no doubt that integrational processes in Western Europe are acquiring a new quality. We do not underestimate the likelihood of the emergence of a single European market in the coming years.

The CMEA has also taken a course towards the formation of a joint market, although we are greatly lagging behind in this respect. The rate of internal transformations within the CMEA will in many respects determine what will undergo a more rapid development in the coming years – relationships between the CMEA and the EEC as groupings or between individual socialist countries and the EEC.

It is quite possible that from time to time this or that form will come to the fore. It is important that they both should fit into the logic of the formation of an all-European economic zone.

The next step in this process is maybe a trade and economic agreement between our country and the EC. We also attach substantial importance to it from the viewpoint of all-European interests. Naturally, we by no means counterpose our contacts with the EC to contacts with other associations or states. EFTA countries are our good and long-standing partners.

It would also be sensible perhaps to speak of the development of relations through CMEA and EFTA channels and to utilise this channel of multilateral co-operation in the building of a new Europe. A common European home will need to be kept ecologically clean. Life has taught us bitter lessons, ecological hazards in Europe have long transcended national boundaries.

To form a regional ecological security system is a matter of urgency. It is quite likely that the CSCE process will evolve most quickly in this really high-priority fields. The first step could be to elaborate a long-term continental ecological programme. Our proposals to set up an urgent ecological aid centre at the United Nations is well known. Such a centre or an agency with a system of warning and monitoring is utterly essential for Europe.

Maybe, the founding of an all-European ecological research and expertise institute, and in due course the establishment of an authority with powers to make binding decisions can also be contemplated.

By a decision of the Vienna meeting, a forum of 35 countries on ecological issues is to be held in Sofia in autumn this year. These problems could be discussed on a practical plane there. Mankind sustains increasingly heavy losses owing to natural and technological calamities that claim tens and sometimes hundreds of thousands of human lives every year. Huge funds are spent for clean-up operations. Scientists warn that the vulnerability of the largest cities to natural calamities is growing.

We know about large-scale projects to combat the mounting global threat. The USSR Academy of Sciences has set up an international institute for earthquake forecasting and is inviting scientists from all over the world to participate in the establishment of a scientific basis to deal with the problems of ecological security of the largest cities, to forecast droughts, and the magnitude of climatic disasters.

The Soviet Union is prepared to provide satellites, ocean-going ships and new technologies for these purposes. It would be useful perhaps to draw the military services of various countries, and first of all medical and engineering ones, into international rescue and clean-up operations.

The humanitarian content of the CSCE process is decisive. A world, in which military arsenals would be cut but in which human rights would be violated, cannot feel secure. We, for our part, have arrived at this conclusion finally and irrevocably.

The decisions taken at the Vienna meeting signify a genuine breakthrough in this sense. A whole programme for joint action of European countries has been mapped out with provision for the most diverse measures. Mutual understanding was reached on many issues which up until recently were a stumbling block in East–West relations.

We are convinced that a reliable legal foundation should be furnished for the CSCE process. We visualise a common European home as a legal community, and we, for our part, have begun moving in that direction.

The resolution of the Congress of People's Deputies of the USSR, says, in part: 'relying on international standards and principles, including those contained in the Universal Declaration of Human Rights, the Helsinki Accords and understandings, bringing domestic legislation in line with them, the USSR will contribute toward creating a world community of states ruled by law.'

Here, too, Europe could be an example. Naturally, its international legal integrity comprises national specific features of states. Each European country, the United States and Canada have their own laws and traditions in the humanitarian sphere. Although there exist universally-recognised standards and principles.

It would be useful to draw a comparison between existing legislation on human rights, setting up to this end either a special working group or something of a European institute of comparative human rights. Most probably, we will not achieve a full convergence of views, considering the difference of social systems. But Vienna and the recent London and Paris conferences showed that common views and common approaches do exist and can be multiplied.

This allows me to speak about the possibility of creating a European legal framework. At the Paris humanitarian forum the Soviet Union and France acted as co-sponsors of the initiative. The Federal Republic of Germany, Austria, Hungary, Poland and Czechoslovakia have joined it. A considerable extension of cultural co-operation, a deeper interaction in the field of humanities and a new level of information exchanges are needed. To put it briefly, the process of getting to know each other better should be intensified. Television could play a special role here, since it makes it possible to ensure contacts among tens of hundreds of millions of people rather than hundreds and thousands.

There are also certain dangers inherent in that. They should be seen. Performing stages, screens, exhibition halls, and publishing houses are flooded with commercial pseudo-culture alien to Europe. National languages are treated with disdain. All this calls for our common attention and joint work in the spirit of respect for the true national values of each and every one.

That may involve sharing of experience in the preservation of cultural heritage, actions to familiarise European peoples with the original present-day culture of each other and collective promotion of language studies. This may also involve sharing of experience in the preservation of historical and cultural documents, joint production of cine-, TV-, and video-films which promote national cultural achievements and the best examples of artistic creation of the past and today.

The Europeans can meet the challenges of the coming century only by pooling their efforts. We are convinced that what they need is one Europe – peaceful and democratic, a Europe that maintains all its diversity and common humanistic ideas, a prosperous Europe that extends its hand to the rest of the world. A Europe that confidently advances into the future. It is in such a Europe that we visualise our own future.

Perestroika, which has as its goal the fundamental renewal of Soviet society, also predetermines our policy aimed at the developments of Europe exactly in this direction. Perestroika is altering our country, in leading it to new frontiers. This process will go further, deepening and transforming Soviet society in all areas – economically, socially, politically and culturally, in all internal affairs and human relations.

We have embarked on this path firmly and irreversibly. The resolution of the Congress of People's Deputies of the USSR 'On the Guidelines of the Domestic and Foreign Policies of the USSR' is a document which sealed with the name of the people our choice, the path of perestroika.

I call your attention to this resolution. It is of revolutionary importance to the destiny of the country which you call a superpower. Once it is implemented, you, your governments, parliaments and peoples will soon deal with a totally different socialist state. This will have a salutary impact, an impact on the whole of the world process.

Source: *Soviet News*, 12 July 1989

PRESIDENT BUSH'S ADDRESS TO THE POLISH PARLIAMENT

10 July 1989 (excerpts)

On behalf of the people of the United States, I am honored to greet the newly-elected representatives of the Polish Parliament. To be here with you on this occasion is proof that we live in extraordinary, indeed, thrilling times. . . .

While I've been to Poland before, I did not expect to return so soon – nor to such altered circumstances. And so, too, perhaps many of you didn't expect to be here – serving in this, or any Polish parliament. . . . Your achievement has surpassed all expectations and has earned all our admiration. . . .

And now, in part because of what you're doing here, the genuine opportunity exists for all of us to build a Europe which many thought was destroyed forever in the 1940s. That Europe, the Europe of our children, will be open, whole and free.

We can make it so in two ways. First, a new East–West relationship must rest on greatly reduced levels of arms. . . . We in the West have proposed dramatic reductions in conventional armed forces in Europe, reductions that promise to transform the military map of Europe and diminish the very threat of war. The new willingness in Moscow to accept this Western framework for reductions in troops and tanks and aircraft and other categories of weapons gives us hope that the negotiations in Vienna will succeed. . . .

Second, reductions in military forces will go further and be more sustainable if they take place in parallel with political change. Excessive levels of arms, we believe, are the symptoms and not the source of political tensions. . . .

Poland's decision to embrace political reform – and Hungary's movement in the same direction – thus have great importance beyond their borders. By creating political structures legitimized by popular will – by that, your reforms can be the foundation of stability, security, and prosperity, not just here, but in all of Europe, now and into the next century. . . .

Your responsibility for your country's future is immense. Poland's friends, including the American people, want Poland to be free, prosperous, democratic, independent – true to the best tradition of your nation's past. And this regime is moving forward with a sense of realism and courage, in a time of great difficulty and challenge. Lech Walesa's Solidarity are deeply committed to institutions in Poland that will serve all its people. This parliament, by its very existence, is advancing pluralism. And the Church has served as a source of spiritual guidance and unity in turbulent times. But above all, there are the people of Poland, people who are steadfastly working toward productive change. . . .

The reform of the Polish economy presents an historic challenge. There can be no substitute for Poland's own efforts. But I want to stress to you today that Poland is not alone. Given the enormity of this moment, the United States stands ready to help as you help yourselves . . . this is where we stand.

Legislation is well underway that will help Polish exporters compete more effectively in the US market through generalized systems of preferences, and that will authorize our overseas private investment corporation to operate in Poland, providing investment insurance and setting up missions to stimulate US investment in joint ventures here.

The United States is proposing a private business agreement that will promote contacts between Poland's growing private business sector and its American counterparts. . . .

I've said that as Poland reforms itself, the United States will respond. . . . So today, I'm pleased to announce that we plan to do more and go farther for the sake of a stable and prosperous Poland.

First, I will propose at the upcoming economic summit in Paris that the nations of the summit . . . intensify their coordination and concerted action to promote democratic reform in Poland and Hungary, and to help manage compassionately the process of change. We will work with our partners at the summit, moving quickly with increased Western aid and technical assistance. This concerted action will complement existing institutions like the World Bank, the Paris Club, and the International Monetary Fund; and address needed economic reforms, credits, management and training initiatives, social safety nets, housing, and other issues important to Poland.

Second, I will ask the US Congress to provide a $100 million fund to capitalize and invigorate the Polish private sector – and we will encourage parallel contributions from other nations of the economic summit.

Third, I will encourage the World Bank to move ahead with $325 million in economically-viable loans to help Polish agriculture and industry reach the production levels they are so clearly capable of.

Fourth, I will ask my counterparts in the West to support an early and generous rescheduling of Polish debt. This could provide deferral of debt payments amounting to about $5,000 million this year, if our allies and friends in the Paris Club agree to join us in offering liberalized terms. . . .

Fifth, economic progress should not come at the expense of our common heritage – our common inheritance – the environment. . . .

Almost two years ago I visited Krakow . . . a city recognized by UNESCO as an international treasure. Today, Krakow is under siege by pollution; its priceless monuments are being destroyed. Krakow must be reclaimed. And the United States will help. I'll ask the Congress for $15 million for a cooperative venture with Poland to help fight air and water pollution there.

Sixth . . . the United States will establish a cultural and information center in Warsaw, and will ask Poland to establish a similar center in the United States. This will be the first time that either of our two countries will be able to conduct educational and cultural programs outside of our embassies and consulates.

. . . The road ahead is a long one, but it is the only road which leads to prosperity and social peace. Poland's progress along this road will show the way toward a new era throughout Europe, an era based on common values and not just geographic proximity. The Western democracies will stand with the Polish people, and other peoples of this region. . . .

Source: USIS, 10 July 1989

US SECRETARY OF STATE JAMES BAKER AND SOVIET FOREIGN MINISTER EDUARD SHEVARDNADZE: JOINT STATEMENT ON ARMS CONTROL

Jackson Hole, Wyoming, 23 September 1989

The Secretary and the Foreign Minister held a thorough and productive review on the range of arms control and disarmament issues. They noted with satisfaction that, since their May meeting in Moscow, the Nuclear and Space Talks, Nuclear Testing Talks, and bilateral consultations on chemical weapons have resumed.

The Secretary and the Foreign Minister had a detailed discussion of nuclear and space issues, including the ideas contained in the letters exchanged by President Bush and Chairman Gorbachev.

Regarding ABM and space, the Soviet side introduced a new approach aimed at resolving this significant issue. Both sides agree that the Soviet approach opens the way to achieving and implementing a START Treaty without reaching a Defense and Space agreement. The sides agreed to drop the approach of a nonwithdrawal commitment while continuing to discuss ways to ensure predictability in the development of the US–Soviet strategic relationship under conditions of strategic stability to reduce the risk of nuclear war. The US side said it would consider carefully the other aspects of the overall Soviet approach. Both sides agreed that their negotiators would consider these issues in Geneva. They also agreed that the negotiators would discuss the US invitation for Soviet Government experts to visit two US facilities involved in strategic defense research.

The Soviet side stated that, guided by its long-standing goal of strengthening the ABM Treaty regime, it had decided to completely dismantle the Krasnoyarsk radar station. The US side expressed satisfaction with this announcement.

At the same time, the Soviet side stressed again the necessity of removing its concerns about the US radar stations in Greenland and Great Britain. The US side promised to consider these concerns, in consultation with its Allies.

In the interest of promoting progress in the negotiations, the Secretary announced that the US side was withdrawing its proposal to ban mobile ICBMs in START, contingent on the funding by the US Congress of US mobile ICBMs. The Soviet side expressed satisfaction with this announcement and the two sides agreed on the need further to develop provisions for effective verification for limits on mobile ICBMs. In this connection, they also reached agreement on additional elements of common ground regarding the verification of mobile ICBMs, building on the elements agreed at the Moscow summit and subsequent work in Geneva.

Both sides noted the need to resolve the ALCM and SLCM issues. On ALCMs, the Soviet side put forward a new idea concerning its approach on how to deal with ALCMs and heavy bombers.

On SLCMs, the Soviet side offered new approaches for dealing with this difficult problem. The Soviet side raised the possibility of dealing with SLCMs in a broader naval arms context. As for the Nuclear and Space Talks, the Soviet side appealed to the American side to concentrate on verification and said that in the context of a verification system for SLCMs, these weapons could be limited outside of the text of a START treaty on the basis of reciprocal obligations. While reiterating its willingness to study the Soviet ideas, the US side for its part emphasized its doubts about the feasibility of a workable verification system for SLCMs, and noted its long-standing view that there are serious problems involved in any discussion of the limitation of naval arms.

The Soviet side responded positively to President Bush's June initiative on verification and stability measures. In this regard, the Secretary and the Foreign Minister had a thorough exchange on the details of the initiative, and signed an agreement encouraging the development of such measures and outlining principles for implementing them. They also completed an agreement on the advance notification of major strategic exercises. The sides examined the other verification and stability measures and agreed to explore these further in Geneva.

The sides also agreed that, for purposes of the 1600 START limit, ballistic missiles will be defined in terms of missiles and their associated launchers, thus resolving a long-standing issue.

New instructions will be issued to negotiators to take account of the exchanges on these and other START issues.

The Secretary and the Foreign Minister reaffirmed the objective of early conclusion of a comprehensive, verifiable and truly global ban on chemical weapons. To intensify efforts toward this goal, and to enhance openness and confidence between the two countries, they signed a Memorandum of Understanding on a bilateral verification experiment and data exchange. The MOU provides for an exchange of data on US and Soviet chemical weapons stockpiles, and for visits and inspections of chemical weapons sites.

The sides adopted a special joint statement on chemical weapons in which they stressed the need to conclude a chemical weapons ban and underscored their concern about the problem posed by the proliferation of chemical weapons.

The Secretary and the Foreign Minister examined the status of the nuclear testing negotiations. They noted that the verification protocol for the 1976 Peaceful Nuclear Explosions Treaty has been agreed ad referendum by their negotiators, and reached agreement to incorporate hydrodynamic and seismic monitoring, as well as on-site inspection, into the verification protocol for the 1974 Threshold Test Ban Treaty, as well as the levels above which these measurements would occur. In order to obtain a statistically significant number of data points to improve the national technical means of each side, each side will guarantee the other side the right to make on-site hydrodynamic yield measurements of at least two tests per year during the first five years following ratification of this treaty. After five years, each side shall guarantee one such hydrodynamic measurement a year thereafter unless otherwise agreed by the two sides. These agreements provide a framework for conclusion of the verification protocols, completing a process that began fifteen years ago. They instructed their delegations to continue intensive work to resolve all remaining issues so that these two documents can be submitted for ratification as quickly as possible.

The Secretary and the Foreign Minister noted with approval the work being done in the negotiations on Conventional Forces in Europe, and called for rapid conclusion of an agreement.

The Secretary and the Foreign Minister agreed in principle to the 'Open Skies' concept proposed by President Bush in May, which could make a genuine contribution to openness and confidence-building. They noted their willingness to attend an international conference on the subject.

The sides noted the importance of joint efforts by the United States and the Soviet Union to prevent the proliferation of missiles and missile technology and agreed to activate bilateral consultations on this pressing problem.

Source: Arms Control Today, October 1989

ADDRESS BY EDUARD SHEVARDNADZE, USSR MINISTER OF FOREIGN AFFAIRS, AT THE 44TH SESSION OF THE UN GENERAL ASSEMBLY

26 September 1989

... The supremacy of universal human values and the observance of the universal rules of the world community are the imperatives of our times. The objective requirements of the age we live in, its trends, character and circumstances leave mankind no other choice than to reject the traditional polarisation. That axiom underlies both the concept and the practical policies of new thinking. Of course, it cannot resolve the existing contradictions overnight; but, for a start, it can alleviate them.

Speaking of the primacy of universal human values, we also imply a mature readiness of nations to accept these. Where that maturity has not yet been attained and where the national idea is being set against the common interest, domestic conflicts go hand-in-hand with, and impel, global destructive processes.

Let me stress this: freedom of choice continues to crown the hierarchy of a nation's supreme values. Every nation is free to choose the ways and means of its own developments – but to do so in a responsible manner. It must not lock itself in the dark rooms of national selfishness or ignore the interests of other peoples and of the entire community of nations. Freedom does not mean irresponsibility towards others, for, in the final analysis, that is irresponsibility towards oneself.

The time has come finally to realise that not all means are good for attaining even the most noble ends. The international community has become aware of the danger of the drugs business and terrorism. It condemns and outlaws them. We need equally determined action against all kinds of violence, whatever the motives or excuses for it. Violence by the state against its own people must be ruled out altogether. Violence on national, ethnic or religious grounds must no longer be tolerated.

To repeat, we advocate freedom of choice. However, we reject its interpretation as a licence to use any means, to commit any violence or to shed blood. Freedom must not be sought at the expense of others. No support or sympathy should be extended to the so-called movements that allow actions humiliating other nations or employ terrorist, barbarous and other inhuman methods in waging their struggle.

It is to be deplored that 50 years after the second world war some politicians have begun to forget its lessons. Let us remember that political and ideological differences did not prevent governments and nations from joining forces to defend universal human values from Nazism and fascism. The dividing line in that battle was drawn not by ideology, but by the rules of and attitudes towards morality. The Soviet Union, the USA, Great Britain and other countries and peoples found themselves in one camp and, fighting together, saved civilisation.

Fascism, which started the war, is the extreme and the ugliest form of nationalism and chauvinism. German Nazism marched under the banner of revanchism. Now that the forces of revanchism are again becoming active and are seeking to revise and destroy the post-war realities in Europe, it is our duty to warn those who, willingly or unwillingly, encourage those forces. The revanchist movement is dangerous and hostile to the march of peace to which President Bush referred here yesterday.

While expressing respect for healthy national movements, let me mention one modern concept of nationhood. It defines a nation as a collective personality endowed with certain rights quite similar to, and even identical with, individual human rights. But there are no rights without responsibilities – either for the individual or for the nation or for the state. The mission of the UN is to promote among the world public the idea of the interdependence of national aspirations and the common good of mankind, and to encourage nations to behave responsibly.

This fundamental position of the Soviet Union is clearly reflected in our bilateral contacts. Relations between the Soviet Union and the USA provide the best illustration of this. I shall permit myself to touch upon the US–Soviet dialogue only because I am convinced that its importance goes far beyond the frontiers of the two states. In the view of the soviet leadership, this is not some kind of privilege but a clearly understood responsibility vis-à-vis the world community. Therefore I include my account of the results of our talks with President Bush and Secretary of State Baker in my report to you.

These talks have demonstrated the increasing awareness on both sides of the need to co-operate for the benefit of mankind, as well as the growing confidence that such co-operation is possible. The agreement to hold a meeting of the top leaders of the Soviet Union and the USA shows that we have moved quite far ahead in solving a number of major bilateral and international problems. Extraordinary efforts at the highest level will be needed to attain the goal of concluding the treaties.

I am referring above all to the preparation of the agreement on 50% reductions in strategic offensive arms. We have proposed to the US side options for resolving the key issues in that agreement – the ABM treaty and space, and long-range SLCMs. Our partners have accommodated us on mobile ICBMs. Our positions on other outstanding problems have become closer. In our view, by the time the summit is held next year in late spring or early summer, we may have passed the last turn on the road towards a treaty reducing strategic offensive arms. Protocols to the 1974 and 1976 treaties on nuclear explosions could also be signed at the summit, enabling them to enter into force shortly.

We are confident that the summit will give a powerful impetus to the talks on major reductions in the armed forces and conventional arms in Europe.

We welcome the proposal concerning chemical weapons put forward yesterday by President Bush. In general, consistent with the well-known initiatives of the Soviet leadership, it indicates to us that we share the desire to rid mankind of those barbarous weapons. The Soviet Union is ready, together with the USA, to go further and assume mutual obligations prior to the conclusion of a multilateral convention:

– cease the production of chemical weapons, as we have done already (I am referring also to binary weapons);
– on a bilateral basis, radically reduce or completely destroy Soviet and US chemical weapons, regarding this as a step towards the global destruction of chemical weapons;
– renounce the use of chemical weapons under any circumstances;
– institute rigorous verification of the cessation of production of chemical warfare agents.

I think that there is no need to say how beneficial that would be for the overall world climate.

In addition to the problems of security, the Soviet–American agenda encompasses the issues of humanitarian co-operation, regional problems and joint efforts in the fields of the environment and economic development, reflecting the ongoing process of bringing together national and universal concerns. More than ever before, we are clearly aware that Soviet–US relations today cannot be built outside the global context, in isolation from the problems common to all mankind. Our conversations in Washington and Wyoming have moved us ahead in our efforts to bridge the continuing gap between the attitudes to one's own and the common good. Much remains to be done, however, to alleviate the disparities of political objectives, for such disparities endanger all of us.

Let us examine the situation, taking nuclear weapons as an example. Why are they dangerous? Not only because of their sheer destructive power. They are unacceptable because they widen the chasm between national and universal interests. The equality of peoples and the unity of the world become empty talk when someone's national selfishness is driven by the idea of nuclear supremacy over the world, camouflaged as national security interests.

I would say that the world community has as yet no reason for complacency or euphoria. The nuclear threat has only been reduced by the Soviet–US treaty eliminating intermediate- and shorter-range missiles. We believe that reliance on nuclear weapons does not serve anyone's national interests. It is also an obstacle in the way of more democratic international relations. Only the complete elimination of nuclear capabilities would help the attainment of real security.

The advocates of nuclear deterrence do not believe this will be possible in the foreseeable future. They respond with concepts of the so-called minimum nuclear deterrence. In our view, that is a step forward, if only a timid one, a step that can be taken. But first we must define what we mean by minimum nuclear deterrence and what capabilities should be considered sufficient. The Soviet Union proposes that these issues be discussed at a meeting of representatives of the nuclear powers and the states on whose territories nuclear weapons are stationed.

Of course, the persistence of the concepts of nuclear deterrence is due not only to the exaggerated emphasis on national rights and interests at the expense of obligations but also to the lack of trust. The problem should not be easily dismissed.

What is the way out of the vicious circle? It lies in asserting glasnost and openness and building a wide-ranging infrastructure of pervasive verification. If we do need to deter each other, let deterrence be transparent and verifiable. To that end, the Soviet Union is proposing that all nuclear powers conclude multilateral agreements on measures to reduce the risk of outbreak of nuclear war. Detailed discussions to work out such an agreement could be held in consultations among the permanent members of the Security Council.

Also in this context, we wish to raise once again the problem of the cessation and prohibition of nuclear tests. Why are we still unable to put an end to them despite the express will of the overwhelming majority of nations? Because there are those who want to maintain their superiority at any cost. Guided by its obligations to the world community, the Soviet Union has revised its nuclear testing programme by reducing the number and yield of explosions. Let me point out, however, that the efforts of one state are not sufficient for a comprehensive solution to this problem. We see a number of possibilities here. First of all, the USSR is ready to reinstate its moratorium on all nuclear explosions any day and hour, if the USA reciprocates. Second, it is time finally to end the procedural impasse at the conference on disarmament and start concrete discussions there on the problem of a complete test ban. Third, as one possible way towards such a ban, we are now considering the possibility of extending the 1963 treaty to cover underground nuclear explosions.

There is an urgent need for a verifiable cessation of the production of fissionable material for military purposes. We have declared that this year we cease the production of enriched uranium, that in 1987 we closed down one reactor producing weapons-grade plutonium and that we plan to close down in 1989 and 1990 a few more such reactors. By the year 2000 all the remaining reactors will have been shut down. In addition, the Soviet Union is proposing that all nuclear powers should begin preparing to conclude an agreement on the cessation and prohibition of the production of such material. We believe that in verifying compliance with it the vast experience of applying IAEA safeguards could prove useful.

It would seem that even the way the second world war began ought to have made clear that weapons do not guarantee security – on the contrary, the more weapons there are, the greater the danger of aggression. And yet, for the 45 years since the war security was sought in the arms race. It is only today that the need is being understood for a fundamentally different concept of security in Europe, a security that relies increasingly on political means and, only as insurance, on a necessary minimum of arms. The Vienna accord heralded a new European situation, opening up broad vistas for humanitarian co-operation and exchanges of people, ideas and information. It holds out the prospect that the European idea will assert itself on a foundation of trust and openness. But the groundwork has to be prepared for that by clearing the continent of excess quantities of arms.

That work has begun. And, whenever the sides do not consign their responsibilities to the far corners of the negotiations rooms, whenever they sincerely want to strike a balance between their interests and those of their partners, progress is always achieved. One example is the Vienna talks between the Warsaw Treaty and NATO countries on reducing armed forces and conventional arms in Europe. In response to our alliance's initiative, the NATO countries have made meaningful proposals which substantially accommodate the positions of the Warsaw Treaty countries.

The talks being held in parallel between the countries participating in the European process to develop a qualitatively new generation of confidence- and security-building measures are marked by the far-reaching approach of the Warsaw Treaty member countries, which calls for a comprehensive set of confidence- and security-building measures and their extension to air force and naval activities.

Going back to the topic of individual countries' obligations to the community. I feel it my duty to emphasise that unwillingness to engage in active talks on reducing naval forces is a sign of neglecting those obligations. Leaving naval forces outside the process of reducing armed forces and arms would be harmful to universal security. The problem of naval forces could be examined, for example, at special consultations to be attended by all states concerned, above all major naval powers. They would discuss mutual concerns in this sphere and exchange views on the mechanism and ultimate objectives of the future negotiations and on how to move towards them step by step.

The dialectic of development of the situation in the European continent urgently calls for the start of talks on tactical nuclear weapons. The situation does not appear to be deadlocked. We propose that mutually acceptable solutions could be sought in an in-depth discussion of this whole set of issues among the USSR, the USA, Great Britain, France and the states where those weapons are stationed. If NATO countries agree to start talks on tactical nuclear weapons, the USSR will respond by further significant unilateral cuts in its tactical nuclear missiles in Europe.

The problem of missile proliferation is also ripe for multilateral discussions. The number of countries that possess such weapons is approaching 20, while the tendency towards its further geographical extension is still strong. The approach to this issue could be two-pronged. Barriers could be put up which, on the one hand, would preclude the proliferation of combat missiles and associated techno-logy across the globe, and on the other, would not impinge on the legitimate interest of countries in gaining peaceful access to space.

No one in the world can as yet bid a farewell to arms. But we can abandon, once and for all – and do it now – the practice of unconstrained and uncontrolled international weapons transfers. To that end, the principles of glasnost and openness should be asserted here as well. The USSR reaffirms its willingness to participate in the establishment of a UN register of sales and transfers of weapons, including in the elaboration of its parameters.

The time has come when the idea of preventing war is being given material expression in relations between the armed forces of a number of countries. A new peace-making instrument is being shaped by the Soviet–US agreement on preventing dangerous military activities and a series of agreements with the USA, Great Britain, West Germany and France on the prevention of incidents on the seas and oceans. Along the same lines, the Soviet Union and the PRC have agreed to start talks shortly on putting an end to their military confrontation. The Soviet Union expresses the hope that other states, too, will engage in this process.

A civilised world is an open world. Breaking the seals on many secrets, the Soviet Union reveals to the international community detailed data about all reductions in its armed forces and arms, their numerical strength and the size of its military budget.

We reaffirm here the position of the Soviet Union: our ultimate goal is not to have a single Soviet soldier outside the country. However, since we are speaking of equal responsibilities, let us for the sake of justice condemn the continuing encirclement of our country – and not only ours – with military bases. The Soviet Union attaches fundamental importance to a transition from individual measures of confidence-building, openness and glasnost in international affairs to a global policy of openness which would become an integral part of compre-hensive security and international peace. President Bush has proposed the idea of open skies. We like it. In welcoming and supporting this initiative, the Soviet Union calls for opening up lands, waters and space. Let us have open lands, open seas and open space. Only then shall we attain absolute transparency and the necessary level of confidence.

In building new international relations our foreign policy looks ahead to a positive evolution of today's world and to its stability. That orientation remains unchanged even in the face of certain changes which affect our immediate interests and the interests of the community to which we have the honour to belong. Still, we are faithful to our avowed principles and continue to affirm that the nations' choice cannot and should not be overridden by force and that stability cannot be achieved by threatening the use of force, by interventions, blockades or other sanctions.

It is no secret that we were not enthusiastic about the Polish communists' election set-back. Nor should it be a secret that we wish them to overcome the crisis. Nevertheless, we see nothing threatening in the fact that a coalition government has been formed in accordance with the will of the Polish people. We are in no way prejudiced against that government. We wish it every success and are ready to co-operate very actively with it.

Tolerance is the norm in civilised political behaviour. But if it is mandatory for us in our attitude towards the current government of Poland, why are others so intolerant as regards, say, Cuba? And if a non-communist prime minister is possible in a socialist country, why should the appearance of a communist as head of a Western government be perceived as heresy? This must not be ruled out either. The days of traditional demarcation lines are numbered. Only one line remains, to be pursued by all of us together moving to a common goal.

It is not the expression of popular will that threatens countries but rather political and ideological intolerance, chauvinism and the extremist excesses of imperial or nationalist mentality. It is only when they engender violence and destabilise the life of countries and peoples that the machinery of legitimate defence must be activated. However different our ideas of the preferable ways of social development maybe, we also have an overriding understanding of our common responsibility for the future of mankind and for the survival of civilisation. We know that only together can we step back from the brink; because an isolated island of development and prosperity would inevitably sink in the ocean of backwardness and poverty, because people and nations cannot be well when mankind is sick. Similarly, mankind cannot survive and avoid devastating consequences if individual nations deplete their resources of vitality in troubles and disputes with others.

There is but one way out of those fateful correlations. As we see it, it is for the world community to move consciously towards a harmony between universal and national principles. It is difficult to attain. But it is possible. It is possible because the collapse of the world is unthinkable. It is possible because we all share a place where individual national efforts unite into a single energy field. The UN is that place. It offers a forum for everybody to talk about their own country and its links with the rest of the world. I shall take this opportunity to say a few words about my country.

We are building a new model of society, a new model of relations among people and nations, a new model of socialism. As a great concept, socialism is by no means a spent force. Indeed, it is revealing its humanitarian potential in the bitter and often dramatic confrontation with the forces and vices that are organically alien to it. In our country we are not just repainting the facade but rebuilding the entire structure, in which the rules of living together must and will be based on the supremacy of law, people's power, openness to the outside world, inter-ethnic harmony and friendship. In every sphere of the common life of our state and our people – the national economy, the political system and the people's intellectual endeavour – rejection of the ossified relics of the past goes hand in hand with the enthusiasm of new construction. And even though, in the words of a poet, we may have a gloomy day or two, we are confident that perestroyka, which began as a revolution of hopes, will keep those hopes alive. Our people, the nation, will keep perestroyka going, for it embodies the aspirations that they cherish.

Today, when some Cassandras hasten to make gloomy predictions, we come up with our forecast. We want its historical optimism to be shared by all those who understand that the destinies of the world are inseparable from the future of our perestroyka. So we are saying to them: our determination to make it irreversible is matched by our confidence in victory, a confidence grounded in the democratic institutions which are ready to ensure that genuine people's power takes root. We are moving along that path guided, among other things, by our awareness of the historic nature and magnitude of the goal which we must attain ourselves, while not rejecting the support of the world community. Believe me, we feel it not only during the tragic days of natural disasters and national misfortunes. It has been voiced in your statements at this assembly, it manifests itself every day in your compatriots' heartfelt gestures, in their deeds and actions. So I am asking you, the envoys of your governments and nations, to convey to them our warm gratitude for that.

Source: BBC Summary of World Broadcasts, 28 September 1989

SPEECH BY US SECRETARY OF STATE JAMES BAKER TO THE COMMONWEALTH CLUB OF SAN FRANCISCO

23 October 1989

Arms control can lend a strong hand in building an enduring peace, but arms control does not proceed in a political vacuum. Let me be clear: We compete militarily because we differ politically. Political disputes are fuel for the fire of arms competittions. Only by resolving political differences can we dampen the arms competition associated with them. To follow Clausewitz, if war is the continuation of politics by violent, military means, arms control is the search for a stable, predictable strategic relationship by peaceful, political means.

That is why our times are now so full of promise. Over the last 40 years, arms control played only a limited role in shaping the US–Soviet security relationship because our political differences were simply too wide to allow enduring and substantial progress. Western strength and Western unity sustained deterrence throughout this period when we all lived in the shadow of opposed values and conflicting purpose. Now *perestroika* in Soviet domestic and foreign policy could, in part, lift the shadow. The political prerequisite for enduring and strategically significant arms control may finally be materializing. Surely the president was right when he wrote President Gorbachev in June, 'We bear enormous – and mutual – responsibility to take advantage of the promise of these extraordinary times to improve international security.'

The president and I have both said that we want *perestroika* to succeed. It would be folly indeed to miss this opportunity. Soviet 'new thinking' in foreign and defense policy promises possibilities that would have been unthinkable a decade ago, such as deep, stabilizing cuts in strategic forces and parity in reduced conventional arms in Europe. Yet *perestroika*'s success is far from assured.

Any uncertainty about the fate of reform in the Soviet Union, however, is all the more reason, not less, for us to seize the present opportunity. For the works of our labor – a diminished Soviet threat and effectively verifiable agreements – can endure even if *perestroika* does not. If the Soviets have already destroyed weapons, it will be difficult, costly, and time-consuming for any future Kremlin leadership

347

to reverse the process and to assert military superiority. And with agreements in place, any attempt to break out of treaties will serve as one indicator of an outbreak of old thinking.

We can take advantage of the new political climate to consolidate deterrence at lower levels of risk. Through sound and verifiable agreements, we can shape and institutionalize a more stable, predictable strategic relationship. The changing political relationship between the Soviet Union and the United States should be reflected in changing Soviet force structures and strategic concepts. In this way, we can help to codify political progress in military reality and by doing so, underpin that progress and strengthen it.

Strategy and the Changing Strategic Environment

Before outlining the tenets of this administration's arms control policy, I would like to say a few more words about the broader strategic environment in which arms control must operate.

Politically, the Soviet Union is in the midst of this revolution of *perestroika*, *glasnost*, and democratization. The new thinkers understand that Stalin's system must change fundamentally if the Soviet Union is – as Mr Gorbachev has said – to enter the 21st century in the manner worthy of a great power. To this end, the Soviet leadership has done much and promised even more for political, economic, and legal reform. While his reforms need to be extended, codified, institutionalized, and made habitual, the political face of Soviet power is being changed already.

The prospects for reform are just as great, in some cases perhaps even greater, in Poland, Hungary, East Germany, Czechoslovakia and the other countries of Eastern Europe. While the trends should not be overstated, the political foundations of a Europe divided by force since 1945 are crumbling away. We can move toward the president's vision of a Europe whole and free.

These great political changes are set in a time of vast technological change. Our military tools are being reshaped by emerging technologies that could offer greater security. Advances in sensor technology, data processing capabilities, and precision-guided munitions present novel ways to strengthen deterrence.

We need to be careful, however, also to see the darker side of changing technological realities. More nations are acquiring the capacity to make chemical weapons and to manufacture missiles. With many of these regimes locked in continuing regional conflicts, the explosive escalation potential of their disputes is obvious.

I would add, too, that these technological changes are taking place in a time of changing defense economics. Everyone has noted the Soviet Union's compelling need to convert some of its vast expenditures for the military into domestic reconstruction. The era of rapidly rising defense budgets is over in the West, too. From the new technologies, we are going to have to pick very carefully those weapons that strengthen deterrence most cost-effectively.

What do these political, economic, and technological changes add up to? Strategically, the world we've planned for since the Cuban missile crisis is increasingly distinct from the world we actually face. Threats to our interests our changing politically and multiplying technologically. Our capabilities are being improved technologically but constrained economically.

Our fundamental values and interests will endure. But as our strategic environment is transformed, we need to look anew at some of our guiding concepts and approaches. Many long-held assumptions may need to be rethought. Strategy aligns ends and means. As both shift, strategy may have to shift, too.

For example, we need to think about the future of both European security relations and the central superpower strategic relationship. Today's historic political transformations in Eastern Europe – if suitably institutionalized – make such reassessments doubly important. In light of the growing threat to our global interests and power projection forces posed by the proliferation of new technologies, we also need to reconsider our strategy for Third World conflicts. Over the longer term, we need to consider if strategic defense options, deep reductions in nuclear and conventional weapons, increasingly powerful conventional munitions, and shifts in Soviet strategy will alter our requirements for deterrence.

To cope with this changing environment, defense programs and arms control must work together. This is a prerequisite for a coherent, integrated strategy that reduces the risk of war by deterring aggression while promoting American values. Both defense programs and arms control can serve the common goals of enhancing stability, ensuring predictability, and bolstering deterrence. As our strategy may change in response to an evolving strategic environment, so, too, our defense programs and arms control positions would also change. Together, security will be enhanced.

Clearly, neither defense programs nor arms control can do the job alone. To maintain the integrity of the Triad, we will need to rely upon the deployment of mobile missiles as a key component of our nuclear modernization program. But START (Strategic Arms Reduction Talks) can play a key role. It can reduce the Soviet threat to our forces and thereby make survivability through mobility more feasible. Without START to constrain the Soviet threat, the job of ensuring reliable deterrence would be less predictable and affordable. Without the START negotiations, the domestic consensus needed to support essential modernization programs – not only mobile ICBMs but also B-2, Trident, and SDI – would be difficult to sustain. Likewise, without our strategic modernization program, the benefits of a START agreement would be sharply reduced. Thus, our force modernization and arms control efforts reinforce one another.

In September, I announced the president's decision to allow mobile land-based missiles in START. Permitting mobile missiles only makes sense if the United States is willing to deploy them. For this reason, this decision is contingent on congressional funding of our mobile missile program. Congress needs now to support START, not undercut it, by funding this program. As Senator Nunn said recently, 'Unless we in the Congress can manage to put our ICBM modernization program back on track . . ., the START negotiations face a very bleak and a very long future indeed.'

Another prerequisite for a successful strategy – for defense programs and arms control that work together – is the need for unity as a nation and as an alliance. This follows from a simple truism: united we stand, divided we fall. We should not tempt the Soviets with exploitable differences between the administration and the Congress, or between the United States and its allies. That does not exempt us, of course, from the need for informed debate. It is imperative that we maintain open and honest discussions about strategy and arms control matters within the strategic community and with the public at large. As we deter possible aggression, we must – as the noted military historian Michael Howard has put it – reassure our peoples that their defense dollars are efficiently and effectively supporting the cause of peace. An open, frank debate is the surest formula for unity. But such a debate must begin and seek to reach some resolution before treaties are signed if we are to bring home treaties in the national interest.

The Goal of Arms Control and the Path to It

As a contribution to such a debate, I would like to move now from the prerequisites of arms control to the basic goal of our arms control policy and the principles for achieving it.

The main goal of arms control is to reduce the risk of war – any war, nuclear or conventional. We hope to prevent war by working toward a stable, predictable strategic relationship. Stability requires military forces and policies such that no one can gain by striking first even in the worst crisis. Beginning a war, especially a nuclear war, must never become a Soviet option – even a least-worst option, as a noted strategist once put it. Predictability requires that sufficient openness and transparency prevails to prevent misperception, miscalculaton, and an inadvertent war – a war no one wanted but no one could stop. The more open and transparent Soviet military affairs, the greater trust and confidence we can have in Soviet intentions.

Four principles guide our search for a stable, predictable strategic relationship. First, we seek reductions in first-strike, surprise attack capabilities. We seek stability through proposals to reduce those capabilities most suited for offensive, blitzkrieg-style actions and preemptive first-strikes. In CFE, we've concentrated on eliminating

Soviet advantages in those weapons must suited to seizing and holding territory: tanks, artillery, and armored personnel carriers. In START, we've focused on reducing the most destabilizing weapons, especially vulnerable, silo-based heavy ICBMs, such as Soviet SS-18s. These weapons are suited principally for preemptive first-strikes and not for retaliatory missions. In Wyoming, we proposed banning short-time-of-flight sea-launched ballistic missile (SLBM) tests, seeking in this way to reduce the capability for a Soviet decapitating first-strike. Our START proposals emphasize the relative merits of slow-flying weapons – such as cruise missiles and bombers which are not suitable for a first-strike.

Our SDI program also supports our emphasis on stability. Effective strategic defenses can contribute to survivable, cost-effective barriers to a successful first-strike. That's why we look favorably on the decision made by the Soviets in Wyoming to de-link the Defense and Space Talks from START. This Soviet decision to no longer hold START hostage to resolution of Defense and Space issues removes a key obstacle to a START treaty while enabling us to proceed with our SDI plans. We remain committed to preserving our right to conduct SDI activities consistent with the ABM treaty. And we will use the Defense and Space talks to explore a cooperative and stable transition to a greater reliance on stability-enhancing, cost-effective strategic defenses.

Our second principle – predictabilty through openness – expands the traditional focus of arms control on capabilities. Every war has its own unique causes, but surely Thucydides made an important general point when he wrote, 'What made war inevitable was the growth of Athenian power and the fear which this caused in Sparta.' Arms control has mainly focused on the first part of this equation: constraining or reducing destabilizing military capabilities. Now in expanding the agenda, we are working to deal with the other aspect of Thucydides' equation: fears of aggressive intent. We are pushing to make Soviet military activities more open and transparent. The more we know and understand, the more we can be assured that our fears are not results of misperception or miscalculation. Greater openness is the surest path to greater predictability and a lower risk of war, especially inadvertent war.

The president's Open Skies initiative is a clear example of this new focus in arms control. Openness about military forces and activities is at the heart of the talks on confidence and security building measures (CSBMs) among all the states of Europe. In those negotiations, we are proposing an all-European military data exchange about our forces and weapons programs. In keeping with the spirit of openness we found at the Wyoming Ministerial, we signed an agreement on notification of strategic exercises and invited the Soviets to visit our SDI facilities. The chemical weapons data exchange will help us move toward a verifiable global ban. Defense Minister Yazov's visit earlier this month is just one of a series of exchanges that provide face-to-face opportunities to understand the Soviet military. And we've pushed the Soviets to publish a real defense budget that reveals the inputs into and outputs from their defense production process.

Openness in military affairs is just part of our overall emphasis in our dealings with the Soviets on creating open, pluralistic institutions. On his recent visit, Soviet Defense Minister Yazov talked of the increasing influence of Supreme Soviet committees over the Soviet defense complex. We hope that Soviet military power may increasingly be exposed to the salutary effects of detailed and searching public debate.

Greater openness combined with force reductions will support political change as well. In CFE, our proposals will reduce the potential not only for a Soviet blitzkrieg but for Soviet intimidation of Western Europe. The Soviet army we face as a potential army of aggression is to East Europeans an army of occupation. The weight of the Soviet military presence in Eastern Europe will be reduced. Freed from the cold shadow of Soviet military domination, political pluralism and free markets should flourish more easily in Eastern Europe.

A more predictable strategic relationship should also be less expensive. Arms control can, as the president wrote Mr Gorbachev, 'introduce predictability into military planning so that we can slow the pace of military competition.' A slower competition could be a cheaper and safer competition. But our desire to save money must not come into conflict with the necessity for security.

The third principle of our policy is a broadened arms control agenda, far wider than its traditional East–West nuclear focus. We are broadening our agenda with the Soviets, both in terms of dealing with pressing, global arms control problems, like chemical and missile proliferation, as well as focusing on regional conflicts. In an increasingly intertwined world, a stable, predictable US–Soviet strategic relationship depend in part on regional stability and vice versa. Earlier, I noted that advanced technologies were proliferating to the Third World. Advanced fighters have gone to Libya, Syria and North Korea. Over 20 states possess the capability to produce chemical weapons. And nuclear proliferation, notably North Korea's reactor program, remains dangerous. Arms control should increasingly focus on such problems.

The president's UN initiative can lead us toward a verifiable global ban on chemical weapons. The president's proposal represents a realistic road map for progress. As a step toward a multilateral ban, we will move bilaterally with the Soviets to reduce chemical weapons to 20 percent of the current US levels. We will further slash stocks to just 2 percent of their current levels within eight years after the multilateral convention goes into effect. This total cut of 98 percent is a substantial acceleration of previous destruction plans. Then, we will move to zero within two years of adherence to the ban by all chemical weapons-capable states.

We realize it may be difficult to persuade problem states such as Libya to join. But we are creating an environment where everyone will have incentives to join and costs to pay for remaining an outlaw. Export controls on precursor chemicals will be strengthened, building on progress made at the recent Canberra Conference. The president has also ordered a study on sanctions to deter and punish chemical weapons use and other violations of a convention. States must know that they will pay a price for their inhumanity.

Our fourth principle is institutionalization of a safer world. The president aims to reduce the risk of war permanently, not temporarily. We want to see Soviet defensive military operations made habitual. We want to see the new thinking concretely built in to the Soviet force structure. We want to see weapons destroyed, not merely removed. And we want agreements that can endure.

Effective verification can ensure that the treaties we sign are doing their job to institutionalize a safer world. Because of the primacy of effective verification in this administration's approach to arms control, our negotiators have already proposed data exchanges and trial verification measures that would be implemented even before the agreements themselves are concluded. Such measures in START and in chemical weapons will help us build confidence and gain practical experience that will facilitate the conclusion of sound, verifiable agreements.

Neither have we stood still in pressing the Soviets to comply fully with agreements already signed. In September, President Gorbachev informed the president that the Krasnoyarsk radar would finally be destroyed. We welcome Moscow's step to come into compliance with the ABM treaty.

A Realistic Path to Risk-Reduction

These four principles of a more stable, open, broader and less reversible strategic relationship offer a realistic path to a lasting reduction of risk. It is a path best travelled by steady steps that build on one another, rather than grand leaps that are often as not unrealistic or undone. In START, in CFE, in all our negotiations – we have made fair, responsible proposals designed to find enduring points of mutual advantage. The Soviets have said yes to much of what we have proposed. Now, we have rolled up our shirt sleeves and set to work together to put principle into practice.

We should be clear about the task ahead. We are not on the verge of a perpetual peace in which war is no longer possible. We cannot dis-invent nuclear weapons nor the need for continued deterrence. Nor can we completely eliminate Soviet–American rivalry. But that rivalry does not require that we stand on the brink of Armageddon as we did 27 years ago this month. Peace need no longer hang solely on Winston Churchill's 'process of sublime irony . . . where safety will be the sturdy child of terror, and survival the twin brother of annihilation.'

Deterrence need not rest only on a delicate, technical balance of terror disturbed by periodic crises. Opportunity invites us, instead, to move beyond containment, beyond the Cold War, to a new strategic relationship based on a sound political footing.

A new relationship in which the capabilities and incentives to attack first are minimized and the possibilities of strategic defenses are pursued. A new relationship in which Soviet military power is open to the naked eye, not just satellites in the sky. A new relationship in which all the peoples of Europe are free of military intimidation. A new relationship in which effectively verifiable treaties lock-in a lower risk of war. And a new relationship in which arms control aids our people in turning the seeds of war into the fruits of peace.

This is the strategic relationship we seek.

Source: USIS, London, 24 October 1989.

WARSAW TREATY FOREIGN MINISTERS' COMMITTEE, COMMUNIQUÉ

27 October 1989

The unconditional respect for the inviolability of existing borders, territorial integrity, independence and sovereignty of countries, and the observance of generally recognized principles and norms of international law, provisions of the Final Act of the Conference for Security and Cooperation in Europe and other documents, adopted within the framework of the Helsinki Process, have fundamental significance for building a common European Home.

. . .

Headway on disarmament, confidence-building, the development of co-operation and the construction of an indivisible Europe will help create a common European system of collective security and simultaneously disband the Warsaw Treaty and NATO.

Source: *Soviet News*, 1 November 1989

PRESIDENT FRANÇOIS MITTERRAND ON GERMAN REUNIFICATION: EXCERPTS FROM PRESS CONFERENCE

Bonn, 3 November 1989

Q. – On the subject of the reunification of Germany, some German politicians are saying that perhaps Germany's neighbours and allies might not be so enthusiastic about that idea, that they might even fear that reunification. Do you fear a possible reunification of Germany?

THE PRESIDENT – It is not just politicians who are talking about it, journalists are too, particularly in Germany, but in France too.

That is quite normal, as it is a dominant issue of the closing years of this century. I attach great importance to this German problem, but we must not look at reunification as something to be feared or approved. What counts above all is the will and determination of the people. Whether the situation evolves – I don't know when that might happen, immediately or later – such that the Germans become a single people in a single State or in a form to be determined – I am definitely not venturing into that territory – is something the German citizens will have to decide. No-one must do it for them. Of course, that will not happen just like that, regardless of the circumstances. People usually say – these are words that may appear conventional, but I say them all the same – peace must not be jeopardized, so it must be a peaceful move.

It must be democratic too, which is taken for granted as we have spoken of the decision of the people themselves. It also concerns the other countries, especially those in Europe. You know there are agreements and special guarantees, not just the world post-war ones, but also those to do with the fact that we live in a community.

All that has to be put on the table. But what counts is what the Germans want to do and what they can do. So there are problems on which I shall express my opinion when the time comes. But what stage has the German Democratic Republic got to? How far will she evolve? What do those who govern her want? What do those who are governed want? How fast, to achieve what status, structures? Has the question of reunification even come up in those circles? I shall wait for the facts before concluding.

In answer to your initial question, I do not fear reunification. I don't ask myself that sort of question as history moves on. History is there. I take it as it is. I think it is legitimate for the Germans who desire reunification; if they want it and can have it. France will adapt her policy so as to act in Europe's and her own best interests. I am not going back over the same ground, I shall say that the answer is simple: as Eastern Europe evolves, Western Europe must become stronger, strengthen its structures and define its policies.

Q. – When will the question arise?

THE PRESIDENT – I am asked to make a forecast ... I can't possibly make one, but at the speed things are going, I would be very surprised if the next ten years went by without us having to face up to a new structure in Europe. I can very well understand that a great many Germans want it. They simply have to understand that history is not made like that. There are countries, which, in some cases for a millenium and in others for hundreds of years, have been used to being neighbours, quarrelling, watching over the balance of their relations. These factors have to be taken into account when people talk about this problem. So my forecast will be based on an obvious observation: things are moving fast, very fast. They won't subsequently go as fast as is wished by those who are talking about reunification now.

But no European politician can now reason without taking that on board, that seems obvious to me. I am not making a specific forecast, reunification poses so many problems that I shall review the situation as things happen.

Source: French Embassy, London, 3 November 1989

AFTER THE BREACH IN THE BERLIN WALL

SPEECH MADE BY MARGARET THATCHER AT THE LORD MAYOR'S BANQUET GUILDHALL

13 November 1989 (Excerpts)

My Lord Mayor, we are witnessing great events.

Fifty years ago the peace of Europe was shattered by the sound of armies on the march. Today the plains of central Europe resound once more, this time to the swirl of people on the move.

The message is clear. When people are free to choose, they choose freedom. They turn their backs on a system which has been discredited – not by western propaganda but by first-hand experience.

An American writer visiting the home of Communism in 1919 remarked:

'I have seen the future and it works'.

Seventy years on we know that it doesn't. . . .

When I spoke at Bruges a year or so ago – in a speech which caused just a little bit of a stir – I reminded people that the European Community is only one manifestation of Europe's identity: that Warsaw, Prague and Budapest are great European cities, just as European as London, Paris and Rome.

Even a year ago, we could scarcely have imagined the extent and the speed of the changes which have since swept the Soviet Union, Poland, Hungary and now East Germany.

We should honour those in the Communist countries who never let repression and dictatorship break their spirit or their unshakeable belief in liberty, and who are now seeing their hopes realised.

We must give them every possible encouragement and support. We are doing just that in all our contacts with the Soviet Union under Mr Gorbachev, and in the practical help – with food, training, trade – that we are giving to Poland and Hungary. We cannot and must not let their brave efforts fail.

In East Germany the objective must be to see genuine democracy, with free elections and more than one party. To attain that in an orderly way which preserves stability in Europe would itself be a huge achievement.

Moreover, as we have already seen in the Soviet Union, it is easier to make political changes than it is to carry out economic reform. Economic reform requires the acceptance of initiative and responsibility by people themselves – and that is very difficult in countries which have never known these qualities.

The way in which we in the West respond to these historic changes could be crucial in determining their success. We want to see democracy extend throughout the Soviet Union and Eastern Europe, and we want it to last. . . .

We must also remember that times of great change are times of great uncertainty even danger. The librarian of the United States Congresss put it very well when he said:

'There is no more insecure time in the life of an Empire than when it is facing the devolution of its power, no more dangerous time in the life of a religion (Communism being after all a secular religion) than when it has lost its inner faith but retains its outer power.' Very wise words.

Now is the time for us in the West to stay true to the policies and the principles that have brought us safely through the years of confrontation and cold war since 1945. I don't believe that the great changes now happening would have come about had it not been for NATO and the strength and resolve it has shown.

And it must be through NATO that we continue to keep the peace by tried and tested means, while welcoming every step that allows us to do so safely at lower levels of forces and weapons.

Source: ACDRU, Foreign and Commonwealth Office

SPEECH OF PRESIDENT MITTERRAND
TO THE EUROPEAN PARLIAMENT

Strasbourg, 22 November 1989

As you know, last Saturday a special session of the European Council was held in Paris.

Its agenda was simple: to consider the events taking place in Eastern Europe and draw the first consequences from them.

After talking to the President of your Assembly, I thought it would be helpful for the smooth operation of our institutions if I, as President of the European Council, could come to speak to you for a moment, without overly prolonging your work, about what happened on that occasion.

Less than a month ago, on 25 October, in this very place, I spoke to you as I am doing today. I talked about the situation in the countries of our East European neighbours, in which, as you can observe, history is being written daily. I referred to that vast movement towards democracy and freedom, that determination of peoples which is dictating the course of events, making walls and frontiers crumble and I said: once again the people are on the move and when they move their action is decisive. On 9 November in Berlin, history on the march offered the world the spectacle, improbable even the day before, of a breach in the Wall which for nearly thirty years had, on its own, signified our continent's scissions.

That day democracy and freedom, inseparable one from the other, achieved, I believe, one of their finest, most significant victories. The people had stirred. The people had spoken and their voices crossed the frontiers, broke the silence of an order they had not wanted, had been imposed on them and which they very probably aspired to repudiate in order to become themselves again.

So I am happy to express here, before Chancellor Kohl and the representatives of the peoples of the twelve Community member States, the deep emotion we felt at those momentous moments. Emotion on which it is unnecessary to comment at length because of the extent to which each one of us has been personally caught up in this history in the making at the same time as experiencing it as a tremendous collective movement, to which I believe we are proud to have been party.

The movement set in train in Poland, pursued in Hungary – to confine myself of course to recent events – as it's already been a long

361

time since the first day free men hoped and free men fought. Many have run the risk of losing their freedom, of death, many have succumbed. In short, when exactly was the first sign and first awakening? However, confining ourselves to the recent events, Poland, Hungary, the movement deliberately encouraged in the Soviet Union, we can never overemphasize Mr Gorbachev's role in all this.

There's a man whose attitude is certainly in keeping with his thinking and his history, that of his country, but who has understood the need to move on to new ways of doing things and that, like the others, his country ought now to accept those dominant forces in human society, which are – it's a pleasure to repeat them – democracy and freedom. To sum up, this movement is speeding up, swelling, spreading throughout Europe and we want – allow me to speak on your behalf even though you have not given me a mandate to do so – we feel of one mind. We even want it to go on. Our hunger is not satisfied: we see what has happened throughout the cities of Poland, East Germany, in Hungary. We hear the appeals of the crowds in Prague and if we cannot hear the voice of the Romanian people, it is because it is still stifled. But we perceive it. That silence is deafening. Some day or other that people will have to rejoin the concert of nations which we already form between our twelve countries, which over this century have grown so far apart and then found their way back together because that was what they wanted and perhaps too because necessity has taught them that was what they had to want.

So why this Paris meeting of 18 November? Should we, on the other hand, have moved faster? I shall not reopen this argument which had some weight and merit and on which it was difficult to decide. I myself pondered the matter from the first day. I thought we should perhaps distance ourselves a little – we didn't let much time pass, it was a week – from the feelings and emotions of the first hours before we could begin to see things clearly, so that the peoples themselves could begin to establish what separates their ambitions, profound desires, sometimes their dreams from today's reality, from the realities governing our political discussions, the meetings of our assemblies, our government decisions. I did not bring the Strasbourg European Council forward for what seemed to me an obvious reason: it is scheduled for 8 and 9 December. There's a time for everything, as you know Ladies and Gentlemen from experience in and outside the Community framework, deadlines are being prepared and projects are coming to a head. The Strasbourg rendez-vous was situated precisely at a turning-point for our Community's future, for increasing the solidity of its structures, defining its principles. I think it was necessary for us to be able to attend there to all those important matters; on Saturday we could talk mainly, indeed almost exclusively both about the events in Eastern Europe and what we, the countries generally regarded as the West, should do. I shall come back to that in a moment. What should we do? We already have some initial answers. They will have to be completed. We have a great deal of work in front of us, both you and I. Today we are all at the workbench, we have to know how we shall forge tomorrow's Europe. However, in actual fact we had a twofold objective: jointly to analyse the situation in Eastern Europe and assess its potential consequences for the European balance and to mark the determination of the Community and its member States to provide aid for all the East European countries who have embarked on the path to reform and, more concretely, more specifically, for those which have taken that direction, not merely giving us their word thereon, but making commitments to that effect in their own countries. The measures already announced provide us with evidence that this approach is indeed one that leads to the establishment of democratic systems.

The circumstances clearly justified that meeting. The subject warranted our giving it detailed consideration without further delay, the issues cried out to be heard by the Community and for it to determine its position in the face of the events directly affecting it. Mr President, Ladies and Gentlemen, you wanted to organize a debate on the political developments in Central and Eastern Europe and their repercussions on Europe's and consequently the Community's future. I congratulate you on that initiative. I am sure your debate will add to the message the Twelve are addressing to the countries of Europe. And, as I am currently presiding over the European Council, I thought I could not fulfil my duty without at some point taking the opportunity to report to you on these matters. In my view it is indeed this Parliament's role to hold such a debate, even though things are in a constant state of flux, and at least mark some of the stages in a significant way, I hope that will be done today.

Don't think this is only a duty. I am also happy, even if it's a bit repetitive, to have this chance to tell you our conclusions. However, as I have referred to Saturday's Council meeting and that is why I have come back so soon, I am going to dwell on it for a moment. The first of these conclusions involves the very future of our Community – I think I can say, as has been said before – the existence of a Community that is growing in solidity and has served as a reference point and stimulus for the events in Eastern Europe. We shall not take the credit for this ourselves, that primarily belongs to those countries' peoples, then to those of their leaders who have understood the necessity for that evolution, have allowed and facilitated it. It belongs too, I am convinced, to this Community which today represents the only real magnet for a structured future of our continent. Then there are the values, the famous values which we often talk about, but we know exactly what we mean. The values from which those peoples claim their inspiration are very close to ours. We ourselves have wanted to express those aspirations, which we share, but which, over the centuries, because of the state of civilization, have seen Europe born, come together, fall apart, come back together again. Those values transcend the focal points for grievances, frontiers, severances of relations, walls: we have the evidence, walls are crumbling, we are meeting again, understanding one another.

I am convinced, as I have already said, that the existence of a strong and structured Community is a factor of stability and success for the whole of Europe. We therefore have to assert our own identity as a Community, confirm our determination, strengthen our institutions, set the seal on our union. That's the first lesson for me, for I see no other alternative between opening up eastwards and completing the Community structure. The two processes go hand in hand. I have told you and want to stress that they complete each other. It is not a matter of withdrawing into ourselves, but of drawing from the Community's success the strength, the reserves of energy and dynamism that will bring together the whole of Europe.

I used that term in the press conference following our meeting on Saturday evening, saying: the major political lesson from all this is that there is an indissociable binomial. As events progress and unfold in Eastern Europe, Community Europe should, at the same pace and – why not? – even a little faster so as to precede the event, achieve still greater consolidation than so far decided on and hasten to establish its identity in its structures. And those structures will strictly depend on the political will it will have displayed in order that all the policies set in train since the Founders conceived Europe may be governed by unity – political unity.

And I think I can say that it was in this spirit that the twelve Heads of State and of Government met. It was what they wanted to express. It was their own will. To encourage and back the progress of democracy wherever we see evidence of it, but also to learn from those factors that the Community must apply to itself the lessons taught us by events.

Make the connection, after what I have just said, between the meeting of 18 November and the one that awaits us on 8 and 9 December. In the interval, admittedly, much has happened and there is more to come. I should like to tell you straight away how the concrete measures were examined, according to situations, which are vastly different from one country to the next, in relation to the East European countries on the march.

Poland and Hungary in the first place. The Twelve stressed the urgency of an agreement being concluded with the International Monetary Fund for those two countries and we decided that the Community authorities would very diligently press that institution to make a decision before the end of the year. Poland and Hungary must, of course, cooperate in order to arrive at a good agreement in accordance with the rules by which our international institutions have to abide. But the matter is so urgent that the Community must stand by those two countries in order to argue a difficult case which, however, deserves a successful outcome.

During the recent visit to Warsaw and Budapest of the President of the Commission and the President of the Council of Ministers,

M Jacques Delors and M Roland Dumas, those countries' needs were ascertained. Poland has to have the use of a stabiliziation fund estimated at a billion dollars, while Hungary is asking for the same amount of 'bridging' finance. I can tell you the principle of setting up these two forms of funding can already be regarded as established.

The Twelve also discussed cooperation with other countries. They considered and fully accepted th signing of trade agreements with the German Democratic Republic.

We might tend to forget Yugoslavia in the flurry of events, but we must remember that that country was perhaps the first to show such a capacity for resistance and such courage that, even though its economy did not benefit, its people nevertheless won the right to a genuine moral obligation on our part to stand beside them and help them, just like the others, especially since, as you know, their country is going through a serious economic crisis.

Going further, and to support the reform movement, we examined what instruments should be established. These are of several kinds as I shall briefly explain in a moment. A debate got under way on a notion that is indeed worth discussing. Should conditions be laid down or not for the countries that need us? Yes and no. It seemed to us that the countries that have been shown a categorically declared willingness to acquire democratic institutions centred round a few simple concepts – human rights observance and announcement of free and therefore secret elections – surely deserved that we should make this extra effort and endeavour right away to obtain for them a number of advantages to which they are entitled, together with their admittance to certain institutions, our view being that the Community (without proposing to enlarge itself in that way or applying any procedures) already considered that a community, a group of nations and peoples existed capable of adopting a comparable approach. So we established a certain linkage for those types of measures to be taken between Poland, Hungary and the Community countries. But all this doesn't mean that we left the countries that are not at the same stage to their fate.

We would not wish our countries' aid in any way to be responsible for introducing a new factor prolonging the totalitarian dictatorial régimes surviving here and there. This would be absurd, and yet at the same time one can well see, having made such provisos, how distasteful it would be to refuse our help to countries simply because they had not been lucky enough to be freed earlier from a system from which they are suffering and so would be denied our assistance and friendship. So we have to consider carefully how to proceed, which is what we are seeking to do. And while we have decided on a course of action and planned a series of agreements, a line of action that is extremely clearly marked out, for Poland and Hungary, we are nevertheless preparing the ground and laying down markers in the direction of all the others, so that everyone knows where they are.

In support of the reform movement we don't have simply to adopt a passive attitude, keeping the score. We also have to accompany the movement, extend its scope. The instruments that will have to be established have been defined and must be discussed again in the days or weeks ahead. I shall mention a few of them, in particular the proposed development and modernization bank for Eastern Europe, which I had in fact talked about on 25 October, speaking on that occasion in my own name. What was decided in Paris was a brief entrusted to the 'Troika'. I think that all who wish to subscribe capital to this bank, comparable to the regional banks for South-East Asia or Africa, should be extensively involved in it, and in the first place the twenty-four countries that answered the call of the Arch Summit on 14 July this year. That is what, until explicit agreement is reached between the Community countries, would make the bank a novel venture. People have, of course, pointed to the EIB, which comes immediately to mind. Whilst we don't feel an obsessive need – I for one do not – to set up new bodies in every conceivable circumstance (I don't like bureaucracies any more than you do), it's just that this is not the EIB's role.

The EIB's work is bound up essentially with the structural funds, its eyes are focussed on another side of Europe, it is made up only of the twelve Community countries, and I think – a few of us think – that this bank must be of specific value to the East European countries and that instead of involving only the Community countries it must gather together all the willing participants in the world and all the capital, whatever its source, so as to release a tremendous momentum commensurate with the task awaiting them.

So that is the feature on which I am insisting and shall insist. The Troika has begun talking about it, attending to it; it will report on 8 and 9 December. I hope that this proposal for a bank for Eastern Europe, which has come from several quarters, several benches of this Assembly and of our national Assemblies and is an idea genuinely conceived in many minds, will really harness itself to development and cooperate in building up new strengths, so as to save those countries at the start from the abyss confronting them.

And from that point of view, action is extremely urgent. I even think that, if there had to be some delays in setting up this bank, if there are and I fear there may be, an immediate solution is required. Which means that, as early as next week, a start must be made on setting in motion the institutions capable of filling this role while awaiting the creation of an institution.

Similarly, I remember a conversation with Mr Gorbachev. I keep private conversations held in that sort of meeting mostly to myself, but this has been said so often that I feel free to recall it. I remember the day when he said to me: 'What we most need is training for our managers'. In how many countries have we heard that? 'We need to train bosses'. Apparently the men and women called upon to run those countries are no longer capable of doing so because they haven't been trained for that, they have been trained for other things. They have not adapted themselves to the new forms of management. After all, it's our role, let's do it, unconditionally. Let's draw up a management training project for all those countries. Similarly, we have decided to open up to the East European countries existing Community programmes for everything to do with education and training. One day we might then see – I am improvising – a Hungarian student taking advantage of the Erasmus programme to do a doctorate at Oxford, a student from Leipzig going on a course, thanks to the Comett programme, in a Dutch, Italian, or – why not? – French firm, a Warsaw French teacher improving his French thanks to the Lingua programme, and so on, you can see exactly what we mean. We aren't keeping those programmes just for ourselves. Already we have begun to take action well beyond the Community boundaries in certain spheres, especially technological ones, and we shall carry on.

Other suggestions, in particular that of admitting certain countries to the Council of Europe and GATT, initially as observers, have been made. Each of these suggestions will of course be examined, to use our civil servants' terminology, in the appropriate framework and under the appropriate procedures. On 8 and 9 December we shall report on the latter to the European Council which will shoulder its responsibilities, and I hope we shall not come back to this matter any more, or rather that, when we do, our object will be to do more and do better, Ladies and Gentlemen.

Has the Community answered the expectations of those who have faith in it? Has it really answered Mr Mazowiecki's anguished appeal asking us not to allow to perpetuate the Europe of the poor and the Europe of the rich? Has it answered your own expectation, which you have voiced on various occasions in a number of proposals? Has the Community fulfilled the hopes of the European men and women who expect it to make its voice heard on all the world's affairs and assert itself both as an active partner in a new European balance and as one of the fundamental active participants in human life on earth?

One never does enough, nor goes fast enough. Speedy action does not imply unthinking action. But we have to realize, and I am speaking to an Assembly that is convinced of this since it constantly reminds us of it – so I wish to be heard beyond these walls – that none of this will be achieved unless we are capable in a few days' time, between ourselves inside the Community, of reaching agreement on the fundamental proposals that will allow our Europe to acquire the instruments for an economic and monetary policy, a social policy and an environmental policy. It will not be achieved unless we complete the internal market at the pace and by the route we have already decided on.

That is what we are now going to work on. That is what we are going to apply ourselves to, those are the questions I shall put in Strasbourg in a few days' time, everyone will have to answer them. And since I want to keep to my subject, I am sure that all of us who bear responsibility, and we all do, will get a flash of insight which won't make everything blindingly clear, but will nevertheless light up the horizon, so that something good, worthwhile and lasting for the others will follow from what we shall be able to do between and for ourselves. In short, in our hands we hold far more than our own fate. We can now show the way totally unpretentiously, with no idea of dominating or lecturing in any way whatsoever, but with a profound democratic resolution that each of our countries has demonstrated a hundred times. We want the way the Community determines its action to serve as an example to the East European countries who are seeking, stirring, suffering anguish, hoping, for those millions who, like us, dream that one day Europe will be Europe. That is what I expect from the Strasbourg European Council. You can see the importance of the stakes. I don't need to tell you; I am addressing an Assembly, of whom the vast majority is convinced that this is where the path and duty lie; we must take that route together.

Source: French Embassy, London, 22 November 1989

SPEECH BY UK FOREIGN SECRETARY, DOUGLAS HURD

House of Commons, 24 November 1989

In 1989, we have experienced upheavals on our continent which have been unparalleled in peace time since 1848, which was also a year of revolutions driven by a desire for political liberty and national self-expression. For the most part, however, the revolutions of 1848 ended in violence and disappointment. In 1989, as this astonishing pace of change continues, we have begun to hope that it may prove to be lasting. There may of course be halts and reverses, but it would be hard now to recreate the Iron Curtain.

Europe has had 40 years of stability, east and west of the Iron Curtain but stability has been assured in very different ways. In the West, we have achieved and held stability after the most destructive convulsion in our history through free political institutions. Internally, we have relied on democracy. Externally, we have built up international institutions freely entered into to draw our democracies closer together. I refer to NATO for our defence, the European Community, to strengthen our prosperity, based on free enterprise, and the Council of Europe to bind us in willing affirmation of these shared values of democracy.

The East has also had stability, but based on enforced uniformity and regimes imposed from the outside. It has been stability based on denying freedom and on one party having a monopoly of power. In the last resort, as we witnessed in the bloodshed of 1953, 1956 and 1968, that stability was based on the readiness of the Soviet Union to employ ruthless force to maintain its nominees in power. The tanks fired in those three years, and the people were forced back into the shadows.

Those systems of coercion are now crumbling fast. It is not hard to understand why. They lacked the basic foundation of consent by the governed. Metternich, who in 1848 symbolised the old regime, understood the appeal of freedom. He once said:
'It is useless to close the gates against ideas. They overleap them.'

For gates, Iron Curtains and Berlin Walls, that is what is happening. In 1989, the idea of freedom is leaping over them all.

I am sure that the whole House welcomes those changes, and we salute the courage and wisdom of those who are using peaceful protest to break down the barriers which separate them from freedom. But it is only the beginning of a long and difficult transformation by the countries concerned.

What should our response be? We, by which I mean the Government, our partners and our allies, are working out and have expressed a careful and clear response. It was worked out in close consultation with our partners at the EC summit last weekend in Paris which I attended with my right honourable Friend the Prime Minister.

To those of us who believe in the European Community, it was heartening to find the Heads of State and Government, not to mention the Foreign Ministers, so clearly united on a response to these events.

We reached the following conclusions:

First, we must do everything we can to encourage the process of political and economic reform in Eastern Europe. . . .

The second main conclusion that we reached in Paris concerned the importance of keeping stability and security in Europe. We all recognise that a time of change is also a time of uncertainty. Neither West nor East should feel that its fundamental security interests are threatened by peaceful change. That is why it has been agreed that it is important to send a clear message of reassurance to the Soviet Union that the West does not intend to seek to use recent events to prejudice Soviet security. For our part, we shall continue to look to NATO as a strong and reliable defence. . . .

To a large extent it is Mr Gorbachev's policies in the Soviet Union that have made possible the changes in Eastern Europe. He has had the courage and clarity of vision to see the writing on the Iron Curtain, and to accept and even to encourage change.

It is emphatically in the Western interest that Soviet policies, which have contributed so much to improved East–West relations and to reform in Eastern Europe, should be sustained. That is also in the long-term interests of the Soviet people. We shall therefore to continue to give Mr Gorbachev support and encouragement.

I believe that it has emerged already that the Community approach which I have summarised coincides with that of the United States. The forthcoming United States–Soviet summit provides a timely opportunity for President Bush to convey Western views to President Gorbachev, and to explore the prospects for East–West relations as a whole. My right honourable Friend the Prime Minister is today meeting President Bush to discuss these and other matters.

On 4 December, President Bush will brief NATO leaders in Brussels on the results of his talks with President Gorbachev. We hope that the summit will provide additional impetus towards further measures of arms control, and especially to the successful conclusion of the Vienna CFE talks next year. There is reason to hope that this goal of agreement next year – it will be a substantial agreement – can be reached. We are playing a full and constructive part in the negotiations.

An agreement at Vienna will mean the elimination of the massive conventional superiority and offensive capacity of Warsaw Pact forces in Europe. Numbers of tanks and artillery in Europe will be cut in half, if the agreement is reached.

Parity in United States and Soviet manpower stationed in Europe at 275,000 a side will mean a cut of over 50 per cent in Soviet forces. Reductions of this size will transform the military security situation in Europe and bring greater stability when it will be most needed, at a time of great change. . . .

I feel strongly that it is a notable privilege to stand here as Foreign Secretary at the Dispatch Box. That would be true at any time, but it is particularly true in this autumn of 1989.

I hope that European's response to events whose drama we all feel has shown that we are not afraid of change. Certainly we want stability, and feel that change must be orderly, but that does not mean clinging to old assumptions. We are ready to modify our policies in the light of events, as we have done throughout the period in which Mr Gorbachev has directed the affairs of the Soviet Union. Our democratic institutions – NATO and the European Community – are strong enough to accommodate and adapt to change: orderly change is our ally.

New opportunities are opening up in Europe as a result of the peaceful changes in the East, and we are well placed to take those opportunities. We are confident in our policies, in our relationships with our allies and partners and in the values on which all else depends.

Source: ACDRU, Foreign and Commonwealth Office

SPEECH BY CHANCELLOR KOHL TO THE BUNDESTAG ON INTRA-GERMAN RELATIONS

28 November 1989

We cannot plan the way to unity from our 'armchairs' or with our appointment calendars. Abstract models will help us no further. We can today, however, already prepare those stages which lead to this goal. I would like to elucidate these using a 10-point programme:

1.   Immediate measures need to be taken. These result from the events of the past few weeks, particularly from the movement of refugees and the new dimensions of inter-German traffic.

The Federal Government is prepared to provide immediate concrete aid where it is needed. We will assist in the humanitarian sector and provide medical assistance as far as is required.

We are also aware that the welcoming money, which is given once a year to every visitor from the GDR, can provide no long-term solution for the financing of journeys. The GDR must equip its nationals with the necessary currency. We are, however, prepared to contribute to a currency fund for the transition period. The prerequisites for this are, that the minimum sum of exchange imposed when travelling to the GDR must be relinquished, that entry into the GDR must be made easier and that the GDR itself makes a considerable contribution to this fund. Our aim is to establish the most unhindered form of tourist traffic possible in both directions.

2.   The Federal Government will, as before, continue its co-operation with the GDR in all areas where it is of direct benefit to people on both sides. This is particularly true of economic scientific and technological co-operation and of co-operation in cultural fields. It is of particular importance to intensify co-operation in the field of environmental protection. Here we will be able to shortly take decisions concerning new projects.

Additionally we also want to help to ensure that the telephone network in the GDR is extended as quickly as possible.

We are continuing negotiations pertaining to the extension of the railway network Hanover–Berlin. In addition, dialogue is necessary concerning fundamental questions of rail traffic within a Europe with open borders, and concerning the linking of the GDR network, with particular reference to modern high-speed trains.

3. I have offered to extensively extend our aid and co-operation should fundamental change of the political and economic system in the GDR be firmly agreed upon and put irrevocably into effect. By irrevocable, we mean that the East German leadership comes to an understanding with opposition groups concerning constitutional change and a new electoral law.

We support the demands for free, equal and secret elections in the GDR which incorporates independent and non-socialist parties. The power monopoly of the SED must be lifted.

The introduction of constitutional state conditions means, above all, the abolition of laws concerning political crimes.

Economic aid can only be effective if fundamental reforms within the economic system take place. Former experience with all Comecon states proves this. The bureaucratic planned economy must be dismantled.

We do not want to stabilise conditions which have become indefensible. Economic improvement can only occur if the GDR opens its doors to Western investment, if conditions of free enterprise are created and if private enterprise becomes possible. There are already examples of this in Hungary and Poland, examples which can be used by the GDR for orientation. Under these conditions, joint-ventures would soon be possible. There is already a large degree of willingness to undertake such ventures both at home and abroad.

These are not official preconditions but factual prerequisites needed before our aid can take effect. Additionally, there can be no doubt that the people in the GDR want an economic order which can also provide them with economic freedom and prosperity.

4. Prime Minister Modrow spoke in his governmental declaration of a contractual community. We are prepared to accept these thoughts. The proximity and the special nature of the relationships between our two states in Germany demand an increasingly close-knit network of agreements in all sectors and at all levels.

This co-operation will also increasingly demand common institutions. Commissions which already exist can be given new tasks and further commissions can be called into being. Here I am particularly thinking of the economic, transport, environmental, scientific and technical, health and cultural sectors. It goes without saying that Berlin will be fully included in these co-operative efforts.

I call upon all social groups and institutions to actively participate in the development of such a contractual community.

5. We are also prepared to take a further decisive step, namely, to develop confederative structures between the two states in Germany with the goal of creating a federation, a federal state order in Germany. A legitimate democratic government within the GDR is an unrelinquishable prerequisite.

We can envisage that after free elections the following instututons be formed:

- A common governmental committee for permanent consultation and political harmonisation;
- Common technical committees;
- A common parliamentary group.

Previous policy with reference to the GDR had to essentially concentrate itself on small steps. These strove to alleviate the results of being a divided nation and uphold and sharpen the consciousness for the unity of the nation. If in the future, a democratically legitimsed, that is a freely elected government, becomes our partner totally new perspectives are available.

New forms of institutional co-operation could be created and further developed in stages. Such a coming together is in the interest of the continuation of German history. State organisations within Germany are always confederations or federations. At this time, we can once again make use of this historical precedence.

Nobody knows how a reunified Germany will look. I am however sure that unity will come, if it is wanted by the German nation.

6.   The development of inner-German relations remains bedded in the pan-European process and in East–West relations. The future structure of Germany must fit into the future architecture of Europe as a whole. The West has to provide pace-making aid here with its concept for a permanent and just European order of peace.

In our common declaration of June this year, the Soviet leader Gorbachev and I speak of the building components of a 'common European house'. I can name, for example:

- The unlimited respect of the integrity and safety of each state. Each state has the right to choose its own political and social system;
- The unlimited respect of the principles and standards of international law, particularly respect for the peoples right of self-determination;
- The realisation of human rights;
- respect for, and the upholding of, the historically-based cultures of the people of Europe.

With all of these points, as Mr Gorbachev and I prescribed, we want to link onto the historically-based European traditions and help to overcome the divisions in Europe.

7.   The powers of attraction and the aura of the European Community is and remains a constant feature in the pan-European development. We want to strengthen this further.

The European Community is now required to approach the reform-orientated states in central, eastern, and southern Europe with openness and flexibility. This was ascertained unanimously by the heads of state and government of EC member-states during their recent meeting in Paris. This of course includes the GDR:

- The Federal Government therefore approves the quick conclusion of a trade and co-operation agreement with the GDR. This would expand and secure the GDR's entry within the common market, including the perspectives of 1992;
- We can envisage for the future specific forms of association which would lead the economies of the reform-oriented countries of central and south-eastern Europe to the EC, and thereby dismantle the economic and social gradients on our continent.

We understand the process leading to the recovery of the German unity to be of European concern. It must, therefore, be considered together with European integration. In keeping with this, the European Community must remain open to a democratic GDR and to other democratic countries from central and south-eastern Europe. The EC must not end on the Elbe, but remain open to the East.

Only in this way is it possible that the foundation of the EC truly include a comprehensive European unity. Only in this way can it maintain, assert and develop an identity characteristic of all Europeans. This identity is not only based on the cultural diversity of Europe, but also, and especially, on the fundamental values of freedom, democracy, human rights and self-determination.

If the countries of central and south-western Europe fulfill the necessary prerequisites, we would also greet their entrance into the European council, especially into the convention for the protection of human rights and fundamental freedoms.

8. The CSCE process is and remains a crucial part of the total European architecture and must be further advanced in order to do this, the following CSCE forums must be taken advantage of:

- The Human Rights Conference in Copenhagen in 1990 and in Moscow in 1991;
- the Conference on Economic Co-operation in Bonn in 1990;
- the Cultural Inheritance Symposium in Cracow in 1991; and
- Last but not least, the next CSCE meeting in Helsinki.

There we should think about new institutional forms for pan-European co-operation. We envisage a common institution for the co-ordination of East–West economical co-operation, as well as, the creation of a pan-European environmental council.

9. The surmounting of the separation of Europe and the division of Germany demands far-reaching and speedy steps pertaining to disarmament and arms control. Disarmament and arms control must keep step with political developments and therefore, might have to be accelerated.

This is particularly true of the negotiations in Vienna for the dismantling of conventional armed forces in Europe and for the agreement upon measures to establish trust, such as the worldwide ban of chemical weapons. This also demands that the nuclear potential of world powers be reduced to a strategic minimal level. The upcoming meeting between President Bush and General Secretary Gorbachev offers a good opportunity to add new impetus to current negotiations. We are trying via bilateral discussions with the countries of the Warsaw Pact, including the GDR, to support this process.

10.   With this sweeping policy, we are working towards the attainment of freedom within Europe, whereby the German people can, via free self-determination, restore their unity. Reunification, the reattainment of German state unity, remains the political goal of the Federal Government. We are grateful that we once again found support pertaining to this point from our Allies in the announcement made at the NATO summit in Brussels in May of this year.

We are conscious of the fact that particularly difficult problems will be encountered on the road to German unity that we can not yet completely answer. This also includes questions pertaining to over-lapping security structures within Europe.

The joining of the German question with pan-European develop-ments and East–West relations, as I have explained in the previous 10 points, enables an organic development which is of concern to all members and guarantees a peaceful co-existence in Europe.

We can only peacefully overcome the division of Europe and Germany together and in an atmosphere of mutual trust. We need discretion, understanding and sound judgement on all sides in order for the current developments to steadily and peacefully continue.

This process could not be hampered by reforms, but rather by the non-acceptance thereof. Freedom does not cause instability, but rather the oppression thereof. Every successful reform step means more stability and increased freedom and security for all of Europe.

Source: Embassy of the Federal Republic of Germany, London 29 November 1989

SOVIET SPOKESMAN G. GERASIMOV ON SOVIET REACTION TO KOHL'S TEN POINTS

29 November 1989

'... realities have to be respected. One is that Europe is divided into two military alliances, NATO and the Warsaw Pact. The second is that frontiers stand as confirmed in Helsinki and the third is that there are two Germanys.

If there were an 11th point, [that Bonn formally renounce a 1972 West German Supreme Court judgement that Germany's 1937 borders were still valid] we might reconsider our position.

Source: *International Herald Tribune*, 30 November 1989

SOVIET–ITALIAN DECLARATION

30 November 1989

At the present crucial stage of international development, when new horizons are opening up and opportunity presents itself for deep transformations of relations among nations on the basis of democracy, universal human values and solidarity.

The Soviet Union and Italy.

– Seeking to promote in every possible way the advancement of these positive processes.

– Aware of the fact that, despite all the complexity of issues and challenges of the modern world, humanity is offered a historic chance.

– Fully aware of their responsibility.

Have jointly arrived at the following conclusions:

1.   The world must be freed from the scourge of war and the threat of a nuclear holocaust. It is necessrsay to try to settle disputes by peaceful means and make every effort to pass from confrontation to dialogue, from enmity to co-operation, from suspicion to openness. The development of political relations should be accompanied by expeditious advances at the talks on nuclear, conventional and chemical disarmament while strengthening universal security.

Specifically, the sides confirm that they will encourage the attainment, at the Vienna talks in 1990, of an agreement on conventional arms. Along with confidence-building measures, it will become a substantial step towards the gradual transformation of military structures on the basis of defence principles and full transparency in this field, including military budgets.

The sides favour the completion in 1990 of the Geneva talks on a complete ban on chemical weapons. They favour the expeditious attainment of an agreement on a 50 per cent cut by the Soviet Union and the United States of America in strategic offensive weapons, which would contribute to the positive outcome of the 1990 conference on the effectiveness of the Nuclear Non-Proliferation Treaty.

They favour the full observance of the 1972 ABM Treaty and the stage-by-stage reduction and cessation of nuclear tests with effective verification.

With the same aims in mind, the sides intend to develop, on a long-term basis, contacts between Soviet and Italian armed forces, exchange experience in converting the military industries and discuss the questions of setting up a centre for reducing the danger of war danger and the threat of surprise attack.

.2. Urgent measures are necessary to eliminate the threat to the environment. The Earth is our common habitat and no state can ignore requirements to maintain the ecological balance. Care for nature, the prevention of ecological disasters, and the ensuring of economic development acceptable and compatible with the demands of universal ecological security are common concerns.

Specifically, the sides intend to contribute to the attainment of agreements, at global and regional levels, on binding ecological standards and stronger international contol in this field. They have agreed to develop co-operation in the field of environmental protection and are beginning an exchange of expertise and technologies, including with the aim of gradual creation of a broader European zone.

3. The sides favour the creation of conditions for the mutual complementariness of the national economies along East–West and North–South lines. Understandings are necessary between economic groupings, as well as the gradual involvement of interested states in international economic and financial organisations, including the International Monetary Fund and the General Agreement of Trade and Tariffs.

They believe that scientific and technical co-operation is a powerful factor in strengthening integration processes in the modern world and hope that the creation of the new climate of trust will result in overcoming obstacles to exchanges in this field.

The sides intend to adjust new forms of co-operation in the fields of road and port buildings, car making, power generation and power engineering as a whole, chemistry and petro-chemistry, agro-industrial and agro-foodstuff complexes, telecommunications and high definition television, health services and training in trades and professions. They have displayed interest in the possibility of establishing in Moscow a centre for Soviet–Italian economic co-operation.

4. The provisions laid down in the universal declaration and international pacts on human rights must be observed by all the signatory states.

The sides proceed from the assumption that the bringing of national legislation into line with international regulations and agreements, including the final document of the Vienna meeting, facilitates work to overcome alienation between the citizens and the governments and creates preconditions for a new type of security in Europe. They regard as positive the results of the first conference on the Human Dimension in Paris in June 1989. They intend to promote the success of the next conference – in Copenhagen. They will spare no effort to ensure the successful holding of the final phase of the Humanitarian Conference in Moscow in 1991.

5. It is necessary to eliminate, step-by-step the barriers of mutual mistrust generated by decades of confrontation and strict ideological opposition.

The future international structure must be increasingly based on the universal values of freedom, national, ethnic, religious tolerance and pluralism.

An in-depth courageous revision of domestic and foreign policies is under way in a number of countries, democratic changes are gaining strength. In every society principles of democracy must be present, as well as respect for the sovereign right of each nation to choose its own way of development. The success of this process meets universal interests. Under the impact of these factors, the curtain of mistrust between East and West is disintegrating.

6. The sides assume that Europe can make a substantial and original contribution to the establishment of peace on the eve of the third millennium. Various global issues are rooted here, but here, too, is concentrated the immense moral and material potential for their resolution. A movement in the right direction has begun in Europe – towards the overcoming of the unnatural rift. Europe is now on the threshold of a new era.

It is quite plausible today to count on the emergence of a peaceful Europe, a common home of all the CSCE member-countries. The basic principles of building the common home were laid down in the Final Act of the Helsinki Conference and the documents of all subsequent all-Europe meetings.

The efforts by the Soviet Union and Italy will focus in particular on the formation, on the European scale, of a greater legal, ecological, cultural and scientific homogeneity.

The sides are convinced that the balance upon which European continental security is based must be preserved. Any destabilising factor is at variance with the striving of every country for peace, and one's own security cannot be achieved to the detriment of another's security. They are equally convinced that each nation is entitled to decide its fate independently, including the choice of a social and political system, its evolution and necessary modifications.

The sides view with optimism the perspectives opening up due to the agreement between the Council for Mutual Economic Assistance and the European Economic Community, as well as the development of relations between the European Community and the countries of Central and Eastern Europe.

7. An international climate is being established facilitating the political settlement of regional conflicts. The Soviet Union and Italy are prepared to contribute to the matter and will make efforts to facilitate the creation of conditions for strengthening confidence and security. Aware of the close inter-relation betwen the situation in Europe and the Mediterranean region, they intend to co-operate so as not to confine the new positive development within the continent but let it spread over the Mediterranean. They also favour the development of co-operation between littoral states.

8. Leaning on their best cultural traditions, the common heritage of humanism and the proximity of the Soviet and Italian peoples, the sides

are convinced that there are conditions for deepening their relations in all fields. They have agreed in particular to invigorate – on the basis of the 1972 protocol on consultations, that fully proved its worth as a foundation for bilateral dialogue – political contacts at all levels. They intend to promote the strengthening of links between their parliaments and the public, among people in general and young people in particular. Humanitarian questions will be resolved constructively and humanely.

The Soviet Union and Italy call for reason and mutual understanding to prevail in international relations. The striving of man for justice, well-being and equal dignity for all is unsuppressible. The Soviet Union and Italy will strengthen their co-operation in the name of a better future for all mankind as a single civilisation.

M. Gorbachev
G. Andreotti

Source: *Soviet News*, 6 December 1989

ADDRESS BY PRESIDENT MIKHAIL GORBACHEV AT THE VATICAN

1 December 1989

Your Holiness,
Gentlemen,

I thank you for your kind attention and for the interest you have shown towards my country, our policies and our views on the world.

A truly remarkable event has taken place. It has become possible due to the profound changes that are sweeping many countries and nations. More than this, we can also expect it to help assure their positive continuation.

We had much to discuss. I feel that my thoughts and concerns have been duly appreciated, as well as my explanations of the problems that exist today in our country, including among them problems between the state and various churches, which we are seeking to solve in a spirit of democracy and humanism and within the framework of perestroika.

The Soviet Union and the Vatican are both participants in the Helsinki process. To the best of their abilities and with due regard for their specific features, both are working to ensure that it proceeds at a normal pace, promotes solutions to common European problems and creates a favourable external environment that will enable nations to make their own independent choice.

Respect for the peoples' national, state, spiritual and cultural identity is an indispensable condition for a steady international environment, something which Europe and the whole world now need in order to cross the historic watershed and reach a new peaceful period.

It is from these positions that we have proceeded in initiating our dialogue with the Vatican – a dialogue which has now been consecrated by this summit meeting. I am pleased to note the high degree of mutual understanding and readiness that exists to fill this dialogue with concrete actions.

We have reached an agreement in principle whereby our interstate relations will be given official status. The form they will take will be determined by our diplomatic officials.

People of many religious persuasions live in the Soviet Union, including Christians, Moslems, Jews, Buddhists and others. Each of them have the right to satisfy their spiritual needs. In the near future, a law regarding freedom of conscience is to be passed in our country.

Within the mainstream of perestroika we are learning the difficult yet indispensable art of comprehensive cooperation and consolidation of society on the basis of renewal.

I greet you and join in the good wishes that we have just heard from His Holiness.

During our talks we discussed a future visit of His Holiness to the Soviet Union.

To conclude, I wish to express my thanks for the opportunity to exchange opinions regarding major issues in the life of the peoples of the world in a benevolent, open and meaningful atmosphere.

Source: Novosti, 1 December 1989

GENERAL SECRETARY MIKHAIL GORBACHEV'S SPEECH TO CENTRAL COMMITTEE, 9 DECEMBER 1989

9 December 1989

Comrades, implementation of the long-term course of perestroika exerts not only a revolutionary influence on all spheres of life of Soviet society, but also influences other socialist countries and developments in the world. At the same time perestroika itself comes under the influence of the world, and needs favourable international conditions.

Proceeding from this, I deem it necessary to report to the Central Committee on the latest international events which directly affect our interests.

This year signified major changes in Eastern Europe. In fact, processes there are developing swiftly. Speaking about the essence of the changes underway, their most typical feature is democratisation and renewal of socialism. It is an open secret that these processes do not proceed easily. The truth, about which we spoke of often in the past few years, has been reaffirmed once again: where there is a delay in dealing with overripe problems, excesses are inevitable.

What is taking place in socialist countries is the logical outcome of a certain stage of development which made the peoples of these countries aware of the need for change. This is the result of internal developmemnt, the result of choice by peoples themselves.

For all the specificity of deep changes in socialist countries, one cannot deny the fact that they proceed in the same mainstream as our perestroika, although we in no way encouraged these processes.

In some socialist countries the situation has been unconventional. Fraternal parties are no longer ruling in Poland and Hungary. Our friends in the German Democratic Republic and Czechoslovakia have largely lost their positions. New political forces have emerged on the arena. They include both those who support the socialist idea and those who seek other ways of social development.

The new situation demands from our friends resolute, well considered actions in order to restore their influence and positions in society and, consequently, to elaborate a new strategy and tactic. The task of consolidating all forces standing on the position of socialism, democracy and progress has moved into the forefront.

Our friends realise this and take account of the situation in their activity, even though they have to master on the move the science of political work in the new conditions of real, rather than declarative, pluralism.

The situation that arises also demands from us the elaboration of a clear-cut approach to both the processes underway there and our contacts with the new political forces, parties and organisations.

Our principled attitude to these processes can be formulated in the following way. We welcome the positive changes while fully realising the difficulties, both domestic and international, that accompany them.

The Soviet Union is building its relations with East European countries – whether they have been carrying out transformations for quite some time, or have only embarked on that road, or are yet to do it – on a single position of respect for sovereignty, non-interference and recognition of freedom of choice. We proceed from the fact that any nation has the right to decide its fate itself, including the choice of a system, ways, the pace and methods of its development.

Our political attitude to the European socialist countries is invariable. They are not only our allies, but also our friends and neighbours. We seek to ensure progress and stability in every way – stability in these countries themselves, the East European region and the whole continent – as well as the inviolability of post-war borders of all the states of Europe. It is precisely for these purposes that our diplomats are engaged in active work with all European countries without exclusion and the United States.

Of course we can see that, despite declaring non-interference, some Western countries cannot resist the temptation to influence the processes under way in socialist countries. We are doing everything possible to prevent interference from outside and to neutralise attempts at such interference, in particular, in regard of the GDR.

We firmly declare that we will see to it that no harm comes to the GDR. It is our strategic ally and a member of the Warsaw Treaty. It is necessary to proceed from the post-war realities – the existence of the two sovereign German states, members of the United Nations. Departure from this threatens with destabilisation in Europe.

Naturally this is not to say that relations between the GDR and the FRG cannot change. Peaceful co-operation between them can and must develop. As for the future, it will take shape in the course of history, in the framework of the developments of the general European process.

On our part, we continue actively supporting the allied countries.

A Warsaw Treaty summit meeting has been held in Moscow recently. We informed the leaders of the Warsaw Treaty states of our talks with the US President and our evaluations of the international situation.

A common position concerning the need to further refine the activities of the Warsaw Treaty was reaffirmed at the meeting. So, our alliance is living through a period of tests, is renewing itself, retaining its value to all members. This is so because the community of our interests in ensuring stability and peace in Europe is maintained.

This was confirmed convincingly enough by the recent visit to Moscow by the head of the new Polish Government. During the talks the Polish side expressed not only interest in the development of relations with the Soviet Union but also devotion to its allied commitments.

Of course, we have a good deal of work to do yet to refine the forms of political and economic co-operation within the framework of collective organisations and to bring it up to a qualitatively new level.

This particularly applies to the activities of the Council for Mutual Economic Assistance (CMEA) where cardinal changes in the mechanism of co-operation are needed and it is essential to put it on a sound economic track, without which it is inconceivable to accomplish one of the main tasks of the present day – to gradually integrate the economies of our countries into all-European and world structure.

And now a few words about the main recent contacts with capitalist countries.

West European countries are obviously conspicuous in this respect. The meetings with the leaders of Britain, the Federal Republic of Germany, France and other countries have not just become more systematic but their political resultiveness has also considerably increased.

It was difficult, it would seem, to count on an additional benefit, say, from the traditionally friendly relations with Finland. But the visit there and the talks with President Mauno Koivisto made it possible to realistically raise the degree of political trust and broaden the scope of economic co-operation. This is of particular importance to our regions that border on Finland – Karelia, the Baltic republics, and the north as a whole.

The results of the talks with the state leadership of Italy proved tangible, too. This country in the past, too, more than once made pioneering moves in the search for new forms of co-operation with the Soviet Union.

This time the agreements and contracts signed – I shall mention an agreement with Fiat on the construction of a car factory – should produce positive results for the Soviet economy and for the saturation of the market.

The Soviet–Finnish and Soviet–Italian political declarations have become the latest word in the philosophical and conceptual substantiation of East–West co-operation.

The meeting with the Pope in the Vatican was of fundamental importance. If the policy of the Vatican, a full and equal participant in the CSCE process, proceeds towards further humanisation and democratisation of inter-state relations, that will also help solve world problems.

An agreement to add a greater official character to our relations with the Vatican may play a useful role.

And finally, it is necessary specially to single out the working meeting with French President Francois Mitterrand in Kiev.

Of course, he was very interested in the results of the Malta meeting. But the rapidly changing situation in Europe was a matter of his principal concern and the central topic of the talks with him.

The French President believes that it is now necessary to show the maximum caution and to take up a well-considered attitude and that the Helsinki principles – and, primarily, respect for the present realities and the inviolability of the established borders – should be the basis for the development of all processes in Europe.

As is seen, the views formulated by him are quite close to ours. And we reaffirmed this, and pointed out that a new mutual understanding between the Soviet Union and France is taking shape and a basis for effective co-operation is being furnished on the strength of the stand set out by the French President.

As regards our relations with Western Europe as a whole, the events of the outgoing year make it possible to single out three main aspects.

The first of them is an undisputable fundamental charge in the West European's attitude to the Soviet Union and to perestroika. Of course, in today's Europe still there are doubts as to how our internal political development will proceed.

But on the whole the Europeans have come to realise that perestroika is a perceptible reality that is not only changing our country but is also having an impact on the rest of the world.

There is gradually growing awareness of yet another circumstance, namely, that we are carrying out perestroika on the basis of our own, socialist principles.

And that, while refining our society and enshrining our economic and social instruments by new methods and forms, we by no means depart from our values but on the contrary we seek to fill them with a realistic, humanistic and democratic content.

At one time, after the October Revolution, as you may remember, our country lived through a period of diplomatic recognitions.

Nowadays we are living through a period of recognition of perestroika as a factor of world-wide significance. This creates a new atmosphere in our relations with the West as a whole and primarily with Western Europe.

The second important aspect is closely interconnected with the first one: West European countries have in actual fact taken a course towards increasing economic co-operation with the Soviet Union.

The West European business community has come to realise that perestroika provides a new market for it. Competition for places in this market has begun.

Hence, not only are new contracts signed with a growing number of West European firms, the contracts that are large but in many respects qualitatively new ones, intended for co-production arrangements and even for a sort of integration with our economy.

And finally, the third important aspect in our relations with Western

Europe is that the drawing closer together of our and West European countries' positions on major international problems is increasingly manifest.

The matter concerns both many aspects of disarmament, primarily the Vienna talks on conventional arms in Europe, and approaches to regional conflicts and ways to resolve global problems that arise on the European continent itself.

All this means that our relations with West European countries acquire both a new format and new contents. A more developed infrastructure of links, capable of growing into a kind of common European mechanism of co-operation, is being set up. In fact, the point at issue is a marked advance on the road of building a common European home.

Changes in the East and West of the continent, the accelerating pace of developments call for increasing the rates and expanding the contents of the general European process. Proceeding from this, we have already proposed to hold a new European meeting in 1990 and not in 1992 as was planned earlier. Such a meeting could be held at summit level. France and Italy supported this initiative. Admittedly, other participants in the European process also view it with interest. We are convinced that its implementation, the hold of the Helsinki-2 meeting would give powerful impetus to the construction of the common European home in all of its main parameters.

For all the advancement of our relations with Europe further normalisation and improvement of USSR–US relations has a multifaceted, truly global significance. It is a fact that the USSR and the US are two major and the most powerful states in the modern world. This does not give them any special rights, but determines their special responsibility for preserving and strengthening peace.

It is also absolutely obvious that political interaction between the USSR and the US on the principles of new thinking can have a powerful influence on the positive development of the world situation.

We were fully aware of all this, when we agreed to a working meeting on Malta proposed by US President George Bush.

Comrades are familiar with the contents of the joint news conference with President Bush. The main thrust of our talks was expressed there, but understandably without special details. Nevertheless, some summing up seems to be needed.

Naturally we wanted the meeting with the US President to give tangible useful results. From the first moments George Bush showed that he also sought a similar outcome.

He started the talks with the problem of improving bilateral relations with the Soviet Union. He especially dwelt on his decision to take the necessary measures in the near future to lift restrictions hampering trade and economic ties between the two countries.

Bush in fact intends to give the USSR most-favoured-nation status, to enable US financial institutions to credit exports, as well as to grant credits and to conclude an agreement on guaranteeing US investments in the Soviet Union. These and some other steps undertaken by the administration give US business circles a signal to act more boldly on the Soviet market. This corresponds to their feelings.

It is also important that the US leadership is changing its approach to Soviet participation in international economic and financial organisations. On the whole, there is an impression that Washington has decided to stop economic war against us.

Summing up the results of the rather intensive discussion of military-political issues, one can say sufficiently firmly that the year 1990 promises to be one of the most productive periods in terms of agreements in this field. Specifically, we agreed with the President that next year will be signed:

– The Soviet–US Treaty on a 50 per cent cut in strategic offensive weapons;

– A multilateral agreement on reductions in conventional armed forces and armaments in Europe, which as we suggested, is subjected to signature at summit level;

– A bilateral Soviet–American agreement on a radical cut in the arsenals of chemical weapons, as part of efforts to full ban chemical weapons and to eliminate their stocks;

– Protocols to the 1974 and 1976 treaties on the limitation on underground tests of nulcear weapons and on nuclear explosions for peaceful purposes.

Besides, we hope that talks will be started in 1990 on new spheres of the limitation of armaments, the building of confidence and stability.

Bush and we agreed that the two sides would actively participate in multilateral talks on 'the open skies' as well as on the concept, which we suggested, of greater openness covering not only the skies but also land, seas, oceans and outer space.

We suggested that talks concerning Soviet and American naval forces as well as full limitation of the naval tactical nuclear weapons be started without delay.

The Soviet Union attaches much importance to this issue, for in the conditions of progress in the efforts to reduce arms in various fields, we cannot put up with a threat to our security and to the security of our allies, the threat emanating from the seas and oceans.

I have already publicly set out our evaluation of the talks on European topics. I would like only to emphasise that Bush and I achieved a reassuring degree of mutual understanding about the need to pursue a well-considered and cautious line in the conditions of deep processes taking place in Western and Eastern Europe.

This also applies to German problems. I think that it is also of importance that we regard all these problems primarily within the context of the CSCE process.

The talks on regional conflicts concerned Afghanistan, Central America, the Middle East, Lebanon, and some other problems.

In general I would like to point out that the talks on these acute topics were this time held in a more business-like and substantive manner.

The two sides showed greater readiness to take mutual interests into account. They showed an increased ability to perceive each other's arguments. In general, the talks in this respect were notable for a markedly unbiased attitude to the evaluations, information and positions of the partner.

Of course, divergencies of opinion, and considerable ones, still remain. But it is important that a different, more business-like and reasonable approach has appeared. Accordingly, we are now taking a more optimistic view on prospects for a peaceful settlement.

On the whole President Bush and we had wide-ranging talks. We consider them as the beginning of a new stage in Soviet–American relations. And, I repeat, great and tangible changes are taking place.

A transition from confrontation to greater mutual understanding has already taken place. We are now moving to a higher degree of mutual understanding and even co-operation. If the US leadership continues to act from the position of high reponsibility, we may move to a business partnership.

And now the last remark. What specifically did the work done in the foreign policy sphere produce for the cause of peace, for our country and for perestroika?

To begin with, it has pushed the threat of war still further away and ensured the consolidation of the foundations of international security. This signifies the hopes for the preservation and strengthening of favourable external conditions for our development are becoming increasingly substantial.

This enables us to carry out the planned cuts in defence spending and in the armed forces and to develop defence production conversion.

While doing all this, we should not of course lose sight of the fact that influential circles in the West have not yet abandoned the position-of-strength policy and still seek to gain one-sided advantages for themselves.

In present-day conditions, just as in the future, reasonable suffi-ciency presupposes absolute ensurance of the defence of the legitimate interests of our country. This is what we proceed from.

That is even an income increment was to be swallowed by the arms race to a considerable extent. We see how this influenced the econ-omic development and deformed it.

It is essential to get rid of such extremes. But the country's reliable security cannot be the subject of discussions. We should have a modern army equipped with the latest weapons and capable of ensuring the country's security.

When the disarmament process began to develop, quite far-fetched proposals were made by some people to the effect that we should even eliminate the army and the entire defence sector.

This is not serious, and one did not even need to react to that. But it must be said that those are attempts at suggesting such views to public opinion, at stirring up some ferment with regard to the army and to those people that are in charge of defence.

I think we should cut off these extremes by directing work into a normal and natural channel. When ensuring the guarantee of the country's defence, one should not fall into any extremes.

I also want to speak of this in the following connection: on the one hand, we want, as a result of disarmament processes, to slow down the arms race, into which we have found ourselves drawn together with America and other countries.

Even for the current five-year plan period, a national income increment – I do not know whether I mentioned it at the Central Committee's plenum or not – was set at approximately 22 per cent while defence expenditures were set at more than 40 per cent.

Normalisation and improvement of relations with the West enable us to further broaden the scope and to extend economic co-operation with capitalist countries. We are increasingly developing new forms of interrelation, extending them, as I already said, to co-operation mechanism and in some cases approaching integration links. Undoubtedly, this considerably enriches our possibilities. Naturally one should realise that we will be able to use them only if we considerably step up our own efforts, responsibility and efficiency, master new forms of co-operation. During the recent summit meetings, in particular, in Britain, France, Finland and Italy we have agreed that, while concluding new agreements and signing contracts, reliable mechanisms should be set up to monitor compliance with them. These mechanisms should also function impeccably from our side as well.

On the whole, one can say that our initiatives in the international arena have returned to the USSR and its foreign policy global recognition as a factor of peace, security and freedom. Realistic attitudes to existing problems and due regard for the interests of all members of the world community ensure the high effectiveness of these initiatives. All this promotes the fulfillment of perestroika, creates an international background necessary for its advancement.

Source: *Soviet News*, 13 December 1989

EUROPEAN COUNCIL: CONCLUSIONS OF THE PRESIDENCY

10 December 1989

Towards European Union

The European Council is conscious of the responsibilities weighing on the Community in this crucial period for Europe. The current changes and the prospects for development in Europe demonstrate the attraction which the political and economic model of Community Europe holds for many countries.

The Community must live up to this expectation and these demands: its path lies not in withdrawal but in openness and co-operation, particularly with the other European States.

It is in the interest of all European States that the Community should become stronger and accelerate its progress toward the European Union.

Countries of Central and Eastern Europe

The Community's dynamism and influence make it the European entity to which the countries of Central and Eastern Europe now refer, seeking to establish close links. The Community has taken and will take the necessary decisions to strengthen its co-operation with peoples aspiring to freedom, democracy and progress and with States which intend their founding principles to be democracy, pluralism and the rule of law. It will encourage the necessary economic reforms by all the means at its disposal, and will continue its examination of the appropriate forms of assocation with the countries which are pursuing the path of economic and political reform. The Community's readiness and its commitment to co-operation are central to the policy which it is pursuing and which is defined in the declaration adopted today; the objective remains, as stated in the Rhodes Declaration, that of overcoming the divisions of Europe.

1. The Community has concluded Trade Agreements and, for the most part, Co-operation Agreements with Czechoslovakia, Hungary and Poland. The Agreement with the USSR should be signed by the end of this year. The Council, will, as soon as possible, instruct

the Commission to negotiate a Trade and Co-operation Agreement with the GDR to be concluded during the first half of 1990.

The European Council welcomes the decisions taken by the Council (General Affairs) on 27 November 1989 temporarily granting Poland and Hungary special trade facilities in order to contribute towards solving their specific political and economic problems.

It noted the decisions taken by the Community to assist economic reform in Poland and Hungary.

The Community took part, in co-operation with its main Western partners, in an operation to supply agricultural products to Poland. In view of the scale and urgency of the needs, the European Council would ask the Council to take a decision in the near future on a further such operation.

2. At their meeting in Paris on 18 November 1989, the Heads of State and of Government asked the Troika of Presidencies and the Commission to make progress in discussion and decision-taking with regard to the following:

   – the European Council approved the principle of granting observer status to the USSR in GATT;

   – the Commission has submitted proposals designed to allow nationals of the countries of Central and Eastern Europe to take part in a number of educational and training programmes similar to Community programmes; the European Council requests the Council to take the relevant decisions;

   – the European Council calls upon the Council to take, at the beginning of 1990, the requisite decisions for the setting up of a European Vocational Training Foundation, on the basis of proposals which the Commission is to submit;

   – the European Council approved the creation of a European Bank for Reconstruction and Developmemnt. Its aim will be to promote, in consultation with the IMF and the World Bank, productive and competitive investment in the States of Central and Eastern Europe, to reduce, where appropriate, any risks related to the financing of their economies, to assist the transition towards a more market-orientated economy and to speed up the necessary structural adjustments. The States of Central and Eastern Europe concerned will be able to participate in the capital and mangement of this Bank, in which the Member States, the Community and the European Investment Bank will have a majority holding. Other countries, and in particular the other member countries of the OECD, will be invited to participate. The European Council hopes that the European Bank for Reconstruction and Development will be set up as soon as possible. The European Council requests that the necessary steps be taken to ensure that negotiations are opened in January 1990. The European Investment Bank will play a key role in preparing the way for this new institution.

3. The European Council confirmed the Community's readiness to participate, under the conditions defined at the meeting on 18 November, in the creation of a Stabilization Fund for Poland. It emphasized that the combined contributions of the Twelve would provide more than half the resources of the Fund, which is to receive 1,000 million dollars. The European Council referred to the need to grant Hungary, after agreement with the IMF, an adjustment loan of the same amount.

    It called upon the Council to take an early decision on the Commission proposals.

4. The European Council confirmed the key importance it attaches to the fact that aid and co-operation projects decided on by Western countries should be as complementary as possible. It reaffirmed the need to maintain and strengthen the procedure established by the Community. It expects the forthcoming ministerial meeting of the 24 Western countries on 13 December to take the necessary substantive and procedural decisions to ensure that the efforts undertaken to facilitate the transition taking place in Poland and Hungary and possibly in other countries of Central and Eastern Europe are co-ordinated and effective.

5. The European Council is following carefully and with interest the important reforms planned in Yugoslavia and confirms the Community's undertaking to examine – once the agreement with the Monetary Fund is concluded – additional measures in support of the programme for improving that country's economic and financial situation.

Source: *Europe*, 10 December 1989

EUROPEAN COUNCIL EUROPEAN POLITICAL COOPERATION DECLARATION ON CENTRAL AND EASTERN EUROPE

10 December 1989

Each day in central and eastern Europe change is asserting itself more strongly. Everywhere a powerful aspiration toward freedom, democracy, respect of human rights, prosperity, social justice and peace is being expressed. The people are clearly showing their will to take their own destiny in hand and to choose the path of their development. Such a profound and rapid development would not have been possible without the policy of openness and reform led by Mr. Gorbachev.

Expressing the feelings of the people of the whole Community, we are deeply gladdened by the changes taking place. These are historic events and no doubt the most important since the Second World War. The success of a strong and dynamic European Community, the vitality of the CSCE process and stability in the area of security, in which the United States and Canada participate, have contributed greatly to them.

These changes give reason to hope that the division in Europe can be overcome in accordance with the aims of the Helsinki Final Act which seeks, through a global and balanced approach and on the basis of a set of principles which retain their full value, to establish new relations between European countries whether in the area of security, economic and technical cooperation, or the human dimension.

We seek the strengthening of the state of peace in Europe in which the German people will regain its unity through free self-determination. This process should take place peacefully and democratically, in full respect of the relevant agreements and treaties and of all the principles defined by the Helsinki Final Act, in a context of dialogue and East-West cooperation. It also has to be placed in the perspective of European integration.

Already the hopes which we expressed a year ago in the Rhodes Declaration have begun to take shape. The progress recorded in the negotiations on conventional and chemical disarmament, the greater freedom of movement of persons and ideas, the greater assurance of respect of human rights and fundamental freedoms, and the different agreements concluded betwen the Community and certain of these countries are substantially changing the climate of relations in Europe.

The European Council is convinced in the present circumstances that all must, more than ever, demonstrate their sense of responsibility. The changes and transitions which are necessary must not take place to the detriment of the stability of Europe but rather must contribute to strengthening it.

Far from wanting to derive unilateral advantages from the present situation, the Community and its member States mean to give their support to the countries which have embarked upon the road to democratic change. They deplore all the more so that in certain countries this process is still hindered.

The Community and its member States are fully conscious of the common responsibility which devolves on them in this decisive phase in the history of Europe. They are prepared to develop with the USSR and the other countries of central and eastern Europe, and with Yugoslavia, in so far as they are committed to this path, closer and more substantive relations based upon an intensification of political dialogue and increased cooperation in all areas. The Community has in particular decided to support the economic reforms undertaken in these countries by contributing – in collaboration with its western partners – to the establishment of healthy and prosperous economies within the framework of appropriate structures.

The European Council has drawn up conclusions which illustrate this intention.

For the future and in accordance with the developments taking place, the Community is willing to implement still closer forms of cooperation with these countries.

At this time of profound and rapid change, the Community is and must remain a point of reference and influence. It remains the cornerstone of a new European architecture and, in its will to openness, a mooring for a future European equilibrium. This equilibrium will be still better ensured by a parallel development of the role of the Council of Europe, EFTA and the CSCE process.

Construction of the Community must therefore go forward: the building of European Union will permit the further development of a range of effective and harmonious relations with the other countries of Europe.

Source: Europe, 10 December 1989

SPEECH BY SECRETARY OF STATE JAMES BAKER TO BERLIN PRESS CLUB

13 December 1989 (Extracts)

Free men, and free governments, are the building blocks of a Europe whole and free. But hopes for a Europe whole and free are tinged with concern by some that a Europe undivided may not necessarily be a Europe peaceful and prosperous.

Many of the guideposts that brought us securely through four sometimes tense and threatening decades are now coming down. Some of the divisive issues that once brought conflict to Europe are re-emerging.

As Europe changes, the instruments for Western cooperation must adapt. Working together, we must design and gradually put into place a new architecture for a new era.

This new structure must also accomplish two special purposes. First, as a part of overcoming the division of Europe there must be an opportunity to overcome though peace and freedom the division of Berlin and of Germany.

Second, the architecture should reflect that America's security – politically, militarily and economically – remains linked to Europe's security.

The charge for us all then is to work together toward the New Europe and the New Atlanticism.

We have moved significantly closer to concluding an agreement limiting conventional armaments from the Atlantic to the Urals. In Malta, President Bush proposed a summit meeting to sign such an agreement in 1990.

Today, I further propose that the ministers of the 23 NATO and Warsaw Pact nations take advantage of our February meeting in Ottawa, where we will launch the 'open skies' negotiations, to review the status and give a further push to the Vienna Talks on Conventional Forces.

I . . . invite allied governments to consider establishing a NATO arms control verification staff. Verification will remain a national responsibility. But such a new staff would be able to assist member governments in monitoring compliance with arms control and confidence-building measures in Europe.

It could provide a clearinghouse for information contributed by national governments, perhaps joining with collective European efforts through the Western European Union.

Regional conflicts, along with the proliferation of missiles and nuclear, chemical and biological weapons, present growing dangers. Intensified NATO consultations on these issues can play an important role in forming common Western approaches to these various threats.

NATO should also begin considering further initiatives the West might take, through the CSCE [Conference on Security and Cooperation in Europe] process in particular, to build economic and political ties with the East, to promote respect for human rights, to help build democratic institutions, and to fashion, consistent with Western security interests, a more open environment for East-West trade and investment.

The future development of the European Community will play a central role in shaping the New Europe.

The European experiment has succeeded because it also held out the higher goal of political as well as economic barriers . . . of a Europe united.

We propose that the Untied States and the European Community work together to achieve, whether in treaty or some other form, a significantly strengthened set of institutional and consultative links.

We suggest that our discussions about this idea proceed in parallel with Europe's efforts to achieve by 1992 a common internal market, so that plans for U.S.-EC interaction would evolve with changes in the Community.

As Czechoslovakia, Bulgaria and the German Democratic Republic undertake political and economic reforms comparable to those already under way in Poland and Hungary, we believe the activities of the Group of 24 [developed nations], centred round the EC, should be expanded to support peaceful change in these countries as well.

Free elections should now become the highest priority in the CSCE process.

We could involve parliamentarians more directly in CSCE processes, not only as observers as at present, but perhaps through their own meetings.

A new Europe, whole and free, must include arrangements that satisfy the aspirations of the German people and meet the legitimate concerns of Germany's neighbours.

As we adapt, as we update and expand our cooperation with each other and with the nations of the East, we will create a new Europe on the basis of a New Atlanticism.

At the same time, the substantive overlap between NATO and European institutions will grow. This overlap must lead to synergy, not friction.

The CSCE process could become the most important forum of East-West cooperation.

As these changes proceed, as they overcome the division of Europe, so too will the divisions on Germany and Berlin be overcome in peace and freedom.

Source: International Herald Tribune 14 December 1989

BROADCAST BY EAST GERMAN PRIME MINISTER, HANS MODROW

15 December 1989, prior to meeting with Chancellor Kohl (Extracts)

Q: Mr Premier, you spoke of this treaty-based partnership pointing to the future. Chancellor Kohl's 10-point programme points to the future and to reunification. If I understand you correctly, there is obviously no consensus here.

Modrow: No consensus exists here. I proceed from the basis that the two sides have their own ideas about the future. I do not claim that I have a monopoly on wisdom, or on the other hand that Federal Chancellor Kohl has. It is my concern that we should assume responsibility today, that we agree on what is necessary and feasible with one another today. Here Chancellor Kohl may have this vision for the future and I may have mine, but our responsibility is not derived from visions of the future but from our present actions.

Q: Nonetheless, I must ask you quite a blunt question that I am repeatedly asked. Can the GDR continue to exist under these current conditions?

Modrow: It must continue to exist, simply in the interests of European security and the expectations which everyone today has of the existence of two German states in the present situation in terms of internal stability in Europe. And of course here too I first of all want to concede to the Federal Chancellor that he himself assumes and has stated that all questions of the future are included in the European process, the CSCE process. Mikhail Gorbachev has stated that he is in favour of a Helsinki II as early as 1990. That is also my standpoint and as in the first meeting, the GDR must sit at that table, make its contribution and it was thus that I also viewed my meeting with the US Secretary of State.

Source: BBC Summary of World Broadcasts, 19 December 1989

NORTH ATLANTIC COUNCIL
MINISTERIAL COMMUNIQUE

15 December 1989

For the past two days, we have met for an intensive review of the accelerating political change in Central and Eastern Europe that is evidence of a profound transformation underway in the nature of post-war Europe. We stand at the threshold of a new era in which the democratic values which are at the heart of our Alliance and part of the European heritage are increasingly shared throughout the continent. Our task is to help advance and consolidate that welcome movement towards greater freedom within conditions of peace and strengthened stability. We have discussed ways to seize new opportunities to bring our vision of an undivided Europe of the future to reality.

I

A Period of Historic Change

1. Since our meeting of Heads of State and Government in May, there have been increasingly dramatic advances towards greater democracy and freedom in most Eastern European countries. Through the long dreamt-of opening of borders, the free flow of people and ideas between the countries of East and West has accelerated. There has been widening recognition of the need for reform towards more market-oriented economies and individual choice.

2. These changes testify to the indomitable spirit of the people in each of these countries. They confirm our long-held conviction that the aspirations common to all people to fundamental rights and freedoms will ultimately prevail in the whole of Europe.

3. Positive change amongst Soviet allies in Europe has been given impetus and unprecedented margin for action by the reforms the Soviet Union has undertaken in the domestic, political and economic spheres and in a reorientation of its foreign policy that breaks with the past in a number of fundamental respects. As the Soviet Union continues to translate such policies into consistent and credible action, the possibilities for increased mutually beneficial co-operation between the countries of the East and the West will substantially increase.

4. There has been significant progress in expanding constructive dialogue and co-operative action into a broader range of fields. Contacts and exchanges, including in the military domain, have

multiplied. There is progress and hope in the ongoing arms control negotiations. Our countries have recently intensified high-level dialogue with the Soviet Union and other countries of the East. In this regard, we have especially welcomed the meetings of Presidents Bush and Mitterrand, Chancellor Kohl, and Prime Ministers Thatcher, Andreotti and Mulroney with Soviet President Gorbachev, and we have noted the bilateral declarations issued.

5. We are aware that the current processes of change underway are still at an early stage and the progress achieved must be consolidated. Many problems remain. The rule of law and democratic government through free elections have yet to be fully institutionalised. In many instances, basic rights are still denied and the pace towards genuine democracy is uneven. Furthermore, we cannot ignore the military realities that our Alliance continues to face and which lie at the heart of Europe's security problems. Important differences remain with the Soviet Union over various regional conflicts, affecting opportunities for overall progress in East-West relations.

Overcoming the Division of Europe

6. We have called for these far-ranging changes since the inception of our Alliance. We have long sought a just and lasting order of peace in Europe, based on full respect for the human rights and political freedoms of all individuals, and on the security of all states from threats of aggression or intimidation. Building upon our dual approach to East-West relations contained in the Harmel Report, the NATO Summit Declaration of this past May reaffirmed out continuing support for the development of these freedoms. At the meeting of the Alliance Heads of State and Government in Brussels on 4th December, we agreed to intensify the implementation of this concerted approach.

7. We want the reforms in Central and Eastern Europe to succeed peacefully and democratically. We are determined to facilitate and promote them without seeking one-sided advantage. We will scrupulously respect all the principles of the Helsinki Final Act, as we expect all other signatories to do. We do not seek to impair the legitimate security interests of any state.

8. We are aware that each country within Europe is unique and that this diversity must be respected and allowed to express itself. As regards Eastern Europe, it is up to each country there to solve its own problems through reforms from within. But we think we also can play a constructive rôle both within the framework of our Alliance and in our respective bilateral relations and regional co-operation efforts.

9. We are witnessing rapid progress towards democracy and freedom in the GDR and the Eastern sector of Berlin. The restoration of freedom of movement was a particularly moving event. The Wall, which has divided Berlin for nearly three decades, has been breached. Fresh opportunities exist to overcome the division of Europe and

thereby of Germany and in particular of Berlin. This new situation opens the way to increasingly close co-operation between the two German States.

We seek the strengthening of the state of peace in Europe in which the German people will regain its unity through free self-determination. This process should take place peacefully and democratically, in full respect of the relevant agreements and treaties and of all the principles defined by the Helsinki Final Act, in a context of dialogue and East-West co-operation. It also has to be placed in the perspective of European integration.

The Continued Importance of the Alliance

10.   These events challenge us to look at our own responsibilities as Allies. The Atlantic Alliance serves as the essential basis for the security of our peoples. By keeping the peace for the past four decades it has enabled our peoples to prosper in freedom, and democratic values to serve as an inspiration for other societies. In the midst of change and uncertainty, the Alliance remains a reliable guarantor of peace. It will provide an indispensable foundation of stability, security and co-operation for the Europe of the future.

11.   To that end, solidarity among the democracies of North America and Western Europe within the framework of the Alliance will continue to be essential. Our Alliance is based on the principle of the indivisibility of security for all member countries and its goal is that of war prevention. For the foreseeable future there is no alternative to the Alliance strategy of deterrence for the prevention of war, based upon both nuclear and conventional forces. We shall ensure the viability and credibility of these forces, while maintaining them at the lowest possible level consistent with our security requirements. The presence of North American conventional and nuclear forces in Europe will remain vital.

12.   We will continue to play a decisive rôle in the pursuit of timely and orderly progress of arms control and disarmament. We remain committed to the full and prompt achievement of the objectives set out in the Comprehensive Concept of Arms Control and Disarmament, adopted in May 1989.

13.   At the same time, the Alliance will increasingly be called upon to carry out its political function. Recalling the origins of the North Atlantic Treaty as a political alliance built upon common fundamental values, our leaders affirmed at the May 1989 Summit that the Alliance must reintensify its own efforts to overcome the division of Europe. In doing so, it must take up new challenges. Our task therefore is to use actively and creatively the potential of our Alliance in the pursuit of political change within stability. Our political approach in support for positive change must be multifaceted and dynamic, seeking to

encourage political pluralism, free flow of information, and co-opera-
ive action in dealing with common problems.

The Future of Europe

14.   Our Alliance will make an essential contribution to the emergence of a Europe no longer divided. This most challenging of our
common tasks transcends the resources of either Western Europe or
North America alone. For that reason the Atlantic Alliance is unique in
bringing together all our democracies in joint effort in support of our
security and political objectives and providing a framework for broad
co-operation among ourselves.

15.   Looking to the future we recognise the outlines of the political
architecture of a Europe made whole and free, in the emergence and
shaping of which we are determined to play a full part. We will further
work to strengthen Western political and economic structures. The
process of European integration will be central to the future of Europe,
and its institutions are already playing a significant rôle in encouraging
the forces of reform forward in Central and Eastern Europe. This
integration process must remain a point of reference and attraction for
these forces. This represents a natural development that goes hand in
hand with the continued close partnership between the North American
and European members of the Alliance, the cohesion of which remains
a critical stabilising factor. We value the rôle of EFTA in this emerging
framework. We also recognise the growing rôle of the Council of
Europe in the larger European perspective.

16.   In this context, the Conference on Security and Co-operation in
Europe (CSCE) is destined to acquire a growing and central importance
in all its aspects. It will continue to offer both an agreed set of
principles for promoting peace, greater co-operation and democratic
values and a means of giving these principles practical substance
and effect.

II

Implementing our Approach

17.   With a view to implementing the approach set out by Alliance
Heads of State and Government at both their May 29th–30th and
December 4th meetings in Brussels we have agreed on the following
lines of action which are part of a continuing process:

18.   We aspire to achieve the full promise of the CSCE process.
Looking to the CSCE meetings scheduled over the next two years, we
are determined to make full use of them as a means to promote peace
and greater co-operation and to strengthen democratic institutions. The
CSCE process in all of its aspects will bear fruit only if implemented in
letter and spirit by all of the signatory countries, without exception.

Thus, we are agreed on a renewed emphasis on full respect for the fundamental freedoms and rights within the Helsinki Final Act and subsequent commitments.

We are also committed to build upon the CSCE process. It has already brought encouraging results in the fields of confidence-building as an important element of security; human rights; economics; science and technology and environmental protection. We will pursue new opportunities in all of its fields. In particular, at the upcoming Copenhagen Conference on the Human Dimension we will explore ways to expand CSCE undertakings to include the explicit right to elections that are free and democratic. We will seek to energize the economic aspects of CSCE to focus on the practical questions involved in the transition to market-oriented economies. In this context, the Bonn Conference on Economic Co-operation could be an important step forward.

The Allies will be considering in the period ahead the usefulness and possible accomplishments of a CSCE meeting at a political level prior to the Helsinki Follow-up Meeting in 1992. A successful meeting would require careful preparation and clarity as to its intended purpose and goals.

19.   Fundamental economic reform in Central and Eastern European countries will be necessary to strengthen and expand the basis for improved East-West economic relations. Consistent with our broad security concerns, we intend to encourage expanding economic and trade relations with the Eastern countries, in a differentiated approach commensurate with the progress of their economic and political reforms and as a means of further strengthening these positive changes. Such relations – based on commercially sound terms, mutual interest and reciprocity – will pave the way to an increased integration of these countries into the international economic system, which we support. An important task of East-West economic co-operation will be to explore means to expand Western experience and know-how to Eastern countries, by establishing co-operative and training programmes and exchanges in technical and managerial fields. In this regard, we support the process of rationalising existing export controls through a co-ordinated approach that allows greater support for reform in the East and for Western investment in those countries while protecting our security interests.

We fully support the efforts of the 24 countries co-ordinated by the Commission of the European Community to provide economic assistance to Poland and Hungary and will continue to respond to the urgent needs of these countries. We welcome the December 13th Declaration of the Ministers of the Group of 24, in which we, in concert with our partners, have renewed our commitment to assistance for the restructuring of the Polish and Hungarian economies and expressed willingness to respond positively to other countries in Central and Eastern Europe, and in particular the German Democratic Republic,

Czechoslovakia, Bulgaria, as well as Yugoslavia, at the time they put into place the necessary political and economic reforms.

20. Recent events have created new opportunities for the Allies to achieve the arms control objectives set out in the Alliance's Comprehensive Concept of Arms Control and Disarmament at the May Summit Meeting. This stressed the rôle of arms control as a vital and integral part of our security policy, and one which is embedded in our broader political agenda. We welcome recent high-level meetings which have helped to accelerate a range of arms control negotiations.

This is in particular true for the two distinct negotiations taking place within the framework of the CSCE process. Thus, the progress already achieved at the negotiations on Conventional Armed Forces in Europe (CFE) in Vienna strengthens our belief that an agreement can be signed in 1990 that would represent an important step towards a stable military balance in Europe at lower levels of armaments. We will intensify our efforts within our High Level Task Force (HLTF) to achieve this agreement and will instruct our delegations in Vienna accordingly. Its entry into force, and the prompt completion thereafter of the agreed reductions and limitations, will be accompanied and supported by arrangements for effective verification. Bearing in mind that verification is a national responsibility, we will consider how the Allies can best organise themselves to contribute to this task.

The conclusion of the CFE agreement will bring us a dramatic step further towards our goal of providing security for all at greatly reduced levels of forces. Building upon this crucial agreement we will look beyond it to discuss among the Allies further steps in arms control as we have affirmed in our Comprehensive Concept of Arms Control and Disarmament.

At the same time we will also work to achieve results in the CSBM negotiations, given the importance of encouraging openness and predictability in military affairs and thereby reinforcing mutual confidence. Recognising the importance of expanded dialogue on military matters, we welcome the Seminar on Military Doctrine to be held in Vienna in January 1990 in the framework of the CSBM negotiations.

Our goals of confidence and security will be further enhanced by an agreement on an Open Skies regime, designed to encourage reciprocal openness on the part of the participating states and to allow the observation of military activities and installations on their territories. Today we have agreed on a common position for the Ottawa Conference to be held in February 1990. The basic elements of our approach are set out in an annex to this communique.

We welcome the intention of the United States and the Soviet Union to accelerate the START process to resolve all substantive issues and, if possible, to conclude a treaty by the June 1990 US/Soviet Summit.

Since the impetus given by the Paris Conference on chemical weapons, new encouraging developments, such as the Canberra Conference, have occurred. We view these events and the recent proposals by President Bush aiming at the accelerated destruction of chemical weapons as important contributions towards the earliest possible success of the Geneva negotiations on a comprehensive, effectively verifiable, worldwide chemical weapons ban.

21.   We will seek to stimulate the free flow of information between the countries of East and West by fostering greater awareness of our democratic societies and institutions and through educational interchange and legislative exchanges with newly vitalised legislatures in reforming Eastern countries. In this spirit, and in keeping with the Declaration of May 1989, we have established the NATO Democratic Institutions Fellowships, the purpose of which is to promote the study of our democratic structures by individuals from both East and West.

22.   We are aware that for our fellow citizens security is more than just the prevention of war and must be seen in a broader perspective. Our consultations within the Alliance will allow us to work together and with other countries in a number of fora to devise common responses to new threats. As part of our international efforts at various levels we are engaging in co-operative endeavours, including with countries of the East, in such areas of common interest as the spread of destabilising military technologies, the fight against environmental degradation, terrorism, drug trafficking and the peaceful resolution of regional conflicts. For example, we are encouraged by the results of the Sofia CSCE Conference on the Environment, which represents a useful step towards the comprehensive and continued attention that all states must devote to this serious problem of common concern.

23.   Current developments in international relations will necessitate intensification of our process of consultation and, where appropriate, political coordination. This will demand optimum use of the procedures of the Alliance. The latter constitutes the only forum for permanent discussion between the Atlantic partners based on an integrated approach to political, economic and military elements of security. Consistent with the decision taken at the May 1989 Summit we have received from the Council in Permanent Session recommendations to this effect. As a result, we are determined to further strengthen our consultation process.

Source: NATO Press Service 15 December 1989

JOINT COMMUNIQUÉ, TALKS BETWEEN FEDERAL CHANCELLOR KOHL AND HANS MODROW, PRIME MINISTER OF THE GDR

Dresden, 19–20 December 1989

At the invitation of the Chairman of the Council of Ministers of the German Democratic Republic, Hans Modrow, the Federal Chancellor of the Federal Republic of Germany, Helmut Kohl, was in the German Democratic Republic for a working meeting in Dresden on 19–20 December 1989.

There was a comprehensive exchange of views about the state of relations between the Federal Republic of Germany and the German Democratic Republic and their potential for development as well as current international questions. The two leaders agreed that these relations were inseparable from East-West relations and embedded in the pan-European process.

The European processes of reform to realize freedom, human rights and democracy must also be directed towards a durable stability in the whole of Europe. The Germans in both states bear a particular responsibility to work with patience and great care towards an organic development, which serves these objectives and at the same time takes into account the interests of all others involved.

Federal Chancellor Kohl and Prime Minister Modrow agreed, that a good-neighbourly relationship between both states, founded in the joint responsibility for peace and a Treaty Community, is of great importance for the stability of Europe and represents a contribution for a new European architecture.

In their view the changes so far give rise to the hope that the division of Europe can be overcome and a new European peace order can be created in accordance with the objectives of the Helsinki Final Act and the other CSCE documents, based on the unrestricted observance of the principles and norms of international law, especially the right to self-determination of peoples and human rights. The European peoples should in realization of their right to self-determination build the common European home on the basis of a sovereign, democratic decision and the free choice of their own path of development.

Both sides will support the active continuation of the CSCE process. They agreed that the proposal for a CSCE summit conference in 1990

can – provided it is well prepared – give stability and new perspectives for the future developments in Europe. They unreservedly accepted
a commitment to all obligations under the CSCE process and declared
the intention of their governments, to act in an exemplary manner in
the implementation of the principles and regulation of the CSCE
documents, including in the area of human rights.

Federal Chancellor Kohl and Prime Minister Modrow agreed, that
disarmament and arms control must keep pace with the political
development, in order to make the positive processes durable. Both
sides welcome the impulses which have emanated from the summit
meeting between General Secretary Gorbachev and President Bush in
this regard. They affirm their willingness to make a significant contribution to the conclusion of an agreement in 1990 about the reduction of
conventional forces in Europe as well as the world-wide prohibition
of chemical weapons. They will also work for an agreement about
Confidence-building and Security Measures.

The bilateral consultation on the appropriate levels of both sides can
support the disarmament and arms control process. The same is true
for talks about issues relating to CSCE and other international subjects.
These consultations will be continued on a regular basis.

Federal Chancellor Kohl informed Prime Minister Modrow about the
development of the European Community, which for the Federal
Republic of Germany remains the cornerstone of a new European
architecture – and, in its willingness open itself – the fulcrum of
a future European balance. He underlined the willingness of the
community and its member states to develop more comprehensive and
closer relations with the Central and East European countries which
have entered the path of democratic change, on the basis of a more
intensive dialogue and improved co-operation. The Federal Republic
of Germany will support the imminent conclusion of an agreement of
trade and cooperation between the European Community and the
German Democratic Republic.

Prime Minister Modrow informed Federal Chancellor Kohl about the
intended further steps towards the democratic renewal in the German
Democratic Republic. He explained particularly the programme of the
coalition government which he leads and emphasized, that the process
begun in the German Democratic Republic towards radical reforms was
irreversible. It involved free, general, equal and secret elections on the
basis of a new democratic election law. A fundamental change of
economic policy and economic reform was envisaged, which would
orientate itself according to market conditions.

Prime Minister Modrow also explained the plans for a change in the
constitution and a reform of the criminal law, which would take full
account of the obligations under the International Covenant on Civil
and Political Rights as well as under CSCE. In this context Federal
Chancellor Kohl expressed his expectation that the notion of political
crimes would be eliminated and all those convicted for such offenses

would be released. Prime Minister Modrow announced, that all persons affected by this would be released from imprisonment soon – if possible even before Christmas. Federal Chancellor Kohl declared for his part, that the Observation Centre [for human rights in the GDR] in Salzgitter can be dissolved when, as a result of the reforms in the GDR, its activities would be no longer necessary.

Prime Minister Modrow explained further that for the problems of those who have left the GDR in recent months solutions should be developed which do justice to the interests of the people concerned.

Federal Chancellor Kohl and Prime Minister Modrow agreed, that the positive changes which are taking place in Europe have added a new dimension to the question of the relations between the two states. There was agreement, starting from the Basic Treaty of 21 December 1972, to extend the co-operation between the Federal Republic and the German Democratic Republic on a more comprehensive basis, raise relations to a new level and develop them more closely, on a more long-term basis.

In view of the special nature of relations between the two states, which is due to historical reasons, a dense network of agreement in all spheres and on all levels will be necessary, which must include Berlin (West) in accordance with the Four Power Agreement. In addition to the existing treaties, a Treaty Community is to be developed with the institutions to deal with common problems of society.

The central element of the Treaty Community is the economy. Federal Chancellor Kohl and Prime Minister Modrow explained, that for this reason they seek to substantially intensify the economic co-operation.

After a detailed discussion of the economic situation there was agreement that a fundamental reform of the economic system, which is also designed to integrate the state economy of the GDR more strongly into the international division of labour, is an essential prerequisite to allow the economic forces of the GDR to unfold and increase their performance.

. . .

Federal Chancellor Kohl and Prime Minister Modrow agreed to remain in constant contact.

Declaration of Intent

The Federal Chancellor of the Federal Republic of Germany, Helmut Kohl, and the Chairman of the Council of Ministers of the German Democratic Republic, Hans Modrow, during their meeting at Dresden on 19 December 1989 jointly declared themselves in favour of the comprehensive development of mutual relations and the creation of corresponding treaties.

They agreed to conclude a joint treaty about the intended Treaty Community governing the relations between the Federal Republic of Germany and the German Democratic Republic about co-operation and good neighbourliness.

Helmut Kohl and Hans Modrow agreed, that representatives of both governments should without delay enter into negotiations about the text of such a treaty. It was envisaged that the treaty should be signed in Spring 1990.

Source: Information Office of the Federal Republic of Germany 20 December 1989
(Translated by Christoph Bluth)

VACLAV HAVEL, PRESIDENT OF CZECHOSLOVAKIA, IN WEST GERMANY

2 January 1990

On German unification:

... many conditions must be met:

The first is that emotions must be kept in check on both sides of the German border.

The second is that the process of German unification be part of the process of European unification.

The third is that unification take place at a time when Germany's neighbours are free of their fears of the greater Germany of the past.

It is conceivable that the two Germanys will be brought together in the future. But I never use the word 'reunification', as it brings up the idea of the 1937 borders.

A democratic system in Germany is more important than the possibility that it might become one nation.

Source: International Herald Tribune, 3 January 1990

DOUGLAS HURD, SECRETARY OF STATE FOR FOREIGN AND COMMONWEALTH AFFAIRS

Windrush Valley, 8 January 1990

Reform in Eastern Europe is being driven by the peoples of Eastern Europe themselves. But if that process of reform is to be sustained and carried through, we in the West will need to give what help we can.

Our response to change must be framed with generosity and imagination. But it must also be based upon a careful assessment of the specific needs of each individual country. Those needs differ in many respects: some countries, like Czechoslovakia, have reached a level of economic development which would make indiscriminate, blanket assistance irrelevant and wasteful. Other countries, such as Poland and Hungary, do not need the kind of help which would only burden them with still more debt. Their debt per head is already the highest in the world. The last thing they need is for us to pile more on top.

For other countries such as Bulgaria and, now, painfully but triumphantly, Romania, we have to apply our minds not only to the most effective forms of economic assistance, but also to the problem of helping to build up a political culture in societies where the practice of politics has been prevented from putting down any roots whatsoever.

The similarities between these countries' problem are more striking than their differences. That comes as no surprise: until recently, they all shared a system which, by suppressing the individual and the well-springs of human creativity, created an economic and, in the worst cases, a cultural desert.

The opening up of those societies has fuelled expectations amongst the peoples of Eastern Europe which their politicians will find hard to fulfil. One look at the richness of the human and natural resources of those countries bring home the full absurdity of the system which has been inflicted on their peoples. their frustration is understandable: we must help make sure that it does not threaten the process of economic restructuring which must now be set in hand.

The countries of Eastern Europe are making a leap between systems based on control and suppression to systems based on free choice. This is difficult in the political field, but it looks as if the crops now being sown will produce a harvest of free elections before 1990 is out. It is much more difficult in the economic field, and the dangers of falling into a chasm of incoherence between the two systems is very real.

Our help will help ensure economic stability while those countries embark on the painful process of reform. The problems they will face are daunting. Poland and Hungary have to manage an enormous burden of external debt. They must also bring runaway public expenditure under control. At the same time, they have to find ways of stimulating the development of a private sector and dismantling the lumbering state monopolies which have failed to deliver the goods which their people want to buy. As if this weren't enough, Poland also has continuing problems with energy and food supplies, as well as spiralling inflation.

Indeed, hidden inflation will be revealed in most East European countries as they move towards more realistic pricing mechanisms. The challenge for the West will be to help the reforming countries to democratise their political systems and rationalise their economies while containing the social pressures that that process will unleash.

So how should we in the West target our help?

First of all, by ministering to the most pressing symptom of economic mismanagement: food shortages and hunger. That is why the Community, at Britain's initiative, has sent £70 million of food and emergency aid to Poland. More is on the way.

The Community has also agreed a budget of £210 million in 1990 for aid projects in Hungary and Poland in agriculture, training and environment. It is fitting that it should be the Community – the most successful expression of our shared values and objectives as Europeans – which is throwing a lifeline to the rest of our family of nations. The European Commission has done a splendid job in co-ordinating the effort of both the Community and the group of 24 donor nations.

It is right that some of that £210 million should be used to tackle the serious environmental pollution which those countries are having to clear up, particularly in their heavily industrialised regions. Protecting and improving the environment is now firmly at the centre of British aid policy: we must put it to work in Eastern Europe as well.

At a time when the barriers in Europe are being dismantled, it is right that trade barriers against Eastern Europe should come down too. That is why the Community is giving Poland and Hungary tariff-free access for industrial products. We are reducing tariffs on certain agricultural products. We are suspending or abolishing quantitative trade restrictions. In addition, those countries are also being made eligible for lending from the European Investment Bank.

We will want to consider next how best to help the other countries of Eastern Europe down the road of reform – a road upon which some of them have only just begun to embark. Wherever it fits, we will want to use aid as a level for change. That is why the European Community's policy of differentiation is absolutely correct: we must target our help upon those countries which carry out the reforms which will lead to democracy and to a free market economy.

That principle must also be applied by the new European Bank for

Reconstruction and Development which is to be set up. If the Bank is to achieve its objectives, it must also scrutinise projects on the basis of sound finance and cost effectiveness. It should be a means of stimulating the private sector and encouraging enterprise. It should not featherbed state dinosaurs.

We will help with debt rescheduling. Wherever possible, we will offer grants rather than loans. We have already announced a 100 million dollar grant to a stabilisation fund to help underpin the foreign currency reforms which Poland's Solidarity-led Government is putting through as part of its brave financial plan.

We will also play a full part in a far-reaching debt rescheduling plan for Poland, which has now come to agreement in principle with the IMF. We welcome that. Altready, the aid is flowing in.

All told, the help which Britain will make available to Poland could total as much as £250 million next year. It will be a major contribution to the collective effort of the international community.

We are following Hungary's negotiations with the IMF in an equally generous spirit. The Strasbourg European Council recommended providing Hungary with an adjustment loan of $1 billion.

The key is to ensure that all these countries make the sort of changes which will help them to generate their own wealth – and, eventually, to stand on their own two feet.

Choice at the ballot-box and choice in the market-place are intimately linked and mutually dependent. It is the only way the societies of Eastern Europe will be able to withstand the strains imposed by the necessary economic restructuring. Political institutions endowed with the authority and legitimacy of popular consent will be the principal means of securing and preserving the people's support through what will undoubtedly be difficult times. In Eastern Europe as in the Soviet Union, abandoning *glasnost* for the sake of *perestroika* is not a viable option.

Strengthening the private sector will be essential. It means building up the private financial infrastructure, by encouraging business institutions to expand their operations in Eastern Europe. Countries like Poland and Hungary desperately need the equity and expertise of the private sector. We are already providing those countries with the sort of advice on privatisation for which Britain has become famous.

That sort of technical assistance is one of the purposes of the pioneering 'know-how' funds which we have set up. Britain was first in the field with that sort of help – help which will promote democracy and the establishment of a market economy. We have recently doubled the fund for Poland to £50 million over 5 years, and a fund for Hungary with £25 million will come into operation in April 1990. Those sums will go a long way, because they are paying for salaries and skills, rather than costly capital equipment.

Now that we are seeing the first stages of liberalisation in the GDR, Czechoslovakia, Romania and Bulgaria, we will want to examine how best to help them as well, as soon as substantial political reforms are in place.

The know-how funds will provide the training, the skills, and the human contacts which are the life-blood of any flourishing and prosperous society. they will help in areas such as financial services and management training, and in imparting the skills which are so badly needed in areas like accounting and auditing. Governments in Eastern Europe lack meaningful or reliable statistics to make sensible choices. They lack accurate costing and pricing mechanisms. They lack many of the instruments they need to embark on successful economic restructuring.

But it is not just a question of training technocrats. Governments can only make sensible choices in the light of criticism, both from experts and from the public. Already, we are helping to train Polish journalists and broadcasters here in Britain. They will help to pump oxygen into the new system. We want to develop our parliamentary contacts with Eastern Europe. We are already giving Polish and Hungarian MPs and candidates a taste of Westminster democracy. We are at last seeing the emergence of effective legislative bodies in Eastern Europe, instead of mere rubber-stamp parliaments. Our own parliamentarians have much experience to share with their counterparts about the process of democratic scrutiny and law-making within a constitutional framework.

We have another precious asset to share: the English language. There is every prospect that English will soon replace Russian as the first foreign language in many of the schools and universities of Eastern Europe. We should be prepared to support and encourage a trend which – quite apart from anything else – is in our own long-term political and commercial interests. It is also a compelling argument for increasing our student exchanges.

Another powerful way of encouraging reform is to invite them into the Council of Europe, in which 23 Western European countries have set out their commitment to democracy and human rights. That club cannot be an exclusive one: it should be ready – I believe it is ready – to accept new members once they have put democracy and the rule of law into practice, and are able to ratify the European Convention on Human Rights. We will greet them warmly as soon as they do. As these countries begin to build up the values of freedom and democracy, we will also want to explore how we can co-operate to defeat the scourges of drugs and terrorism.

We must make a strenuous and imaginative response to the extra-ordinary effort which is being made by the peoples of Eastern Europe. Diplomacy and ordinary human communication will matter in the 1990s as never before. We have to help them replace a mean, starved stability based on communist repression with a firmer stability based on free institutions putting down roots into every city, town and village. It will not be at all easy. But for them, the cost of failure would be too high and they have suffered enough already.

Source: London Press Service, Central Office of Information, 8 January 1990

FEDERAL CHANCELLOR HELMUT KOHL ON 'THE GERMAN QUESTION AND EUROPEAN RESPONSIBILITY'

The Centre des Conferences Internationales, Paris, 17 January 1990
(Extracts)

With the reduction of East-West confrontation and the democratic change taking place in the countries of central, eastern and south-eastern Europe, for the first time a realistic opportunity is emerging to overcome peacefully the division of Europe and the division of Germany. Let there be no doubt: this is a task we will only be able to manage jointly. A unilateral national approach to solving the German question would be presumptuous and doomed to failure.

It would also be disastrous if, on the difficult road we have ahead of us, mistrust were to take the place of mutual confidence and doubts were to enter into our mutual intentions. It must be our common objective to see to it that the reforms initiated in central, eastern and south-eastern Europe continue to develop stably and successfully.

Not all questions that have arisen in connection with the ongoing developments can be answered definitively today. Similarly, we would at present not yet be able to definitively resolve all the questions that would arise concerning reunification.

The interest of our neighbours in this context is, of course, focussed on the question regarding the future borders of a united Germany.

In this context I would like to make it very clear that no-one with political responsibility in the Federal Republic of Germany, no serious political group, has dreams of a 'greater Germany', to use this unfortunate term from an unfortunate period of our past.

For this reason alone, the debate being conducted on this subject – not least of all in our own country – is artificial and indeed superfluous. Many of the statements made in the context of this debate clearly bear the mark of an incipient election campaign.

Let me state two things clearly here and now:

I. The legal situation

In the Warsaw Treaty of 1970 the Federal Republic of Germany and Poland reaffirm the inviolability of their existing borders now and in the future and mutually agree to unreserved respect for their territorial integrity. They state that they have no territorial claims of any kind against one another and that they will not make any such claims in the future. At the same time both sides state that this treaty does not affect bilateral or multilateral international agreements previously concluded by the parties. The Moscow Treaty, concluded prior to this, contains similar and in part identical passages. In both treaties the then Federal Government took into account that no peace treaty exists and that the Federal Republic of Germany cannot act as a sovereign authority for all of Germany but rather only on its own behalf. This situation is no different for the Government of the federal Republic of Germany today.

Incidentally, in Article 7 of the Bonn Treaty of 1952–54 it was agreed that the final definition of Germany's borders would have to be postponed until such time as a freely-negotiated settlement for all of Germany based on a peace treaty has been attained.

II. The political side

Another question is what the vast majority of Germans – whose democratic will would determine the posture of a future all-German government – think about this. The Germans, and there should be no doubt about this in anyone's mind, do not intend to initiate a debate on borders in a Europe of tomorrow, a debate that would necessarily pose a threat to the European peace order we are all working to achieve.

The Germans want permanent reconciliation with their Polish neighbours. This includes guaranteeing the Poles that they will be able to live within secure borders. No-one wants to see a second expulsion, given the horrors of the expulsion that Germans experienced themselves. As such, no-one wants to associate reunification with changes in existing borders, borders that will lose importance in a free Europe of the future.

In the post-war period, France and Germany have provided a unique example as two neighbouring nations who have travelled a long road from a rivalry with destructive effects for all of Europe to an 'entente' that has been fruitful for the other European partners as well. We will not deviate from this road in the future.

Source: Federal German Embassy Report, London, 19 January 1990

ADDRESS BY PRESIDENT OF THE EUROPEAN COMMISSION, JACQUES DELORS, TO THE EUROPEAN PARLIAMENT

Strasbourg, 17 January 1990

What an astounding series of events have unfolded virtually on our doorstep since I spoke to you this time last year of the challenges facing the Community. I referred then to Mr Gorbachev's dream of a 'common European house' and our slightly different vision of a 'European village' built around a solid house called the 'European Community'.

The Community has progressed apace since then. Its economy has strengthened further thanks to job-creating growth fed by investment. The persistence of this cycle has led to production in the Twelve rising by some 20% since 1984, 8.5 million new jobs being created and European business displaying a new-found assertiveness at home and abroad – though it could still do even more. The Community's influence has grown economially and politically. The Community is now respected, courted, held in awe.

And yet recent events in Central and Eastern Europe should give us pause for thought. Why has it taken us more than thirty years to respond tentatively, with moves towards Economic and Monetary Union, to the objective of a political Community set by the founding fathers, whereas the Germans of the East, released from former constraints, have taken no more than a few weeks to re-open the Brandenburg Gate in an act full of symbolism for the future unity of the German nation?

Why is it taking us eight years, of what we regard as intense activity, to create a single market and an organized economic and social area, while our Eastern neighbours have taken no more than a few months to discover the heady wine of liberty and democracy?

It is a striking contrast, when seen against the tremendous surge of history in the making, as nations cast aside the old régime to embrace a new era holding the promise of peace, pluralist democracy, and economic and social progress.

Today more than ever the Community is faced with challenges: the challenge presented by aims, strategy and method as the Twelve face up to their responsibilities in the East and elsewhere in Europe, in the Mediterranean and in the developing world; the challenge of reaffirming our values through our day-to-day activities; the challenge of implementing the Single Act, which remains our top priority and finds practical expression each year in the Commission's programme.

But, first and foremost, how, in a new and shifting situation, can we ignore the fact that time is running short, that events in Europe are challenging the Community to respond?

The challenge of events in Europe

It was in the name of freedom that millions of men and women, far from remaining resigned to servitude, took to the streets, roused from their inertia by the decline of the régimes which had governed them and the relaxation, sometimes deliberate, of the iron grip which had held them in thrall.

But let there be no mistake: the prosperity and freedom of our Community – free from hegemony, governed by the rule of law, where even the smallest country has a say – served as a lodestone, a lodestar in terms of ideals and actions. Over the last few months it has not been the ambitions of politicians, but the will of the people that has made history; a will manifested with dignity and joy in some countries, in the midst of drama and bitterness in others, and above all with a collective spirit that is all the more impressive because it seems so sadly lacking in our privileged Western half of the continent, hamstrung by ridiculous quarrels rooted in nostalgic yearning for past glories.

Our admiration for the people of Central and Eastern Europe must not, however, blind us to reality. The changes under way give cause for hope, but they are also fraught with danger. As Tocqueville wrote in the aftermath of the 1848 revolution '[it] has ceased to be an adventure and is taking on the dimensions of a new era'. There is still a danger of back-tracking, of things going wrong, as is amply illustrated by differences between the people and their leaders in Leipzig and in Bucharest, not to talk of the upheavals taking place within the Soviet Union. And who can ignore the yawning gap between the determination of the people and the precariousness of their situation, between their clearly-expressed aspirations and uncertainty about the eventual outcome?

There are economic dangers, given that most of the countries of Eastern Europe are experiencing stagnant growth, low investment and high debt – particularly when compared to export earnings from trade with the rest of what used to be the Communist world. We must, of course, be wary of generalizations since situations differ in a number of respects – investment in Bulgaria, growth in Czechoslovakia and debt in Romania – and levels of development vary. And national differences are even more marked when traditions and political structures are borne in mind. But all the countries of Eastern Europe are in a difficult situation calling for new political structures and radical economic reform.

Neither must we underestimate the political dangers facing Eastern

Europe – and hence also of concern to us – in the uncharted waters leading to the free, multi-party elections scheduled for the spring, and indeed in the post-election period should political reforms fail to materialize, should economies collapse, should there be moves towards Balkanization.

The Community, too, is running enormous risks because the pace of events has fuelled the debate on European integration. I have heard it argued in some quarters that the Community, as a product of the Cold War, should die with the Cold War, completely disregarding the experience accumulated over forty years on our difficult but exciting journey to pooled sovereignty. I interpret this variously as a return to facile nationalism or a temptation to play the Metternich card. It is as if a changing world had created openings for those driven by vanity and for would-be statesmen seeking to play yesterday's hand.

I know, too, that others are talking in terms of immediate Community membership for the countries of Central and Eastern Europe, as if they were ready, economically and politically, to embrace pluralist democracy and operate a market economy; as if this scenario raised no financial or institutional problems. Perhaps I should remind them that Spain and Portugal spent seven years preparing for Community membership. This goes a long way towards explaining their success and the outstanding contribution they have made to reinforcing the Community spirit.

I quote this example deliberately because it demonstrates that the Community is a unique testbed for plural democracy, that is to say, democracy exercised by a concert of nations. But we must be wary of raising unrealistic expectations. Of course, the principle is quite clear: any democratic European country is free to apply for Community membership. But, leaving aside the fact that the Community has chosen to concentrate on the improvement of present structures in preference to expansion, it all comes down to ways and means and, while we will not abandon our basic approach, the substance of practical arrangements can vary over time. The question put to every applicant for membership is simple: are you, or are you not, prepared to accept the marriage contract in its entirety, with all that it holds for the future?

But to come back to our neighbours in Central and Eastern Europe: we are duty-bound to help them as they embark on the unique experiment of moving from Communism towards a market economy – a complete reversal of the process to which so many have given so much thought, often blinded by a tendency to equate capitalism with the market economy. How can we help without being paternalistic? How can we lend our support without getting in the way? This is of course principally a matter for the countries concerned. But the Community must commit itself to solidarity, within a new framework for cooperation, which we intend to define as a matter of urgency.

Solidarity has been in evidence from the moment that the Paris

Summit in mid-July asked the Commission to coordinate Western aid to Poland and Hungary. Less than two weeks later, experts from 24 countries met in Brussels to assess needs and consider what form action should take. Three meetings were held, the last – a month ago – at ministerial level. At the same time, the Community decided to send emergency food aid, which was already on its way to Poland by the beginning of September. Cooperation is taking shape, the Commission adding its ideas to those of the countries concerned so that coordination can make the entire operation more effective in terms of quality and quantity.

You can see that when there is an urgent need – for food aid and medical supplies – or when the issues involved are relatively well-defined – financial assistance, the opening-up of markets, extension of generalized preferences – the response is swift. Helping these countries rebuild their economies, when the machinery of State is fast disintegrating and individual initiatives are still in their infancy, will be more difficult and will take time. There will be ups and downs. But we are ready to deal with whatever comes.

The decision taken at the Paris Summit envisaged assistance to Poland and Hungary only. Developments since then have made our task infinitely more ambitious, as the Foreign Ministers of the 24 countries have acknowledged. This will inevitably raise the issue for the Twelve – as this House is well aware – of what Community instruments and what resources are available.

To take Community instruments first. We are in the process of negotiating, or have already signed, trade and cooperation agreements with all these countries. But these agreements are now unlikely to meet *our* requirements and *their* individual and collective needs. We must therefore look beyond them to devise new forms of cooperation and provide a framework for future political cooperation between democratic States.

This could be our goal in drawing up new, revised association agreements. If the six countries so wished, these agreements could include an institutional aspect, the creation of a forum for genuine dialogue and economic and political consultation, the extension of cooperation to the technical, scientific, environmental, commercial and financial spheres; but not necessarily involving a common market, since such ill-prepared economies could not cope with one for a number of years.

This would emphasize the necessarily open-ended nature of cooperation, setting it apart from ordinary trade agreements, which, while they have their uses, merely reflect the balance of interests at a given point in time.

All this presupposes a new series of instruments. Two decisions on training and youth exchanges have already been adopted by the Heads of State or Government of the Twelve and the Commission's work on these projects is already at an advanced stage. At the General Affairs

Council on 5 February, the Commission will be proposing the creation of a European training foundation, a loose arrangement for promoting exchanges, collecting information and fostering contacts, but also for guaranteeing loans and credit insurance and providing financial assistance, areas in which the new European Bank for Reconstruction and Development will have a major role to play.

It is important to remember, however, that additional financial resources will have to be found for these ambitious plans. This will lead inevitably to a revision of the financial perspective, though there can be no question of going back on budgetary discipline, which must continue to be our guiding principle. I would like to quote some figures to give you an idea of the scale of the problem. If we were to confine ourselves to extending our own internal arrangements for helping regions lagging behind – what we call 'Objective 1 regions' – to the six countries on the road to democracy, we would need an extra ECU 14 billion a year. If we were to add European Investment Bank intervention in these same regions, another ECU 5 billion would be required. Finally, allowing for the capacity of these economies to absorb financial aid as they undergo major upheaval, our programme would have to extend over a period of five to ten years. There we have it. It might be a good idea to bear these considerations in mind during the coming months, since the Commission will be making fresh proposals under the Inter-institutional Agreement to adapt resources and instruments to the new situation. In February 1988 the European Council took a historic decision to underwrite the internal solidarity and further development of the Community. Another 'February 1988', equally significant, equally historic, is needed to demonstrate our solidarity with Eastern Europe and the rest of the world.

Finally, I would stress, that, whatever the solution found, it will be impossible from now on to separate the Community's economic role from its political one. This is one of the major lessons to be learned from developments in the East.

The Community's responsibilities elsewhere in the world

Given developments in the East, renewed détente and the emergence of a multipolar world, the Community and its Member States must be in a position individually and collectively to influence the course of events and the future shape of a Greater Europe so that it reflects their interests and values. This will be a crucial topic for discussion and political debate. We must tackle it head-on.

It immediately raises the German question. Rapprochement, or even reunification, of the German people is clearly a matter for the Germans themselves. But the Community has an interest too. Let me explain why. The preamble to the German Basic Law of 23 May 1949 links the principle of German reunification, on the basis of self-determination by the German people, to the issue of European unity – and may I say in passing that this text, which predates the Treaty of Rome by nine years, testifies to the perspicacity of the German leadership.

Furthermore, the Treaty of Rome itself makes reference to this issue, in the Protocol on German internal trade, in the declarations on German nationality and the status of Berlin, and in the 28 February 1957 declaration by the Bonn negotiators.

This makes East Germany a special case. I would like to repeat clearly here today that there is a place for East Germany in the Community should it so wish, provided, as the Strasbourg European Council made quite clear, the German nation regains its unity through free self-determination, peacefully and democratically, in accordance with the principles of the Helsinki Final Act, in the context of an East-West dialogue and with an eye to European integration. But the form that it will take is, I repeat, a matter for the Germans themselves.

The Community as a focal point

As you will no doubt appreciate, the Twelve have no choice but to remain a focal point, a rock of stability for the rest of the continent. This is not a role they have inherited from history but one they have earned by constant effort and resolve as the pioneers of European integration.

But this does not mean that the Community is the only European organization with a role to play. In the economic sphere there is EFTA, of course, but there is also COMECON. After undergoing radical changes, COMECON must consolidate its function, if only to keep up a flow of trade in products which cannot yet compete on the world market because of their quality. It seems that this was the conclusion reached by COMECON leaders at their meeting in Sofia despite the strong reservations expressed by some delegates about the organization. Should COMECON countries decide to embark on reforms, the Community will be prepared, at their request, to give them the benefit of its experience in economic cooperation.

Then there are the alliances which the two superpowers are resolved to retain as a source of stability, if not control, and which, to judge from certain pronouncements, are to be given new powers. And last but not least another organization offers a broad perspective: the Council of Europe. It must continue to work in the areas of cultural affairs, human rights and education and at the same time help the countries of Central and Eastern Europe to rediscover their cultural roots and refamiliarize themselves with the ways of multi-party democracy.

Source: European Commission, 17 January 1990

SPEECH BY FOREIGN MINISTER HANS-DIETRICH GENSCHER AT THE CFE CONFERENCE

Vienna on 25 January 1990 (Extracts)

Disarmament and arms control are a fundamental concern of both German states, which have the largest concentration of conventional and nuclear weapons. A conventional conflict in Europe would mean the end of the indivisible German nation; that is why we are striving particularly hard to develop a security system in Europe based on cooperative structures. We are determined to contribute our share to stability, which also means we Germans – whether separated or united – have no territorial claims against anyone now or in the future.

Among the main preconditions for increased stability in Europe are eliminating remaining imbalances in the conventional sphere and the capability for surprise attack and large-scale offensive action. Highly mobile conventional weapon systems with heavy firepower still constitute the biggest threat to security in Europe. Their reduction to levels absolutely essential for defence is our primary short-term objective.

The CFE (Conventional Forces Europe) negotiations in Vienna have proved to be a disarmament forum with a new quality. The clear determination in recent months of all the states taking part to make early substantial progress is something new in the history of multilateral arms control. In the meantime a broad basis of conceptual convergance has evolved between East and West, which has added unusual momentum to the negotiations.

With this momentum – due not least to the American President's courageous initiative last May – we must conclude the negotiations in the coming months. The dramatic developments of recent weeks make achievement of substantial results this year still more urgent.

The peoples of Europe and North America expect an agreement on conventional disarmament to be signed before the end of 1990. If this schedule is to be kept, the crucial problems must be solved by the summer. This fifth round of negotiations will be the one in which the main decisions regarding an agreement will have to be taken. The period of unprecedented conceptual rapprochement is over: what is now needed is real negotiation structured to solve the many concrete problems and to produce results.

Time is pressing. In the autumn the heads of state and government must sign the first agreement. We must already look beyond the next six months. The first CFE agreement will be only an initial, albeit decisive, step towards a new security system for Europe.

It does not yet signify establishment of lasting stability, hence there must be a break in the arms control dialogue. Immediately after the first CFE agreement the negotiations for a second phase must begin.

In the proposals presented on March 9 1989 the members of the Western Alliance envisaged further steps towards disarmament:

- Further reductions and limitations of conventional forces;
- Restructuring of forces to strengthen their defensive character and further reduce their offensive capability.

This implies lower ceilings for categories of major equipment already included. It also implies reducing not only stationed forces but the forces of the basing countries as well.

As a new element, logistics should also be included and agreements reached on the limitation of ammunition and fuel supplies with a view of reducing offensive capabilities and, with less equipment, restructuring forces for a defensive role. In addition, the process of restructuring should be intensified by reducing the degree of operational readiness and force generation capabilities, and at the same time increasing the transparency of mobilization procedures. Overall, future negotiations should focus not only on the strength of armed forces but on rules governing the use of military power.

That is why, within the scope of this comprehensive drive to establish stability in Europe, we also attach special importance to expanding the system of CSBM (Confidence- and Security-Building Measures) adopted in Stockholm. Confidence-building is an indispensable complement to disarmament; it is vital to the consolidation of a new, co-operative safety structure in Europe. We must therefore make every effort to conclude as well this year the negotiations on a new set of CSBM in which all participants in the CSCE (Conference on Security and Co-operation in Europe) process are involved.

As soon as the implementation of a CFE agreement is under way it will be time to put arms control on a broader basis, i.e., negotiations on short-range nuclear weapons will have to be started, but nuclear artillery, too, must be made part of the disarmament process. Notwithstanding the changes in Europe's security situation that will ensue from successfully ending the Vienna negotiations, the maintenance and further development of our partnership with the US remains the basis and guarantee of our security. The political and military presence of the North American democracies continues to be the precondition for peace and stability in Europe.

The alliance whose member-states are working hard in these negotiations to find solutions for the sake of peace in Europe play a special role in this process.

The object is to develop the alliances increasingly into instruments not only of defence but of confidence-building, dialogue and co-operation in all areas of security policy. Their political dimension and function will grow.

The old security structures based on antagonism are no longer in keeping with political developments: on the contrary, they could put the brake on comprehensive rapprochement among the nations of Europe. Our goal must be to establish security through co-operation instead of confrontation. This is the challenge of our age.

The architecture of a Europe undergoing such dramatic change must be based on genuine stability throughout the continent. An intensified CSCE process is the proper framework. We need a partnership for stability for the whole of Europe, embracing political and economic relations and security. The CSCE process and its agreements must become the Magna Carta for stability in Europe.

A CSCE summit meeting in 1990, as called for by EC foreign ministers in Dublin on January 20, is therefore an urgent necessity. That meeting could:

Reaffirm in binding form the principles embodied in the Final Act of Helsinki;

Discuss the future of our continent, common pan-European structures which would also embrace security;

Establish pan-European institutions which will foster the coalescence of Europe within the CSCE framework; and

Agree to continue the CFE and CSBM negotiations and to co-ordinate both sets of negotiations – with a view to forging co-operative security structures in Europe.

We are called on to prepare a blueprint for a peaceful order in Europe and to give it substance step by step.

Source: Federal German Embassy, London 29 January 1990

PRIME MINISTER MARGARET THATCHER

25 January 1990 in Wall Street Journal

[German unification] must come at a rate which takes account of other obligations and which gives us time to work things out – otherwise, that could destabilize everything. And if I might way so, the person to whom that would be most bitterly unfair is Mr. Gorbachev, without whom it could never have come about.

Source: Interview with *Wall Street Journal* published 25 January 1990

PRESIDENT FRANCOIS MITTERRAND

Interviewed on Italian television, 27 January 1990 (Extracts)

Q. In your end-of-year message you proposed the creation of a European confederation which would include the East European countries once they had become democratic. How can this be done in concrete terms?

THE PRESIDENT – In that same statement I said in the first place that the events in Eastern Europe and the problems they were setting us highlighted the need to strengthen the European Community of the Twelve, its structures, to give more marked expression to a common political will and therefore to acquire the instruments with which to exercise that will.

I then said that I would like a European confederation to be created once all the fast-evolving East European countries had established democratic institutions and democratic practices for themselves. Why? Because where are they, the countries such as those which were first to move into the limelight, Poland, Hungary, Yugoslavia and the others? Admittedly still within the Warsaw Pact alliance, still of course inside the order created forty-five years ago, but also outside it. Those countries are all going through a serious economic crisis and a political crisis. They are all striving towards democracy. Beside them they see the European Community, today the world's number one trading power and which, in the normal course of events, must in all areas aspire to rank very highly in world affairs.

So what is going to happen to them? Will they have to seek other alliances? To form between themselves confederations of minor States, even though all of them have always contributed to Europe's culture and history and belong to Europe geographically? They have to have a goal. That goal can't be the hope, after a given lapse of time, of joining the Community which demands constraints, abandonments of sovereignty considerable discipline and a certain economic standing. So are they to be left with nothing, the prospect of remaining isolated countries with just an agreement now and again, in a state of subordination at any rate in the economic sphere?

No, that must not be. Why not create a framework as things materialize, enabling those countries to be linked to each other – the European countries – and, through a range of contracts covering cultural exchanges, trade and common security, to have direct ties with the European Community of the Twelve and with each of its countries? I don't exclude any European States from this prospect. Those who make this choice who will exercise self-determination. I think that prospect will answer an expectation.

Q. – You said on another occasion that you hoped the Soviet Union would join in this confederation. Yet Mr. Gorbachev, who will . . .

THE PRESIDENT – I said that it was not for me to determine in advance which countries would be ready to adopt a democratic system. Any European country with democratic institutions is a potential participant in that confederation, which will be our common framework. Europe will at last recover its identity and will have successfully overcome the Yalta period. It will be itself. That's all. In fact, wasn't it in Italy that people said Italy would come into being of her own accord? It's a very fine phrase, which can be applied to Europe.

Q. – Mr. Gorbachev, whom you know very well, is in difficulties. You have always said that he must be helped. How can he be helped to cope with the serious nationalities problems facing him today?

THE PRESIDENT – We obviously cannot take over from him and the Soviet authorities the task of settling the Soviet Union's internal problems. We can, of course, say what we think and, if asked, advise, give an opinion. It seems certain, for instance, that it is in the flexibility of the Soviet institutions that Mr. Gorbachev will find an answer, not, I would say, to nationalist demands, but to the awakening of nationalities among the various peoples who today belong to the Soviet Union. Whether the answer will suffice I have no idea.

But we can't take over from him. The better the Soviet Union does economically – and there is much to be done – and the more headway we make on disarmament, i.e. on reducing the unproductive costs weighing down both the Soviet Union and ourselves, the more we shall facilitate Mr. Gorbachev's task, give him room to breathe and avoid the demands that today risk seriously compounding all the difficulties, the awakening of the nationalities, the economic crisis, the unnecessary costs, etc., etc.

The psychological aspects are more difficult. If the inhabitants of the various regions, parts of the Soviet Union feel that a system based on confidence is being re-established in Europe, that detente is growing between East and West, that prospects are improving thanks to economic aid of all kinds, agreements and trade, then the positive factor is rather more likely to outweigh the negative ones. Direct assistance in relation to the Soviet Union's internal problems is not possible, but there are possibilities of helping indirectly by creating a better climate, better channels for exchanges.

Source: French Embassy, London, 27 January 1990

SPEECH BY TADEUSZ MAZOWIECKI, PRIME MINISTER OF POLAND, TO THE COUNCIL OF EUROPE

Strasbourg, 30 January 1990

Europe is living through an exceptional period. Part of our continent torn up from its roots almost half a century ago is now aspiring to return. Back to Europe! This expression is gaining currency these days in the countries of Central and Eastern Europe. Politicians and economists are speaking of a return. The same applies to members of the cultural world, although it was easier for them to feel they still belonged to Europe: Europe was felt to be their spiritual home, a community of values and traditions. Perhaps the expression 'back to Europe' is too feeble to describe the process we are experiencing. One should speak rather of a European renaissance, the rebirth of the Europe which virtually ceased to exist after Yalta.

My presence here among you is a sign of this rebirth, a sign of the renascent feeling of European togetherness and solidarity which was all too often forgotten in the past. With these remarks, I also wish to call to mind all those among whom a sense of European community and solidarity has remained alive. I am thinking of those who publicly voiced their protest against acts of violence such as the invasion of Hungary in 1956 and of Czechoslovakia in 1968. I am also thinking of all our Western friends who, after the establishment of the state of emergency in 1981, afforded us both moral and material support. At various times throughout these difficult years for us, the personal contacts established in this way helped to create a most valuable network which still subsists and which now offers a priceless foundation for rebuilding the political and economic components of a true community with the other countries of our continent.

The Polish people are acutely aware of belonging to Europe and the European heritage. They are as conscious of this as are the other European peoples situated at the cultural crossroads adjacent to the superpowers, experiencing alternating phases of political existence and non-existence and hence feeling the need to strengthen their identity. In all these situations, Europe has always remained a beacon, an object of affection which the Poles felt ready to defend. The idea of being the 'ramparts of Christendom' and, by the same token, of Europe itself has remained alive in Poland throughout three centuries. Europe is therefore present in the Polish conscience as a value which it is worth living for and sometimes, indeed, dying for. But at the same time, Poland has borne a grudge against Europe and this sense of reproach has remained engraved to the present day in our collective consciousness. We continue to regard Europe as an ideal, the home of liberty and the rule of law, and we continue to relate closely to it, but we also continue to feel reproachful because of Yalta, because of the division of Europe and for having been left on the other side of the Iron Curtain.

Today, however, now that the return to Europe, the renaissance of Europe as a single entity is becoming more and more of a reality, we are wondering more and more frequently what we have to offer, what our contribution can be today to the European treasure house. I believe that we do have a lot to offer. Our contribution to Europe is both our strength and our weakness.

We are like someone recovering from a serious illness. For years we have undergone the tremendous pressure of totalitarianism but we have stood firm. However, we are still convalescing. Our economy is still in a critical condition which we are trying to alleviate; the democratic institutions of our state are only just being resuscitated and rebuilt. But we have acquired experience which we shall not forget and which we shall pass on to others.

If we have managed to survive as an entity, we owe this partly to our deep attachment to certain institutions and certain values regarded as the norm in Europe. We owe it to religion and the Church, our attachment to democracy and pluralism, human rights and civil liberties and to the ideal of solidarity. Even when we were unable to give these values their full potential or put them into practice in our public life, we still held them in esteem, we clung to them and struggled for them and therefore we know them and know their value. We know the price of being European, the price of the European heritage which Westerners today have inherited without even having to pay the rights of succession. We can remind them of this price. We therefore offer Europe our faith in Europe.

Today, we are lodging an application for membership of the Council of Europe. We desire to 'achieve a greater unity between its members for the purpose of safeguarding and realising the ideals and principles which are their common heritage and facilitating their economic and social progress'. We wish to share in promoting human rights and fundamental freedoms. The Council of Europe, which has performed wonders in the defence of rights and freedoms and which is a rich fountainhead of European ideas and initiatives seems the right place for Poland, which has itself achieved a great deal in the defence of these same rights and freedoms.

Ladies and gentlemen, the gash across Europe symbolised until recently by the Berlin Wall can now begin to heal. This can be a fascinating process, although undoubtedly a very complex and lengthy one. And yet today, as opposed to yesterday, the principal political requirements exist, or are taking shape, which will make this process possible.

Our country is confronted with the enormous task of reconstituting the rights and the institutions which characterise modern democracies and rebuilding a market economy, after an interruption of several decades. Added to this, there is the need to overcome enormous economic problems. We not only have to recreate rights and institutions but, in cases where they were non-existent, we have to start from scratch. Otherwise our two European worlds will never manage to live in harmony.

Poland has already set to work. The government which I have been leading for barely five months has drafted and had enacted numerous laws which provide a legal framework for the independence of the judiciary, for freedom of the press and freedom to organise, for freedom to found political parties, and for local self-government which, with the forthcoming municipal elections, will soon become effective. We are preparing a new Constitution of the Polish Republic which will become a democratic State subject to the rule of law.

Since the beginning of this year, we have embarked upon a very difficult economic programme, one which aims not only to check inflation but also to establish the foundations for a modern market economy, after the pattern of the institutions which have proved their worth in the highly developed European countries. We intend to continue along this path, successively introducing new elements, among which importance will be attributed to reforming the system of ownership and introducing certain forms of state intervention and social protection within the market economy. We shall gradually develop this system in accordance with our possibilities. We wish our future economic system to combine effective mechanisms for stimulating production with adequate protection for the social groups which require assistance within a free and competitive market economy.

Furthermore, in collaboration with our partners in the CMEA (COMECON), we have taken far-reaching steps to reform the organisation which, in our view, should be based on free consent between the states which feel it is in their interest to be members and deal jointly with matters which they believe call for concerted measures and action. We have no desire to create closed associations cut off from the rest of the world, not only by frontiers but by customs barriers. We wish to avoid this so as not to create a Europe where economic walls have replaced the political ones.

We know you also favour an outward-looking policy and this is all to the good, for otherwise there would be a hidden obstacle preventing us from making the progress towards each other, despite the desire for rapprochement which is clearly expressed in all the current appeals for an undivided Europe.

Just as the Berlin Wall not so long ago was both the symbol of the divided Europe and a physical barrier splitting Germany into two separate states, so its collapse, while offering an opportunity to unite Europe, at the same time raises the problem of German unification. No people can be denied the right to live within the same state. But the division of Germany resulted from a major disaster caused by the Nazi state which destroyed tends of millions of human lives. It is therefore not at all surprising today if, at a time when the prospect is emerging of a reunited German state, the memory of this disaster arouses anxieties which cannot be alleviated even by obviously weighty counter-arguments such as the fact that today the situation is different and the Germans themselves are different. We acknowledge these arguments. But we must understand these anxieties and overcome them by settling the German question with the agreement of all the interested parties and in a manner which, from the outset, will offer a credible sense of security to all those who require it and which above all will guarantee the inviolability of the Western frontier of Poland.

The upheavals in Central Europe and the Soviet Union are creating unparalleled opportunities but also carry risks. In some countries the supporters of the old regime are no longer in a position to determine the course of events but can still impede it. In others, although they are on the defensive, they have not given up hope, and have not lost the capability, of regaining their former position. If severe symptoms of destabilisation, together with economic chaos, were to persist, these people's chances would increase. They will diminish if the peoples in our region, who at the moment are proving active, can carry through the crucial transformations resolutely but as calmly as possible, and above all if they can resist the temptation to try to achieve everything at once. That approach is often counterproductive.

Another danger is that of Balkanisation of part of the European continent, or of the various countries, because of acute tensions between the peoples or states, tensions whose origins lie in the present as well as the past. If partisan or national interests were to surface and the notion of regional or European interest were to be lost sight of, it would be a major obstacle to establishing healthy co-operation and mutual understanding in this continent of ours which is in the throes of change.

But the events unfolding in Central and Eastern Europe, although they carry risks, are first and foremost an unbelievable and historic challenge. And although obviously the challenges are mainly for us, the people of Central Europe, they are also a historic challenge and a task for the whole of Europe. The scope is vast. There is room for Western Europeans who see what we are trying to do and believe in our aims. With them – with you – it will be easier to narrow the distance between us. The wall which divided free Europe from enslaved Europe is down. Now we have to fill in the gulf between poor Europe and affluent Europe. If Europe is to be a 'common home' whose door is open to all, such great disparities cannot be allowed to continue. A huge job of work awaits us all.

We now need new guidelines to point our endeavours down a common European road, to no-one's exclusion and everyone's advantage.

It is not easy to chart such a course, for it takes thought and collaboration. But as, in your part of the continent, post-1992 Europe is even now taking shape, why not start thinking in terms of a Europe of the year 2000? To be realistic, what kind of Europe might that be if we unite our efforts?

It will certainly not be a European area with free movement of goods, capital and people but it might be a Europe where borders and tariffs would be much less of an obstacle, a Europe wholly open to the young. For the fate of our continent depends on what kind of young people we bring up.

It might be a Europe in which contact between the creative and the scientific communities, fostering permeability of national cultures and thereby bringing them closer together, will be richer than it is today.

It will not be a Europe with a common currency but it might be a Europe in which economies will be complementary and where differences in living standards will be smaller and international economic exchange richer.

It might also be a Europe with a healthy climate, pure water and unpolluted soil, an environmentally clean Europe.

But above all it will have to be a Europe which has made distinct progress towards disarmament, a Europe which will make an impact on the rest of the world as a factor for peace and international co-existence.

By applying our minds, we could find many other spheres of social life which we could arrange better in this last decade of the 20th century. We need but apply ourselves to the task.

In this continent of ours there are institutions in which a labour of this kind has long-term prospects, because it has already been going on quite a while. One of these institutions is the Council of Europe, one of whose aims is to achieve greater unity among its members for the purpose of safeguarding and realising the ideals and principles which are their common heritage and facilitating their economic and social progress.

Now that events are speeding up in Europe, it is beginning to be possible for us – states, groups and organisations – to reflect about these matters together, and we can glimpse the possibility of and need for pan-European structures to take change of these tasks.

I think the time has come to realise the 'common home' and the European confederation which eminent statesmen have recently proposed. It is time to establish institutions genuinely encompassing the whole of Europe.

That is why I would draw attention to the suggestion I recently put forward in our parliament, for a Council for European Co-operation, embracing all signatories to the Final Act of the Conference on Security and Co-operation in Europe. The council would have two functions: firstly to make preparations for summit meetings of the CSCE states and secondly to examine pan-European problems arising in between regular meetings of CSCE states. We think this would lend needed impetus to the CSCE process and at the same time facilitate future initiatives concerning our continent and aiming to secure its unity.

I am addressing you in Strasbourg, the capital of Europe. A city which, like our country, has often been caught up in the turmoil of history. A city which has several times changed hands and has wondered about its identity. But also a city which, though the capital of a region which has been fought over since time immemorial, a place that has suffered the ravages of revolution, is now an oasis of peace and prosperity. This city is a symbol of hope for us who live in the heart of Europe, where echoes of age-old quarrels are still audible. Today the whole of Europe is faced with the historic challenge of restoring its unity. Will we be equal to it? That depends on us and on you. Over a year ago, Pope John Paul II, addressing the Parliamentary Assembly, said:

> The member countries of your Council are aware that they are not the whole of Europe: in expressing the fervent wish for intensification of co-operation, already sketched out, with other nations, particularly in Central and Eastern Europe, I feel that I share the desire of millions of men and women who know that they are linked by a common history and who hope for a destiny of unity and solidarity on the scale of this whole continent.

When he said this, probably no-one suspected the climate would become auspicious and that his hopes would begin to be realisable.

Among Strasbourg's many symbols, on the cathedral façade, are statues of the wise virgins and the foolish virgins. Let us be wise virgins. Let us be capable of recognising a historic juncture and rising to its challenge – cautiously, boldly and clear-sightedly.

Source: Text issued by Polish Government, 30 January 1990

SPEECH BY FOREIGN MINISTER HANS-DIETRICH GENSCHER, AT A CONFERENCE OF THE TUTZING PROTESTANT ACADEMY

31 January 1990

To serve world peace, to be an equal partner in a united Europe, and to preserve their national and political unity, that is the mandate which the German people have been given by their constitution. Our constitution thus places our national objective in the European context and evokes our responsibility for peace. That constitutional mandate is a renunciation of the power politics of the past; it requires us to pursue a policy of responsibility.

As early as 1953 Thomas Mann impressively stated what that means: We want not a German Europe but a European Germany. The Germans in the GDR are in the process of defining their position on Germany's and Europe's future. The programmes of the parties who intend to contest the election on 18 March show that they, like ourselves, seek a united Germany in Europe.

The people taking part in the peaceful demonstrations are in many ways even more insistent than the party programmes. On the evening of 18 March the world will be in a better position to judge which way the people in the GDR want to go. We will know as a result of their decision taken in free, secret and equal elections, and we will know more accurately because the central theme of the election campaign, apart from the future economic and social order, will be the question of national unity.

It would be a mistake to assume that nothing or only little can be done before then. The coalescence and interlocking of political, social and economic forces is proceeding at full speed; unification from below is in progress. Many individual contacts are developing, tourism and twinnings are increasing. These links are being established right down to club level. They are creating irreversible facts.

This intra-German saturation is by no means a one-way street from West to East. I repeat what I have said before: Nothing will again be like it was, either in the GDR, or here, or anywhere else in Europe. The political culture in the Federal Republic of Germany is bound to be influenced by the fundamental democratic awakening in the GDR. Here, too, more and different questions are again being asked. Many of them present themselves in a new light, new ones arise. This calls for a new thinking on our side, too, and some of the affirmations of German unity will still have to pass the litmus test.

Cooperation between the two states is already possible and urgently necessary. Assistance for the development of infrastructure and tele-communications, environmental protection and radical improvements in medical care, brooks no delay. The GDR's social insurance system requires support from us if it is not to collapse.

The effectiveness of private investment depends largely on the extent of the economic reforms which the acting government decides to carry out. By private investment we mean investment by the Germans in the GDR themselves and investment from the West. Economic reforms are also called for in order to establish the foundations for an urgently required economic and monetary union between the two German states. Good pay for good work is a legitimate demand for GDR citizens too. Everything I have mentioned here can be started now.

'Unity in national solidarity' can and must start immediately. It is unity being brought about by practical steps. It does not infringe upon the rights of any other country. It does not violate any of the treaties and agreements between the two German states. Nor does it affect their respective alliances. Much more can be achieved in practice than most people presume.

'Unity in national solidarity' developing in this way lies within the perspective of the unification of the two German states. It will open up real prospects for the Germans in the GDR. This is urgently necessary in view of the growing numbers of resettlers from there. Their departure creates problems for the Federal Republic of Germany, too, of course, though probably to a lesser extent, thanks to its huge capacity for integration, than an excited public discussion suggests. The real problem arises in the GDR which, owing to quantitative and qualitative erosion, will have additional difficulties to cope with.

Through 'unity in national solidarity' we can anticipate much of political unity. In giving practical assistance we have no time to lose. The bringing forward of the election for the People's chamber to 18 March means that in less than two months it will be possible to continue the negotiations with a democratically elected government.

In this phase the policy of the Federal Republic of Germany should be to increase public awareness of the need for sizeable contributions to enable the GDR to make a new beginning and to start with those contributions as soon as possible.

German unity cannot be had for nothing – either economically, financially or politically – this last aspect I shall be referring to again later. But it can already be said that all this assistance will be more advantageous to the Germans in East and West in the long run than a continuous and possibly increasing flow of resettlers. It will also help ensure stability in the GDR and hence in Europe.

Our determination to develop wide-ranging cooperation with the GDR and to provide assistance will not be at the expense of our cooperation with the other countries of Central and Eastern Europe. The revolution for freedom in 1989 has evinced a close connection between the movements towards freedom in the Warsaw Pact countries. This is also true of their consistency, their momentum, and their success. Any stagnation or failure of the reform and democratization process in one country may have serious repercussions for the others.

If de facto and through intra-German agreements a great deal can already be done today, prior to 18 March, then after that date the time will have come to determine the future relationship between the two German states and the future of the German nation through their democratically elected goverments.and parliaments.

The statements made by Soviet Foreign Minister Shevardnadze in December 1989 and January 1990, and especially yesterday's statement by President Gorbachov concerning the unification of the two German states, reflect an accurate analysis, a sense of realismf and far-sightedness. They open the way to a constructive European and intra-German policy aimed at vigorous progress on a stable basis.

The Basic Treaty incorporates a *modus vivendi* as regards the future of the Germans. Side by side are the Federal Republic's insistence on national unity and the GDR's insistence on the permanent existence of two states. A further treaty will have to provide the answer to the question of Germany's future and determine the route to national unity. It will have to create the framework for the process of German unification. It should not put this process in a straitjacket, nor should it apply any constraints as regards the time factor. By concluding such a 'treaty charting the course to German unity in Europe' the two governments will be fulfilling the hopes of the Germans. They would be well advised to let the people in both German states elect a constituent assembly and thus give them an opportunity to voice their opinion at the right time.

The draft of such a treaty charting the course will vest intra-German relations with a quality which will no longer affect us Germans alone. That new quality will have to make allowance for Europe's structure and architecture. It touches upon the four-power responsibility for Germany, and the present alliances.

Both German states are therefore called upon to give not only a German but also a European response as they pursue the goal of national unity. Those responses must dovetail with Europe's future architecture.

That is the Germans' European vocation. It originates in German history, in Germany's geographical position, and in Germany's importance for future developments in Europe. The Germans thus have an opportunity to provide the thrust on the way to ending the division of Europe. The aim, therefore, is to develop the German framework for the process of unification, and the European framework within which that process can take place.

The aim is to define Germany's position in a future Europe. This issue is of greater concern to our European neighbours than the details of the German unification process.

Let there be no doubt: We Germans, like all Europeans, want more security and stability, not less. We do not want to be united to the detriment of others. The question we Germans have to answer is: What should be united? The answer is obvious: The two German states including Berlin. No more, but no less.

The first joint act by the two freely elected German parliaments and governments must be a declaration guaranteeing the frontiers of all our neighbours. The Federal Republic of Germany will then have to answer the question what happens as far as its membership of the European Community and the Western Alliance is concerned if Germany is united. The answer is clear: Our membership of the European Community will remain irrevocable. So too will our determination to continue the process of integration leading to political union. The same applies to our membership of the Western Alliance. We do not want a united, neutralist Germany.

The European Community will be one of the components of a European peaceful order stretching from the Atlantic to the Urals, the common European house. It is already an anchor of European stability. The Soviet Union and the other European members of COMECON are recognizing this fact by their energetic efforts to intensify relations with the European Community. Cooperation and association agreements are to be negotiated. Some of these countries view cooperation and association in the perspective of subsequent membership.

The President of the European Commission, M. Jacques Delors, has proposed three options for the GDR, all of which take account of the GDR's special relationship with the Community since it was established. They are:

1. a cooperation and association agreement;
2. an application for membership on which the two sides, as an exception to the general rule, could negotiate before 1 January 1993;
3. entry into the European Community via union with the Federal Republic of Germany.

These three options the GDR will have to decide upon for itself after 18 March. The acting government has already decided in favour of the first option in its aide mémoire of 24 November 1989.

These options for the GDR should be accompanied by realistic community options for all European COMECON countries, including the Soviet Union:

1. Trade, cooperation and association agreements as well as political consultations with EPC.
2. Participation in the work of the international economic and financial institutions such as GATT, IMF, World Bank and

OECD. Participation in stages, including observer status, may be expedient.
3. Membership of or observer status in the Council of Europe. Accession to the European Human Rights Convention and the extension of cooperation within the European Court of Human Rights to the whole of Europe.
4. Membership of the newly founded European Development Bank with all rights and obligations.

These possibilities can help considerably to form a Europe-wide network of economic and financial cooperation. This will be conducive to the unity of all Europe. It is at the same time part of the process of embedding German unification in the European structure. The pan-European network of cooperation must have as its framework the CSCE process. The pan-European architecture will grow from the CSCE process. The CSCE framework must provide the stability framework for the dynamic, dramatic and in some respects revolutionary developments in Central and Eastern Europe including the Soviet Union.

An East-West partnership to maintain stability is now called for. The CSCE process must serve as the foundation for that partnership. All CSCE participating states must want to maintain the momentum of development in stable conditions. The Western offer of partnership for stability, which has a political, economic and security dimension, is a significant contribution to the success of the process of reform and democratization.

In view of developments within COMECON and the Warsaw Pact it will be necessary to give special attention to the security interests of the Soviet Union. We cannot clearly foretell the results of developments in Central and Eastern Europe, but there are two trends:

1. The European members of COMECON, including the Soviet Union, are increasingly focusing on the European Community, a fact which can be taken into account by the treaty policy I have mentioned. This is a contribution to stabiflity, especially as regards the operation launched by the Group of 24.
2. In the Warsaw Pact countries Poland, Czechoslovakia and Hungary there is a growing demand for the withdrawal of Soviet forces. We cannot say for sure at present what impact this will have on the structure, and on the future, of the Warsaw Pact. This matter solely concerns the Warsaw Pact. The principle of non-interference must be taken particularly seriously in this respect.

What NATO must do is state unequivocally that whatever happens in the Warsaw Pact there will be no expansion of NATO territory eastwards, that is to say, closer to the borders of the Soviet Union. This security guarantee is important for the Soviet Union and its conduct. It must also be the Western perception that the transformation in

Eastern Europe and the process of German unification must not be allowed to impair Soviet security interests.

Creating the necessary basis for this will require a large measure of European statesmanship. Any proposals for incorporating the part of Germany at present forming the GDR in NATO's military structures would block intra-German rapprochement. The important thing is to clearly define the future role of the two alliances. They will move away from confrontation towards cooperation and will become elements of cooperative security structures throughout Europe.

The Western Alliance will – according to the will of its members – continue to exist since the alliances will continue to have a peace-keeping and stabilizing function. This also means that we will remain a member of NATO. German neutralism would benefit no one.

Through its involvement in the CSCE process the United States shares responsibility for Europe's future. Both superpowers consider America's participation important and useful, as was confirmed at the recent US-Soviet summit in Malta. The American role in maintaining security and stability in Europe depends on the continued existence of the Western Alliance, whereas the Soviet Union's role is already determined by its size and position in Europe and by the landmass on the Euro-Asian side.

But both alliances are called upon to define their role more and more along political lines. The armed forces will play an increasing role in the process of confidence building and verification. The part played by the alliances in the pursuit of disarmament and stability should not be underrated, especially in the current phase of development. The development of cooperative security structures – in which the alliances could later be absorbed – must provide the contractual basis for the alliances' progress from confrontation to cooperation.

Their missions and doctrines must keep abreast of political developments. If those developments proceed faster the alliances will lose their stabilizing influence. In assessing the threat from the East and the balance of power the West should not disregard the emergence of democracies in the Warsaw Pact. Nor should Eastern Europe ignore the fact that the West, as an alliance of democracies, has neither the intention nor the capability to attack the East.

Nor must the disarmament process be allowed to lag behind political developments. Without resolute steps towards disarmament there can be no united Europe and no united Germany. No one can get by this fact.

The purpose of disarmament is to secure drastic reductions of the military elements of the East-West relationship and to cut forces to the absolute minimum necessary for self-defence. The American initiatives towards reducing conventional forces are major contributions to the achievement of this objective.

But the forces of the basing countries must also be included in Vienna II. Here it is becoming clear that the Soviet policy of greater openness makes bold disarmament steps possible. The Vienna I conventional disarmament negotiations must be followed without a break by Vienna II negotiations. The same applies to the Vienna negotiations on confidence-building measures. Here, too, Vienna I must be followed immediately by Vienna II. Once the implementation of Vienna I begins, the way is clear for negotiations on short-range nuclear missiles. Nuclear artillery must also be included in disarmament. If 1990 is to become the year of disarmament, the two Vienna I agreements must be concluded by the end of the year. The same applies to the global ban on chemical weapons and the halving of the two superpowers' strategic nuclear arsenals.

The CSCE summit, at which the two Vienna disarmament agreements are to be signed, will mark the beginning of a new chapter in European history. At their meeting in Dublin, the EC foreign ministers agreed on such a summit. France and the Federal Republic of Germany regard the holding of the summit in 1990 as an important contribution to stability and East-West rapprochement. I appeal to all countries to recognize its importance and to make the institutional preparations.

This summit will differ significantly from all previous CSCE meetings, especially the 1975 conference in Helsinki. At that time countries from antagonistic systems with confrontational security policies came together at the conference table, alongside the neutral and non-aligned countries. They adhered to different values and hence to completely divergent political and social orders. In retrospect, the adoption of the final Act seems like a miracle. The faith that the Final Act's supporters had in its momentum was borne out, and the faintheartedness of its opponents refuted. The disinterest of those who voted for the Final Act but did not take it very seriously was very quickly superseded by keen interest.

The relationship between the two German states then was as antagonistic as that between the alliances to which they belong. And yet they had made an indispensable contribution to bringing about the Helsinki conference. The Federal Republic of Germany had concluded treaties with the Soviet Union, Poland, Czechoslovakia and with the GDR. The Quadripartite Agreement on Berlin had been signed. But the two German states had different ideas about a common German future. This time the CSCE summit will not be marked by a spirit of confrontation between the 35 countries. This applies politically, economically and militarily. And it must be borne in mind that concepts now coincide. That the commitment to human rights and human dignity enshrined in the Helsinki Final Act is beginning to become reality everywhere. Without wishing to anticipate the results of the GDR elections – this remains the sovereign decision of the people in the GDR – it can be assumed that at the conference table of the 1990 CSCE summit there will be two democratically elected German governments, which will be at one in their quest for unity and will already have embarked on the road to that goal. Their attitude will to a decisive extent again determine whether a new chapter can be started in the history of Europe. Once more the European mission and shared responsibility of the Germans must prove their worth. They must be a driving force for strengthening and intensifying the CSCE process, East-West cooperation and disarmament.

At this summit we shall have to discuss the future structure of Europe, whether it is to be structured in a confederate manner and whether this confederate order should ultimately lead to European federalism. President Mitterrand's call for a European confederation is an important and constructive contribution. What form should cooperative security structures take? We Germans will have to make it clear what shape Germany's future should have. The basic elements of a treaty on German unity in Europe should be defined by then. The CSCE summit can also contribute towards an East-West partnership for stability and a peaceful European order by dealing with the establishment of European institutions, such as:

1. An institution to coordinate East-West ceconomic cooperation. The European Development Bank must also be seen in this context.
2. A pan-European institution for the protection of human rights. The application of the Council of Europe's human rights convention to the whole of Europe suggests itself.
3. A centre for the creation of a European legal area aimed at legal harmonization.
4. A European environment agency.
5. The extension of EUREKA cooperation to the whole of Europe.
6. Collaboration between ESA and corresponding Eastern institutions.
7. A centre to develop European telecommunications.
8. A centre to develop European transport infrastructure and policy.
9. A European verification centre.
10. A European conflict-management centre.

To keep the CSCE process moving, one might also set up a council for foreign ministers of the CSCE countries, which would meet at regular intervals.

It will be essential that by deepening and reinforcing the CSCE process all participating states are prepared to create a framework of stability and network of security for foreseeable and unforeseeable developments in Europe. This includes an assurance by all participants that they will not strive for unilateral advantages at any stage and that they will strive for security through cooperation and not through confrontation. We must vigorously work for a peaceful European order from the Atlantic to the Urals, for the construction of the common European house.

The process of German unification must be placed in this context.

I realize that in neighbouring countries there exists a fear that the Germans will play a dominant role. This fear is unjustified in respect of Germans living in freedom and democracy. It can be dispelled still further by the resolute advancement of integration within the European Community and by pan-European integration, i.e. in the CSCE and disarmament process. But the pan-European process of unification requires the active and constructive participation of everyone concerned. We Germans seek this integration. Here at home there are some who fear the CSCE summit might become a conference on Germany. This, too, I consider unjustified, provided that we Germans in the two states are determined to make it a conference for overcoming the division of Europe and hence a conference for German unity, too.

German unity will not be achieved without Europe, and European unity will not bypass the Germans. The Germans should not therefore refuse to participate in Europe, nor should the Europeans refuse to participate in Europe so as to slow down the process of intra-German rapprochement. The convergence of the Germans in an ordered European framework is just as important for Europe's stability as a stable framework for the revolutionary developments in Central and Eastern Europe. Within such a framework of stability the process of German unification, to be defined in the 'treaty on German unity in Europe', can take place without causing a shift in the balance of power or destabilization in Europe. We owe it to Gorbachov to create a stable framework for Europe.

The offer of a partnership for stability must include not only the political and disarmament dimensions, but also the economic dimension. The Federal Republic of Germany will use its economic potential to this end. And we owe it to the peaceful revolutions for freedom not to upset the process of democratization by the old bloc-based approach, by national egoism or power politics of the past.

A European-minded Federal Republic of Germany faces its national and European responsibility in its commitment to German and European unity. The Germans in the GDR are just as good Europeans as we are. All countries in Europe can perceive that the yearning of the Germans in the GDR for German unity is growing ever stronger. That coincides with the feelings on our side. 'We are the people; Germany, a single fatherland' – this must not be overheard by anyone, by any state or government, in a Europe of self-determination and democracy. And nobody must overlook the fact that, given its economic and political problems, the GDR may become a threat to stability in Europe if it has no realistic prospect of unification. Gorbachov realizes this. Nobody benefits if developments in the GDR move away from intra-German and European policy. The present situation is not the outcome of an irresponsible policy pursued by the Federal Republic of Germany, but the legacy of 40 years of SED rule.

We do not want to go it alone or to follow a separate German path. We follow our path with a sense of responsibility for Europe. We seek a dynamic development in conditions of stability. We appeal to our neighbours in West and East to open up the European perspective together with us. We want to place the process of German unification in the context of EC integration, of the CSCE process, the West-East partnership for stability, the construction of the common European house and the creation of a peaceful European order from the Atlantic to the Urals. The Germans, who pin their hopes on Europe, must not have their European aspirations dashed. The nations of Europe should realize that we Germans want nothing but to live in peace and freedom with all our neighbours. New thinking and a sense of responsibility are demanded of everyone – first and foremost of us Germans, but not of us alone.

Source: Text issued by West European Union, 31 January 1990

PRESIDENT GEORGE BUSH: STATE OF THE UNION ADDRESS

31 January 1990 (Excerpts)

Nearly 40 years ago, in his last address to the Congress, President Harry Truman predicted such a time would come. He said: 'As our world grows stronger, more united, more attractive to men on both sides of the iron curtain, then inevitably there will come a time of change within the communist world.'

Today, that change is taking place.

For more than 40 years, America and its allies held Communism in check, and ensured that democracy would continue to exist. Today, with Communism crumbling, our aim must be to ensure democracy's advance. To take the lead in forging peace and freedom's best hope – a great and growing commonwealth of free nations.

To the Congress and to all Americans, I say it is time to acclaim a new consensus at home and abroad – a common vision of the peaceful world we want to see.

Here in our own hemisphere, it is time for all the people of the Americas – North and South – to live in freedom.

In the Far East and Africa, it is time for the full flowering of free governments and free markets that have served as the engine of progress.

It is time to offer our hand to the emerging democracies of Eastern Europe. So that continent – for too long a continent divided – can see a future whole and free.

And it's time to build on our new relationship with the Soviet Union – to endorse and encourage a peaceful process of internal change toward democracy and economic opportunity.

We are in a period of great transition, great hope, yet great uncertainty. We recognize that the Soviet military threat in Europe is diminishing, but we see little change in Soviet strategic modernization. Therefore, we must sustain our own strategic offense modernization and the Strategic Defense Initiative.

But the time is right to move forward on a conventional arms control agreement to move us to more appropriate levels of military forces in Europe – a coherent defense program that ensures the United States will continue to be a catalyst for peaceful change in Europe. I've consulted with leaders of NATO – and in fact, I spoke by phone with President Gorbachev, just today.

I agree with our European allies that an American military presence in Europe is essential – and that it should not be tied solely to the Soviet military presence in Eastern Europe. But troop levels can still be lower. So tonight, I am announcing a major new step – for a further reduction in US and Soviet manpower in Central and Eastern Europe to 195,000 on each side. This number reflects the advice of our senior military advisors. It is designed to protect American and European interests – and sustain NATO's defense strategy. A swift conclusion to our arms control talks – conventional, chemical and strategic – must now be our goal. That time has come.

Source: United States Information Service, 1 February 1990

OBSERVATIONS BY PRIME MINISTER HANS MODROW ON GERMAN UNITY

1 February 1990

In these days and weeks the European peoples look to the two German states. The complicated process of democratic renewal in the GDR and the future relations between the GDR and the FRG exercise considerable influence on the Europe of today and of this decade. More than ever, peace, security and stability on this continent hinge on how the Germans succeed in solving their problems. For this I am submitting a blueprint.

Germany is to become a united fatherland to all citizens of the German nation again. It takes a sense of responsibility, circumspection and an awareness of what is feasible and bearable for Europe to ensure that Germany will never again be a threat to the existence and welfare of its neighbours.

This can be assured if German relations are bound tightly into the development of Europe as a whole. To the extent that the GDR and the FRG in their quest for a new quality of their cooperation and for drawing closer together see themselves as part of the process of European unification, they will mould their common future for the good of their peoples rather than to the detriment and at the expense of others.

What is needed therefore is to give a sense of direction to the understandable urging of large parts of the population in both states so that a peaceful development will be possible with the discernible prospect of a reasonable time-frame for the unification of the two German states. The way the necessary steps are coped with will determine that time-frame.

The GDR has in the past repeatedly tabled concrete proposals on the restoration of German unity. Those proposals, including the one for a German confederation, did not however meet with an adequare response at that time. It must not be permitted that the chance we have today of achieving dramatic qualitative changes in German-German relations is again left unused and that the practicable road to that goal is blocked by unbalanced or illegal demands.

As a matter of logic and purpose the process of German unification will be closely bound up with the creation of the European home and the European confederation. That European home must have no room for strong-arm politics. The understanding is that as early as at the confederative stage both German states, step by step, disengage from their obligations as allies of third countries and that they attain a status of military neutrality. The border between the GDR and the FRG will then cease to be the dividing line between the two military blocs with everything that this entails.

The blueprint entitled 'For Germany – United Fatherland', which I am going to propose to you, envisages that the two German states move together step by step and in a way that is transparent and calculable for the European peoples. Nothing must happen that would run counter to efforts to overcome the partition of Europe and create new dangers. Existing all-European structures like the CSCE process should serve as a framework.

The blueprint offers suggestions as to how the division of the German nation could be conceived in the context of a European order of peace. This opens up entirely new prospects for disarmament in Europe and beyond. Germany, but not Germany alone, has a real chance of ridding itself of weapons of mass destruction. It is the purpose of all this, and I know that many politicians and countless citizens of both German states feel the same, that the German's achieve the unity of their fatherland through free self-determination and that that process be embedded in the common effort for a peaceful and cooperative Europe.

Europe is entering a new stage of its development. The post-war chapter is being closed. The conditions for peaceful and good-neighbourly cooperation among all peoples are taking shape. The unification of the two German states is being put on the agenda.

The German people will find its place in the construction of a new order of peace where both the partition of Europe into two hostile camps and the division of the German nation will have been overcome. The hour has come for closing the book on the Second World War and concluding a German peace treaty. It would settle all issues that are related to the agression of Hitler Germany and the downfall of the Third Reich.

A final solution to the German question can only be achieved through the free self-determination of the Germans in both states, cooperation with the four powers, and by taking account of the interests of all European states. It must be a solution that encourages the European process which is to free our continent from military dangers once and for all. The drawing together of the two German states and their subsequent unification must not be taken as a threat by anybody.

This prompts me to propose a national dialogue inspired by a sense of responsibility. Its object should be to identify concrete steps which lead to a unified Germany destined to become a new factor of stability, confidence and peace in Europe.

Through such a dialogue and equality-based negotiations represent-atives of the GDR and the FRG could try and find best possibile answers to the question about the future of the German nation.

Steps on the road to German unity could be the following:

- Conclusion of a treaty on cooperation and good-neighbourliness as a contractual community, which should already contain essential confederative elements like an economic, currency, transport and communications union as well as the harmonization of legal provisions.
- Establishment of a confederation between the GDR and the FRG including joint authorities and institutions such as a parliamentary committee, an assembly of the lander, and joint executive bodies in certain areas.
- Transfer of sovereign rights of the two states to authorities of the confederation.
- Establishment of a single German state in the form of a German federation or a German 'bund' following elections in both parts of the confederation, convening of a single parliament which would decide on a single constitution and a single government having its seat in Berlin.

Necessary prerequisites for this course of action would be:

- Each of the two German states takes care that any steps towards German unity can be reconciled with their obligations vis-a-vis other countries or groups of countries and with what is necessary in terms of reforms and changes. That includes the division of the GDR into lander. The maintenance of stability, law and order internally is just as indispensable as the strict observance of treaties concluded earlier between the GDR and the FRG and which provide, among other things, for non-interference into each other's affairs.
- Upholding the interests and rights of the four powers and the concern of all peoples of Europe for peace, sovereignty and secure borders. The four powers should declare that they intend, once a single German state is formed, to definitively settle all issues arising from the Second World War and the post-war period, including the presence of foreign troops on German soil and the affiliation to military alliances.
- Military neutrality of the GDR and the FRG on the road to becoming a federation.

The process of the unification of the Germans evolves on the basis of agreements between the parliaments and governments of the GDR and the FRG. All sides give expression to their will to engage in political debate in democratic and non-violent form and create the necessary guarantees, including by plebiscite.

This blueprint is pledged to what has been handed down from our common history and recent past in the way of democratic, patriotic and progressive ideas and movements to the benefit of the unity of the German nation. It is pledged to the humanist and anti-fascist traditions of the German people.

This blueprint turns to the citizens of the GDR and the FRG, to all European peoples and states and to world public opinion with the request for their support.

Source: Embassy of the German Democratic Republic, London. Press Release, 2 February 1990

SPEECH BY BRENT SCOWCROFT, ASSISTANT TO PRESIDENT BUSH FOR NATIONAL SECURITY AFFAIRS, WEHRKUNDE CONFERENCE

3 February 1990

We have seen breathtaking changes since the last Wehrkunde Conference – changes of a kind that the allies have long worked to bring
about. We now face an unprecedented opportunity to reduce the
military confrontation in Europe, and – if present trends continue – to
achieve a strategic transformation.

Here is how we plan to go about it:

- As Dick Cheney told our Senate on Thursday, we will continue to
anchor our strategy in the enduring principles of deterrence, flexible
response, forward defense, strong alliances, and prudent arms
reductions. The extraordinary year just past – the 'Revolution of
1989', as President Bush called it – does not mean we should
abandon this strategic foundation.
- Within this framework, some adjustments in the infrastructure for US
forces in Europe are being made, as you have heard, in our new
budget. We hope to achieve efficiencies through modernizing and
consolidating functions, in consultation with allied governments.
But these adjustments do not reduce our capabilities – or commitments. The big decisions on our force posture in Europe remain
linked to the negotiation on conventional armed forces (CFE) – in
which the president just made an important new initiative with allied
concurrence. Our adaptation to a reduced threat will be a deliberate
process, conducted by consensus and guided by a sound assessment of the security requirements of the new environment.
- The United States intends to remain engaged in Europe with a
substantial military and political presence. We are a European
power, with an abiding and permanent interest in European security.
As the president said in Brussels, our forces will stay as long as
needed in the common effort. Whatever the level of Soviet forces
deployed outside their borders, the United States has an enduring
responsibility to remain here – as a counterweight to the Soviet
Union's permanent, geographical advantage on this continent. That
too, is part of the philosophy of our new CFE position. As Foreign

Minister Genscher said recently, the American presence is a 'pre-condition for peace and stability.' History has taught Americans – and, I believe, Europeans – that our destiny is intertwined with yours.
- Since its inception, the alliance has adapted to change and served many goals, political as well as military. One of its original aims was to shield the process of West European recovery – and integration; since the Harmel report it has also helped frame our common approaches to the East. Today it faces a qualitatively new situation; we need to do some hard thinking. Yet, we know the alliance is grounded in common values. Unlike the Warsaw Pact, it is a natural framework for cooperation in a new era of diplomacy.
- Finally, America will remain engaged as a global power. Part of the adjustment in our defense posture will be toward active forces that are smaller, more global in their orientation, and having a degree of agility, readiness, and sustainability appropriate to the demands of likely contingencies. It will not be a retreat into isolation.

This is the American resolve – to remain engaged; to help maintain the balance of power; and to be partners in change.

A New Europe

Today, as we look around us, we see so many things changing in the political map of Europe. Some of the most important things are happening in Western Europe. We categorically support West European integration on fundamental strategic grounds. As the president has said, there is no ambivalence about that in his administration. The strengthening of Europe strengthens the West. European unity has healed old enmities and promoted unparalleled prosperity. Today we can see the European Community as the core of a new Europe – a magnet to the East Europeans, a powerhouse of progress that, by sheer economic dynamism, will help overcome Europe's division.

We not only support your economic unity; we also support West European political and defense cooperation, and we hope to develop new forms of political cooperation with you as you develop your own. We should try, as Secretary of State Baker has suggested, to strengthen the institutional and consultative links between the United States and the EC.

The scope of change in Eastern Europe is, of course, a political earthquake. This year will be a year of free elections throughout Eastern Europe – what an extraordinary development. And it will probably see communist parties removed from office throughout the region by peaceful means – even more extraordinary.

The underlying change here is really the change in Soviet policy. The Soviet Union, having embarked on a course of promoting reform in Eastern Europe, wisely chose not to resist the popular will in these countries even when it went far beyond Moscow's probable original intentions.

Soviet policy changed because the burden of empire became too great. Aggressive Soviet foreign policies of the past were discredited by failure. Their quest for military superiority failed because the West rebuilt its strength and demonstrated its solidarity. Soviet domestic policies were discredited by economic paralysis. Meanwhile, the West was charging ahead into a new technological revolution, and democracy was proving a vital force everywhere.

It happened as George Kennan foresaw in 1947: If the West stayed firm and patient and blocked Soviet advances, then sooner or later the internal stresses of their flawed system would begin to shake the structure; then we might see, as he put it, 'the breakup or the gradual mellowing of Soviet power.'

The lesson for us all is that this didn't happen by accident. No country, least of all in today's interdependent world, is immune to the environment in which it finds itself. Forty years of common fidelity to the alliance helped create the conditions that have now had their inevitable effect. The Soviet leaders deserve credit for wise decisions, but so do our own leaders over more than a generation.

Our Continuing Responsibility

If this is true, then we have a continuing responsibility – all of us. Even as we enter an era of unprecedented hope for peace, we cannot neglect the basic conditions of security that are bringing it about. Basic facts of geography don't change. Many uncertainties remain about the Soviet future. The balance of power must still be maintained – though it can be done at lower levels of forces. We must pursue firm policies that make moderation the Soviets' only choice – because other options are foreclosed. We must see the transition through, until we see thoroughgoing changes in Soviet force structure, deployments, spending levels, and policies that can't be easily reversed. We're still in the beginning stages of an enormously promising process of change.

- However, at present, Soviet strategic forces continue to be modernized across the board. While there is some sign that their programs are being adjusted to correspond with the projected START treaty, they enter the 1990s with highly advanced, mobile and modernizing force.
- For the foreseeable future, even with projected cuts, the Soviet Union will remain the preponderant military power on the Continent. Even as its economic weakness takes its toll, it will not have unlimited incentive to dismantle the military strength that represents its main claim to great power status.

We will still live in a nuclear world. Nuclear deterrence has helped prevent war since 1945, and continues to do so. World history is replete with wars whose recurrence demonstrates how unreliable conventional deterrence has been.

In a new era, we have no doubt that success in reducing the strategic, conventional, and chemical threat will call for changes in alliance force posture. We need to work this out together, systematically, and not as a pell-mell stampede of unilateral national decisions.

In the political dimension, America and its allies have another common task – to manage a transition to a transformed Europe. This, too, we can only accomplish together. The EC has a pivotal role, but so does the alliance, since the political, economic, and security dimensions all overlap. We are in the midst of what will be a turbulent process in the East; there are bound to be setbacks – and even risks. The issues are so important, and our interests are so intertwined, that unilateral policies by the EC can no more succeed than unilateral policies by the United States, in our dealings with the East. There must be coordination and, in our judgement, the alliance is the natural framework.

Arms reduction is closely intertwined with the political evolution in Europe. coordination among us is imperative. It's crucial that arms reductions enhance security, and not create the sense of a power vacuum that magnifies insecurities. The CFE forum enables us all to manage the process in a way that bufilds confidence and enhances the conditions for democratic change.

President Bush is committed to rapid success in CFE. That is why he just unveiled a new proposal – to reduce US and Soviet manpower in Central and Eastern Europe to the lower ceiling of 195,000 on each side. This responds to the new realities in the region; it will help us achieve an even better outcome in CFE this year.

An important point needs to be made. Behind those numbers, there is no symmetry, in a deeper sense, between the two sides. CFE must not be used as an excuse to maintain Soviet troops where they are not wanted. America's democratic allies have made clear they want a substantial American presence. So we will remain. There is a funda-mental difference between the long overdue departure of an occupying force and the cooperation of free peoples to ensure collective security. The US force level proposed makes military sense, is designed to support forward defense and flexible response, and represents a level we intend to sustain for the foreseeable future.

The democracies have a responsibility, as well, to develop the full potential of CSCE. As the president said in Mainz, for example, it's time to broaden CSCE to promote democratic pluralism and free elections. Clearly, CSCE is one of the institutions that will help us end the division of Europe and promote freedom and security. But here, too, the West should have a common strategy.

The United States is still considering the question of a CSCE summit this year. We have already proposed a summit to sign a CFE treaty. In any case, we see value in one CSCE summit this year, not two; it should include the signing of a CFE treaty, review all three baskets, and prepare for (not replace) the next main CSCE follow-up meeting scheduled for 1992.

Strategic arms reduction, of course, is the subject of a bilateral US-Soviet negotiation. Nevertheless, the outcome will have enormous importance for Europe. Our strategic forces are – and will remain – the basis of extended deterrence. Soviet strategic forces will, even when reduced, represent a standing challenge to the balance of power. The START treaty that we seek will bolster stability as well as reduce numbers sharply. We hope for a treaty by June, and we will continue to keep our allies fully informed as the process unfolds.

Chemical weapons are another danger, particularly as they proliferate in Third World regions of festering conflict, and in conjunction with ballistic missiles to deliver them. The world's experience with this kind of warfare is grim; tragically, the inhibitions that the world labored so hard to construct earlier in this century are breaking down in some quarters. We propose to reverse this trend by seeking a global ban. The problem is complex, because of the links with legitimate commercial and scientific activities. But we must make this a priority.

America and Europe

In a new environment, there are bound to be changes in the balance of relations between America and its European allies. We need just as much creativity in this area as in negotiating with the East.

A stronger Europe could assume increased responsibility for its own defense – and here, European defense cooperation could become more important, within the alliance framework. We support the Western European Union, French-German military cooperation, and the British and French nuclear forces. We welcomed the European presence that the WEU helped organize in the Gulf. It's time for a 'European pillar' to be built in the security field – now, more so than ever.

It can be assumed that Europe will take on a greater political role as well. We welcomed the EC's active efforts in Eastern Europe. We also expect Europe to develop its global role, taking on more responsibility in diplomacy, security, and economic assistance outside of Europe, as its countries have done on an individual basis in the past. There are so many global issues on which the industrial democracies need to work together – such as trade, terrorism, the environment, energy, Third World conflicts, and proliferation of high-tech weaponry.

Our institutional mechanisms of cooperation need to be sorted out – the relationship among NATO, the EC, the G-7, the G-24, the WEU, on our side and how we relate to the East bilaterally and in CSCE. We need to be imaginative, and perhaps make some choices. But whatever the mechanisms, one thing is clear: The more equal partnership that has long been foreseen between America and Europe is now at hand.

America and Germany

Germany's role in all this is pivotal. For Germany's growing strength may be a most prominent feature of the new European balance.

President Bush has reiterated America's long-standing commitment to German self-determination and German unity. These have been common goals for 40 yers. The president spoke in Mainz of our admiration for the Federal Republic's steadfast commitment to democracy, its economic genius, and its value as a trusted ally.

No one should stand in the way of the freely and peacefully expressed will of the German people – least of all, West Germany's friends. As Chancellor Kohl has said many times, unification is a process that is consistent with and indeed facilitated by a wider process of East-West reconciliation in Europe. We see a natural evolution, already in train, supported by Germany's strong commitment to the European Community and the Atlantic alliance.

Conclusion

Taken all together, the message I have come here to deliver today about American policy is one of both continuity and change. I don't apologize for repeating traditional principles of American foreign policy, such as our commitment to NATO, nuclear deterrence, the EC, and other policies – policies that now stand vidicated. They embody enduring values that are our compass as we navigate in a world of change.

We're ready for a new era. We see a new Europe being born, conceived in democracy. We see a new structure of true security in Europe. Our new CFE initiative can bring both those goals closer. As that initiative demonstrates, America will play a part in Europe, supporting our allies and their efforts. We expect to be a major factor ourselves – a factor of security, reassurance, economic support, and, when needed, leadership.

There will be a different kind of European balance, but it need not threaten anyone. There will be a different kind of partnership between Western Europe and America, but America welcomes it. There will be a different kind of relationship between the United States and the Soviet Union, but it should be one that enhances Europe's freedom.

The outcome, however, is not foreordained. It depends on our wisdom and statesmanship. It depends also on our continued strength and solidarity as an alliance. That remains America's conviction – and America's commitment.

Source: United States Information Service, London, 12 February 1990

SPEECH BY UK
FOREIGN SECRETARY DOUGLAS HURD

Bonn, 6 February 1990 (Extracts)

For the countries of eastern Europe, the phase of smashing statues and hunting secret policemen is almost over. They are engaged now in something more difficult, namely the building of free political institutions – and something more difficult still, the building of market economies . . .

Since the future is unsettled, though no longer massively threatening, it would clearly be foolish to suppose that our defence and security problems have in some way been solved and that we need no longer to think seriously about them.

All history warns us against such empty optimism. We need now, in Europe and in the Atlantic Alliance, to undertake a rapid and rigorous review. We need to establish which of our present policies we need to retain on the grounds that they will be as important for our future as they have been for our past. Then we need to identify those policies which can and should change in order to ensure that flexibility which will be needed for our future success.

As regards the European Community, I believe that it would be sensible to think in terms of keeping steady its present basic institutions and broadly the present membership, at least for the next three years.

We have a massive workload which will test those members of those institutions to the utmost, without adding the complication of a further major round of accession negotiations. We have to complete the last great reform agreed by the Community in the Single European Act, and thus open up to our peoples the practical realisation of a citizen's Europe.

We have to create and then constantly enrich the right framework for our relationships with the newly democratic countries of eastern Europe.

The British Government believes that this is best done on the basis of individually tailored association agreements, flexibility drafted, so that their content can increase as the country concerned travels further towards the kind of market economy which makes our association more fruitful and worthwhile . . .

We need to continue and intensify the discussion within the Community about the best route towards economic and monetary union . . .

The Treaty of Rome is a charter for economic liberalism, and so is the Single European Act. The 1992 drive for a genuine Single Market has wholehearted support in Britain . . .

As regards Nato, how do we distinguish between what must be permanent and what can be adapted to new circumstances?

Adaptation includes a radical, but orderly, process of disarmament negotiations. President Bush's proposals have contributed to that . . . I would regard the following as necessary continuing attributes to NATO – its present membership; the US strategic commitment; the presence of significant stationed forces, including US, Canadian and British on the continent of Europe; a sensible mix of nuclear and conventional forces; an integrated command . . .

As far as one can see into the future, NATO offers us the promise of stability in a world which will certainly remain turbulent to the east and to the south of our part of Europe . . .

Together with the European Community, NATO offers its European members the guarantee that its members will not in future revert to conflicting, and therefore self-defeating, national policies in the fields of defence and foreign policy . . .

I also agree with the concept of a fuller political role for NATO and believe that this could be reconciled without too much difficulty with the growing importance of political co-operation within the Community of Twelve . . .

It is in the context of these themes that Germany's friends and allies consider the prospect of German unification.

We in Britain do this in a spirit of constructive friendship. We have accepted, and indeed advocated, the right of self-determination by the German people for many years. We still do.

It is inconceivable to us that of all the people in Europe, only the German people should be denied that right. That is our commitment and our conviction.

The amazing success of the Federal Republic of Germany, not just in developing its economy but in founding and maintaining the institutions of a stable democracy, has naturally enough acted as a stimulus.

It is not surprising that so many East Germans have already voted with their feet or that others might feel inclined, once they have the chance, to vote in the ballot box for a united Germany. That is a matter for them.

We, with the other friends and allies of Germany, will work with full energy and goodwill to fit their decision into the framework of a stable and harmonious Europe.

If this path is to be trodden, the first need is obviously an undisputed expression of the wish of the peoples of the FRG and the GDR: an act of self-determination.

I recently visited the GDR and realised how fragile is its stability as it seeks to move towards free elections on March 18.

It seems to me highly desirable for the stability of Europe that these elections should take place in a fair and orderly way, under a process which gives equal access to all contenders and which is sustained as widely as possible by the emerging political groups and parties within the country.

I pay tribute to the courageous men and women in the GDR who risked their freedom to bring democracy to their fellow countrymen. I also pay tribute to all those in the Federal Republic without whose political and economic support the cause of freedom could so easily have foundered.

For all the uncertainties, the prospect before you is a bright one and we in Britain share your excitement as the Berlin Wall comes down and the old, divisive order is swept away.

In the next stage, a number of highly practical problems would arise in which, as the Federal Chancellor has often pointed out, Germany's friends and neighbours would be intimately involved.

The conclusions of the European Council at Strasbourg last December, endorsed the following week by the NATO Council, set out the context, and we stand clearly by these words:

'We seek the strengthening of the state of peace in Europe in which the German people will regain its unity through free self-determination.

This process should take place peacefully and democratically, in full respect of the relevent agreements and treaties and of all the principles defined by the Helsinki Final Act, in a context of dialogue and East-West co-operation. It also has to be placed in the perspective of European integration.'

In the perspective of integration in the European Community, for example, there obviously could be no place for a command economy.

The concepts under which the GDR economy is at present run, and in particular its total dependence on subsidies and state aids, would need to be radically changed. So a period of transition would be required.

As regards NATO, it seems to me that none of us has yet begun to think with any rigour of the consequences for the Alliance of German unification, if that was the Germans' choice.

When I wrote these words a few days ago, they were true. But since then a number of interesting and constructive suggestions have been made.

If there is truth in what I have sketched above as the essential elements of NATO, then among those elements German membership will continue to be a crucial element in the security of us all.

We must together find some way of reconciling German membership of NATO with the persisting anxieties of the Soviet Union, however unrealistic we may believe these anxieties to be in view of the proven record of NATO as a defensive alliance and the proven democratic record of the Federal Republic.

These anxieties also, of course, cover the question of the eastern frontiers of Germany. I welcome the growing recognition here in the

Federal Republic of the need to use our imagination and energy in devising the best answer to this particular aspect of the problem. We shall be glad to join in this work.

These considerations are part of the reality of the situation. I believe that reasonable periods of transition would enable us to find tenable answers to the questions which will be posed if a decision in principle is taken by the inhabitants of the FRG and GDR.

The Germans, for their part, would need time to think through and resolve the many questions involved in amalgamating the two countries.

Certainly the friends and allies of Germany would have no wish to obstruct the process, and have every sympathy with the underlying aspiration.

Equally, it would not be in the interests of the German people to achieve unification in circumstances which aroused anxieties or sent nerves jangling throughout Europe. Such reconciliation would be a test which should be beyond our wits to pass.

I can readily envisage that, at the end of orderly transition, German unity and stable architecture in Europe should come about together.

Source: *Daily Telegraph*, 7 February 1990

SPEECH BY NATO SECRETARY GENERAL MANFRED WORNER

Hamburg, 8 February 1990

The question of European security is one that must now be looked at afresh. The rigid military confrontation of past decades is increasingly giving way to a concern for enhanced security and to the active pursuit of peace using a combination of military and political elements.

Two tasks have to be faced in the coming years:

- the development of a new security structure, and
- the creation of a new political order in Europe.

Both tasks are equally indispensable for the preservation and strengthening of peace in the long run.

The Alliance therefore faces a dual challenge. It must be a driving and guiding force in the dynamic process of change from the status quo, helping to establish a new continental order of peace and freedom. In the second place, it must be a source of stability, guaranteeing security in Europe, especially in the face of erratic developments in the Soviet Union and a difficult transitional period in Central and Eastern Europe.

The task of working out a new European security equation for the 21st century offers a historic opportunity. Under pressure for comprehensive change in its system the Soviet Union favours a new security order. The basic premises of Western security and stability – the presence of US troops on the European continent, the continuation of the Atlantic Alliance and an ultimate nuclear deterrent to uphold peace – are today increasingly acknowledged by the Soviet Union as being prerequisites for stability and fundamentals of a future security structure.

I believe the following points to be important:

- Only the transatlantic link, the continued integration of America in our security structures, can guarantee stability in the long term. The US commitment to European security is the cornerstone of the Western system that was created after the Second World War, and which has given us peace. Without the active participation of North America it will not be possible to balance the Germans' interest in unity, their neighbours' concern and the Soviet Union's legitimate security interests, and to reach a common position.

- The Alliance, which is the concrete expression of this transatlantic link, remains indispensable for a future security scheme. At the same time, the Alliance will still have the function of guiding the ongoing arms control process.
- The starting point for the future European security structure is provided by the Vienna negotiations. Initial results must lead to yet further reductions in force levels and new defensive structures. The latest US proposal to reduce American and Soviet troops in Central Europe to less than 200,000 shows the way. Future conventional disarmament in Europe must not remain a matter of mere bean-counting, however. It must not merely cover force levels, but also build-up capability, logistics, infrastructure, modes of deployment, force structures and exercise patterns, under conditions of increased transparency.
- A new European security equation must also comprise a residual nuclear deterrent as an ultimate guarantee of peace, with agreement on a minimum level of nuclear armament. On this point, the most recent pronouncements of Soviet spokesmen, including even Gorbachev, are encouraging.
- It is necessary to develop co-operative mechanisms to promote understanding with the East – for instance more exchanges between military academies, reciprocal troop visits, seminars to enhance shared learning.
- Comparison of NATO with the Warsaw Pact is only conceivable or useful if the latter changes fundamentally to become a voluntary alliance of free and equal partners. Until this happens the two cannot properly be equated, although they often are, through thoughtlessness or for transparent reasons. Even to refer to both these alliances as military blocs is grossly misleading. The Warsaw Pact itself is no longer a bloc, let alone NATO. The Atlantic Alliance is a free association of democratic, self-determining nations of the free world, and is purely defensive in nature. Up till now the Warsaw Pact has been a military alliance lacking the legitimation of a free expression of will by the peoples involved. We hope for a change, which would decisively improve the prospects for fruitful co-operation.
- Nevertheless we cannot and will not become guarantors of the Warsaw Pact. We are arguing neither for its dissolution nor for its continuation. Its fate will be determined by its members alone exercising free choice. This must also be allowed for in the arms control process.
- Even if the Warsaw Pact does dissolve itself that is no reason for disbanding NATO. On the contrary there is every reason to argue that our role as an agent of stability would then become even more important.
- To equate the stationing of Soviet troops in Central and Eastern Europe with the presence of American troops in Western Europe is

neither acceptable nor helpful. The American and Canadian troops are here with the agreement of free parliaments and governments. The same is not true of the Soviet forces in Central and Eastern Europe – on the contrary, the free governments of Czechoslovakia and Hungary have demanded their withdrawal. Once again, the removal of Soviet troops can and indeed will lead to the reduction of American force levels, but not to a complete US withdrawal. There are also geostrategic reasons for that. The current arms control negotiations should not be used to legitimise the presence of Soviet troops in Central and Eastern Europe against the will of the stationing countries, nor to make their withdrawal conditional on that of the North American forces.

A future European political order must build on the right of free self-determination of peoples. From the debate in the West the outlines of a European architecture for peace are already visible. It is based on existing institutions which represent the outstanding accomplishment of the post-war period:

(1) The process of European integration with its goal of political union;
(2) the Atlantic Alliance;
(3) the CSCE process.

In this context the CSCE framework for a pan-European peace systems assumes special significance. The CSCE system must be extended and deepened. Such an overarching structure, however, cannot replace but only complement the Atlantic Alliance. How should a body of 35 states, which will can exercise veto rights, really guarantee security. Only the Atlantic Alliance is able to supply the structural base for the growing European architecture, to overcome crises and conflicts which can never be excluded, even with the current changes in the European landscape. The Alliance is the umbrella under which European integration is able to grow dynamically and continually. EC and CSCE would be overburdened if they had to carry out the task of guaranteeing peace in the foreseeable time. They do not dispose of the necessary structure nor the corresponding instruments in their present and foreseeable state of evolution.

Whether we are concerned with security arrangements or a peaceful political order in Europe, we inevitably find the German question to be central.

German unity will come. We, who have striven for the triumph of democracy and for an end to the division of Europe and of Germany, must accept the crucial role of the peoples who are shaping the new order in the revolution in the East. The timetable for the achievement of German unity will not so much be determined by planners and governments as by the course of events in the GDR, as part of the tremendous restructuring of Europe, and by the free choice of the people there and in the Federal Republic. What politicians and diplomats can do is to recognise these facts and develop a framework so that the process is smooth and harmonious and avoids crises or erratic developments with the attendant risks for all of Europe.

The Alliance has been pledged to German unity since the entry of the Federal Republic in 1954/55. This is true of the three Western powers as well as of all the other Allies. The alliance is not an obstacle to German unity, any more than it is to European integration. It helped to bring more democracy and freedom. It seeks to overcome the division of Germany and Europe. It is promoting reform in the East.

The continued existence of NATO and progress towards German unity are perfectly compatible. Indeed I would say they were mutually dependent. Now I hear sometimes: It is not realistic to assume that a reunified Germany could exist in the Atlantic Alliance. I would confront these voices with the insight drawn from our historic experience: To make the dissolution of the Alliance a sine qua non of German unity would deprive both Germany and Europe of a basic force for stability. Only firm anchoring in the West can provide the fundamental stability for the difficult process in which we are engaged.

A drifting, neutral Germany cannot be a solution, given the country's geostrategic position and its political, economic and military potential, and this is the view of all the Allies. It would not even be in the enlightened self-interest of the Soviets. The history of the last two centuries demonstrates this.

Thus there is no acceptable alternative to Germany remaining anchored in the Atlantic Alliance – and belonging to the European Community. Please understand that it would be a mistake to consider the German question in terms of a dynamically unfolding future while, at the same time, viewing the role and function of the Atlantic Alliance as merely static. The latter is another part of the same series of rapid, interdependent developments.

The Soviet Union is adapting to this movement towards German unity. Foreign Minister Shevardnadze's speech in Brussels and General Secretary Gorbachev's latest pronouncements show this. Soviet security interests and their definition have changed dramatically in the past four years. The Soviets' forward deployment in Europe since 1945 sprang partly from an expansionist drive for world power, but also from a deep-seated need for security. That need has lost its justification with the now unequivocal recognition that there is no threat from the West.

As a result, the Soviet perception of their security has changed. They no longer need a Western glacis. The Soviet Union will have to accept – and is probably already on the way to doing so – that its security will be enhanced rather than impaired by the loss of its Central and East European buffer zone. New, stable structures and increased prosperity as well as new and closer forms of international co-operation in Central and Eastern Europe will above all benefit the Soviet reform process.

The Soviet Union's security interests – in stability, freedom from threat and co-operation along the borders of the Soviet state – will be better served in the long term by the intensification of the disarmament process and the further reduction of military forces, by taking advantage of the Alliance as a co-operative partner in the management of peace, and by the extension of the CSCE system and the resulting reduction of confrontation.

In addition, special arrangements could be devised to take account of Soviet security interests with a united Germany as a member of the Atlantic Alliance.

A component of such an arrangement could be a special military status for the territory of the GDR, or perhaps an agreement not to extend military integration to that territory. These are just two possibilities out of many which could be conceived. German unity and membership of the Atlantic Alliance are perfectly compatible within a security architecture which would preserve European stability in the interest of the Soviet Union as well as of other states.

The members of the Alliance must as a matter of urgency incorporate such considerations into a common concept for progress towards German unity.

The important thing is that the European Community, the Atlantic Alliance and the CSCE should be developed as a framework for German and European unity. Omission of any of these structural elements would disrupt the balance which is so vital for the future of Germany and Europe. The Soviet Union can be sure that we take their ideas seriously, and more: we will respect their legitimate security interests.

Source: NATO Press Service, 8 February 1990

ROLAND DUMAS, FRENCH FOREIGN MINISTER

Interview 9 February 1990

The right to self-determination is inviolable. I do not lay down preconditions: reunification will take place.

. . .

The security of France is played out beyond her frontiers, and our country has always been interested in surrounding herself with solid allies. A neutral Germany would be the heart of an unstable Europe.

. . .

The [Franco-German] friendship will remain strong. It rests on a solid basis. France is a power that maintains her rank. Germany will have more inhabitants. Her economic potential will be superior. But her constraints will also be heavier. West Germans are beginning to realise that. It will not be entirely rosy either for a reunited Germany.

Source: The Independent, 9 February 1990

JAMES BAKER, US SECRETARY OF STATE

Press Conference 9 February 1990

Our preferred position is that Germany remain a member of NATO, but NATO is going to change ... We don't favour neutrality. We favour continued membership or association with NATO.

Source: *Financial Times*, 10 February 1990

SOVIET-AMERICAN JOINT STATEMENT

10 February 1990

Soviet Foreign Minister Eduard Shevardnadze and US Secretary of State James Baker, met 7–9 February 1990 in Moscow as part of the preparations for the Soviet-US summit to be held in June in the United States. Proceeding from their common goal of building a more stable, constructive and cooperative relationship, they reviewed the broad range of issues on the Soviet-US agenda. The Secretary of State was also received by President Gorbachev for an open, wide-ranging exchange of views.

The Foreign Minister and the Secretary of State discussed developments in Soviet-US relations since the Wyoming ministerial meeting and the Malta meeting between President Gorbachev and President Bush. They examined the prospects for the summit, with the particular aim of advancing the objectives and priorities defined by the two leaders in Malta.

The Foreign Minister and the Secretary of State noted with satisfaction the progress that is being made in Soviet-US relations. While certain significant differences remain between the sides, their relationship is increasingly marked by understanding, cooperation and the search for mutual advantage. The Foreign Minister and the Secretary of State believe that candid dialogue and continuing efforts at finding practical and concrete solutions will further the signficant progress that has been recorded to date.

In this context, the Moscow ministerial meeting was a useful and important step in preparing the ground for a productive summit. The high-level discussions were complemented by expert working groups on arms control, regional, human rights, transnational and bilateral issues, as well as an informal group on economic questions. Specific agreements were reached in several areas of the agenda.

I.

The Foreign Minister and the Secretary of State held a thorough exchange of views on arms control and disarmament issues. With respect to the treaty on the reduction and limitation of strategic offensive arms [START], they reaffirmed their common objective of resolving all major issues by the June summit in order to allow signature of the treaty by the end of the year. To further this goal, the sides reached agreement or exchanged new proposals in a number of areas. ´

469

On air-launched cruise missiles, the sides made substantial progress on a package approach, agreeing on all remaining issues with the exception of the range threshold.

The sides also made good progress on sea-launched cruise missiles [SLCMs]. The sides agreed that such missiles would be dealt with by parallel, politically binding declarations for the duration of the START treaty. The Foreign Minister and the Secretary of State agreed that the remaining issues involving SLCMs would be addressed at the negotiations in Geneva.

The sides agreed that there would be numerical limits on non-deployed ballistic missiles and the warheads attributable to them for all ICBMs of a type that has been flight-tested from a mobile launcher. Other non-deployed heavy bomber weapons will not be subject to numerical limits. The sides further agreed on a regime governing the location and movement of all non-deployed ballistic missiles.

The sides reached agreement on major elements of a regime to ensure the non-denial of telemetry data during flight tests of START-accountable ballistic missiles. These provisions will be included in the START treaty, but will be implemented early, at the time of treaty signature, through an exchange of letters.

The US side presented new proposals on verification of mobile ICBMs, duration of the treaty, phasing of reductions, and attribution of warheads to future types of ballistic missiles. The Soviet side presented new proposals dealing with non-circumvention. The Foreign Minister and the Secretary of State instructed their negotiators to discuss these new proposals and to expedite efforts on resolving remaining differences in the text of the treaty and its associated documents.

The sides discussed the Vienna negotiations on conventional force reductions and reiterated their determination to conclude an agreement as soon as possible in 1990. The sides discussed President Bush's January 31 proposal on manpower which was presented by NATO in Vienna on February 8, as well as NATO's aircraft proposal presented on the same date. As a result of the discussions in Moscow, the differences on personnel were narrowed. The sides agreed to continue their discussions in the context of the negotiations in Vienna and at the ministers' meeting on 'open skies' in Ottawa.

The Foreign Minister and the Secretary of State had extensive discussions on how to proceed toward their common goal of achieving, through the negotiations in Geneva, a global ban on the development, production, stockpiling and use of chemical weapons and of their destruction. The Soviet and US delegations in Geneva were instructed to proceed with developing means of practical cooperation in the area of chemical weapons elimination. The sides issued a separate, more detailed statement on chemical weapons.

In discussions on nuclear testing, the sides made progress on resolving the remaining issues. They believe that the task of completing the verification protocols to the 1974 and 1976 threshold limitation treaties for signing at the summit is realistic. The sides agreed on the right to simultaneous use of hydrodynamic and in-country seismic yield measurements. The sides also resolved several longstanding problems regarding the implementation of the hydrodynamic yield measurement method. The sides identified the three seismic stations in each country to be used for in-country seismic yield measurements. The side reaffirmed their adherence to the agreement reached in September 1987 with regard to the negotiations on nuclear testing.

The Foreign Minister and the Secretary of State expressed their hope that the Ottawa 'open skies' conference – which they will both attend – would be a success and lead to early agreement. They believe an 'open skies' regime can make a genuine contribution to openness, transparency and stability.

The Foreign Minister and the Secretary of State noted the recent consultations between their experts on chemical weapons non-proliferation, missile technology control and nuclear non-proliferation. They agreed to prepare a document for consideration by their leaders covering both principles and concrete steps of cooperation in all areas of non-proliferation – chemical, missile and nuclear.

The sides conducted a discussion of the problem of non-proliferation of missiles and missile technology. They noted that they both adhere to the export guidelines of the existing regime relating to missiles, which applies to missiles capable of delivering at least 500 kilogrammes of payload to a range of at least 300 kilometres. They further agreed to continue joint discussions on this problem in the interim before the next ministerial meeting.

Source: *Tass*, 12 February 1990

SOVIET-GERMAN JOINT STATEMENT

10 February 1990

Mikhail Gorbachev met Helmut Kohl, Chancellor of the Federal Republic of Germany, in the Kremlin on February 10.

Although this meeting was held in a substantially different situation, it was directly connected with the results of their previous meetings in Moscow and Bonn, was based on all principled provisions of the joint Soviet-West German statement signed last June and was held in an atmosphere of deep mutual understanding and confidence in the political and personal respects.

'We live at a time when we have to maintain constant contacts. The Chancellor is right in saying that everything we have to do should be done, proceeding from the spirit and letter of the joint statement,' Gorbachev said.

This was a frank and substantive meeting with full understanding of the responsibility of the moment and the importance of decisions which could be made as a result of this exchange of thoughts and appraisals of the current events.

The discussion was conducted along two lines in accordance with two inseparable objective processes.

The German question can be resolved at the present time only in the context of the European development, taking into account the security and interests of neighbours as well as other states in Europe and the world.

Gorbachev stated, and the Chancellor agreed with him, that there are no differences now between the USSR, the FRG and the German Democratic Republic that the question of the unity of the German nation should be settled by Germans.

The Germans themselves should make their choice as to what state structures, what periods, at what pace and under what conditions they will be realising their unity.

Gorbachev referred to his recent meeting with GDR Prime Minister Hans Modrow. He stressed that all Germans, both in the East and the West, should know the Soviet Union's position.

But while resolving their national question, they should remember the realities of life: there was the war, and the war, as well as the post-war period, has left its heritage.

We are thinking about all this anew. We have departed from confrontation, and the European process is gaining momentum.

German rapprochement should not damage the positive results achieved in this sphere, East-West relations as a whole, or upset the European balance.

On the contrary, this rapprochement can and must proceed in such a way as to make a contribution to the constructive European development, Gorbachev said.

Therefore, only such a policy is acceptable which takes into account all realities and all possible aftermaths – domestic, foreign policy and economic consequences and, naturally, the psychological reaction of Germans and other countries, especially those which participated in the war.

The solution of the German question is inseparable from the success of the disarmament talks in Europe, from the changing role of the two military and political alliances and from questions concerning the presence of foreign troops in European states.

Helmut Kohl confirmed the Germans' firm determination: a war will never be unleashed from German soil. He advanced the formula that 'only peace should emanate from German soil'.

The construction of German unity and a search by Germans for a new place in the European and world structures should constantly take into account basic realities of our times.

'I said long ago that history would settle the German question. It has now begun to work at an unexpected pace. We should act in a balanced way, taking into account really historical criteria,' Gorbachev noted.

'In the new situation we should cooperate without breaking the achieved mutual understanding at the state level, and without damaging the new character of relations between the German and Soviet peoples. We should cooperate to develop and enrich these relations,' he added.

The two leaders agreed to continue comprehensive, frank and fruitful talks, which should be conducted in contact with other interested parties, above all the United States, Britain and France. Current events imperatively demand this.

Completing the main part of the meeting, the chancellor said: 'We agreed in Bonn that we turn a new page in our relations. It is clear now that the need for cooperation in this spirit has increased rather than diminished'.

Agreeing with this idea, Gorbachev noted that at the present, very significant stage, it is very important to raise the level of interaction, to increase confidence-building efforts, to abide firmly by understandings reached, and to call on each other immediately, if need be.

A meeting was then held with the participation of Eduard Shevardnadze and Hans-Dietrich Genscher, who informed the leaders of the parallel discussions they had held. The sides summed up the results and expressed the opinion that the visit was timely and useful.

Soviet and West German Foreign Ministers Meet

There follows the full text of the official announcement on the meeting of Soviet and West German foreign ministers:

On February 10, Soviet Foreign Minister Eduard Shevardnadze met West German Foreign Minister Hans-Dietrich Genscher, who had arrived in the Soviet Union together with Chancellor Helmut Kohl.

The ministers noted with satisfaction that the working meeting between Mikhail gorbachev and Helmut Kohl shows that contacts at the highest level have become more intensive, and this proves the two sides' desire to observe the programme of joint actions set forth in the Soviet-West German statement of June 13, 1989.

It was emphasised that the implementation of the policy of new thinking was opening up a unique chance of ending the period of confrontation and mistrust, overcoming the division of Europe, building a common European home and creating structures which would ensure the security and prosperity of countries and peoples.

The sides had a detailed exchange of views on the German affairs. The Soviet side emphasised that a search for ways of rapprochement of the two German states and the working out of forms and conditions for implementing the idea of eventual German unity require special responsibility and caution. It is necessary to find such solutions that would meet the interests of the German Democratic Republic and FRG, the interests of the Soviet Union and other European countries, and would take into account the responsibility of the four states with treaty interests in Germany's affairs, and in relation to West Berlin, legal and political realities.

People should have a guarantee that the threat of a new war will never again come from the German soil and that the current changes will not upset the existing balance in Europe.

They should also be sure that claims on revising the postwar borders in Europe will not be made.

Eduard Shevardnadze stressed the need to give the people of the GDR the opportunity to make their choice in a normal situation, without any pressure and outside interference.

It was emphasised that the movement of the GDR and FRG towards each other should be carried out in phases and be synchronised with the development of the Helsinki Process. It is important that it should promote stability and security in Europe.

Special attention was paid to questions of deepening the European process. Hans-Dietrich Genscher supported the Soviet Union's proposal to hold an all-European summit. The sides believe that such a summit would contribute to working out a view on the future European architecture that would be common to East and West, and to a further substantial lowering of military confrontation. It would promote trust and ensure advancement towards disarmament.

The foreign ministers discussed the state of affairs at the Vienna talks on conventional arms in Europe, and announced their intention to work towards their earliest completion by concrete and substantial results. This would create favourable conditions for passing over to the second stage of the Vienna talks.

The two ministers favoured the expansion of economic and scientific-technological ties between the countries of the East and West Europe, and attached great importance to their intensification and removal of the still existing barriers and restrictions. The forthcoming economic forum, to be held in Bonn in March-April, will be an important step in this direction.

'The sides also considered the course of implementation of agreements reached during the Soviet-West German summits, as well as some practical issues of bilateral relations.'

Source: *Tass*, 12 February 1990

CHANCELLOR KOHL

Press conference following visit to Moscow, 11 February 1990

General Secretary Gorbachev told me unmistakably that the Soviet Union will respect the decision of the Germans to live in one state and that it is up to the Germans themselves to decide on the timing and the path to unification. He acknowledged our position that German neutrality is out of the question.

Source: *Wall Street Journal*, 12 February 1990

SOVIET GOVERNMENT STATEMENT ON TROOP WITHDRAWAL PLEDGE

11 February 1990

Europe is witnessing positive dynamic processes of restructuring of domestic and inter-state relations.

The Cold War period has ended, and a transition to a qualitatively new international order based on fundamentally different relationships between European states has begun.

For the first time in the post-war period, there has arisen a realistic possibility of the gradual dismantling of the outdated model of the European balance of forces that took shape over the Cold War years and was based primarily on military confrontation.

Instead, a new system of relations is to be established to ensure stability and security on the European continent.

In this situation it is of importance not to miss the historic chance but to supplement political detente by relaxation of tension in the military field in good time.

This task becomes increasingly pressing, and there are good pre-requisites for accomplishing it. The successful headway made at the Vienna talks on reductions in conventional armed forces on the territory stretching from the Atlantic to the Urals is the main one of the prerequisites.

At the same time there are misgivings that the results of the Vienna talks may lag behind the pace of reforms in Europe. This should not be allowed to happen.

It is known that the Soviet Union and other Warsaw Treaty member-states, without waiting for the conclusion of Vienna accords, are already preparing to make unilateral cuts in their armed forces and ensuring that they are structurally incapable of attack.

The withdrawal of troops and the elimination of bases on other people's territories are also of basic importance for the relaxation of tension in the military field.

We reaffirm the Soviet Union's commitment to the earlier declared stand – to work to secure the withdrawal of all foreign troops from other people's territories in Europe by 1995–1996 and the elimination of all military bases on foreign territories by the year 2000.

Since only Soviet troops are stationed in Warsaw Treaty countries outside the Soviet Union's national territory, the USSR is prepared, by arrangement with the allied countries, to withdraw or reduce Soviet troops in Warsaw Treaty countries after discussing practicalities connected with this.

The Soviet Union has already begun talks with Czechoslovakia and Hungary for the withdrawal of its troops from these countries.

There is every ground to expect that the talks will end in agreement on all aspects of troop withdrawal, including technical and social ones, and that Soviet soldiers and officers will be able to return home as quickly as possible.

Apart from these two countries, Soviet troops in Europe are now also stationed in Poland and the German Democratic Republic.

If the government of the Republic of Poland expresses an appropriate desire, we could discuss with its representatives the question of Soviet troops in that country.

As far as the Western group of Soviet troops stationed on the territory of the German Democratic Republic is concerned, the Soviet Union is already unilaterally reducing its troops stationed there.

Further steps in this respect will be possible within the framework of accords at the Vienna talks where all aspects of cuts in conventional armed forces in Europe are under consideration.

Besides, the stay of foreign troops in both the GDR and the Federal Republic of Germany is a special issue connected with the four powers' obligations arising from the outcome of the Second World War, and it may be tackled only with due regard for the security interests of all the states concerned.

Of course, the above-mentioned activities should be carried out with due regard for the established post-war realities in Europe, taking account of the interests of all-European stability and within the broad context of further evolution of the political situation in Europe and in the world as a whole.

Source: Tass, 11 February 1990

EDUARD SHEVARDNADZE, SOVIET FOREIGN MINISTER

Press conference, Ottawa, 13 February 1990

I'm not saying that neutrality is the only way for Germany, but in my view it is the best way. But there is room for negotiation.

Source: *The Guardian*, 13 February 1990

STATEMENT BY THE FOREIGN MINISTERS ATTENDING 'OPEN SKIES' CONFERENCE

Ottawa, 14 February 1990

The foreign ministers of the Federal Republic of Germany, the German Democratic Republic, France, the United Kingdom, the Soviet Union and the United States had talks in Ottawa. They agreed that the foreign ministers of the Federal Republic of Germany and the German Democratic Republic would meet with the foreign ministers of France, the United Kingdom, the Soviet Union and the United States to discuss external aspects of the establishment of German unity, including the issues of security of the neighbouring states. Preliminary discussions at the official level will begin shortly.

Source: Foreign and Commonwealth Office

INTERVIEW BY THE FRENCH PRESIDENT, M. FRANCOIS MITTERRAND, WITH FRENCH REGIONAL NEWSPAPERS

14 February 1990 (Excerpts)

Q. – Mr. President, what can Western powers do to help Mr. Gorbachev?

THE PRESIDENT – Not much, and a lot. Not much, indeed nothing, as regards political and institutional reforms inside the USSR, such as the problem of nationalities. A lot, to give the economy a shot in the arm. What the Soviet Union lacks most, for example, is managers trained in the modern skills and the laws of the market. Hence the Community project to set up a European foundation to train these managers. It will be established soon. Also, the Western powers should provide various forms of urgently needed aid, notably food aid, together with substantial, long-term financial assistance. The latter will be made possible by institutions such as the Bank for the Reconstruction and Development of Eastern Europe, a French initiative. I hope also that we shall see a proliferation of joint ventures between the USSR and the Western nations. There are also indirect ways to help Mr. Gorbachev. To begin with, by disarmament and establishing a climate of peace and cooperation in Europe, which will encourage the nations of East and West on our continent to devote their investment to productive ends.

Q. – Since you stated that you were not afraid of German reunification, have you not felt alarmed at the accelerating pace of events?

THE PRESIDENT – Don't forget we have experienced some magnificent moments, with the collapse of the Berlin Wall. That really was history, and what a tale it is: the victory of freedom being written before our very eyes. The fact that events are moving faster in no way alters the principles that ought to inspire us. I have never set any precondition for German self-determination, neither today nor in the past. Unification is essentially a matter of their will, for them to decide. That is a fundamental right. That said, the Germans must remember that we are bound together by certain commitments: security in Europe, the future of the Community, and the balance of power in Europe. The declaration unanimously approved by the twelve member countries of the Community in Strasbourg, on 8 December 1989, was a useful reminder of this.

Q. – You mentioned commitments. Isn't an unambiguous recognition of the Oder-Neisse frontier indispensable?

THE PRESIDENT – Yes.

Q. – Haven't Franco-German relations – until now the driving forces behind French and German diplomacy – 'caught cold' as a result of the holes in the Berlin Wall?

THE PRESIDENT – Other people have already asked me that question, and certain French and German newspapers have taken up the theme in a polemical tone. Let's try to clarify the issue. If we are normal (and in keeping with agreements) that France should express her opinion. That is what I have done in saying that it was above all up to the German people to decide democratically. This is probably what will happen this year. How? By progressing from a simple contractual community to absorption of the GDR by the FRG, via confederation or federation. There are many possible scenarios. Who can fail to understand the yearnings for unity of this people so long divided? As a Frenchman, that is why I took part in the Resistance when France was occupied and divided by German forces. It would be unjust to hold the present generations responsible for what happened half a century ago. Especially as the French and Germans have since been reconciled and become firm friends. I want the Germans to know that, like the majority of the French people, I send them my fraternal wishes for a happy fulfilment of their destiny. But, whatever form it takes, France has a direct interest in the consequences that unification will entail: the content of the peace settlement, the fixing of frontiers, integration into the Community, the stationing of troops, the state of the alliances. My duty in all things is to ensure the security and fundamental interests of France.

Q. – But isn't there a risk of France falling behind Germany?

THE PRESIDENT – Once they are reunified, 80 million Germans will be a mighty nation; and when Prussia and Saxony roll up their sleeves, the world will look up. But France, gathered behind its natural frontiers, with the strength born of a great history and rich in its cultural influence, with its healthy economy, its international role and its ability to provide for its own security, will be able to stand the comparison. It has already done so for ten centuries.

Q. – This German unification will inevitably raise the problem of the alliances. What would you regard as a formula acceptable to all?

THE PRESIDENT – Today, 380,000 Soviet soldiers in East Germany, a few more Atlantic Alliance soldiers in West Germany, including the four

Berlin zones. Tomorrow, a military frontier and armies facing each other within a unified country, in peacetime: that would look strange and impermanent. It is up to the members of the two alliances to decide on this, and for the members of the Conference on Security and Cooperation in Europe (CSCE) to express their views. In any case, the Atlantic camp would be wise to signal straight away its intention not to advance NATO's defences beyond their present limits, pending a general agreement incorporating the new situation in Eastern Europe into the balance of forces.

Q. – Aren't the Soviets already talking about demilitarizing the whole of Germany?

THE PRESIDENT – Yes, by linking the two terms unification and neutralization. But neither West Germany nor the other members of NATO would agree to that.

Q. – Wouldn't a neutral Germany finally be more reassuring for everyone?

THE PRESIDENT – Neutral, why? Neutral, how? Both German States have their armies, like any sovereign country. The FRG has undertaken not to possess nuclear weapons. What more can one ask?

Q. – And what about the foreign forces stationed on German soil, on either side?

THE PRESIDENT – Military dispositions will flow from the political decisions.

Q. – Couldn't the present-day FRG follow the French course and drop out of NATO's integrated command while staying within the Alliance?

THE PRESIDENT – The FRG will do as it sees fit. France has an autonomous strategy because it has atomic weapons. Germany does not.

Q. – Why did you propose a confederation?

THE PRESIDENT – The idea is simple. The countries of Eastern Europe now recovering their freedom and full sovereignty, about to try to rebuild their economies, will want to be neither isolated nor assisted. They will not want to join the Community, not for the time being at least. And the latter wouldn't be ready for it. Will they be satisfied with regional agreements among themselves, and with organizational agreements with the Twelve? Their dignity and their interests would not be satisfied. Will they remain within the Soviet-dominated COMECON?

That's unlikely. So what then? On 31 December 1989, in my New Year address to the French, I said that I would like to see the emergence of a confederation in the coming years, in which the democratic nations of our continent would come together within a common, permanent body. Initially, it would handle economic and cultural exchanges and mutual security, and it would provide a forum for regular meetings between Foreign Ministers. That would offer a grand perspective for those nations. That way, they could become clearly aware of their European identity and their natural solidarity, within an institution made up of partners that are equal in law.

Q. – How does your projected confederation differ from the project for a common European home, Mr. President?

THE PRESIDENT – The confederation would give political and legal substance to the house we want to build.

Source: Record of Interview, Paris, 14 February 1990

PRIME MINISTER MARGARET THATCHER, SPEECH TO BOARD OF DEPUTIES OF BRITISH JEWS

18 February 1990 (Extracts)

The whole European scene has changed beyond recognition in this last year, changed for the better. Of course that has brought forward new problems, and we shall have to overcome them. But let's first of all allow ourselves to feel *glad* about what's happened.

It's not so long ago that Communism was seen as the way of the future, the irresistible force which would rule the world. Now it lies in ruins, a discredited and bankrupt system, while democracy and the market economy are gaining ground everywhere.

We have seen revolutions – for the most part peaceful – sweep through the countries of Eastern Europe, ending the Communist Party's monopoly of power. Now the Soviet Union, too, is about to take the historic step of accepting a multi-party system.

At the same time, the Soviet Union has made substantial unilateral reductions in its forces: and the negotiations in Vienna on conventional forces in Europe promise further reductions on both sides, though the Warsaw Pact will have to make greater reductions than NATO: nearly 4000,000 Soviet troops as against about 100,000 US troops. It is likely that Soviet forces will withdraw altogether from some Eastern European countries. The Soviet Union's capacity to mount a surprise attack against Western Europe – which has been one of our great fears for more than 40 years – will be dramatically reduced.

All this is good news. It represents a success for the West, for NATO and for the resolve and determination of its individual members. We should recognise, too, how much it owes to the vision and the courage of Mr. Gorbachev. But above all, it is a triumph for our ideas – for democracy, for the rule of law, for the market economy – and the free institutions which we have built upon them.

It becomes even more important to maintain these institutions in the new situation which we now face. At best, we are bound to enter a period of uncertainty. Democracy will take time to put down roots in Eastern Europe. We are already seeing a renewal of disputes and problems between nationalities, which is reminiscent of the days before the First World War – and we remember how other countries can all too easily be dragged into such disputes.

There is a lot of talk in the West about a peace dividend. Our real dividend is the failure of the Communist system and the reduction of the military threat. We should not squander it by allowing the very institutions – above all NATO – which have kept us secure to be undermined: or by dismantling our defence, when the Soviet Union continues to have vast military capabilities.

If we had had something equivalent to NATO in the 1930s, we would never have had a Second World War. We shall always have to keep adequate defences because you never know where a new threat might come from. One has to bear in mind that 12 countries outside NATO and the Warsaw Pact already have ballistic missiles; and many more than now *could* be in a position to acquire nuclear weapons by the end of the century.

Hopefully, there will be an opportunity to make *some* reductions in our forces, as part of balanced reductions by both NATO and the Warsaw Pact. But we shall not do anything which will put our defence and our security at risk nor to weaken our capability to undertake out-of-area tasks: and that means that we shall continue to need our independent nuclear deterrent, as well as strong and well-equipped conventional forces. No-one should doubt our determination on that score.

German unification

One aspect of these developments which I know will be of particular concern to this audience is German unification. I say 'unification' rather than 'reunification' because we are not talking of Germany with its 1937 borders, but of the coming together of the *existing* Federal Republic and the GDR.

There is no doubt that this coming together of the two parts of Germany is going to happen. The Western allies have always supported the principle of unification, provided that it comes about as the result of the freely-expressed choice of the people of the two German states.

But it is understandable that, for some, bitter memories of the past should colour their view of the present and future.

As Chancellor Kohl and Foreign Minister Genscher have themselves acknowledged, German unification must take into account not only the feelings of the two German states, but the sensitivities and interests of others in Europe as well.

It must respect:

- existing treaties and agreements, including the commitments of the Helsinki Final Act which recognises *existing* borders in Europe; and
- the rights of the four powers in Germany. After all it is on the basis of four power rights and responsibilities that the allies have preserved West Berlin's freedom for over 40 years.

Nor must it make *any* of us, in Eastern or Western Europe or the Soviet Union, feel less secure. That means that we want to see Germany remain part of NATO with American and other troops stationed there, with some special arrangements for East Germany, to meet the Soviet Union's security concerns. Indeed it would be quite reasonable for some Soviet troops to remain there at least for a transitifonal period.

These are major questions and they need to be thought through and satisfactory answers found. They do not involve Germany and the four powers alone. For instance, we understand and indeed fully support Poland's wish to see its western border guaranteed by treaty. And other neighbouring states will have their particular views too.

Our aim all along has been to see a framework within which the full implications of Germany's unification could be properly worked out. That we have now achieved, with the agreement at the Open Skies Conference in Ottawa to start meetings of the four powers and the two Germanies. I very much welcome that.

In all this, we want to ensure that Germany's unification upholds peace and prosperity in Europe, and does not become a new source of instability. Chancellor Kohl and his colleagues share this aim and I am sure they will remain staunch supporters of NATO.

Source: Official Text

SPEECH BY TADEUSZ MAZOWIECKI, PRIME MINISTER OF POLAND

21 February 1990 (Extracts)

We do not intend to negotiate on [the Polish-German] border with anyone. It is a fixed part of the European order. We think, however, that one cannot enter the new phase of history which the unification process of Germany poses with any ambiguities on the border of a united Germany.

Source: *International Herald Tribune*, 21 February 1990

INTERVIEW WITH ITALIAN FOREIGN MINISTER, GIANNI DE MICHELIS

15 February 1990

The fact that the two Germanies have kept their commitment to consult with the four powers is significant because it represents the explicit recognition of the importance that foreign interests place on the question of unity; but for Italy it remains clear that such interests cannot be fully explored in the forum of the four power guarantee.

The common management of Berlin is an example [of the special reponsibilities of the 'four powers']. But the final communiqué cites the 'security of the bordering countries' as one of the external problems trusted to the negotiations of the 'Two plus Four', and to us it seems that, to give another example, the security of the Polish borders cannot be discussed without at least Poland. And we are also interested.

. . . Ottawa is an important starting point for a year which will bring great changes. One cannot foresee exactly when German unification will take place, but now events will have to unfold rapidly. To cite an urgent problem, in a few months East Germany may be included in the European Economic Community, and this means that negotiations on the entry of Austria into the EEC have to begin immediately, especially from the Italian point of view. In a common market always more weighted towards the center-north of the continent, we run the risk of remaining attached to Europe by only a strip of border with France, obtaining insufficient advantages from the open borders.

Source: *La Repubblica* 15 February 1990 (Translation by David Boren)

INTERVIEW BY PRESIDENT MIKHAIL GORBACHEV TO *PRAVDA*

21 February 1990

. . . With all respect for their national right to it, the situation makes it impossible to imagine that the Germans will come to the terms between themselves and then let the others merely endorse decisions already made.

There are some fundamental matters, which the international community is entitled to know about and which must leave no room for ambiguity.

It should likewise by made clear right from the start that neither the process of rapprochement between the FRG and the GDR nor a united Germany should spell a threat or harm to the national interests of neighbours or anybody else for that matter. And, of course, any encroachment upon the borders of other states must be ruled out.

In addition to the inviolability of the post-war borders, which is most important, it also had other consequences. Nobody cancelled the responsibility of the four powers. And only they themselves can decline it. There is no peace agreement with Germany. It is this agreement that can finally determine Germany's status in the European structure in terms of international law.

Security, however it can be, has been maintained for a long time by the existence of two military-political alliances – the Warsaw Treaty and NATO. The prerequisites for forming a fundamentally new system of security in Europe are only emerging now. Therefore these alliances retain their role although it is radically modified as the armed confrontation decreases, the military component of security diminishes and political aspects of its activity increase.

Consequently, the reunification of Germany should take account of these circumstances, namely the inadmissibility of disrupting the military-strategic balance of these two international organisations. There should be complete clarity on this.

And the last thing. It follows from what has been said that the process of German unification is organically linked and must be synchronised with the general European process, with its core – the formation of a fundamentally new structure of European security which will replace the one based on blocs.

The task [of the 'two plus four' talks] is to discuss in a comprehensive and stage-by-stage way all the external aspects of German reunification, to prepare the issue for inclusion into the general European process and for considering the fundamentals of a future peace agreement with Germany.

Moreover, the effectiveness of such consultations, and their prestige depend on the degree of trust and openness between all parties involved. Naturally sovereign states can exercise any contacts, including the German issue, on a bilateral and any other basis. But we rule out an approach when three or four will initially arrange things and then tell the other participants the already agreed-upon position. This is unacceptable.

. . . , [We] link the 'two plus four' mechanism with the general European process and at the same time understand the special interest of other countries, left out of this formula. And, consequently, their legitimate right to protect their national interests. I refer primarily to Poland – the inviolability of its post-war borders, like the borders of other states, must be guaranteed. Only an international legal act can provide such a guarantee.

. . . As is known, we have proposed that all troops be recalled to within their national boundaries by 1995–1996, and that all foreign military bases be eliminated by the year 2000. Negotiations about the withdrawal of our troops from Hungary and Czechoslovakia are being conducted with their governments.

In short, the agreement about the reduction of the US and Soviet military presence in Central Europe is fully in keeping with the main tendency of international development and promotes peace.

Source: *Soviet News*, 28 February 1990

SPEECH BY FOREIGN SECRETARY, DOUGLAS HURD, HOUSE OF COMMONS

22 February 1990

Up till now the challenge for the West was to manage a relationship between adversaries. The overriding need was to avert war. After that to seek progress with arms control, and greater respect for human rights.

Much of our effort was directed to limit the damage of the Cold War; to expose the abuse of human rights; to counter the disruptive influence of the Soviet Union worldwide. This traditional effort needed perseverance and sometimes it needed courage. We did not need to look beyond existing alliances, political systems, certainties but now, including the Soviet Union, those countries are being transformed.

We shall still need steadiness and courage. But we have to welcome fresh ideas and original thought. That is undoubtedly the new mood in this country, in the rest of Europe, and across the Atlantic.

This came across very sharply in the remarkable series of meetings in Ottawa last week. Ottawa turned out to be a diplomatic festival as well as a formal conference. Foreign Ministers of NATO and the Warsaw Pact were there to discuss the 'open skies' regime. In practice, the talking ranged much more widely. It was less a case of 'open skies' than of 'open house'. It was an extraordinary experience for example to talk to, to listen to, the Polish, Czech or Hungarian Foreign Ministers and hear, for the first time in nearly half a century, genuinely national points of view emerging.

I came away with a strong sense that the Soviet Union is no longer sure of its moorings. The Warsaw Pact is no longer biddable. Democracy is starting to encroach. Soviet Foreign Policy is certainly much more sensitive than before. I have the impression that, perhaps for this reason, that policy at present contains more questions than answers. I admire the Soviet leadership for riding the tide of events but the pace and strength of that tide will increase over the next few months.

The dominating issue at Ottawa was German unification. The Western allies, as the house knows under different Governments in this country, have always supported the principle of German unification, to be brought about as the result of the freely-expressed choice of the peoples of the two Germanies. We can be glad as friends of the new and democratic Germany that the years of painful division are coming to an end.

The momentum towards unification has built up fast, and it is now likely to happen sooner rather than later. There is the political momentum, due largely I would say to the continuing flow of people from the GDR to the Federal Republic, and the desire of those who stay behind to share in the prosperity of their fellow Germans in the West. There is also as we can all understand an emotional momentum, which in a way is the most powerful of all.

But there are other realities, equally important, which can now be taken into account. Because German unification closely, of course, affects the interests of other countries: the immediate neighbours of Germany, her partners and allies in the EC, in NATO, and the Four Powers who retain rights and responsibilities in Germany. So there are also external aspects to the German question. Alongside self-determination goes the need for joint determination of these external issues.

We felt before the Ottawa meeting that these external aspects were not always being adequately heeded as the German Government grappled with the rush of events in the GDR. Until last week, we lacked a framework for discussing these external aspects of German unification.

We were not alone in that concern. Others too were worried that we seemed to be getting into a scramble towards unification, without having this framework for handling the external aspects, including membership of NATO by a united Germany: the implications of this for the territory of what would be the former GDR and the Soviet troops there; the status of Berlin; the final settlement of borders; the implications of unification for the European Community. Our message was not one of obstruction. It was that we risked muddle and instability if these issues were not addressed in some orderly way.

As I say, many felt these anxieties and told us about them. We were probably foremost in spelling them out. Because of that, a notion grew up, particularly in parts of the German press, that we were in some way going back on our traditional support for the principle of unification. I hope that notion has now been dispelled, to the comfort of us all. . . .

When I visited Washington on 29 January, I stressed to the President and to the Secretary of State this view that a framework was needed. We did not discuss in detail what form that framework should take. By the time I went to Ottawa at the beginning of last week our thoughts had become more precise. My right honourable Friend the Prime Minister and I were clear that I should press at Ottawa as hard as possible for a meeting, or meetings, of the Six – the four former occupying powers and the two Germanies. There are other external aspects which need to be discussed elsewhere, for example in the EC, in NATO, and with Poland. But a Six Power meeting seemed the first step. And I found when I got to Ottawa that I was knocking on an open door because the minds of our allies had moved in precisely the same direction. Only the Soviet Union was reticent, and at Ottawa that reticence was overcome within twenty-four hours.

We think this forum of the Six offers some obvious advantages. It brings together those most immediately concerned – the two Germanies themselves – with the four countries which have a unique standing in terms of legal rights and responsibilities in Germany. . . . We therefore achieved what has been our aim – a channel which can guide the discussion in future. We welcome this. Plenty of hard work lies ahead. But we are now optimistic that German unification can be achieved in a way which fits a pattern of European stability and security which is acceptable to all.

I cannot help adding that, now that this framework is beginning to take shape, everyone is beginning to say how important it is. Everyone is happy to climb aboard now. Analyses of the importance of discussing the external aspects of German unity, were regarded as unrealistic footdragging when the Prime Minister and I spoke about them a few weeks ago, but I must tell the House that such analyses about the importance of the external aspects were two a penny round the table at Dublin on Tuesday. But here I would say a word of appreciation for the way in which the German Minister of Foreign Affairs, Herr Genscher, has throughout, in private and in public, stressed the importance of consultation and the particular role of the Four Powers. . . .

It is not just on procedure that we have begun to make good progress. There is a coming together of ideas on substance as well.

First, there is the concept of a united Germany in NATO. This is clearly important for the West. It is also important for the security of Europe as a whole, as a number of Eastern countries now for the first time recognise. A neutral Germany outside the existing security arrangements in Europe would weaken that stability, and we believe the Federal Government has rightly rejected that option.

American and other foreign troops and their nuclear weapons will need to remain in Germany in significant numbers as a stabilising element in European security and on this point too there is a growing consensus. But we need, as we have said before, to take account of Soviet concerns. That means finding special arrangements for the territory of what is now the GDR, including perhaps the continued presence of Soviet troops for a transitional period. It is too soon to be precise about details. I do not think it is sensible at any rate for the Government to try to be precise about details but the principles are becoming clear.

I believe that the Soviet Union will come to accept that its own interest in stability will also be served by having Germany with the special arrangements I mentioned as a member of the defensive Western alliance, especially as arms control reduces the level of forces on both sides in Europe.

Second, there is the question of the Eastern border of a united Germany. No-one with any sense of history can be surprised at the Polish emphasis on this subject, stressed to us by the Prime Minister

Mr Mazowiecki last week. The German government have made it clear that the substance of their position is not in doubt on this issue. I have heard Herr Genscher say several times that a united Germany will comprise the territory of the Federal Republic, the GDR and Berlin. Not more, not less. Nevertheless we believe that there should be a formal and binding agreement to settle this matter once and for all. A Treaty is the obvious solution. And of course Poland will need to be closely involved in this discussion.

Third, we need to consider seriously within the EC the implications of an enlarged Germany. The economy of the GDR is clearly ill-suited to Community life. It is massively state-aided; it offends every EC environmental directive; its industrial and manufacturing standards are to put it mildly not those of the Single Market. So the Germans will need derogation from Community law, and we shall all need some transitional arrangements. And that is why the Irish Government, as The Presidency, proposed a special Community Summit to discuss this after proper preparation towards the end of April. We welcome that initiative. The European Commission agreed in Dublin at my suggestion that detailed work should begin now in preparation for that meeting. . . .

Fourth, there is the question of Berlin. The Western allies have defended freedom in their sectors of Berlin during the long period when the city and Germany itself was divided. Now that the Berlin wall is coming down and unification is in prospect, we do not want needlessly to perpetuate the occupation regime. It has served a particular and worthwhile purpose during a particular period in Berlin's history. The allies will consult the Russians about the future status of the city, and the two Germanies should be associated with the rather more formal process here of Four Power consultation about Berlin.

I am particularly anxious that, in all these matters, we should work as closely as possible with the French. We have long had a virtual identity of interest in many of these matters. I hope that we can work for a virtual identity of view. . . .

The second important decision at Ottawa was the agreement to hold the CSCE summit later this year at which, and this is very important, an agreement on conventional force reductions in Europe should be signed and which would establish a framework for future European cooperation.

For years our negotiators, including our British negotiators, struggled to secure, in the Helsinki process, a common standard of human rights. It was a long drawn out business under several Governments, painstaking and painful. But the governments of Eastern Europe were in the end brought to sign up to a set of standards by which their own people could apply a test. And we have all been able to make very good use of that Final Act. People like President Havel and Doina Cornea would have been lost to view – they might have disappeared for ever – if we had not had a standard which could be waved on their behalf and a mechanism by which we as well as others could keep pressing for their freedom and their rights.

All that has been proved worthwhile. It has been vindicated. The new governments of Eastern Europe, many of whose individual members benefited personally from this process, want to build on it for the future. We agree. We believe this process can now play a greater role than ever before in strengthening peace and stability in Europe. It has the right membership. It has the right broad agenda.

We need to make human rights, democracy and the rule of law as secure as we can. As permanent as we can and that needs an underlying framework of stability, to support and nourish the wider growth of human rights, democracy and the rule of law, because all history shows us that the survival of these things is fragile and sometimes at risk. The CSCE process is there to hand. We believe it should be adapted and strengthened for this purpose.

I see it rather like a motorway which at the moment carries a good deal of the traffic of East-West relations. But the traffic has been moving uncertainly in the past.

The political work of the CSCE is going to become more important in the future. If this motorway for carrying the traffic of East-West relations is to fulfil its potential to carry the additional traffic, we need to widen it: to increase the number of lanes, and find other ways of keeping the traffic flowing. So we are going to look for practical new elements with which we can strengthen the CSCE's contribution to European security. . . .

Last year, Britain, with the United States, launched a proposal in this context on free elections. We put forward another on respect for the rule of law.

In Ottawa, I put forward another British proposal. It seems to me that the Cold War has had many of course undesirable effects, but one effect which perhaps was neutral was to freeze many of the old nationalist emotions and tensions which for centuries have been flashpoints in Europe. Now that the Cold War is melting, the ice is thawing there is a risk, we can see it in every newspaper, particularly in central and Eastern Europe, that national reawakening will be accompanied by some of the uglier aspects of nationalism, as the old rivalries reassert themselves. In the West we have made a reasonable job of overcoming such rivalries in freedom, but Communism, the enforced, the artificial uniformity there, denied that chance to our Eastern neighbours.

I think the CSCE could provide a means of resolving disputes between its members to defuse tension and avert the threat of conflict, alongside of course the established machinery of the UN.

I do not think the process should get bogged down in machinery. It would be perhaps quite easy to get arrangement on a piece of conciliation machinery and then find that most countries spend their time finding excuses for not using it. We need to encourage the countries of Europe to talk and think collectively, and more often, about some of these issues, eg minority rights and their protection, which may be at the heart of existing or future disputes between countries and within them.

The third important agreement which came out of those 2½ days in Ottawa was perhaps in some ways the most surprising. It was the agreement reached between the US and the Soviet Union on the reduction of the stationed forces in Europe. Alongside that was a consensus between the Alliances that the negotiations going on in Vienna should press ahead as quickly as possible, so that we can reach an agreement this year.

Britain will work hard to achieve this outcome. There are problems remaining. We have not solved the problem of aircraft, we have not solved the problem which always dogs these negotiations about effective verification. But I came away from Ottawa with the feeling that the political will was there to achieve this result.

We need now to begin to look beyond these Vienna negotiations to the future needs of European security. Because obviously further measures of arms control will be part of this. So too will be the political aspects of security, which I have already mentioned. I suggested to Ottawa that we should set this work in hand, and we shall follow this proposal up in NATO and in the CSCE. . . .

All these developments raise the question of the future of our own Atlantic Alliance. I do not think we need to be dominated here by thoughts of symmetry, ie, by thoughts about what is happening in the Warsaw Pact. The implications for the Warsaw Pact of democracy among its members are certainly going to be profound. Either it will be transformed or it will fade away. But only its members can decide what its future should be. NATO too is going to be affected by the changes in Eastern Europe. It too will need to adapt. But, it is different. It does have proper foundations in the consent of governments and peoples, and therefore it will endure. We need to distinguish as rigorously as we can between those attributes of NATO which will remain important in the future, and other aspects which should change in response to events. Our security needs will change. But the need for security will not.

Among the permanent characteristics, I would list: The present membership of NATO; the presence of significant stationed forces, including those of the US, Canada and Britain, on the continent; a sensible mix of nuclear and conventional forces, and an integrated command structure. These essentials taken together would mean that we would continue to have a strong European defence. For the UK they include, among other things, the retention of the independent nuclear deterrent.

As for change, we envisage the Alliance will become more deeply involved

— in the management of change in Europe;

— in dialogue with the East;
— in arms control and its verification;
— in consultation about security problems outside, as well as inside, Europe; and
— in developing the new ideas I mentioned for the 90s, such as minimum deterrence.

An Alliance which can change with the times still has a lot to offer for the security of its members. It offers a sure link between Europe and North America; a sound framework for cooperation in defence and arms control; and the cheapest insurance policy against the uncertainties and possible turbulence of the 90s.

The long-term security and stability of Europe obviously can best be maintained if what is happening now, the democratic renewal in the Soviet Union and in Eastern Europe remains on track. There may well be reverses and upheavals. I do not think myself that any such reverses and upheavals in Eastern Europe are likely to bring back the Cold War, but they could send tremors of danger through the whole of our continent . . . We need the process of democratic renewal to succeed. To the extent that we can, we should provide practical support for reform. . . .

I should like to stress the key role in this of the European Community. The Community's response to events in the East has been fast and effective. It is the Commission which, at the request of the United States and others coordinates the work of the wider Group of 24 Western countries. We are sending aid of many kinds. We, the Twelve, have launched the idea of a European Development Bank whose emphasis on helping the private sector owes much to British urging.

We are acting to develop trade and cooperation agreements with the Eastern countries and, as a British initiative before Christmas, to look for closer forms of association between the Community and these countries in the longer term. We want to enable the emerging democracies to develop their economies and align themselves more closely with the Community as reform proceeds.

I hope myself that this process will lead eventually to full membership of the Community. That is for the future and a matter for them as well as for the Community . . . Already the Community provides a stable political, economic and legal framework for European development. The relationship with the Community will enable these countries to cope better with the economic and political travail through which they will pass over the next few years.

We have also provided bilateral help. It is increasing all the time, it is extremely well targetted help and increasingly effective. I would like to make a new statement today. We want to look, on an all party basis, at what help Britain can give to the political parties in Eastern Europe and perhaps elsewhere. We shall be in touch shortly with others in the House. . . .

We have to encourage these countries in every way possible in the amazing task which they have set themselves. In their societies they are transforming the nature of the relationship between the State and the individual. And that sounds easy as a general statement, extraordinarily difficult in practice day by day.

I have touched on the three main efforts in which we, the British Government, are engaged – the moving towards German unification and our interests in the external aspects of that; the developments of the European security framework; and supporting reform in Eastern Europe. All these tasks stem from events of which the whole House was glad – the breaking down of walls, and the freeing of people. Lech Walesa said to me when he was here before Christmas that he and his fellow-amateurs, as he put it, had done their bit by proving to us professionals that the impossible was possible. Then he added, and this was the thrust of it, the rest was up to the professionals. So professionals, the parliamentarians and the diplomats, the business-men and the bankers, the journalists and the broadcasters, we have to show the skill and imagination to follow up in a worthy way the work of those – for example, the shipyard workers of Gdansk, the crowds in St Wenceslas Square, and those who through the years defied the Berlin Wall.

Source: Central Office of Information, 22 February 1990

SPEECH BY CATHERINE LALUMIERE, SECRETARY GENERAL OF THE COUNCIL OF EUROPE TO ROYAL INSTITUTE OF INTERNATIONAL AFFAIRS, LONDON

28 February 1990 (Excerpts)

... Our constituent bodies, the Parliamentary Assembly and the Committee of Ministers, as well as the Secretariat, have lost no time in initiating dialogue, in forging contacts which have already proved their worth.

In the last two years, a whole panoply of ideas and projects has been launched to meet the needs and expectations of the Eastern countries rapidly.

— The first was special guest status with the Assembly, which was introduced in June 1989, and which has allowed parliamentarians from the USSR, Poland, Hungary and Yugoslavia to sit alongside our own parliamentarians in Strasbourg. Czechoslovakia, the German Democratic Republic and Bulgaria have just applied for this status as well.

— The next was the forging of legal and operational ties through accession to various European conventions (including the European Cultural Convention, which gives the new signatories a full part in our activities in the fields of education, culture and sport).

— Another is the launching of genuine co-operation to allow these countries to take advantage of the Council of Europe's work and expertise in everything that touches on the rule of law, human rights and the principles of pluralist democracy. This programme of co-operation and assistance has been christened the 'Demosthenes Programme'.

— The last, and this chapter remains to be written, may be full accession to the Council of Europe. Hungary applied for membership in November 1989, followed by Poland in January 1990, and Yugoslavia. . . .

... By what might be termed an entirely natural process, the Council of Europe has thus become the pan-European forum of the democracies. Today, with 23 member states, not a single democracy is lacking. Tomorrow, we shall be ready to welcome and assist the young democracies which are emerging in the East of our continent.

What we offer these new regimes is thus a stable anchorage which they can find nowhere else, and we are playing our part, with all the European nations, in forging a new cultural and political identity for a wider Europe.

What structure should be used for dialogue and co-operation involving all the countries of Europe?

The CSCE and the Helsinki process might, perhaps, suggest themselves here. That Conference has played a vital role in the process of détente, and will retain a central function in matters of security. It also has the advantage of bringing in the United States, which has an important say in European security.

At the same time, the CSCE, which marked a very important stage in the process of East-West rapprochement, does not seem capable of assuming the full range of roles today.

In fact, the extent of the changes in the East has somewhat overtaken the old efforts at rapprochement. They – and one can only welcome this – are increasingly a thing of the past. Of course, CSCE-type machinery will still be needed for continued work on security and disarmament, for this is a task which is far from completed. As far as the third basket – human rights – is concerned, however, the emphasis has shifted away from the old, painstaking efforts to get the Eastern countries moving, and now lies in co-operation to consolidate democracy and freedom in those countries.

In other words, the problem itself has changed: it is no longer a matter of laying down principles, which are now being accepted gradually by everyone – but of implementing and monitoring those principles – something which the CSCE is scarcely equipped to do. In the European Convention of Human Rights and the European Court of Human Rights, however, the Council of Europe possesses not only a precise text, but a supervisory court which has no equivalent anywhere else in the world. This is why, where the third Helsinki basket is concerned, wisdom would suggest that, at one of its future meetings, the CSCE should entrust implementation of that basket in Europe to the Council of Europe, whose machinery for protection of the individual is undoubtedly the most highly-developed and effective in the world.

It would thus be both logical and reasonable for the Council of Europe to be given a mandate by the CSCE to continue that Conference's work by implementing the principles which it has laid down.

But the Council of Europe's future role can extend beyond this human rights mandate. It is the role of an organisation capable of taking in all the countries of Europe and making it possible for them to work together in a whole range of fields, provided only that they are democracies.

The Council of Europe is something we have already, and that is its first advantage. In fact, the countries of Central and Eastern Europe urgently need a structure capable of accommodating them and assisting them on the path of democratic reform. The countries which lost no time in knocking on the Council of Europe's door knew what they were doing. Step by step, the Council can involve them in its decision-making process and admit them to membership. For them, it represents the way into the democratic camp.

As well as taking them in and helping to meet their most pressing needs, the Council of Europe can also, by virtue of its Statute, enable them to engage in genuine co-operation with the other countries of Europe.

First of all, it can provide, and is already providing, the means of co-operating in various technical areas, such as the different branches of law, human rights, European cultural identities, education, health, audio-visual media, etc . . . The 135 Council of Europe Conventions form a remarkable web, linking the countries of Western Europe, and this web can be extended to cover the countries of Central and Eastern Europe as well.

Beyond this technical co-operation, the Council can also provide a forum for political co-operation, a forum where all the countries of Europe can discuss their shared concerns, starting with the painful problem of minorities, which will certainly be among the hardest to solve, and among the gravest threats to the new Europe's stability. And there is the burning question of German reunification and its consequences for its neighbours and the whole of Europe.

Source: Council of Europe

COMMENTS AT JOINT PRESS CONFERENCE BY CHANCELLOR KOHL AND PRESIDENT BUSH

27 February 1990

President Bush: The United States formally recognizes the current German-Polish border.

Chancellor Kohl: The border question will be settled definitely by a freely elected, all-German parliament . . .

. . . there is a particular interest on the part of the Poles, and I'm sure that in the course of this process, we will find ways and means of adopting solutions satisfactory to everybody.

Source: *International Herald Tribune*, 27 February 1990

POLISH GOVERNMENT STATEMENT

1 March 1990

Mr Vogel's statement [spokesman for the FRG government], another one made by Chancellor Kohl and representatives of the Chancellor's Office in recent days, aroused our surprise, mainly in the question of linking the settlement in a treaty of the Oder-Neisse border to the issue of guarantees of rights for Polish citizens of German origin living in Poland.

We fully meet our obligations we have taken towards the German minority in the statement signed by Chancellor Kohl and Premier Tadeusz Mazowiecki in November 1989 and we would like to remind that the statements were reciprocal. The FRG side committed itself to similar obligations towards the Polish minority in the FRG.

As concerns resignation from reparations, or to be precise confirmation of the treaty of 1953 signed by Poland, Poland did not want to link the question of the settlement of the Oder-Neisse border in a treaty to any other issues. If the FRG side wants to extend the subject matter, Poland will put forward the question of compensations for over a million Polish citizens who were forced labourers in the Third Reich during World War II.

Source: Polish Embassy, London

POLISH-FRENCH SUMMIT MEETING

9 March 1990

A French-Polish meeting attended by President Francois Mitterrand and Wojciech Jaruzelski, Premiers Michel Rocard and Tadeusz Mazowiecki and the French and Polish Ministers of Foreign Affairs was held on 9 March in Paris. At the subsequent press conference the following statements were made:

President Mitterrand: France considers the Oder-Neisse border, that is the border between today's East Germany and Poland, as inviolable. Therefore, any declarations which will not clearly contain that will be insufficient. Hence France supports Poland's position that this inviolability of the border on the Oder and Neisse be proclaimed and confirmed by an international legal act. That means that our French interpretation goes further than the declaration adopted by the Bundestag. Anyhow, we think Poland should be granted access to any deliberations which will be taken on the matter.

I also want this international act to become subject to negotiations as soon as possible, anyway before the probable unification of both German states. Therefore, it seems normal to me that Poland should be given access to all negotiations which will pertain to her own border. This is simply the minimum. We will support this Polish postulate as the forum of the Six, that is Four plus Two.

I was very satisfied at the decision taken by the German authorities, by the German Parliament. It seems to me that the decision to a greater degree corresponds with our mutual interests, to European balance and the future of all Europe. I nonetheless think that this declaration should give more detail to some issues. Of course it would be good to say that the matter at stake is not some border, but the border on the Oder and Neisse.

President Jaruzelski: It would be a good and a sound thing for the security in Europe, if the process of Germany's unification were synchronised with the process of European unification and with ensuring the sense of security to every country, that is it should be accompanied by decisions which would reduce armed forces to proper ceilings not only in the dimension of coalitions but of particular countries as well. And solutions should consistently strive at ensuring defensive orientation of all countries and their armies. These should be solutions which will allow the building up of confidence by means of considerable enrichment of measures serving to this confidence. To sum up, the organizational, structural shape should stem from this fundamental objective.

Prime Minister Mazowiecki: We think that following elections in the GDR, but before unification, a treaty of a peace treaty character should be initialled between the Governments of both German states and the Polish Government with the participation of the four great powers, finally acknowledging the existing Western border of Poland and the Eastern border of the future united Germany. The united German state, the Government of this united German state, its Parliament should then ratify this treaty.

We think that Poland should be present in this cause. The formula of consultations does not satisfy us. We think the point is not in us not being consulted but in our participation in the settlement of this matter because it directly concerns us.

Polish society is very sensitive to this matter, it fears all sorts of decisions about us without us, it fears any repetition of some new formula of Yalta and therefore we think it is important to respect the rights of our society which in recent times has given evidence of their readiness to struggle for human rights and freedom, a struggle which also helped Germany towards this forthcoming unification. And we respect their right to unite.

Source: Polish Embassy, London

PRESIDENT GORBACHEV INTERVIEW TO SOVIET AND GERMAN JOURNALISTS

6 March 1990 (Excerpts)

We cannot agree to [a united Germany's participation in NATO]. It is absolutely ruled out. We believe that the process of unification of the two German states is a natural process which fits in well with a concept I used to expound before as well: the shape of the reality that history has bequeathed us will be decided by history itself.

Now, as we say, history has begun to accelerate. And I think that in this case the interests of the Germans must, doubtless, be accommodated. We are prepared for this. But the Germans, too, and all those associated with this process, must take into account the natural interests of the neighbours of the two German states, of all Europeans.

... On big and crucial questions, affecting such fundamental things as the interests of peoples, the Germans themselves, the Europeans, the whole world, it is inadmissible to act hastily, 'all of a rush', so to speak. This approach is not suitable for big politics.

... [I]f the European and the Vienna processes go on, we shall reach the point of Helsinki-2, and NATO and the Warsaw Treaty will be changed from military-political into political organisations – this will be one situation and in this case there will be no need for bargaining on where the united Germany must be. In a recent conversation one of the representatives of the leadership of a Western power told me: well, strictly speaking, why are you, Mr Gorbachev, concerned over this issue, for the Germans are already not those Germans, they are other Germans! Yes, the Germans both in the East and in the West are committed to peace and they have achieved a lot. All this is true. But in this case, I answered him, let us agree this way: why should they enter NATO, let them join the Warsaw Treaty, if this is of no consequence whatsoever. Immediately this objection followed: well, no. Why? In this way, this counterproposal of mine made many things clear. Let us weigh everything seriously, make calculations, in short, pursue business seriously.

Source: *Soviet News*, 14 March 1990

ARTICLE BY M. ROLAND DUMAS, FRENCH MINISTER OF FOREIGN AFFAIRS, PUBLISHED IN THE *NEW YORK TIMES*

13 March 1990

It is time to build a greater Europe. The desire for liberty and democracy has overthrown outdated ideologies. Everywhere we hear the same demands: a society based upon democratic values, separation of powers to protect against arbitrary acts, multiparty systems that safeguard the will of the people, an end to suffocating bureaucracy.

The German question lies at the heart of the challenge of building this new Europe.

I always believed that the arbitrary division of Germany was senseless since no-one can permanently divide a nation, a people, a country. German unity will put an end to one of history's anomalies. And it is up to the Germans themselves to determine the pace and internal conditions of this unification. But the situation inherited from the war cannot be improved without the participation of countries other than the two Germanys.

With this in mind, six countries will meet before the end of this month: both Germanys and the four victorious powers, France, Britain, the U.S. and the Soviet Union. Together, we will decide what new international agreements may be needed. Together, we will discuss borders, the peace settlement, the status of Berlin, security and other subjects of common interest.

German unification can be achieved only if it is accepted by all European countries. For Germany's neighbors, and most of all for Poland, it must be absolutely clear that borders cannot be altered. This must be recognized in and of itself.

Everything revolves around a simple idea: a German unification must be accompanied by a strengthening of European stability and the opportunity lends itself to this. The reduction of East-West tensions favors disarmament, even if considerable arsenals still exist. Agreements will be signed in 1990, and further negotiations should then follow.

But will the structures of security be both strong and flexible enough to withstand the shock of German unity? Should we not review our old alliances and establish new bonds that take into account Europe's changing balance of power?

The existing alliances were born of confrontation between East and West. In the coming months, serious reconsideration will undoubtedly be given to their structure, role and doctrines.

The Atlantic alliance reflects common values and the sense of belonging to the same sphere of security. This is why I hope a unified Germany becomes part of the alliance. This is its natural place. I welcome statements by West Germany's leaders rejecting neutrality.

NATO should, of course, adapt to the changes resulting from German unification and from progress toward disarmament. Yet, trans-Atlantic ties and the American presence in Europe must continue to be recognized as key elements in the future stability of our continent.

Another important element of security is the distinctive friendship between my country and Germany. Common elements in the area of defense are already in place.

Together, we must discuss all aspects regarding the future of Europe. The Conference on Security and Cooperation in Europe is the ideal forum for this. It is within the Helsinki framework that we have made significant progress on human rights. It is within this framework that we shall reach an agreement on reducing military forces and develop new forms of cooperation.

This is why France immediately supported the idea of holding a major summit of the heads of the CSCE's 35 member nations before the end of this year. Everyone now agrees to this. The summit meeting will take place, and Paris, need I add, is willing to host it.

However, the Helsinki framework is not a political model for Europe. Western Europe has been built around the European Community, and the community's success has certainly influenced events in the East. France has always expressed its commitment to progress toward European union in all its aspects, including political union based on new institutions. A unified Germany will have to be part of this strengthening of the community.

Beyond this, France's President, François Mitterrand, wishes to promote another approach, one embracing all aspects of relations between our countries: the European Confederation.

Confederation is the most flexible form of association between countries that want to come together on what is most important. It is within this framework that we, together, can build a future of peace and prosperity for Europe.

Source: French Embassy, London

AGREEMENT CONCERNING THE WITHDRAWAL OF SOVIET TROOPS TEMPORARILY STATIONED ON THE TERRITORY OF THE HUNGARIAN REPUBLIC

11th March 1990

The government of the Hungarian Republic and the government of the Union of the Soviet Socialist Republics (henceforth referred to as the parties),

guided by the endeavour to develop friendly and good neighbourly ties between the Hungarian Republic and the Union of the Soviet Socialist Republics,

consistently observing the basic principles of international law as endorsed in the United Nations' fundamental document and in the Final Act of the Conference on Security and Co-operation in Europe, including the observance of sovereignty and of non-interference in internal affairs,

regarding the issue of the withdrawal of Soviet troops temporarily stationed in Hungary as an organic part of the common endeavour aimed at the strengthening of European and international trust and security,

agreed the following:

Article 1

The withdrawal of the Soviet troops temporarily stationed on the territory of the Hungarian Republic, will take place during the period of 1990 and 1991. The withdrawal of the Soviet troops from the territory of the Hungarian Republic will commence on 12th March 1990 and be concluded on 30th March 1991.

The entire personnel of the Soviet troops will be withdrawn, including civilians who are Soviet citizens, as well as all arms, military technology and material equipment.

The schedule of the withdrawal of Soviet troops from the territory of the Hungarian Republic is contained in the supplement to this agreement, and comprises an indivisible part of that.

Article 2

The government of the Hungarian Republic will co-operate in the withdrawal of Soviet troops from the territory of Hungary, by securing the necessary conditions for the implementation thereof.

Article 3

The transportation of the Soviet troops, and the leaving behind and destruction of various materials and waste, will be implemented in keeping with the interests of the civilian population and with the observance of the laws of the protection of the environment.

Article 4

There will be a limit to the movement – including flights – connected with the military training and activities of the Soviet troops stationed on the territory of the Hungarian Republic.

Article 5

The parties will appoint authorised agents to secure the implementation of the provisions of this agreement, to oversee the withdrawal of the Soviet troops from the territory of the Hungarian Republic, and for the recording, valuation, handing over or the selling, by agreed methods, of the objects, equipment or other material implements.

Article 6

Until the permanent withdrawal of the troops from the territory of the Hungarian Republic, the legal status of the Soviet troops, and the property laws and other issues pertaining to the temporary stationing of the Soviet troops in Hungary, will be decided by the agreement made on 27th May 1957 between the government of the Hungarian People's Republic and the government of the Union of Soviet Socialist Republics regarding the legal situation of the Soviet troops temporarily stationed in the Hungarian People's Republic, as well as by the regulations of other Hungarian-Soviet agreements currently in force.

Article 7

Those property, financial and other economic queries, arising from the withdrawal of Soviet troops, which are not settled by contracts already in force, will be brought under regulation by separate agreements. The parties shall make arrangements as soon as possible, aimed at the solution of the above queries until the complete withdrawal of the Soviet troops.

Article 8

Any disputed questions in connection with the understanding and implementation of this agreement, and with the execution of the withdrawal of Soviet troops according to schedule, will be settled by the parties within 30 days of their submission to the Hungarian-Soviet mixed committee, formed by the government of the Hungarian Republic and the government of the Union of Soviet Socialist Republics on the basis of Article 17 of the agreement made on 27th May 1957 regarding the legal position of the Soviet troops temporarily stationed on the territory of the Hungarian People's Republic.

Should the mixed committee prove unable to reach a decision in a question submitted to it, the dispute will have to be resolved by diplomatic means.

Article 9

The regulations of this agreement do not touch such obligations in force between the parties which originate from bi- or multilateral agreements, including those arising from the friendly co-operation and mutual assistance pact made in Warsaw on May 14th 1955.

Article 10

This agreement comes into force on the day of its being signed. Two original copies of it were prepared in Moscow on March 10th, 1990, in Hungarian and Russian; both texts are eqully authentic.

Source: Hungarian Embassy (translation Judith Roman)

THE POLISH BORDER: TEXT OF BUNDESTAG RESOLUTION

*Text of the resolution on the Polish border
adopted by the Bundestag on 8 March 1990*

With reference to its declaration of 8 November 1989 the German Bundestag proposes that, as soon as possible after the elections in the GDR, the two freely-elected German parliaments and governments issue an identical declaration essentially stating the following:

The Polish people are assured that their right to live in secure borders will not be questioned by us Germans through territorial claims either now or in future.

The purpose of this declaration is, in accordance with the principles of the CSCE Final Act, to reaffirm in the light of German unity the inviolability of the borders with Poland as the indispensable basis of peaceful relations in Europe.

In this spirit, the border question should be settled in a treaty between an all-German Government and the Polish Government that seals the reconciliation of the two nations.

Poland's waiver of reparations from Germany dated 23 August 1953 and the joint declaration made by Prime Minister Tadeus Mazowiecki and Chancellor Helmut Kohl on 14 November 1989 remain valid for a united Germany.

Source: Embassy of the Federal Republic of Germany, London

EUROPE: A GOLDEN OPPORTUNITY NOT TO BE MISSED

Gianni De Michelis, Italian Foreign Minister

Rome – How is it that, in a mere decade, Europe has made the transition from Eurosclerosis to Europhoria? I believe Europe has entered the ascendant phase of a new Kondratieff cycle – the more or less 50-year generational cycle of change in which technological and political innovation overcomes stagnation and generates a new economic boom.

The new momentum began with a decision by the key European powers to integrate by 1992. In effect, integration was the political response to the necessity of moving from an industrial to a post-industrial society. Already linked by television, fax machines, rapid trains and air travel, Europe's well-educated consumers required more than a vast internal market for merchandising manufactured goods. They required a real, unified economic and cultural space.

This idea of 1992 produced exactly the same psychological effect in the minds of the Japanese, Americans and East Europeans. Japan and America began to fear a prosperous Fortress Europe from which they might be shut out. East Europeans, especially the young, saw a model of prosperity to which they wanted to belong. This helped trigger the mass migrations and the evolutions toward reform in Eastern Europe that (thanks to Mikhail Gorbachev's restraint) produced the revolution of 1989.

Today's Europhoria is well-founded. Europe will experience in the 1990s the most important economic boom of the century for three reasons:

- Extension of the market economy to Eastern Europe will boost West European businesses, from revamping phone systems to the installation of pollution-control equipment.
- 140 million new consumers from the East will eventually generate huge demand for such items as cars, cameras, stereos and washing machines.
- Disarmament is expected to free at least 0.8 percent of Western Europe's GNP for new investment.

The average growth rate in Europe during the 1990s will therefore likely be 5 percent – twice that of the projected U.S. rate. The combined GNP of the 18 countries of Western Europe, with their 400 million people, could be as high as $6 trillion by the mid-1990s

– 1.5 times the size of the U.S. economy and two to three times the Japanese economy. As long as the world trading system does not splinter into blocs over these projected spoils, America, Japan and Europe together could produce the greatest economic boom in history. All this points to Europe recovering its role as the core of the world economy. The next 10 years will make evident Japan's big short-comings: its relatively small population and its political weakness. (If Japan and the United States moved toward some form of integration, of course, this assessment would change.)

While Europe is not yet integrated, the political momentum to do so has never been stronger. To shape this momentum, a medium-term framework of integration must be built to counterbalance the weight of a united Germany. Practically speaking, the integration of East and West means the integration of Central Europe. Because West Germany and Italy are the two countries of the West, besides neutral Austria, that border the East, integration in these places will occur more rapidly. Apart from the security issue, German integration will be a relatively easy matter. But for us, nothing is unified. Our neighboring countries not only have different economic and social systems, their people speak different languages and have varying cultural backgrounds.

For this reason, Italy, Czechoslovakia, Hungary, Yugoslavia and Austria have organized a regional association. Together, these countries will contribute to a more even balance of power in the future Europe.

Above all, Europe must remain open. A Fortress Europe engaged in economic warfare with Japan would destroy all that the postwar order has built. It would be a terrible mistake to drift in that direction.

For the moment, that is why the Helsinki conference – the Conference on European Security and Co-operation – is the most important political body for Europe. Japan should be brought into the Helsinki conference. Everyone, including the Japanese, would benefit from this closer political association.

The model to which the East Europeans aspire is not that of Japan or the United States, but of Western Europe. That model comprises democracy, pluralism, a market economy and the welfare state. Despite its recent setback in the East German elections, social democracy will undoubtedly have a broad, even dominant appeal in an integrated Europe.

A formalized all-European Union of Social Democratic Parties will be set up this year, including former Communist parties from Hungary to Italy, and perhaps someday the Soviet Union. Whether in power or opposition, such a united European left will guarantee the endurance of Europe's singular legacy – the welfare state.

The institutional form of European integration will itself be subject to innovation. Such 18th and 19th century democratic mechanisms of integration as federation or confederation do not correspond to modern reality. Democracy will have to be reinvented.

Inevitably, in a global marketplace faced with ecological threats as well as problems of economic coordination and North-South inequality, political power must be transferred from sovereign nations to supranational institutions. The resultant democratic deficit will have to be offset by a redistribution of power to autonomous regions, cities and citizens. In the 21st century, neither the global nor the local level can work without the accountability of one to the other. All that is certain is the obsolescence of the nation state.

In psychological terms, 1989 was very much like 1945. It marked the end of a period of war and division. Unfortunately, the way we set about reconstruction in 1946–47 created the basis for the next war, the Cold War.

Thus the crucial issue of 1990 is how to end East-West conflict in a way that does not create the basis for a new world war – a war between North and South. If conflict, whether in conventional terms or terrorist terms, proliferates, the promise of boom and prosperity will collapse.

Above all, we must avoid the schism of one interdependent world with two civilizations. The environment, with its related issues of poverty and development, and religion, especially Islam, pose the greatest risk to the promise of integration. The Salman Rushdie affair offers a sobering preview of the deadly conflict between the modern promise of integration and the counter-revolt against interdependence.

The realities of global interdependence are a fait accompli. The ecological consciousness, disarmament and the open global market are examples of the integrative tendency.

Attempts at fragmentation out of fear and uncertainty are the negative reaction to interdependence. Protectionism, ethnic nationalism and religious fundamentalism are examples of the disintegrative tendency.

The future of mankind lies in the success of integration. So for me, Europe is the test for all humanity. Europe today stands at the nexus of the most important challenges of integration: the integration of the sovereign states of the West, on the one hand and East-West integration, on the other. If we do not realize during the next 20 years the optimism of our will, a new Dark Age of nationalism, fragmentation, racism and violence may well be the price of our failure.

Source: *Los Angeles Times*, reprinted in *International Herald Tribune*, 26 March 1990